OUT THERE

AND BACK

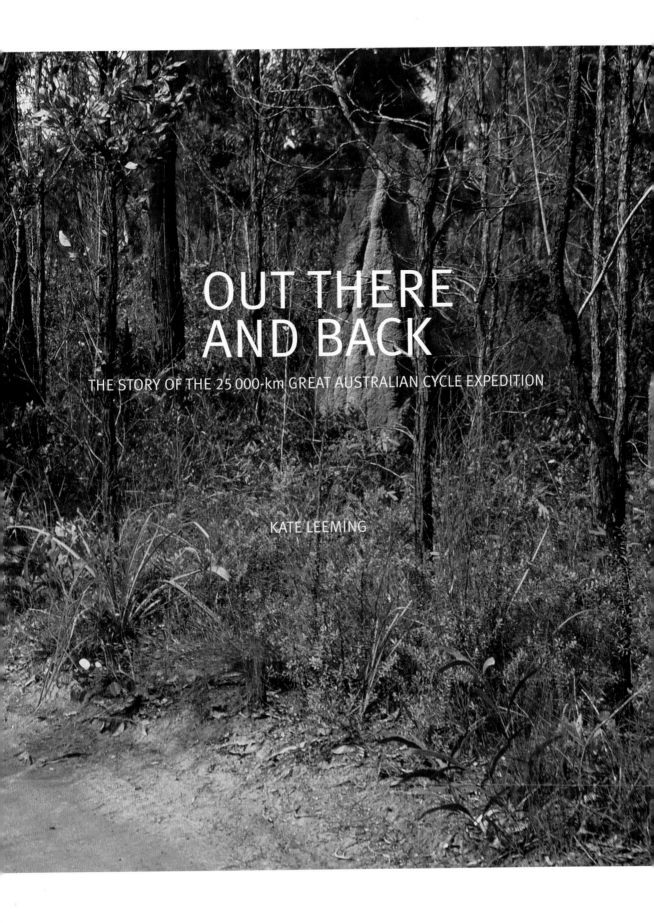

OUT THERE
AND BACK

THE STORY OF THE 25 000-km GREAT AUSTRALIAN CYCLE EXPEDITION

KATE LEEMING

Published by Kate Leeming
www.gracexpedition.org

National Library of Australia Cataloguing-in-Publication entry
Leeming, Kate.
  Out there and back: the story of the 25 000-km Great Australian Cycle Expedition.

  1st edition.
  Includes index.
  ISBN 9781920892463.

  1. Leeming, Kate. 2. Cyclists - Australia - Biography. I. Title.

796.6092

Designed and typeset by David Constable
Edited by Susan Powell
Maps by James Lee
Produced by Publishing Solutions
www.publishing-solutions.com.au

Printed in China

To my parents

Lorna and Ted Leeming

Acknowledgements

The GRACE Project has involved organising and completing an expedition, making a contribution towards education for sustainable development, and writing a book. None of this would have been possible without the support I have received from family, friends and associates, and those involved in relevant businesses and organisations, all of whom have generously donated their time, energy and know-how.

Sincerest thanks go to the sponsors of the GRACE Expedition: Alcoa World Aluminium Australia, Australia Post, UNESCO, Hewlett Packard, Giant Bicycles, Cycleworks (Box Hill, Melbourne), SRAM, Schwalbe, Jax Presentation Concepts (website design), Callum Sneddon (website development), Wilderness Wear, Mountain Designs, Leatherman Tools, Green People, SkyTrans, Polar, Fujifilm, Aktiv8, Phillips and Father Printing, Red Mist, Going Solar, Canning Expeditions, Victorian Association for Environmental Education (VAEE), Alasdair Cooke, Wiluna Club Hotel, Kimberley Hotel (Halls Creek) and Moonlight Bay Apartments (Broome).

Due to the scale of the project, to list everyone who has contributed would just about involve writing another book! In particular, I thank: Greg Yeoman, Yuri Trusov, Don Walker, Andrew Rickard, Arnaud Domange, Danny McCoppin, Simone Hewett, Andrew Campion, Jane Leeming, Tony and Megan Leeming, the Alcoa team (Erin, Wendy, Brendan), Gary Lee, Craig Williams, Mark Arapakis, Doug Sullivan, Philip Endersbee, Rob Eva, Richard Allen, Merrick Ekins, Dr Michael Wooldridge, Dr Brendan Nelson MP, Senator Bob McMullen, Mick Gentleman MLA, Catherine Holmes à Court, Bill Deuchar, Dick Friend, Kelly Linaker, Seth Eccelston, Justin McKirdy, 12 Parasols (PR), and the Australian Association for Environmental Education (AAEE), and all the other people who kindly provided me with food, accommodation, information and various kinds of assistance during the course of the expedition.

With regard to the production and publication of this book, I am indebted to the contributions, professional expertise and advice of: Publishing Solutions (Ken Yendell, Elena Cementon, David Constable), Susan Powell, Robert Swan, Barney Rivers, Ruth Siems, Diane Rolfe, James Lee, Robert Sessions, Arthur St Hill, Ted Leeming and Alice Wheeler.

Any factual errors in this book are entirely mine. Unless otherwise indicated, all photographs were taken by myself (or someone using my camera).

Contents

Foreword
by Robert Swan, OBE

By the age of thirty-three I had achieved my childhood dream of becoming the first person in history to have walked to the North and South poles. In the years since that time I have tried my best to inspire people, most importantly young people, about the issue of looking after our world.

One way I have done this is to find 'real' people doing amazing things and support them. I first met Kate Leeming in London back in 1993 when she was organising the Trans-Siberian Cycle Expedition, a 13 400-kilometre journey across the 'New Russia' from St Petersburg to Vladivostok. I was totally in awe of what Kate was attempting to achieve and very impressed that she was going to use the journey to aid the children of Chernobyl. It was an honour to become the patron of the successful expedition.

After five months of battling across some often very inhospitable terrain, she (and travelling companion, Greg Yeoman) arrived in Vladivostok one day ahead of schedule. This made Kate the first woman in history to have cycled unsupported across Russia. Talk about dreams coming true...she had done it!

Ten years after the Russian adventure, living back in Australia, Kate brought another dream to fruition when she organised the Great Australian Cycle Expedition (GRACE), a 25 000-kilometre journey through her own country, 7000 kilometres of which were to be 'off road' on isolated tracks.

Again Kate's plans had a greater purpose, this time to promote the importance of and contribute towards education for sustainable development. The project was selected as Australia's first Demonstration Activity for the United Nations Decade of Education for Sustainable Development (2005–14). Inspiring sustainable development means leading by example and Kate's expedition would be a great example for young people.

The nine and-a-half-month expedition demanded tremendous physical and mental stamina and strength. In the face of extreme heat, dehydration, sand and corrugations, headwinds and personal hardship, Kate maintained a challenging program: a daily average of approximately 130 kilometres on tarmac and 100 kilometres on unsealed roads while carrying between 30 and 50 kilograms of equipment and supplies on the bike.

Out There and Back is Kate's personal chronicle of the GRACE Expedition. At the same time it raises awareness of the importance of education for sustainable development, underpinned by the author's beliefs and fuelled by her experiences cycling across Russia. I greatly enjoyed this detailed, often graphic, account of an amazing journey into the heart of Australia, told with style, humour and insight. A highlight is Kate's description of the first bicycle crossing of the Canning Stock Route (CSR) by a woman. The CSR, the world's longest, most arduous stock route, bisects four deserts and approximately one thousand sand dunes.

Cycling without the aid of a support vehicle (for all but the CSR), and alone for the second half of the expedition, Kate celebrates the close connection and respect she developed with the Australian people and landscapes, skilfully weaving in information about early explorers, pioneers and colourful characters who shaped the outback. She gives vivid impressions of her visits to Indigenous communities and glimpses of life on cattle stations and remote outposts and in country towns.

I know that this book, illustrated by hundreds of full-colour photographs, will appeal to a wide readership around the world. I am proud to have played a small part in this fantastic story.

Robert Swan OBE
Greenwich, London

Prologue
Into the heart of the New Russia

Making a close connection with the locals, Sim, Ural Mountains
(photo: G Yeoman)

'Could you do that again, please, so I can capture it on video?'

This was Greg's reaction to witnessing me and 45 kg of bicycle slither from perhaps the highest point on the landscape, the hump in the middle of the road. It was as if I was pedalling on ice. Torrential overnight rains had turned the main route to Vladivostok into a quagmire battlefield, with wheel ruts deep enough to be trenches. Venturing into the rough fields beside the M5 Siberian highway in search of a more solid path had led, during the course of the day, to being ambushed by swarms of giant mosquitoes. These vicious insects possessed the ability to bite right through most of my clothing, with the exception of the two pairs of cycle shorts I was wearing to ease the raw consequences of sitting on an unsympathetic, callous-forming saddle for eight hours at a time. Most people take the train.

Winded from landing heavily on my left side for the third time that day, I didn't know whether to laugh or cry at my travelling companion's comment – it hurt to do either. We all heard the ominous crack of a broken rib as I clambered to my feet. My tears were of shock rather than pain – of the sudden realisation of how easily one small error could thwart the five-month expedition that had begun six-and-a-half weeks ago in St Petersburg. I was annoyed at myself for allowing this to happen. If the fractured rib had punctured a lung, Day 47 of the Trans-Siberian Cycle Expedition on the soggy Barabinskaya Steppe, halfway between Omsk and Novosibirsk, would have been my last.

Timely, light-hearted comments like this one of Greg's were valued because coping with the daily frustrations of travelling across the 'New Russia' definitely

Not feeling too comfortable just after breaking a rib on the Steppe
(photo: G Yeoman)

required a sense of humour. In this case, there was absolutely nothing I could do except carry on. A doctor would have only prescribed rest, but taking time-out was not an option. We had to persevere to reach Vladivostok by 1 October, before the onset of the severe Russian winter.

Crudely scraping away the excess mud which had caked up its working parts, I wheeled my bike back out to the mosquito-ridden field. Progress to the village of Pokronka through the sludge was heavy-going and painfully bumpy, but at least I wouldn't slip. I had convinced enough friends and sponsors that this journey was possible, that it would take more than a broken rib to stop me.

◆ ◆ ◆

The Trans-Siberian Cycle Expedition had set out from the monument of Peter the Great in the Decembrists' Square, St Petersburg, on 1 May 1993. The choice of the starting date and the site were no coincidence.

Some two metres (6ft 7in.) tall, Peter the Great, after whom St Petersburg is named, had immense presence. Probably the most powerful of the Tsarist rulers, he carved out a new capital city because of his hatred of Moscow. Founded in 1703, this 'Venice of the North' emerged from the swampy delta of the River Neva as a showpiece; at a cost of 30 000 lives, it demonstrated Peter's obsession with the West.

In 1825, revolutionaries known as the Decembrists conspired to revolt against the draconian policies of the autocratic rule of the Tsar. They wanted to transform Russia into a British-style constitutional monarchy, abolishing serfdom and granting equality before the law. Freed peasants were to be given a small plot of land. Although the Decembrists' attempted coup was a fiasco, the conspirators rounded up and either hanged or banished to Siberia, they take their place in history as ideological martyrs.

In 1896, Vladimir Lenin designated the first of May, May Day, as a time to incite the working classes to show solidarity and protest for their rights. In Soviet times May Day became a patriotic occasion with military parades glorifying the worker. In the post-communist era, May Day is still an annual Labour and Spring Day holiday, but street demonstrations, especially in the major cities, include a broad spectrum of activists such as communists, monarchists and fascists, who openly display their grievances.

Steering clear of any demonstrations, it was an immense relief to wobble off down Nevsky Prospect just after noon on 1 May with Greg and our first two Russian cycling companions, George (an orthopaedic surgeon) and Vladimir (a factory machinist). The planning and preparation were over and I was exhausted yet excited at the prospect of the adventure which would unravel itself over the next five months. Apart from satisfying the spirit of adventure, the purpose of the 13 386-km Trans-Siberian Cycle Expedition from St Petersburg to Vladivostok was to aid the cause of the children of Chernobyl.

To sum up the progress of the first few days, we were like bears waking from winter hibernation, clumsy and eternally hungry. As foreigners, we were in culture shock, sensory overload. Our daily routine of cycling, eating and sleeping had to be moulded around the Russian way of life, where even the most simple tasks such as shopping, making telephone calls, obtaining directions and being accepted into Russian hotels was frustratingly complex. At the same time as getting to know each other and battling with the language, we were also initiated into *banyas* and *dachas*.

The *banya*, or Russian sauna, is an integral part of Russian life. Most villages have them (not all functional) and many people build their own private *banya* at their *dacha*. (A *dacha* is a second country residence – anything from a mansion to a shed – usually located on a small, private plot of land. People from the cities and large towns fortunate enough to own a *dacha* grow much of their fresh food there.) I much preferred the latter variety of *banya* because of the privacy element; I could relax and sweat out days of road grime without feeling like a travelling side-show.

The private *banya* consists of two rooms: a tiny change room, often cluttered with heavy overcoats and bear hats which are stored there for the winter, and the sauna itself. This chamber is heated by a wood-burning furnace, which also serves to heat the small cauldron of water above it to near boiling point. Adjacent to this contraption is a vat of cold water. The general idea is to blend the two in a standard enamel wash bowl until the desired temperature is achieved and then dump the water over one's body in a fashion as traditional as downing vodka in a Russian toast. I was entertained by the extravagance of being able to slop the water to all four corners of the steamy room. After a good scrub down with a loofah (which Greg called his 'Martin' after Martin Luther King), the customary skin-toning session which followed involved whipping oneself with a bundle of birch branches. As if I needed any more punishment after seven hours on the road!

The communal *banya*, such as 'Bath House No. 2' in Marilinsk, was almost as invigorating. Before arriving in this industrial central Siberian town, the only wash we'd had was a swim in the River Tom'. In hindsight, this was an extremely unhealthy move as I later learnt that the Tom' was one of the country's most polluted waterways.

A queue of about twenty-five women meandered back past the ticket office and out onto the street. Judging by the state and stench of some of the *genshinas* (ladies), either the women's section of the communal *banya* had been out of order for quite some time or everyone was spreading manure on their *dachas*! It was times like these when our Russian companions were invaluable. Yuri and Eugene (who had replaced Vladimir in Novosibirsk) ensured my third place in line after a quick negotiation with the cashier and a fee of four roubles (less than one Australian cent). The boys disappeared through an equally dilapidated entrance to their side of the bath house. The locals did not seem too perturbed by my jumping the queue; in fact, my pathetic attempt to converse with those around me was probably an entertainment.

Entering the changing area, I felt even more conspicuous, especially as I peeled off my 'second skin' of salt-encrusted cycle clothing. I became embarrassed and self-conscious about my ridiculous suntan; the lines of my socks, cycle shorts, tee-shirt and sunglasses were all accentuated by the road grime. Many pairs of eyes glanced shyly across, careful not to let 'the alien' catch them gawking. I blended in about as well as McDonald's in Moscow. In Western society, my height of 170 cms (5ft 7in.) is fairly average, but here I towered over the average Russian, and was definitely more athletic than the assortment of figures before me. A harsh existence of years of manual labour, climatic extremes and a poor diet had sculpted the weather-beaten bodies into a visual age which far exceeded their actual age. Life expectancy here is about fifteen years less than the Western average.

Pretty soon, the ebb and flow of conversation, the splashing of water and the ringing of enamel bowls as they were plonked down on the concrete benches resumed. After slopping a few bowls of water over myself, I was beginning to feel like a local – that was, until I produced a razor from my bag and proceeded to shave my legs. This, I had discovered, was the most efficient way to remove the dirt! Confused by this very foreign action, one of the more wrinkled figures, flashing a gleaming silver-toothed smile, came over and presented me with a loofah. Politely accepting, I finished off my underarms and then paid a visit to the steam room. The atmosphere here was so dense I could only hear the din of voices punctuated by the birch 'floggings'.

Deciding I was cleaned, refreshed and toned enough, I returned 'Martin' to its owner, dressed and left the *banya*, passing the filthy queue still awaiting their turn. My companions looked relaxed as they waited for me in the evening light. 'How was it for you?' I asked.

◆ ◆ ◆

Perhaps the main value of travelling unsupported by bicycle is the opportunity to develop a strong relationship with the people and the land. Locals open their hearts to you. It seems to bring out the brighter side of human nature, or in the case of Igor and Vassili, nature and humans.

On Day 78, one day out from Krasnoyarsk, the rim on my rear wheel split after one bump too many. Sasha, our new guide (who had just replaced Yuri and Eugene), and I left Greg to watch our belongings at the traffic police checkpoint and hitched a ride to the nearest town, Uyar, to telephone our expedition base, Centre Pole. Communicating with Centre Pole was always my department. Patience was required for even a simple task like telephoning from an office. This could take an hour or more because there were too few internal connections.

Centre Pole, in Ryazan, a city 200 km south of Moscow, immediately organised for someone to personally accompany the needed equipment. This involved them driving to Moscow, buying a plane ticket, taking the four-hour flight to Krasnoyarsk, which was like flying from Perth to Sydney, and finally making a 120-km train journey to Uyar. This is the only way it could be guaranteed that we received the equipment. We were to be stuck in Uyar, a dull-looking village of 10 000 inhabitants, for four days.

Sasha and I returned to find Greg wearing a policeman's cap and with his feet up inside the traffic police station, practising his Russian with one of the officers, Igor. I had noticed that in Russia names such as Sasha, Vladimir, Olga and Svetta recurred often, but this Igor was only one of four who worked in the traffic police depot. Igor offered to take us on a special outing into the forest the following day.

Our time spent with Igor and his friend, Vassili, epitomised our journey into the heart of Siberia. They arrived at 8am, as promised, Igor on his brother's motorbike on which I sat for the journey, and Vassili on his twenty-two-year-old, two-stroke machine with a tray attached, on which Greg and Sasha were to endure a bone-rattling ride.

As we set off, all we knew was that we were heading to a place where no one but locals had been before. The dirt track became progressively less used and more overgrown. More nimble on our slick pair of wheels, Igor and I often paused to wait for the others and look around. He pointed out a region across the valley of the Rybnoye River where Stalin used to hunt sable and another spot where there used to be a *gulag* (concentration camp). It was virtually impossible for prisoners, like the Decembrists (some of whom were sent there after their failed coup attempt in 1825), to escape, Igor explained. They would have had no idea where they were and the climate was inhospitable for most of the year.

Turning away from the valley, the track now became merely a set of deep wheel ruts which snaked a path through the wild taiga. In wet patches, the single pair of tracks gave birth to a maze of alternatives which required an intelligence test to navigate. While we were enjoying the tranquillity of our surroundings, waiting for the others once more, Igor explained that we were heading for the place where we were most likely to spot bears. This was not a comforting thought, but on hearing the lawnmower-like noise of Vassili's approaching machine, I realised we were pretty safe.

Filling our water-bottles at a crystal-clear stream, we clutched at flecks of gold. Beside the water's edge, we saw the footprints of a mother bear and cub. Then we all had to hold on tight and trust our new friends' instincts as the finale to the trek was virtually trail-blazing through 1.8 metre (6ft) high grasses, where vision was nil. It was a miracle that Igor and I only came off once. Every time I glanced over my shoulder, Greg and Sasha were balancing in precarious positions on their little tray.

Bear footprint in the forest near Uyar
(photo: G Yeoman)

Somehow, we arrived at our destination, some 40 km from Uyar. There we perched on granite overhangs and looked out over a perfect sea of green. We were hoping to spot bears which regularly fished in the river, about 200 metres below. There were no chimney stacks in sight, and unfortunately no bears. Despite all the reports of the lethal legacies of industrial pollution brought about by years of foolhardy neglect and mismanagement in the former Soviet Union, the majority of what I had seen of the countryside was relatively unspoilt. We were enjoying a corner of the largest forest in the world: the Siberian taiga covers an area more than twice the size of the Amazon.

The picnic: Greg, Sasha, Vassili and Igor deep in conversation

Descending to the water's edge, it was not bears I was face to face with but red and purple wild geraniums. Then 'Kate, don't look' came the belated warning as our Russian friends, egged on by our twenty-year-old, body-builder guide, stripped off and dived in. That was about all the wildlife I saw that day.

We had earned our picnic lunch by the time we had climbed back up to the bikes. Our hosts constructed a smoky fire to ward off the mosquitoes while the three of us collected bilberries to make tea. I realised how fortunate we were to have Sasha's excellent interpreting skill as we conversed over a jar of Vassili's home-made rose-petal jam, which we spooned straight into our mouths in true Russian style.

The hub of the conversation was an exchange of ideals and values, which in theory could have ended the Cold War and solved many of the problems of the 'New Russia'. I learnt that the view I once had of the Soviet Union was in line with the image Igor had of the West. There was a never-ending stream of questions – 'What is it like to live in Australia and England?' 'How is it different from Siberia?' 'Could you live in Russia?' In their view, Siberian people were poor, poorer than European Russians and Western society in general, because they couldn't afford the same material assets.

I replied that it depends how you define wealth. In terms of average material wealth, there was obviously no comparison, but they would be hard pushed in the West to find the type of hospitality we were experiencing in Siberia. Igor, Vassili and typically most Russians use their natural wealth by collecting seasonal resources as an essential part of their diet. As we were discovering, an excursion to the forest to gather mushrooms, berries and pine nuts, pick herbs for medicines and catch fish was as much a part of their culture as a visit to the supermarket is for Westerners. The refreshing differences here were that fruit and vegetables were not graded into uniform size in plastic wrapping, milk did not come in a carton and there was no question that the eggs were free range. The 14-cm (5in.), 'not too bent' Euro-banana would look out of place here.

While our new friends' knowledge of Greg's country and my own was surprisingly detailed, it was evident that Russians were receiving confusing signals as a result of a gradual increase in exposure to Western culture, mainly through the medium of television, now uncensored. They were starting to be conscious of 'being poor'.

Sasha's situation is an extension of this point. At the early age of sixteen, this intelligent medical student had earned himself an opportunity to visit the USA. His first culture shock came when he entered the toilet while in transit at Shannon Airport in Ireland. He was so gob-smacked by what he found that he forgot he needed to use the facilities! His three weeks in Seattle ended all too soon. Returning to Ryazan, Sasha locked himself in his room for days and cried. His visit had instilled an insatiable appetite for anything and everything American, and he felt trapped between wanting Western culture and living in Russia and being Russian. This longing had driven a wedge between him and many of his friends with whom he had little in common any more. On this day, though, he was proud to be Russian.

From Igor, we learnt about the stresses and dangers of policing. Although there were still laws, it had become impossible to enforce them. Now the Russian mafia seemed to control everything and Igor cited the razed shop we had seen near the market – the price for not paying protection money.

Vassili was a member of a powerless ecological society of Uyar which was attempting to advise the local ceramics factory about ecological management. The industry, however, continued to do as it pleased. Despite being ignored, Vassili's organisation had an important role in increasing awareness, as care of the environment was obviously an issue low on the list of priorities under communist rule. During the seventy years of this regime, industries strove to achieve their five-year productivity targets by whatever means it took, with the most outstanding factory workers rewarded as 'town heroes'.

We found that people we met in Russia who lived in regions which were obviously contaminated by industrial pollution were either not aware of this fact or did not understand the threat it posed to their environmental and personal health. They accepted dangerous levels of air pollution or the unrestricted use of asbestos, for example, as being normal and unchallengeable.

A worrying instance of the public's lack of awareness occurred when I was speaking with a well-educated woman, Diane, in the city of Ufa on the western edge of the Ural Mountains. On a walking tour of her city, Diane seemed to be pointing out an unusually high number of hospitals. When I asked what the main health problems were, she replied, 'The children are sick'. 'Why are they sick?' 'The air is dirty.' She explained that most of the hospitals concentrated on mother and child care, and that the most common illnesses were respiratory disorders and cancer. She said this was due to the many factories in and around the city. When I enquired whether the series of nuclear accidents which occurred near Ufa in the 1950s had anything to do with these health problems, Diane's response was, 'I don't think that affects us now because it happened a very long time ago'.

We later found out that the amount of radiation released over a ten-year period from Cheliabinsk-65 near Kyshtym, 130 km north of Ufa, was equal to 60 per cent of the total radiation expelled at Chernobyl. One of the principal dangerous isotopes which escaped from the 1957 accident was Plutonium-239, which has a half-life of nearly 24 000 years. This isotope has a direct effect on the respiratory system and children are the most susceptible.

From our discussions at the picnic, I hope Vassili and Igor got the message that what they were doing was important. As promised, our spare wheel was delivered and we continued towards Lake Baikal, eager to make up for lost time.

◆　◆　◆

The Siberian Swamp had always loomed as the biggest challenge on our quest to cross from the Baltic to the Pacific. The only overland connection in this region lying between Chita and Blagovechensk, east of Lake Baikal and north of the NE Chinese border, is a 1500-km section of the Trans-Siberian Railway line. No through roads were shown on our US air military maps because any tracks that were made were regularly washed out.

Winter maintenance tracks ran parallel to the railway line. Heavy vehicles could use the tracks in winter when everything was frozen, but they often disappeared under water during summer. We used the railway line to navigate

People are living and working in the shadow of heavy industry. The residents of Togliatti (western edge of the Urals) grow their food on their *dachas* beside the Order of the Red Banner of Synthetic Rubber Works.

Isolated 'Swamp people': residents from a hamlet near Arksenovo-Zilovskoye who gave us lunch and directions

through this region and hauled our loaded bikes up onto the railway itself when the terrain became impassable. Without bridges, this was also the only way we could cross the massive rivers.

Small villages were fairly evenly spaced along the route. They relied on the train as their lifeline and we, in turn, were totally reliant on the villagers for directions, food and accommodation. It was often too wet to camp and not very safe in the bear-infested taiga.

Before we left Arksenovo-Zilovskoye, Sasha went through the usual rigmarole of asking a number of locals for directions to the next village, Sbega. Few people ventured far from their homes except to pick berries and mushrooms or to cut hay, so obtaining accurate information was sometimes near impossible. We would not only ask for directions, but also when they had last travelled on that route and whether they owned a vehicle. If they had not used the road that season, we did not count on their responses as being too reliable.

We were pleased with our progress when we arrived in the small settlement of Uryum after 61 km of reasonable track. We had only needed to use the railway line a few times. It was mid-afternoon and I asked for directions to Sbega. 'Straight on over the railway line, turn left.'

After three or four steep climbs and fording a shallow river, we came to an intersection. The left fork, which headed towards the railway line, was merely a conglomeration of mud and puddles. The right branch had a superior surface, but headed off into the mountains. I favoured the railway track because it surely had to be the most direct route. The other track with its smooth surface appeared far more tempting. Being a forestry track, this may have been an alternative – a less direct but potentially faster path to our destination.

Sasha in particular was adamant that we should take the forestry route and impatiently set off before we had made a team decision. We seemed to be travelling in completely the wrong direction, and after about three kilometres I convinced Greg that we should try the wetter alternative. Sasha reluctantly accepted our democratic decision-making process.

A typical section of inundated 'winter track': it was this or the railway line

The track we were now on, which followed parallel to the railway, became impenetrable – all mud, rocks and puddles. We regularly had to navigate through the dense undergrowth to avoid the obstacles. Half an hour and two kilometres later, we were halted by a huge expanse of water. The forestry track once more had greater appeal than the sodden, cross-country excursion which required us to lift and drag our gear back onto the railway line. We needed machetes rather than Swiss Army knives. Before we had a chance to retrace our tracks, Greg's rear rack broke again and we had to wait for him to re-wire it.

The favoured forestry track deteriorated into deep gutters and soft sand as we ascended steeply. Together with my low state of health (constant diarrhoea), this difficulty was responsible for a serious energy 'bonk', when all energy seemed to drain out of the holes in my shoes, my legs turned to jelly, I broke into a cold sweat and got the shakes, and everything seemed to happen in slow motion. My mind was consumed by negative thoughts, the gradient became steeper, the sand softer, I worried about a bear wandering on to the road in front of me, and wondered when the hell the others (those bastards) ahead were going to wait. To stop and push would be defeatist in my mind and I was carrying no ready-to-eat food. There was no option but to persevere. This meant standing on the pedals while pulling on the handlebars just to turn the cogs.

Lost on the steep forestry track which led to nowhere out of Uryum
(photo: G Yeoman)

Finally, distressed, I caught up with the boys, who had only been waiting a couple of minutes.

'Where the f— were you?'

'I'm out of food. Quick, I need food...please?'

A tin of Russian-style Spam (which had been sitting in Greg's pannier since Chita as we hadn't been desperate enough to use it until this emergency), bread, cucumbers and halva were produced, and we ate our second lunch for the day, at 6pm. A little further on, we were able to scoop up some water from a tiny stream.

We kept together for the remainder of the ascent, struggling to avoid the deep crevasses caused by water erosion. The summit rewarded us with a sweeping panorama which we took a few minutes to absorb. A temporary relief.

The track became increasingly overgrown as we descended the dark side of the mountain. The hope that it was leading us to Sbega ebbed as we ducked under and wove around the encroaching vegetation. Eventually the path disappeared completely into the swampy, mosquito-infested taiga. We were lost.

We considered our options after donning our waterproofs and insect repellent, second nature by this stage. A quick scout around the area confirmed that there was no way forward. We had to turn back. Our extra effort had been a waste of time and energy.

It was 8.15pm by the time we had decided to at least return to the top of the climb where there would be more daylight. Greg and Sasha had both suffered from energy 'bonks' during the sandy climb. I passed them as they dived into a bag for the last of the Kendal Mint Cake and was waiting at the top for them this time. We decided to return to Uryum rather than camp as our supplies were now low.

The light was failing, as were our brakes, which ran hot as we descended. The screeching sound they made penetrated the otherwise tranquil forest. Passing the notorious fork in the road for the fourth time, it felt as if we knew the area like the back of our hands. By the time we returned to Uryum, at 9.30pm, we had clocked an extra 50 km.

Sasha spoke to the pot-bellied silhouette of a man who was returning home with a bucket of mushrooms. The 'mushroom man', as we called him, directed us to some goldminers' quarters nearby. I always accompanied Sasha when asking for help because the presence of my filthy-dirty foreign female face markedly increased our chances of being accepted. Sasha was only partway through his well-rehearsed speech when Vladimir, the director of the miners'

Sasha studying the Decembrists' graves near the Shilka River

quarters, welcomed us as his guests. All facilities were laid on for us. We were stuffed full of vulgarly sized portions of fatty meat, potatoes, tomatoes, bread, compote, biscuits and, of course, vodka. Exhausted, we accepted the invitation of a rest day. We had fallen on our feet once more.

As had been the case with previous unscheduled stops in Ufa and Uyar, our experiences in Uryum with the Ukrainian goldminers in this remote part of Siberia were some of the most valued of the whole expedition.

The following day was spent resting, eating, washing, eating, catching up on diaries, repairing and cleaning bicycles, talking and eating. We were always so tired on rest days that these mundane chores seemed almost as challenging as the struggles of the previous days spent cycling. The warm sunshine gave us the opportunity to spread out the entire sodden contents of our panniers all over the yard to dry: tents, maps, clothes, packets of soup and dried fruit.

That evening, our new friends organised a special banquet for us. Just prior to tucking in, Nikolai (Vladimir's brother) and Misha (a young truck driver) asked us to stay another day in order to visit their goldmines and also to see where some of the Decembrists lived out their years in exile. We were ahead of schedule, and considering the starting point of the expedition, this was an opportunity not to be missed. Of course, not having to cycle the following day and being in such friendly company created the ingredients for a very merry evening. We could really let our hair down.

Toast after toast, red *champanski*, white *champanski*, vodka and finally 'spirit' (a form of 'moonshine', pure alcohol mixed with water) – the Ukrainians were in fine voice as they reeled off a seemingly endless repertoire of national folk songs with hearty pride. Then they insisted it was our turn and waited expectantly for our response. What song could an Australian, a Briton and a Russian possibly know in common? Not *Waltzing Matilda* or *Advance Australia Fair*. *Land of Hope and Glory*, or perhaps *God Save the Queen*? A wave of inspiration enveloped the three of us almost simultaneously...Let's do it! The only song we could competently recite was *Bounce Your Boobies*, a ditty from my hockey days which I had taught Greg and Sasha to liven up some of those long days in the saddle, and also save us from any more Russian jokes. As well, it was a bit a private joke for me because I had grown tired of Sasha's habit of removing his shirt and flexing his pectoral muscles, which seemed to happen pretty often.

The Ukrainians were clearly impressed with the gusto of our rendition. Obviously they had not understood a word and probably thought it was some kind of national song. Fortunately I had not taught the boys the hand actions or that would have given us away.

The evening gradually spun itself into oblivion, the table cluttered with empty bottles, glasses, and plates of cold food now set in congealed fat. The Russian word for 'enough', *dastatichna*, which had taken me three days to perfect while sober back in Yekaterinburg, proved to be just as elusive once more. Blaring from the television, Russia's weekly dose of MTV all seemed a blur. There was more than one reason for forgetting that we were in such a remote part of the world.

OUT THERE AND BACK

I certainly didn't feel like sitting in the cramped cab of Misha's truck the following morning for a 100-km journey over potholed, winding and bumpy roads. Our destination was Ust Kharst, a village trading post on the Shilka River. The word *shilka* means 'death', so it was an aptly named destination given our delicate conditions. The dirt road was an ancient trade route into China.

About 15 km from Ust Kharst, the valley floor began to show the scars of the gold-mining operation. The river had been dammed into square sections, giving a patchwork effect to the valley. The earthworks dominated the scene so much that at first I did not notice the derelict building beside the operations. The jail, which once housed the Decembrists, was now in ruins. Keeping an eye on proceedings were some of the graves of their children and, adjacent, a newly erected monument in their memory.

Once Misha had completed his work errands, we paid a visit to the mine. Its young director explained that two kilograms of gold a day were extracted from sifting the valley floor. The profits from the stockpile of 600 kg sitting in the storehouse were funnelled straight to Moscow. The mining community of 120 staff was fairly self-sufficient, and the miners well-rewarded for their labours.

At the same time, there was plenty of evidence of negligence and inefficiencies, drunk machine operators, for example. There were environmental guidelines set by the government, but the director explained that by paying a few backhanders to the right people, his staff were saved the extra effort. As a result, the topsoil was never replaced and only a handful of trees replanted. Regeneration in the area was very slow, although in time, at least this land would recover. Of most concern to me was the attitude. We had already seen some of the results of large-scale industries displaying the same reluctance to respect and care for their environment and their people.

As we left the region, another magnificent rainbow beamed over the valley. A pot of gold was guaranteed at the end of this one. The following day, we retraced our route out from Uryum back to the intersection, hauled our bikes up on to the railway line and pushed on towards Sbega. Our bicycles were very much worse for wear but we made it through the Swamp to Blagoveschensk relatively unscathed.

Despite my breaking a rib on the Steppe (which took about six weeks to heal), crossing the Swamp and dealing with all the red tape and frustrations of travelling through the world's largest country undergoing extreme economic, political and social upheaval, we arrived in Vladivostok on 30 September 1993. We had beaten the onset of the Russian winter and were one day ahead of schedule.

Leaving Uryum on the Trans-Siberian railway line, the only route to Sbega

1

Trainer wheels

William Snell, before his epic 2000-mile journey across the Nullarbor, from Menzies to Melbourne on his Rover Road Racer, May 1897

The desire and inspiration to explore by bicycle is most likely inherited from my great-great-uncle, William Snell. In 1897, five months after the first bicycle crossing of the continent, twenty-five-year-old Uncle Willy cycled from Menzies, in the Western Australian goldfields, to Melbourne, 'leisurely looking for pastoral land'. Snell's 2000-mile (3200-km) journey on his Rover Road Racer was the second crossing of the Nullarbor and took only twenty-six days. At the time he was, according to one newspaper account, 'just what a long-distance rider should be: the impersonification of health and strength'.

Snell's fast pace was attributable to the fact that his real motive was to propose to his childhood sweetheart. He was accepted, and after the wedding he left his young bride to travel by ship to Fremantle while he cycled back across the Nullarbor. Snell was to become known as the 'bike rider'. Even in the 1930s, at sixty years of age, he would round up his cattle on his push-bike and was seldom seen riding a horse.

I have vivid memories of William Snell's niece, my grandmother, telling me about his exploits, which inspired me to buy my first 'proper' bike. I earned my Malvern Star by collecting cow manure. At the age of eight or nine, I used to drive the ute out into the cow paddock and collect the drying cow pats with shovel and bucket until I had a full load. One of my parents would then drive the precious cargo 32 km into Northam, the nearest town, and deliver the pre-ordered fertiliser. I used to earn seven dollars per load: my second-hand Dragster, complete with plastic 'flower power' seat, was worth four loads of manure.

Cycling at that stage was really a passing fad for me. Ullaring Rock, the 830-hectare (2000 acre) wheat and sheep farm (we had a few cows too) where I grew up with my two sisters and two brothers, was mainly sand plain country and not very conducive to push-bike riding. All five of us possessed strong sporting ability, but it was evident from a very young age that I – number four in the family – had perhaps the most competitive and driven nature. I achieved success in mainstream sports, which in country Western Australia included hockey, athletics and tennis, while five years of boarding at Perth College added squash, cricket, cross-country running and a few others to the list.

My desire to travel and natural interest in geography probably evolved from constantly studying the map of the world which always hung on our kitchen wall. Whenever something happened in the news or I read about a place, the map was there as a constant reference. My grandfather (mother's father), who lived with us for the last few years of his life, fuelled my curiosity with stories of his World War I battles – he was fortunate to survive the trenches in France – and of his early life in England. In the 1960s, at the age of seventy, he and a long-time friend and fellow war veteran journeyed overland from Rome to Bombay, an adventure which captured my imagination.

The opportunity to travel came after I completed my Bachelor of Physical Education degree at the University of Western Australia and helped to organise and co-captain a University Hockey Club Tour of Great Britain. Thirty of us, a men's and a women's team, left in January 1990 for London, to play twenty fixtures over the following month. We managed to win more than we lost, but hockey aside, the time abroad enabled the personality of each tour member to flourish, and we developed friendships for life. After the tour, only six of the thirty flew home, the rest of us staying on in the UK for varying lengths of time, taking the opportunity to travel and work there and in Europe.

Back in Australia I had dreamt of cycle touring in France and Italy, but never imagined what I could actually achieve on a bicycle. Not that I would have had the confidence to ride by myself, especially in countries where I didn't speak the language. All that was about to change.

My first taste of bicycle travel came after the hockey tour when I was touring in Ireland with one of my good hockey friends, Dave Albrecht. Although he was not usually one for this type of exertion, I somehow convinced him that we should hire some bikes and cycle from Cork through south-west Ireland. Perhaps it was the recent visit to kiss the Blarney Stone that gave me the gift of the gab – at least for a brief moment. As there were no bikes available for hire at any of the dozen bicycle shops in Cork, we caught a bus down to a coastal village called Crosshaven where we found a fisherman with three rusty mountain bikes for hire. The third bike was for George, a New Zealander whom we had met in Cork and who was keen to join our little adventure.

We were completely ill-prepared, especially to be pushing into some wild weather in early March. The fisherman dumped us on the side of the main road with three wrong-size bikes and no spare tubes, helmets, pump, tool kit or even a lock. He did give us a piece of chain and suggested we buy a padlock at the local hardware store. At the first service station we pumped up our tyres and added a few spots of oil to the bikechains before heading on our way.

I had promised that we would not do more than 50 km per day. So when on the first day we did 64 km before pulling into a pub in Dunmanway with sore backsides and aching, tired muscles, Dave, who is usually placid and easy-going, hissed with disdain. Every memory – good and bad – of that five-day adventure is still etched in my mind, ranging from being accosted by a dribbling drunk in a pub in Bantry, exploring a mountain near Glengarriff and crossing the windswept Healy Pass to receiving a puncture in Kenmare (the only town on our route with a bicycle shop) and getting lost on Macgillycuddy Reeks before descending through the stunning Gap of Dunloe to arrive in Killarney. Even after fifteen years, I have not had to refer to my diary to write this story (except to spell Macgillycuddy Reeks).

I was now hooked on this different form of travel. Back in London, I was soon kitted out with all the proper touring equipment and was planning my first escapade to France and Spain. Initially I travelled with hockey friends, but by the time we reached Clermont Ferrand in the Massif Central in France, we realised we had different agendas, abilities and expectations. They went off to meet friends in Toulouse and I stuck to my original plan, riding solo. Suddenly I was alone in a country where I didn't know anyone and didn't speak the language.

I thrived on the freedom of cycling on my own. There was particular satisfaction in reaching each goal under my own steam and making a line on a map come to life. And, of course, there was much more of a connection with the people and the land. This mode of travel enabled me to experience the heart of a country or region. If each country could be represented by a human body and its roads by its own blood-vessel network, then I can make the analogy that the act of cycling is like the flow of life-giving oxygenated blood through the major arteries (highways), which finally ends up at a specific destination by travelling through capillaries (minor roads) to the cells. Out in the open, moving at speeds closer to walking than driving, meant I was a lot more receptive to the surroundings than one ever is in a car. I experienced the heat on my forehead and the rain on my shoulders, felt the effect of each pothole and bump, smelled the farms and heard the streams. I became part of the landscape, enjoying merging harmoniously into its natural momentum. A car by contrast stays outside, an alien object conveying occupants in a climate-controlled bubble, removed from the immediate environment.

Cycling, especially alone, is perceived as a positive action: you have the confidence, interest and trust to immerse yourself in a certain region and culture. Cyclists are not considered to be wealthy – or they wouldn't be riding a bike. Contrary to my own initial concerns, and those of people who haven't experienced bicycle travel, cycling with loaded panniers is relatively safe. As long as you remain alert and don't take unnecessary risks, on the whole I consider cycling a safer and pleasanter mode of travel than using public transport.

Locals are generally interested in cyclists and respect the effort involved in pedalling a pile of metal around their neck of the woods. The bike is often an instant conversation starter: 'Where have you come from? How many kilometres do you cycle each day? How many flat tyres have you had? How many gears do you have?' After a while it is difficult to patiently answer the same questions over and over, especially when tired and hungry, but tolerance and good humour are usually rewarded with acts of kindness and the making of new friends. The bike is a great leveller, for people can see that there is nothing to hide and their streets are not being filled with noise, dust and fumes. Cycle touring breaks down barriers, and it makes one humble, which is the greatest virtue any traveller could wish for.

Unexpected opportunities are one of the many joys of bike touring. Nearly anything can happen. As I pushed on through Spain on my major 9000-km 'personal discovery' of Europe, flippers and snorkel would have been a more appropriate mode of travel to reach the centre of Barcelona than a bicycle. The persistent summer deluge transformed the roads into raging torrents. Looking for a specific youth hostel, I referred to my map, which now more closely resembled papier mâché, and decided I needed some help. The two elderly gents I consulted, who were sheltering under a doorway, had no comprehension of what I was asking as they spoke Catalan rather than Spanish. At that point, a car pulled up and a young man came over to see whether he could assist. Estevez, who spoke English, knew where I needed to go and asked me to wait. He parked his car, pulled his mountain bike out of the back and proceeded to escort me in the driving rain wearing only jeans and a shirt. We wound our way for a couple of kilometres through cobblestone streets and finally up a steep climb to arrive at the hostel. Soaking wet, Estevez waited to see that I was able to book in, gave me his telephone number and insisted I call if I needed any more help. Then he disappeared back out into the rain.

Chivalrous Spaniards, generous French or exuberant Italians – priceless interactions seemed to occur with such amazing regularity that I would have to remind myself not to take kind actions and hospitality for granted. Such respect was not isolated to cycling-friendly countries like France, Spain and Italy. I can recall an equal number of rewarding experiences during a total of 15 000 km of pedalling through the Mediterranean region to Turkey, through Central Europe and even beyond the Arctic Circle in Norway. As time passes, any negative experiences tend to be either erased from memory or at least stored away in a 'WinZip' file and archived in the back of my mind. I have had more negative experiences travelling with someone else than on my own, probably because I take fewer risks alone.

Travelling solo in Italy was one of the few times I felt fearful. Although I was asked many times for *un caffè* by young hopefuls who followed on occasions on their Vespas, a polite 'No' and then ignoring them completely usually did the trick. My experience on the road between Pisa and Florence was far more threatening. The driver of a white van had noticed me checking out my map on the side of the road, changed direction and started following me. He kept passing me and then slowing down, so much so that I had to cycle around the vehicle. I ignored him completely and dropped a gear or two on my bike. Spinning the pedals faster, even if moving at the same speed, gave the impression that I was strong and had plenty of energy. This cat-and-mouse game continued for about five or so kilometres, until I ran out of patience and decided to confront the man. This was not a time to be humble. I stopped at the car window, looked him in the eye and asked assertively, 'What the f— do you want?' Maybe this was not a wise choice of words because even though I did not speak Italian, his answer was clear and he then lunged at me, grabbing at my shirt. I reacted by tensing up my body and breaking away with a twisting motion. Striking him could have inflamed the situation; my aim was to demonstrate that I was more than he could handle and that I was not interested. I started pedalling again and he continued to pass, this time waving money at me. I ignored him and cycled confidently. It was important that he did not realise that, behind the facade, I was very scared. Eventually he gave up, and spurred on by adrenaline, I pushed on to Florence in extra quick time.

Rare encounters like this are a sobering reminder to combine caution with adventure. Trusting one's own instincts and taking care to avoid potentially dangerous situations are part of the deal.

◆　◆　◆

With such a cocktail of experiences behind me, self-belief and confidence in my cycling ability soared and my goals became more ambitious. It was time to raise the bar. The idea of traversing Russia had been a dream ever since I had studied the world map on the kitchen wall at home. The fact that the Soviet Union was a mysterious land which wrapped halfway around the globe evoked particular fascination. My plans to cycle through Russia germinated somewhere in Arctic Norway on a cycling journey to the Nord Kapp in the summer of 1992. On my return to London, where I worked as a fitness counsellor in a gym in Chelsea Harbour, I started researching this grand adventure to see if I could make it a reality.

I had been safely located in the Southern Hemisphere, studying at university in Perth, at the time of the Chernobyl nuclear accident on 26 April 1986. Although the news of the world's worst nuclear catastrophe, caused when 100 million curies of radioactive materials were released into the atmosphere, sickened me, I was glad I was so far away. There was nothing I could do about it.

In 1986, my image of the Soviet Union was the communist enemy, the Cold War, the nuclear threat of the arms race, espionage, the KGB and, above all, the Iron Curtain preventing freedom of expression. I pictured onion-domed churches, ballet dancers, Olympic domination, vodka and potatoes. Siberia I imagined as a frozen wasteland of salt mines and Stalin's concentration camps. Independent travel across the USSR was restricted to a censored journey on the Trans-Siberian Railway.

With the subsequent advent of Gorbachev's *glasnost*, and the break-up of the Soviet Union into the Commonwealth of Independent States (CIS), unrestricted travel was becoming possible. By 1992, most of what we in the West heard about Moscow and St Petersburg concerned bare shelves in shops, bread queues, dire poverty, the mafia and alarming reports of crime and corruption. I wanted to know what else the 'New Russia' had to offer.

The ball was really set rolling in early January 1993, when I wrote to Russian cycling clubs to try to find cyclists to join my expedition. At this point I met Robert Swan, the first man in history to have walked to both the North and South poles, and at the time a United Nations Goodwill Ambassador for Youth and the Environment. Under Robert's guidance, the project which I named the Trans-Siberian Cycle Expedition, and which features in the Prologue of this book, was streamlined into a more marketable plan, and he became its patron. Traversing what was now the largest country in the world would involve cycling from St Petersburg on the Baltic Sea to Vladivostok on the Pacific Ocean. Few people would have backed such an ambitious proposal, especially since I had only three-and-a-half months to organise everything from scratch – itinerary, the 'Russian side', sponsorship, equipment, the charity aspect and publicity – while working full time.

Rather than simply satisfying my own spirit of adventure, I realised that such a journey could have a greater value. I already knew Ted Johns, the European Director of the charity Children's Aid International, and had learned of the organisation's excellent work aiding children affected by the Chernobyl disaster. Although the accident had occurred in the Ukraine, Belarus and Russia were also seriously affected. Belarus, in fact, received approximately 70 per cent of the total amount of radiation which spewed out of the No 4 reactor for ten days and nights. About 14 million people from the former Soviet Union still suffer the effects of the world's worst nuclear mishap, which released one hundred times more radiation than the atomic bombs dropped on Hiroshima and Nagasaki. Aiding the children of Chernobyl by supporting the American-based charity Children's Aid International and its Belarusian partner organisation, RESPONSE,

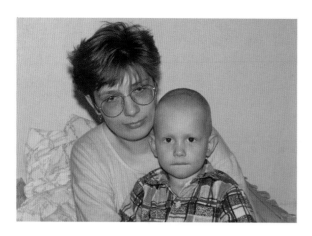

Children of Chernobyl – mother with her child who is suffering from thyroid cancer, Borovlyani Centre, Minsk, April 1994

was a means of directly helping the people of the former Soviet Union, something I would not have considered a few years previously.

This, then, was the context of the Trans-Siberian Cycle Expedition. When the expedition was over, I travelled to Belarus to see some of the problems for myself, meeting and learning from the volunteers of the RESPONSE charity who were working tirelessly for their people. In Minsk I visited the Paediatric Oncology Department of the Borovlyani Centre where the eighty times increase in the rate of child cancer made a gut-wrenching impact on me. The most alarming rise is in the incidence of thyroid cancer. I arrived at the centre armed with my camera ready to capture a record of the situation. Overwhelmed by the number of gravely ill, bald children with great wads of dressings over their necks – some walking around, others too sick to leave their bedside – I took only two photographs and put my camera away. I would have made a poor investigative journalist but I got the impression these proud people – the children and their families – did not wish to be photographed in such a condition. As I pressed the shutter, it felt as though I was taking away some of their dignity.

I travelled next to Gomel, close to the Ukrainian border, where I toured one of the city's twenty-six orphanages. The director of this orphanage, Vladimir Kleyner, was particularly impressive as he had relinquished the opportunity to live in the USA with some of his family to stay on in Gomel and look after the 365 children and young people, aged between six and nineteen, who lived in the institution. As I discussed the situation with him, like everyone else in the area I had no way of knowing whether the food I had eaten had been contaminated with dangerous isotopes. Radioactive elements such as iodine-131, caesium-137, strontium-90 and plutonium-239 circulate through the Gomel region via the water cycle and as dust in the atmosphere, and are readily absorbed into the food chain.

Money raised from the Trans-Siberian Cycle Expedition provided a Russian-English computer translation system and the remainder was contributed towards some of the costs of setting up a research program to chart the effects of sending children from contaminated regions to neighbouring radiation-free zones. Children's Aid International/RESPONSE helped develop summer respite camps in Poland and within non-contaminated regions of Belarus, where costs could be kept to a minimum. Recuperating at these camps meant the children did not suffer from the culture shock of visiting Western countries nor the depression which often followed their return to Belarus from further afield, when all the things they were missing out on impacted on them.

By the time this book is published, the Chernobyl catastrophe will have marked its twentieth anniversary. Such is the nature and magnitude of the worst nuclear accident in history that its most serious effects will not diminish for more than one thousand generations. The full extent of the impacts on health, the environment, the economy and the social aspects are yet to be fully assessed. About 97 per cent of the radioactive materials from the Chernobyl plant remain inside a hastily constructed, crumbling sarcophagus in urgent need of repair.

◆　◆　◆

The first Greg Yeoman knew of me or the Trans-Siberian Expedition was an out-of-the-blue telephone call he received on his way to work one Monday morning. I had met his brother at a party in London, and he had given me the number. I said something like, 'Hello Greg, you don't know me, but I met your brother at a party on the weekend and would you like to cycle to Vladivostok with me?' I knew he was the right man for the challenge when he told me how he had once cycled 800 km with a broken arm on a charity ride to Greece. Once Greg committed, a partnership was born which was central to the success of the venture.

Forming the 'Russian side' of the expedition was Robert Swan's friend and fellow Polar explorer, Dr Misha Malakhov, and his Ryazan-based company, Centre Pole. With unrivalled expertise, the company organised expeditions in the Russian Arctic. I was invited to Ryazan one month before the start to negotiate a contract. The agreement ensured that there was always an accompanying cyclist to help us with language and steer us through a country in chaos, that we had a base for communications, storage for excess equipment, a safe to store cash and practical advice based on years of experience. In return, we supplied all the equipment and funding. Throughout the duration of the expedition, we were to keep in contact with Centre Pole by sending a weekly telegram, as this was the most reliable form of communication.

The itinerary I had devised involved pedalling an average of 130 km per day (except in the Swamp region, where no roads were marked on our maps). This was extremely optimistic according to Dr Malakhov, who warned, 'You don't know Russian roads'. The plan included not only crossing the seven time zones by the most direct route but also took in a further 1600 km of diversions in order to explore places of interest. Greg and I broke the journey down into manageable sections: European Russia, the Steppe, the Sayan Mountains, Lake Baikal and Environs, the Swamp and Far-eastern Siberia. I had to be accurate with the planning because there was a time limit. We needed to start by 1 May in order to have a chance of covering the 13 386-km distance within five months, by 1 October, to avoid the onset of the severe Siberian winter. During October the weather can change at any time, with the freezing conditions potentially making the roads impassable.

When Greg and I started out as planned from the Decembrists' Square in St Petersburg, just after the midday bells had tolled from the Sts Peter and Paul Cathedral, we could not possibly have predicted the adventures which would unfold for us over the next five months.

It only took until the end of the first day for us to become immersed in the culture of Russian village life. Arriving in a tiny *paseoloc* (hamlet) called Ribovo we were invited to stay in the *dacha* of a man named Sasha. We slept in a basic, dusty, wooden cottage with no running water; it was nestled in the midst of the owner's vegetable garden, and surrounded by his chickens, rabbits, dogs and cats. Our host donated as many potatoes as we could eat. George, one of our first two guides, negotiated for another villager to milk her cow for us. The five of us, Sasha, George, Vladimir, Greg and I, dined on potatoes, bread, salami, pickles, onions and six litres of milk by the light of flickering flames. Communicating embraced a variety of techniques. George could speak a little English, we knew a few words of Russian, we constantly consulted the phrase book and by mixing all this with sign language and other gestures we managed to get by. This was what we had come to Russia to experience. We never looked back.

By the time we reached Moscow after covering 800 km in the first week, we had seen as much as most Westerners ever see of Russia. At this stage I was cursing the salesman at my bicycle shop in London who recommended that I use a leather seat as it would be the most durable and would only take about 800 km to wear in. In the meantime, my backside was literally wearing out; I hoped the raw skin would soon be as resilient as a tanned hide. The effort of the first week was certainly marred by the fact that it took me at least twenty minutes after every break to numb the pain and be able to sit on my bicycle saddle with full body weight.

We still had almost five months to go, four of them in Siberia. Greg and I certainly were privileged to witness the 'New Russia' emerging from the ruins of communism as we crossed seven time zones and travelled a distance equivalent to three-and-a-half times across Australia. The five Russian cyclists who joined us for various sections of the journey also learnt more about their country and about our Western culture, although it would have been difficult for them to imagine many of the things we described, especially in face of the language barrier.

The reality of Siberia, its diverse nature, stunning landscapes, intense summer heat (up to 40°C, turning the tarmac into the consistency of treacle at times), the people – ethnic minorities, Caucasian majorities – and how they live, is in complete contrast to the general perception of the country as a land of frozen plains and salt mines. The level of hospitality was constantly humbling and rarely did we experience any hostility. There were times when we realised that our hosts were giving us far too much of the little food they had left to sustain them through the following winter. Despite being hungry, we restrained ourselves from devouring what was generously offered so they wouldn't go without.

Having survived the Swamp, and left the city of Kharbarovsk in eastern Siberia behind, it was now on to Vladivostok. To arrive on schedule, we needed to cover a similar distance to that of our first week, when we rode from St Petersburg to Moscow. This is where the similarities ended. In Moscow, President Yeltsin's leadership was in the process being challenged and a battle took place to oust the militants who had seized the White House. The president had responded by ordering his national forces to send in the tanks to blast out the offenders. Despite the political unrest in the west, the people of Kharbarovsk, Vladivostok and Ussuriland – the region sandwiched between the two cities – continued on as usual, unaffected by the drama unfolding so far away in their capital city. They were used to looking after themselves, and the process of business privatisation was more advanced here than elsewhere.

In communist times, the Ussuriland region, home of the threatened Siberian tiger, was a closed military zone and Trans-Siberian trains would travel through at night, non-stop with the shutters down. A day south of Kharbarovsk, we spotted some MiG fighter jets through the bushes, found a hole in the fence and walked into the back of a military air field. The whole area was dilapidated. Yuri and Sasha took delight in climbing over the bomb casings of the once-feared weapons of the mighty Soviet Red Army. There were bombs stored in the aircraft hangars which I hoped never fell into the wrong hands. Realising we had stumbled across a sensitive military outpost which we had no permission to enter, we hastily recorded the moment and ate our picnic on the other side of the fence.

On the penultimate night of the Trans-Siberian Cycle Expedition we ended up in a village called Kremovo. The hotel was full of Chinese in town doing business with the locals so we were directed to the derelict railway station which was by contrast now a relic of the communist era. The woman in charge allowed us to

Signs of the times, Russia 1993

President Boris Yeltsin with the Canadian prime minister, in the Kremlin, 9 May 1993

Lone bus stop on the Siberian Steppe – a symbol of how the communist regime revered the worker, with the most diligent and worthy awarded the status of 'town heroes'

Tuvan men in Ak Durug, Sayan Mountains, near the north-western Mongolian border; ethnic minorities were not recognised under Soviet rule

In the village of Chudovo (near Novgorod, Day 2), the church had recently been restored and reinstated. These villagers were queuing to kiss the main icon which was being returned to the church after seventy years of religious prohibition

Slavic and Nicholai – their dairy farm had just converted from being a collective farm to a cooperative where villagers bought shares in the 350 hectares

Sasha climbing over a MiG fighter jet, once a prized fighting machine of the Red Army

Champanski – arriving at the Vladivostok city boundary on 30 September 1993, one day ahead of schedule after five months on the road

stay in the *Krasney Oogolok* or 'Little Red Corner', a room that had been the meeting place for railway officials – an important site in view of the fact that communism glorified the worker and, by extension, the railways. Everything was covered with a thick layer of dust which had not been disturbed for quite some time. Dominating the far, dimly-lit wall were two massive framed portraits, one of Lenin and the other of Marx. It felt as though the 'Fathers of Communism' were watching over us as we cooked one of our last meals on our leaking, petrol-burning Russian primus (stove) – soup with extra pasta followed by rice pudding. Every time a train thundered by, dust and pieces of plaster dislodged from the walls, one fragment almost landing in our soup.

The mayor of the town of Kiparicovo, where we stayed on our final night, presented us with a Russian flag. Sasha was over the moon as he had never held the new national flag before. He attached it to a stick and for the last seven kilometres to the Vladivostok border he proudly waved it – upside down. No Russian corrected his mistake, which I took to be a sign of the times.

We miraculously managed to find a bottle of *champanski* in a village shop just before Vladivostok (for the entire trip, we had rarely been able to find what we needed in Russian stores) and celebrated in style. Having sampled the quality of Russian bubbly previously, I am sure it was better to shake it up and spray it everywhere rather than actually consume any of it. We spent a few days in Vladivostok trying to arrange flights back to Moscow, an unexpected challenge due to the political unrest. The Australian consulate was very helpful and we were soon out of there, via a nine-hour domestic Aeroflot flight.

◆ ◆ ◆

Not only was I accurate about the timing of the Russian journey, but also the budget. I arrived back in London with fourteen pounds to my name, but far richer for the experience. It took a few weeks to get my head around being back in Western civilisation and much longer to put everything into perspective.

When I found work at the Harbour Club in Fulham managing the swimming pool, little did I realise that I was about to discover the game of real tennis and a whole new career opportunity. Tucked in behind the underground pool was the first real tennis court built in London for about eighty years.

Real tennis, also known as *jeu de paume* in France, court tennis in the USA and formerly known as royal tennis in Australia and Scotland, is the precursor to all modern racquet sports. The 10 000 exponents of the game (approximately) around the world know it simply as tennis. The game which most of the world know as tennis is officially named lawn tennis, and began around 130 years ago in Leamington Spa, England, when players were unable to play on the indoor tennis court and decided to take their racquets and balls on to the lawn outside. The game of lawn tennis they devised had a different court design from real tennis, simplified rules and demanded fewer technical skills. This made it more accessible than real tennis and led to it becoming more popular.

I stepped into a new world when I walked out onto the Harbour Club court for the first time for my introduction to real tennis. I was intrigued by the court's asymmetric architecture and the vastness of the three-dimensional playing space. (A tennis court can fit four squash courts within its walls.) After two group lessons I was thrown straight into the deep end. There was nothing like the pressure of competition to accelerate learning. I very quickly re-discovered my competitive spirit and relished the opportunity to learn a new game which I simply enjoyed with no expectations – initially. Although a completely different field from the Russian cycle expedition, the level of commitment, determination and focus required translated to my new challenge. I was able to draw on and adapt a range of skills from most of the sports on my curriculum vitae and my standard steadily improved when I volunteered in my spare time to play virtually anyone at the club using the accurate handicap system. Expectations were gradually raised and I approached my new sport with greater intensity.

After two years, I had established myself as one of the strongest women, winning the 1996 Australian Open singles and doubles titles and making at least the semi-finals in the British, French and US Opens. With positive encouragement to take it further, I accepted the opportunity to become a training professional, one of two working women professionals in the world at the time, and moved to The Oratory School in Berkshire.

Becoming a real tennis professional was a decision of passion for the 'modern game' rather than of economic opportunity. Unlike with its more popular cousin (lawn tennis), prize money for real tennis professionals generally amounts to little more than pocket money. Real tennis professionals earn a living from the game by working as club professionals.

As a player, I wanted to give it my best shot to reach my potential, whatever that may be. As a club professional, my role was to be involved in all aspects of running a club and promoting the game. Every discipline, from coaching, hand-making the balls and hand-stringing the racquets, organising tournaments and umpiring matches, is highly specialised. Attempting to achieve my goals as a pro therefore demanded total devotion and was far more than a nine-to-five job – it became a rewarding, all-consuming way of life.

In joining the small and supportive world of real tennis, I embarked on an adventure of a completely different kind. Its demands dried up any

Real tennis – a new focus. Warming up for the 2003 World Championships, Royal Melbourne Tennis Club
(photo: T Collens)

opportunities for re-creating anything like the Russian expedition. Other doors opened, however. I met and fell in love with Arnaud Domange, when he came to England from France to work as a training professional. In my first few years as a pro I was privileged to work in some very special places – The Oratory and Hardwick House, Cambridge, and Arnaud's home court in Fontainebleau (in a chateau 60 km south-east of Paris). Arnaud and I were married in Fontainebleau in 2002, before we returned to Australia at the end of that year. I accepted a position as Deputy Head Professional at the Royal Melbourne Tennis Club while Arnaud decided to change careers altogether. When I first ventured to the UK on the hockey tour, I never imagined that I would be away from Australia for a total of twelve years.

Experiences as a professional, however, took me on a more personal journey and forced me to dig deep within, not always in the direction that I wanted to go. A knee injury sustained during an overly competitive match back in 1996, just before I became a pro, has remained problematic during the course of my playing career. Sheering articular cartilage directly off the head of the femur (thigh bone) meant I entered a cycle of surgery followed by painstaking, expensive rehabilitation and comebacks. Seven operations in total ensured that I was off the court for more time than I was on it, despite being fortunate in having access to the best technology available. In between the time-outs I managed to work my way to World No. 3.

◆　◆　◆

After the 2003 World Championships in Melbourne, my knee was definitely not happy and I felt like I was going through the motions; any opportunity to improve as a player was restricted as I was unable to put in the maximum effort required without a strong reaction. Giving lessons while masking the discomfort was mentally draining day after day. The reactions I was experiencing were a sure sign that the grafted cartilage was wearing thin. This unhappy development destroyed the balance between being a club professional and being able to explore opportunities to improve my game. Although I still had a passion for real tennis, it felt as though I was stagnating.

An MRI scan and doctor's advice verified that if I continued to train and play at the level I had been maintaining over previous years I would compromise my ability to move without pain. Cycling, however, would not be detrimental to my injury because it is a weight-supported activity where legs work in a single, controlled plane. Twisting and changing directions on a concrete surface was doing my knee in.

In light of this unwelcome news, I started to toss around the ideas which had been in my mind since the Trans-Siberian Expedition. I pulled out old plans that had been hatched during the coldest, darkest European winters. Cycling through vast open spaces and desert sands in the Australian heat had seemed a very attractive proposition from there. Arnaud was of the view that I really needed to have a go at the expedition I had been thinking about ever since he had known me. Originally he had wanted to be a part of it, but came to realise that his new career brought other priorities. He insisted that I must go ahead or put the whole idea to rest. There was only a small window of opportunity in my life in which to do so, and that was now.

First, I had to analyse what it was I wanted to achieve, work out what was realistically possible, and settle on a purpose and route which best signified my intentions. Over the next month, the plan for the Great Australian Cycle Expedition (GRACE Expedition) evolved, and the concept formalised in a prospectus detailing who, what, why, when and how, along with logistics, budget and equipment. With this I hoped to attract sponsors and publicity. Overall, I aimed to travel by bicycle unsupported into the heart of my country and to explore remote regions off the beaten track. I planned to pedal the entire 25 000-km, nine-and-a-half month journey and hoped to attract cyclists to join me where possible. I also needed to find supporters to help coordinate the project off the bike.

The process of organising such a huge project is similar to setting up a new business – developing an original idea into a strong concept about which I felt passionate, being confident the goals were achievable, and creating a product I could sell. From a solid base, the idea was refined by networking and persisting over many long hours, with personal sacrifice and sheer hard work.

It took me nine months (three months longer than I had planned) to carry out this organising phase. Tasks undertaken while I was also working full-time included developing the concept, planning the route, logistics, coordinating and writing material for the website (including educational activities), finding a team to help out and join me where possible, organising publicity, and keeping fit.

One of the major selling points was the route. Every year many people cycle around Australia, usually choosing a path closely following Highway No. 1. While this is still a noble feat, whether it be for personal reasons and/or raising money or awareness for a particular cause, it is difficult to sell because it has become a popular journey. Cycling this route means riding about 15 000 km and generally hugging the bitumen. I wanted to extend myself and build on previous cycling achievements. A journey around Australia on its main highway would be relatively straightforward compared with the Russian Expedition, and did not present enough of a challenge to satisfy me.

The route I planned was much more of an exploration of the country. Of the 25 000 km of pedalling planned, about 7000 km would be 'off-road' cycling on isolated, long-distance tracks. I had already learnt that cycling unsupported evokes an incredible 'sense of place'. The distance involved was the equivalent of St Petersburg to Vladivostok and back again, further than many so-called around-the-world tours. The long-distance tracks I intended to travel included the Cape York Peninsula Development/Telegraph Road, the Gulf Track, the Tanami Track, the Great Central Road, the Gunbarrel Highway and the Canning Stock Route.

The Canning Stock Route is the world's longest and perhaps greatest long-distance stock route; approximately 2000 km in length, it crosses four deserts and around one thousand sand dunes. The only people living near the route are a small Indigenous community, at Kunawarritji halfway along, where limited supplies are available. If I was successful in cycling the route, I believed I would be the first woman to do so.

My projected program was unusually intense for an unsupported cyclist over a long period of time. To keep to my schedule and complete the sections through the north and central deserts during the Dry season meant covering at least 3000 km a month where there was tarmac. Appealing to the romantics among my supporters was the fact that I would be retracing two of the feats of my great-great-uncle William Snell by tackling the Canning Stock Route and later following his tyre tracks across the Nullarbor. In fact, Snell reconditioned the wells of the first two-thirds of the route back in 1929. A man of many talents and great fortitude, his achievements are detailed in later chapters.

As with the Trans-Siberian Cycle Expedition, I wanted to derive some benefit for the people of the country I was travelling through on the GRACE Expedition. I thought long and hard about how my plans could relate to my passions. In keeping with the theme of the purpose of the Russian journey, and as a result of the heightened awareness that had developed during its course, the Belarusian visit and a total of 30 000 km of bicycle travel, I realised that my interests were specifically allied with the concept of sustainable development. This is defined by the Brundtland World Commission on Environment and Development in its significant 1987 report *Our Common Future* as 'development that meets the needs of the present without compromising the ability of future generations to meet their own needs'. A connectedness I knew would develop with the people and the land during my journey would contribute to my understanding of many attitudes toward and issues of sustainability within Australia. My belief was that the greatest value of my expedition would lie in motivating others to take action.

At the heart of my concept was that cycling unsupported is a model for sustainability. The introduction I wrote on the website about the team sums this up, as follows.

> To succeed with the Great Australian Cycle Expedition, the team must adopt a completely sustainable approach. Pedalling an average of 6–8 hours per day, 3000 km per month for over nine months we must travel at a workload (intensity, frequency, duration) which is sensitive to our personal thresholds so it can be maintained. If we cycle too hard, carry too much weight, don't look after our bodies by drinking enough water, eating enough of the right food, getting enough sleep or fail to protect ourselves from the elements or to plan ahead, we will 'blow out' and the expedition will not succeed. We are all individuals from very different backgrounds. To reach our common goal we must cooperate, respect and accept each others' differences and support each other.

We will have to work hard to overcome obstacles and difficulties as they arise.

To achieve a sustainable future, communities (local, national and global) need to adopt a similar model of approach to the GRACE team. Population control, reduction of poverty, education of women, maintaining the biodiversity of species, short-sighted use of finite energy resources, creating excessive waste and continuing with unsustainable land clearing practices are a few examples of issues which will threaten the health of communities, the environment and the existence and function of life as we know it. In other words we need to 'look after our global body'.

Education is the key to sustainable development. Sustainability should be in everyone's mindset and needs to be adopted as a normal part of life. This positive, optimistic project is about taking action and every person must feel responsible and empowered to make a difference.

If we can contribute to the motivation of youth to be proactive towards sustainable development, then the project has succeeded.

UNESCO, the United Nations Education Scientific and Cultural Organisation, adopted the Great Australian Cycle Expedition as Australia's first, and one of the world's first, Demonstration Activities for its Decade of Education for Sustainable Development which was to begin in 2005. It identified that the ethos of my project was in line with its vision for a sustainable future. UNESCO's vision of education for sustainable development states:

There can be few more pressing and critical goals for the future of humankind than to ensure steady improvement in the quality of life for this and future generations, in a way that respects our common heritage – the planet we live on. As people we seek positive change for ourselves, our children and our grandchildren; we must do it in ways that respect the right of all to do so. To do this we must learn constantly – about ourselves, our potential, our limitations, our relationships, our society, our environment, our world. Education for sustainable development is a life-wide and lifelong endeavour which challenges individuals, institutions and societies to view tomorrow as a day that belongs to all of us, or it will not belong to anyone.

The GRACE project was selected as a Demonstration Activity because it satisfied the main criteria due to its focus on the educational and learning dimensions of sustainable development, innovative nature, ability to make a difference, likelihood of having a sustainable effect and potential for replication.

Education for sustainable development (ESD) has no universal model and is equally relevant for both developed and developing nations. According to UNESCO, ESD is about learning to:
- respect, value and preserve achievements of the past;
- appreciate the wonders and peoples of the Earth;
- live in a world where all people have sufficient food for a healthy and productive life;
- create and enjoy a better, safer, more just world;
- be caring citizens who exercise their rights and responsibilities locally, nationally and globally.

I planned to communicate these messages by means of a website where observations would be reported in the diary section and educational activities would be made accessible, by visiting schools, people and organisations where possible en route, and via the media on local, state and national levels.

UNESCO's sponsorship enhanced the credibility of the project and was an important selling point which helped sway a number of potential sponsors. Although the expedition had what I considered an important purpose, it was often difficult to sell because it was slightly ahead of its time and many didn't comprehend the importance of the concept. The purpose was not as tangible as raising money directly for a cause.

An essential part of the organisation of the project was finding good people to help behind the scenes and accompany me where possible during the route. I sent emails to various contacts and cycling organisations around the world, in Japan, Mexico, India, the UK, USA, Canada, New Zealand, Russia and other countries. There were many interested potential fellow cyclists but either they could not afford the time or the financial commitment. The intense schedule also weeded out many when they realised this was no holiday.

Greg Yeoman, back in the UK, must have had feelings of *déjà vu* when he first received my email detailing the plans. It was roughly ten years since I had called to ask whether he would like to cycle to Vladivostok. His first exclamation this time was 'What a huge journey!' Since the Russian expedition he had been working at the same job, managing mountain biking holidays for a British adventure travel company. He agreed with me that it was time for a new challenge, time to move out of his comfort zone. He had extra considerations this time including his relationship and financial commitments. Greg's background both as an experienced, strong cyclist and his previous employment as an ecologist stood him in good stead for being a major part of the expedition. Not only did he agree to join me for the first 12 000 km of the ride – as far as Wiluna at the end of the Gunbarrel Highway – but he committed much time and effort to finding sponsors and working, where possible, on the education for sustainable development side. The strength of Greg's commitment shored up my belief in the project in times of doubt, when there was so much to do in so little time, and when I received the inevitable knock-backs from potential investors whom I had targeted as likely supporters. Greg had to hand in his notice at work three months in advance, committing his time well before I had secured most of the sponsorship and was able to hand in my own resignation.

The other most significant support came from Andrew Rickard at the Victorian Association for Environmental Education (VAEE). He responded to a general letter I had sent out in the hope of creating networking contacts and ended up not only coordinating support for the educational aspect of the project from within the VAEE but also volunteering his personal time. Andrew was to act as the base, coordinating the educational side while I was cycling; he planned to join me at some stage of the journey if his work commitments would allow.

The final few weeks were totally mad and there was barely any time to sleep. I could not leave Arnaud unless I had secured everything financially. The main sponsor, Alcoa, made its generous commitment three weeks before the expedition was due to begin. I had already adjusted the starting date as far back as I could: to set off any later would have meant I would not have been able to cover the planned route through northern Australia and the deserts within the Dry season. I also had to keep my real tennis work and my expedition separate until I had sufficient financial backing. There were all sorts of technical difficulties with the website and that side of things wasn't progressing as I had hoped. In addition, I was still writing the educational worksheets.

Pressures continued to mount from all directions. I was overwhelmingly busy writing emails trying to sort out the publicity, website, sponsors, equipment, insurance, the start in Canberra and the team. When Greg arrived in Melbourne to help out in the final week, I was yet to receive any of the sponsorship funds and therefore could not buy any of the equipment which I had lined up. It was difficult to convey to the organisations involved my heightened sense of urgency. These financial restraints meant I had to work up until the final weekend. The thought of leaving my husband for so long was really starting to hit home: I didn't want to leave him for a week, let alone nine months. Fortunately, I received just enough funds in time which, along with Greg's and my personal investments, allowed us to purchase the bikes and all essential pieces of equipment. The last couple of days were a bit like Christmas except my brain was too overloaded to understand any instruction manuals. I would have to learn how to use all the technology, such as the iPAQ palm-sized computer, a digital SLR camera and a video camera, on the road.

Suddenly the leaving day was upon us. Greg and I had divided all the equipment up and carried out several 'dummy' packs to determine how it would all fit in. The two front and two rear panniers had to be balanced, with the most-needed items made easily accessible.

And then the hardest part of all – leaving Arnaud. Although we would be able to telephone each other regularly and he would be able to visit me on occasions during the expedition, the thought of not being with him for so long was tearing me apart. He supported what I was doing and said it would give him time to consolidate his own career. I didn't want to let go but I had to. Before we set off, Greg left us alone for quite some time. Eventually, I took the driver's seat of the hire car and squeezed Arnaud's hand as I started the engine. He didn't let go until I let the vehicle roll forward. I still don't know how I did it. That moment was to haunt me for the duration of the expedition.

QLD

Brisbane ●

Border Ranges

Lismore ○ — ○ Byron Bay

Great Dividing Range

Waterfall Way ○ Grafton

Armidale ○ *Waterfall Way*
Uralla ○

NSW

Thunderbolts Way

Great North Rd ○ *Myall Lakes*

Maitland ○

Katoomba ○
Oberon ○ *Blue Mountains* ● **Sydney**

Canberra ○ Goulburn

● **ACT**

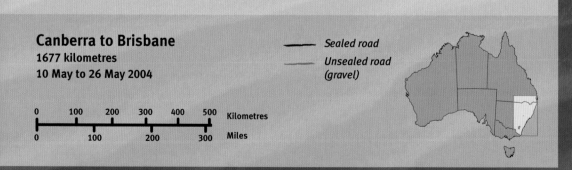

Canberra to Brisbane
1677 kilometres
10 May to 26 May 2004

—— *Sealed road*
—— *Unsealed road (gravel)*

| 0 | 100 | 200 | 300 | 400 | 500 | Kilometres |

| 0 | 100 | 200 | 300 | Miles |

2

Out there

(The Start: Canberra to Brisbane)

At Cape Byron, the most easterly point of the country

The tenth of May 2004 was a typically crisp late autumn morning in Canberra. We returned our hire car to the airport depot and loaded our gleaming new bikes for the first time with all our equipment. Everything had to fit securely and in balance – a real intelligence test, a three-dimensional jigsaw puzzle. Whatever couldn't be packed into the front and rear panniers and bar-bag was held on with elastic bungy straps: tent, water-bags and sandals. The eight kilometres from the airport to our official starting point at Parliament House was the first time we'd ridden the bikes at all, let alone with such a load.

Clattering over speed bumps, we wobbled off toward the main road. Our machines sat heavily on the tarmac, their normally rigid aluminium frames flexed, looking more like prime movers than agile mountain bikes. Peak-hour traffic was banked up all the way into town, so we mostly crept down the hard shoulder about as deftly as an elephant on a tightrope. Finding our way through the unfamiliar road network, however, wasn't so straightforward and pressure mounted as we started to doubt whether we would arrive in time for our meeting with the federal Minister for Education, the Hon. Dr Brendan Nelson.

I had chosen Canberra as the start and finish point because I thought it most appropriate, considering the purpose of the expedition. We would be able to deliver our message to those who make the decisions. To time the journey to fit in with the seasons, we needed to start in the south-east of the country, and Canberra seemed to be the 'apolitical' choice between Melbourne and Sydney. The word Canberra is a hybrid of 'Canberry' and 'Kamberra'. Canberry was the name Joshua Moore gave to the first land grant on the Limestone Plains on

With Dr Brendan Nelson,
Parliament House

which the federal city was later built, after he heard local Aboriginals using the word 'Kamberra' in their conversations. The word Kamberra meant 'a meeting place' of either rivers or of tribes joining together to feast on Bogong moths. We too were using Canberra as a meeting place, minus the Bogong moths.

We began the 'warm-up' ride rugged up with fleeces and cycling longs, the cold, dry air rasping on the back of our throats. Grappling with the unaccustomed workload and the brief panic that we might be late, we pushed up Parliament Hill, arriving with steam rising off our bodies and only a few minutes to spare. The press had started to gather around the ministerial entrance, making us feel nervous. Surely the media release which had been circulated couldn't have been this successful? What was I going to say? I tried to practise the answers in my mind. Why were we about to pedal 25 000 km through Australia over nine months? What is sustainability? Why is it so important? How do you feel with 25 000 km to go? How did I feel? I couldn't tell the press that I was absolutely exhausted and highly stressed. I'd had little sleep over the last month and the final few days were completely mad. What was I doing? I'd left behind my husband, my safe, full-time job and my whole comfort zone. I was concerned that the website wasn't ready and that I was yet to receive the bulk of the sponsorship money. We were here, though, waiting at the ministerial entrance of Parliament House with all the hard work done, and what wasn't quite ready should fall into place over the next few weeks. Enough people had invested their time, money and belief in the project and I had put myself on the line. The opportunity had been created and it was all up to us to pull it off.

All of a sudden an official car pulled up and the press swarmed toward the federal treasurer like a flock of enthusiastic schoolchildren. I had been so blinkered during the final few days that I had failed to register that the federal budget was due to be delivered the next day. The press weren't interested in us at all! But Dr Nelson soon appeared with his secretary to meet us and took the time to chat about the expedition, its purpose and specifically (and predictably) the importance of the educational aspect. He remained positive about the task ahead even after straining to lift my bike with its entire load to give him more of an idea of what I was pushing. We were careful to record the moment before he disappeared back into Parliament House for a cabinet meeting.

Eventually we set off just before midday, feeling satisfied that we had made the most of the official start. The chill which remained throughout the clear, sunny day reminded me of Yuri's quote about starting out on his part of the Russian expedition and seemed equally as appropriate: 'We were like bears waking from winter hibernation; clumsy and eternally hungry'. As we left Canberra's leafy, pristine streets and climbed out of the hills which form the capital's natural amphitheatre, I was overwhelmed by a sense of relief. Finally being out on the open road was like releasing the steam valve on a pressure cooker – the expedition had become a reality. The busy Federal Highway was somewhat of a rollercoaster ride as we scaled a series of long, steady hills.

Although not exceptionally challenging, the degree of difficulty was plenty enough for someone who had not yet found her cycling legs.

Three months into organising the project I had vowed that I did not want to start the GRACE Expedition without adequate physical preparation. I had done a few longer rides to test out my knee and my cardiovascular engine before I started accepting any sponsorship deals. I had managed 130 km without too much problem, although that was on my nimble racing bike rather than my workhorse of a mountain bike with all the baggage. As the departure date drew nearer, there was no way that I could afford the time to spend hours on the road so I had to be content with the odd intensive cycling session in the gym. During the last few weeks, I had managed nothing at all. Greg's physical preparation was equally as unsatisfactory. We spent much of the first day searching for cycling rhythm, taking a break every hour to an hour-and-a-half to stretch, eat and take in the sights. It was all about pacing ourselves.

Our first rest stop was at the top of the escarpment overlooking Lake George. The lake, normally a shallow, saltwater expanse, was bone-dry for the first time in sixty years. It had been about three years since it had held any water. The draining of Lake George was a strong indication that the surrounding land (and, in fact, most of eastern Australia) was in the grip of a severe drought. A mob of sheep stirred puffs of dust as they followed in single file across the lake bed. Being May, farmers would be hoping for the first breaking seasonal rains. We hoped the drought would be broken very soon, preferably after we had passed through!

The final hour into Goulburn seemed to last an eternity. I struggled to get my head around how I was going to occupy my mind for six to eight hours in the saddle every day: this journey promised to be a test of mental endurance just as much as a physical challenge. The first day had been long and emotionally charged and the evening nip in the air extracted every last ounce of energy. We rolled at a snail's pace into the large rural town just on sunset, diverting directly to the camping-ground. My body behaved like a car engine spluttering on its last few drops of fuel. Remarkably, after 100 km of pedalling, we had managed to average 21 km per hour, the same daily median we had clocked over the five months of the Trans-Siberian Cycle Expedition, ten years previously. From experience, we knew that while this was good for one day, the big test was whether we would be able to sustain the workload day after day.

Preparations for Day 2 on the road seemed to happen in slow motion. Yuri's analogy about bears and hibernation certainly rang true once more, although at that point we were arthritic old bears. From Goulburn it would have been

Pedalling through drought-affected countryside on an unsealed section of the Oberon Road, west of the Blue Mountains, Day 3
(photo: G Yeoman)

simplest to brave the busy Hume Highway traffic and head straight for Sydney, but as would be the pattern for the whole expedition, I chose a route away from the major arterial roads in order to experience a closer connection with the country we were travelling through. We stocked up at the last major town for a couple of days and headed north, skirting the western edge of the Blue Mountains on the Goulburn-Oberon Road.

The long, rolling hills of Day 1 soon seemed like mere ripples as the undulations condensed into a series of short, tortuously steep climbs. The residual tiredness from the previous day combined with the fact that our legs were not yet strong enough meant the quadriceps soon burned with lactic acid. The back, neck, shoulders and triceps also complained vigorously at this sudden physical shock. It was a rude awakening and I started to wonder whether, given the terrain, it was expecting too much of us that we would arrive in Sydney within four days (450 km).

We were soon passing through a high plain almost 1000 metres up at an embarrassingly low average speed. A bitter polar wind whistled across the open grassy paddocks, chilling us to the core. We were careful to keep moving and stretching on our snack breaks to avoid rigor mortis setting in, otherwise we may have ended up gnarled and twisted like the trunks of the majestic snow gums which dotted the scene. Cattle grazing on the rich pastures remained oblivious to our passing, as if we blended in to the landscape, although I am not sure whether we were 'merging harmoniously into its natural momentum' just yet.

Windswept, ravenous and lagging miserably behind schedule as we were, our spirits were lightened by the welcoming sign 'Taralga – Smile, You Are In A Happy Town'. This historic town of about 370 people has remained largely unchanged over the decades because the road through the village is not a major thoroughfare.

It is said that this country's economy grew on the sheep's back and today Australia is the world's biggest producer of wool, with an average total flock of over 100 million (at least five sheep per person). Although we had noticed herds of cattle on the way from Goulburn, Taralga is known for its pioneering contribution to the sheep industry. John and Elizabeth Macarthur were the most famous of the pioneers. In 1796, they imported merinos into Australia from South Africa. The Spanish breed thrived in the harsh, drier conditions and became prized for its high quality, fine wool. The Macarthurs refined the bloodlines on their farm at Parramatta and then at Camden, 60 km south-west of Sydney, and by 1803 they had a 4000-strong flock. Macarthur's son, James, and nephew, Hannibal, moved to the Taralga area in 1824 and continued to expand and develop the wool industry. It was James who established the village on his land, with the aid of convicts in clearing it.

Today, the main street is lined with old, well-maintained stone buildings: hotels, churches, shops and homes. We took sanctuary from the icy draft on some steps opposite the general store and let the sun's rays thaw us out as we made short work of our sandwiches. It was tempting to stop there longer, but that would have delayed our arrival in Sydney. We left the 'Happy Town' via an avenue of yellow-leafed poplars displaying their full autumnal splendour, certainly in more jovial spirits than before, although my leaden legs were not particularly happy as we resumed.

To add to the challenge of the hilly terrain, the road north of Taralga intermittently ran out of tarmac. At times the gravel surface was perfectly acceptable and, at other times, usually on the steep climbs, the path was adulterated with testing sections of wash sand, washouts, potholes and corrugations. We had chosen thin road tyres for the first 5000 km to Cairns as they would be far more efficient for all but these tedious sections of unsealed road. It was surprising that we were so close to the country's largest city, on a through road between two reasonably-sized towns, and yet we were struggling on gravel tracks, out of mobile phone range. On the upside, the extra concentration required to negotiate the obstacles diverted the mind away from the pain and time passed more quickly. It suddenly seemed as though we were in a remote region, and the stresses of the previous week became a distant memory. The golden late afternoon light romanticised the vistas on the western edge of the Blue Mountains.

The finale to the day was a long, steep descent, down, down and further down through a labyrinth of switchbacks to the Abercrombie River, where we set up camp. Usually in May the river would have been a raging torrent but in this drought-affected season it was reduced to a few stagnant pools. I hadn't factored in the diminishing hours of daylight as we approached the winter solstice, and in the mountains the sun set just after five o'clock. We had little time to sort ourselves out – erect the old tent we had used in Russia, collect firewood for warmth, and set up the new petrol-burning stove for the first time – before it was completely dark. We hadn't expected to be camping wild so early during the expedition.

The night under the stars was unnervingly silent and peaceful. As I wrote my diary by torchlight, nocturnal animals, especially kangaroos and wallabies, could be heard bounding about at the pond. The Abercrombie River is known to be a haven for platypus but there was no sign of the shy, secretive creatures. I was so tired that sleeping on the hard ground in sub-zero temperatures was no problem.

◆ ◆ ◆

I've had some birthdays in memorable locations during my travels over the years. Greeting me this time, on the third day of our trip, was the steepest climb in New South Wales (NSW). The road followed the river for a couple of hundred metres and then it was straight into a 17 per cent gradient. Keeping to the outside of the hairpin curves gave a minor respite. Greg made it all the way; I simply wasn't strong enough at this stage and had to stop twice, my heart feeling as though it was leaping through my mouth. The constant grinding sounds of the disc brake pads contributed to the pressure – we had been warned that they would take about 500 km to wear in and the added friction whittled away my patience.

Happy birthday – climbing up from the Abercrombie River, the steepest climb in NSW
(photo: G Yeoman)

The remainder of the day was a continuous trial through hilly farmland and forests via Oberon, the highest town in the Blue Mountains. We arrived at Hampton, having struggled to reach our 'minimum distance' in the pitch dark.

The 162-km ride from Hampton to my friends' place in Sydney the following day was an epic which could have been divided into about five chapters. It was not the type of challenge our bodies should have been forced to undertake on Day 4. Chapter 1 involved about 20 km of blissful downhill from the wind turbines at Hampton to the historic village of Hartley on the Great Western Highway. The layers of warm clothing were rapidly peeled off as we began to pay for our free-wheeling extravaganza. Nothing ever comes free. Newton's Third Law of motion, 'For every action, there is an equal and opposite reaction', was certainly a theory I was to experience during the course of the day, and in fact the whole expedition. While descending long hills I was never able to fully relax because there would always be a corresponding ascent to test the legs and lungs although I did attempt to divert my attention from harsh reality and enjoy the moment. Conversely, when a climb seemed as though it would never end, I would remind myself that, for every serious up, there has to be an equally significant down. Chapter 2 of the epic involved a severe climb up Mt Victoria Pass. During the effort, I tried to maintain positive images, such as thinking what a wonderful downhill run we were going to enjoy all the way to Sydney and what good views we would have at the summit.

The third chapter was the reward. Heading into Katoomba in the Blue Mountains, we wove our way through the steep streets, passing rows of tourist buses to reach the Echo Point Lookout on the edge of town. I felt as though we had really earned the views, more stunning than any picture postcard could convey. The mountains were on their best behaviour, the midday sun burning away the morning cloud cover and warming the dense eucalypt forest sufficiently to evaporate the eucalyptus oil which gives the range its blue appearance. In the foreground, the famous Three Sisters rock formation made an indelible impression on me. The sandstone pillars are the subject of Aboriginal myth: according to the legend, the 'Sisters' were turned into stone to save them falling into the hands of a monster which lurked in the sea of green which is the Jamison Valley below.

The Blue Mountains have evolved from an eroded plateau rather than from being pushed up by tectonic activity. This is why they are relatively low in elevation (1065 metres) but still undeniably dramatic. They presented an impassable barrier to the early European explorers, and it was not until 1813 that a path was finally carved across the rugged, heavily forested sandstone uplands, leading to the opening up of fertile farming land west of the Great Dividing Range.

Just 100 km to do after lunch and mostly downhill, we thought. If we kept moving we would make it to my friends' place in Sydney before we ran out of daylight. For those who are of a less materialistic disposition and believe in the Great Law of Destiny, whereby every success or pleasure must be offset by a corresponding fiasco or a certain number of minor vicissitudes, chapters 4 and 5 were the counterbalance for the highlight of the Blue Mountain panoramas. The final two stages were the most dangerous sections of the day and, probably, the whole expedition. The descent was indeed long and fast, but also terrifying. Constricted by deep roadside cuttings and sharp turns, the lanes of the highway seemed far too narrow for the steady stream of huge juggernauts which hurtled passed with no respect. The loaded bikes gained momentum quickly, making it difficult to maintain control and balance at speeds of 40 or 50 km per hour.

The Three Sisters rock formation – the Blue Mountains from Echo Point

For once I didn't mind that the brake pads were rubbing; they were certainly highly efficient when needed. Cruising on the hard shoulder, we had to fight to prevent the bikes accelerating beyond a point of no return, the smooth road surface engendering a false sense of security. Then, without warning, the edges of the road would crumble away and we would be left balancing precariously on the white line as trucks and buses forged past, stirring up destabilising eddies of air. At alarmingly close quarters, the tourist busses particularly tended to suck us towards their wheels. Overcorrecting by a few inches would have resulted in slipping into the gravel and down a steep embankment, no doubt resulting in horrific injuries. Somehow we kept our nerve and survived the white-knuckle descent hemmed in on the white lines. We arrived on the western fringe of the urban sprawl mesmerised – spent from the intense concentration the stint demanded. Fortunately everything was intact except for frayed nerves.

It may have been a relief to finally arrive in Sydney but we still had a further 60 km to go. From Penrith we were able to slip down the hard shoulder of the M4 which was uninspiring but by far the most efficient way to reach our destination. Tempers dangled on tenterhooks as we found our way across the chaotic peak-hour traffic to the M2, constantly cut off by blinkered drivers. Greg became more and more agitated as we gradually lost another race against the daylight. Our bikes did not have adequate lighting – we managed with just head torches – as it was difficult to attach anything else with all the baggage. I hadn't planned to ride after sundown and for the last two days we had been forced to push on for over an hour in the dark. I didn't like it either, but there was no choice...we just had to get on with it. Flowing with a river of headlights was in stark contrast to the opacity of the country road we had blindly followed into Hampton.

Running only on adrenaline and the thought of two days rest, we navigated from Macquarie University down the busy Epping Road to my friends' house in Northbridge. By the time one of my hosts, Helen, drove out to meet us we were almost there. She was surprised at our fast progress; we were surprised that we'd made it in one piece. It felt as though we had survived the ride into Sydney relying far too much on luck rather than good management.

Our journey's start had been more difficult than I imagined. Even though I wished I could have prepared better physically for the expedition, it was always going to be a case of biting the bullet. I hardly felt like 'the impersonification of health and strength' a good long-distance cyclist is supposed to be!

◆ ◆ ◆

The adventure of the first four days served as a microcosm of the journey ahead, at least up to Brisbane. It was all about setting a pattern and finding a rhythm which we could sustain for extended periods. Apart from visiting friends, seeing a few sights and catching up on all the administration, the two days off the bikes in Sydney were essential to let our bodies catch up and adapt to their new way of life. The GRACE Expedition was more than a full-time job. Each day was approached as if it were another day at work except that rather than being in an office for eight hours, we would be turning the pedals. Remaining on schedule required a disciplined work ethic, although in reality the short-term goals had to be flexible to account for all sorts of unpredictable situations such as changing weather and road conditions, tiredness, breakdowns and meeting people. Expecting the unexpected is synonymous with bicycle travel, usually providing the highlights and lowlights. We would wake each morning with a planned course of action but by the time we hit the sack, our day had often featured any number of unpredictable turns.

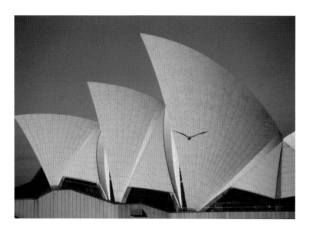

Sydney Opera House
(photo: G Yeoman)

We thought leaving Sydney early on a Sunday morning would alleviate some of the pressure of the traffic. The Pacific Highway was still busy but it was certainly less stressful than our arrival in the dark – that was, until Greg came within inches of death courtesy of an inattentive driver who was totally consumed by her mobile phone conversation. Sydneysiders certainly take the national prize for having the least regard for cyclists – a product of a fast-paced lifestyle, higher population density and the geography of the city. Steady streams of vehicles are funnelled through narrow bridges and streets which weave a convoluted network over the many waterways and hilly terrain.

Accompanying us for the first couple of hours out of Sydney were three old friends, David Stoate, Andrew Campion and Andrew Love. The last time I had cycled with David was in the Massif Central in France fourteen years previously. He had been a member of the British hockey tour and stayed on to travel through some of Europe by bicycle. Since living in Sydney, he and Andrew Love had become enthusiastic cyclists, regularly enjoying their Sunday escapades through the northern suburbs. David's father owns Anna Plains, a million-acre (400 000 hectare) cattle station 250 km south of Broome on the Kimberley coast. Although I was planning to visit Anna Plains, given our struggles of the first few days, it was impossible to imagine myself pedalling all the way to the diagonally opposite end of the continent, even without the scheduled diversions. I was looking forward to seeing the station but it was another world away and much was to pass beneath my tyres before then.

Andrew Campion was at the time visiting with his family from Perth. In recent years he had become a keen mountain biker and promised he would try to join me when I neared Perth. It was a pleasure to have the boys' company as we tried to maintain conversations up some sharp climbs. Greg and I really struggled to keep up as they managed the steady pace with ease on their efficient racing bikes. The two Andrews returned to other commitments after about 25 km, but David continued with us through Ku-ring-gai Chase National Park, one of Australia's oldest national parks, and down across the Hawkesbury River. I tried to tempt him to join me later during the expedition but family and work responsibilities did not permit.

At Calga we left the Pacific Highway to head for the Hunter Valley via the Singleton Road. We paused at the town sign for what has to be one of the country's most strangely named villages, 'The Letter A'. (Perhaps it should be twinned with a fishing village in the Lofoten Islands, arctic Norway, called merely 'Å'. I stayed there back in 1992 during my journey to the Nord Kapp.) At Bucketty we joined the convict-built Great North Road.

When the Hunter River region was opened to free settlers, there was no overland connection with Sydney as the maze of sandstone mountains with deep gorges and razorback ridges which we had just crossed isolated the area. The only way to reach Newcastle and the Hunter River hinterland was by sailing ship. Eventually, a road was surveyed by connecting existing tracks with a number of Aboriginal paths which followed the ridge tops. Extending north from Sydney to the fertile alluvial soils of the Hunter Valley region, the 240-km long Great North Road was built between 1826 and 1836. The labour force consisted of convicts who had re-offended after arriving in the penal colony. Up to 700 of them worked on the road at any one time, clearing timber, digging drains, blasting and shaping stone and shifting it into position. They mostly used small hand tools and were bound by leg irons weighing up to six kilograms.

I noted some of the precise dry-stone masonry as we rode by a retaining wall and some culverts but once again we were racing against the diminishing light and searching for places to camp. We fiddled around in Laguna asking at the hall and the shop but no one was particularly forthcoming. When the shop owner refused to help us due to concerns about public liability we realised we were too close to Sydney. 'This would have never happened in Russia,' I heard Greg mutter. Eventually someone suggested we call to the Mulla Villa Guesthouse eight kilometres further on. After another freezing, cautious 45 minutes riding virtually blind in the pitch dark we finally had a place to stay, food and accommodation provided. The guesthouse itself is a relic of the convict era, originally owned by the magistrate of Wollombi.

At Wollombi the Great North Road divided. One section continued north to Singleton while the option we took headed through the Lower Hunter River region to Cessnock and over the fertile floodplains to Maitland. Greg had travelled extensively during the previous ten years he had spent designing and leading mountain bike holidays on various continents. As we moved from one Australian landscape to another, each reminded him of different places he had visited. During the first couple of weeks we just about travelled around the world – South Africa, Kenya, Morocco, Spain, France, Greece, along the Danube, Russia and various parts of South-east Asia. The Hunter Valley floodplain seemed to be able to grow almost anything. As we passed small market garden plots, citrus orchards, rows of olive trees and vines, turf farms, dairy farms and other various forms of intensive agriculture, Greg claimed the landscape was just like 'Nam'. The conversation then diverged off about all sorts of experiences he had travelling through Vietnam. Most recently, Greg had taken his folding bicycle to Antarctica and pedalled a few hundred metres along a stony beach. He has just one continent to go before he can claim that he has cycled on all seven. I prayed that none of the landscapes we were to travel through would conjure up memories of Antarctica!

The range of landscapes we passed in one day of 140 km of cycling was astonishing at times, and it was difficult to comprehend that we were doing it all under our own steam. We began the day in frosty hills scattered with the remnants of early European settlement, followed a river valley out to its floodplain, struggled to find our way through the major rural centre of Maitland, and were intimidated by a steady stream of huge trucks back on the Pacific Highway before we turned east across to the tranquil coastline at Hawks Nest. As I lay in my sleeping bag listening to the waves rhythmically washing onto the shore, I pondered what the next jam-packed twenty-four hours might have in store.

The geographical theme was straightforward; we were to follow the Myall River from its mouth to its source. In cycling terms that meant a lot more ups than downs. In short, water from the Upper Myall River spills into the Myall Lakes – a series of three interconnected lakes – before eventually flowing out from Bombah Broadwater via the Lower Myall River to empty into the ocean at Port Stephens. We made a special diversion to include the Myall Lakes in the expedition. These stunning, internationally recognised wetlands need protection because they are one of the most popular and accessible parks in NSW for water sports and outdoor activities. They are also vulnerable because it takes almost two years for some parts of the lake system to totally change

Bombah Broadwater,
Myall Lakes

their volume – from the time fresh, nutrient-rich water flushes into the lakes from the two rivers which feed them to when the brackish water flows out to sea. This time-frame means the lakes are particularly susceptible to algal blooms caused by the washing of nutrients and other pollution from upstream.

Starting at sea level, the road ran between the Lower Myall River and the coastal dunes to the littoral (coastal) rainforest at Mungo Brush. As the road was enclosed by coastal scrub, which produced a claustrophobic ambience, there was little to see until we reached the open expanse of Bombah Broadwater. A boat ramp just before Bombah Point cleared a window through the dense bush through which to view the lake, whose edge was fringed with reeds and paperbarks. Beyond the flock of pelicans which fished the shallows, the water met the sky in a continuum of shades of pale blue broken only by a narrow strip of 60 000-year-old sand dunes and distant hills.

'Myall' is an Aboriginal word meaning 'wild'. Crossing the neck between the two lagoons, the gravel road to Bulahdelah left an indelible impression very much in tune with the Indigenous term. At Bulahdelah we were shown a shortcut along the partly unsealed Markwell Road up the Myall Valley to Gloucester, our planned destination. Attracted by the thought of trimming 30 km from our daily total, we ignored the fact that the man who showed us the shortcut did not look like a cyclist and therefore probably had no conception of the degree of difficulty of the route he advised. Accordingly, we crossed the narrow gauge forestry railway line and headed out of town. The heavy feeling in the pit of my stomach was not only due to eating far too much lunch but also knowing there was bound to be plenty of pain ahead. We followed parallel to the course of the river through some rich pastures, steadily gaining altitude.

In 1866, writer and pioneer Rachel Henning preserved, in her diary, a record of her journey down the Myall River and a snapshot of the area.

It is quite unlike the deep, dry rocky river-beds of the North, but very beautiful in its own way, not very wide but very deep, so that the great timber-punts can go up and down it, and the banks shut in by very dense forest so that you cannot see any light through the beautiful vines hanging from the trees and dipping into the water. Then you turn a corner and come upon a bright little clearing with a settler's wooden house and a patch of maize and perhaps an orange orchard or a vineyard. Further on the forests shut you in again.

In Henning's time the river would have been bordered by stands of majestic red cedar trees, but now pine plantations grow in their place. It was generally easy to identify with her description, although now much more of the farmland is open. We finally climbed over the watershed and out of the valley. The bitumen returned and after a long, chilly descent to Gloucester, my limbs felt so numbingly brittle they could have been coated with glass. I felt stronger than a week ago but the high workload and piercing cold worryingly caused my knee to stiffen and ache.

The only real inkling of what lay ahead came from a motor cyclist at the campsite who had just ridden down our intended route from Gloucester to Armidale from the opposite direction. He warned that we would have a hilly, convoluted path with one particularly long, steep climb up onto the New England Tableland. This classic route, called Thunderbolt's Way, joins Gloucester to Walcha and Uralla. Originally a forestry track, it was first pushed through in 1961 and only completely sealed in 1999. There was some controversy over deciding to name the road after a bushranger who had many hide-outs along the route and in the region.

Frederick Wordsworth Ward, alias Captain Thunderbolt, was born in about 1836. He learned about horses working as a groom and horse-breaker on Tocal Station near Maitland. Seconded into a horse-stealing racket, he escaped from his second stint in prison; a cycle of ill-treatment there had hardened him, and he slipped into a fugitive life as a bushranger. Many details about the legend of Captain Thunderbolt are hazy. The only two points not in dispute are the quality of the horses he stole and rode, and the fact that he never killed or injured those whom he robbed. He was occasionally shot at by police but never returned the fire, relying on the magnificent horses he rode to get him out of trouble. His philosophy was that a racehorse was a better weapon than a revolver. (If only more people around the world also believed this.)

**Captain Thunderbolt,
Uralla**
(photo: G Yeoman)

By the time he was supposedly shot in 1870, he had carried out eighty major hold-ups and robberies which netted him about 20 000 pounds. Some 300 people viewed the dead body, identifying it as that of 'Thunderbolt', not as Fred Ward. Three days after he was killed by police at Uralla, two policemen saw his horse at a race meeting at Glen Innes. 'Thunderbolt' managed to give them the slip as they chased him to somewhere near Ebor, not far from where his sister lived. At his funeral in Uralla, a local newspaper reported as being present a tall, unidentified woman dressed entirely in black clothes and wearing a veil. As she left, it was noted that she walked away with a manly gait. Family tradition claimed it was Fred attending his brother Harry's funeral.

Having pedalled in the Cotswold region of England, I could see how some Australian towns, such as Gloucester and Stroud, had come to receive their names. In the Antipodean setting as in the original, bald, steep-sided hills dropped away to fast-flowing creeks and rivers. The size of these mounds gradually swelled as we pushed west. It was the warmest day yet and at the Barnard River we stopped at a property to refill our bottles. With no one around, we slipped in through the back gate and helped ourselves to the rainwater tank. It didn't feel right traipsing through someone's private property, but we weren't exactly stealing horses or money.

Our bodies were struggling – Greg stretching out on the road after climbing for six kilometres up Thunderbolt's Way

A horse would have been pretty handy at that point. The house was at the foot of the big climb. We weren't quite sure what we were in for: my map was not nearly detailed enough and information from motorists was sketchy so I dropped into my lowest gear and tried to pace myself. Between us, Greg and I had endured some difficult climbs over the years, in Europe, Asia and Africa. As Australia is the flattest continent in the world, surely it couldn't be as tough as some of our previous experiences? It will all be over in a couple of kilometres or so, I thought. Greg stopped for a breather after two kilometres as I caught him up and continued to crawl past. I daren't stop for fear of not being able to restart with my load on such a steep incline which appeared to rise out of the Barnard River like an exponential line on a graph. In this situation it is best not to look up as the path ahead can seem insurmountable. A wiser option is look to the side or behind at the view or at fine details on the roadside. Another kilometre passed...surely we must be nearly there. I'd look expectantly at each light-filled clearing around a hairpin curve ahead, mistakenly thinking the road was levelling off. Then from the 'heavens' above I could hear screeching brakes and engines roaring as drivers changed down a gear or two to control their descent – still a way to go. I longed for the massive downhill which must await us at some point. There was nothing left in my tank, but I wasn't going to be beaten by this climb. Six kilometres later, the road flattened out, conning us into thinking we had finished. There is always a sting in the tail and after a token downhill, we were confronted with another two-kilometre, back-breaking climb before reaching Carson's Lookout. It may not have been the longest climb I had ever done, but it was certainly one of the most difficult.

We didn't lose much altitude as we had ascended onto the New England plateau. From Nowendoc, Thunderbolts Way bisected vast, fertile, heavily grassed plains, gradually rising to 1100 metres just before Walcha and then over more subtle undulations to Uralla, where the legend of Captain Thunderbolt was officially laid to rest. We milked the last rays of the day sprinting along the New England Highway to the university city of Armidale.

Carson's Lookout showing the valley of the Barnard River below

The altitude of the tableland means the region experiences a cool temperate climate and is one of the few parts of the country which has four distinct seasons. Like the rest of the eastern seaboard, New England was in the grip of a severe drought and cattle stirred the dust as they scoured the paddocks for something to eat.

◆   ◆   ◆

After ten days on the road, our metabolisms were finally cranking up to be able to consume the obscene quantities of carbohydrate required to meet our energy usage. Any major stop, such as the morning in Armidale, would include a visit to the supermarket. Mindful of our strict budget and limited carrying capacity, we would comb the shelves for foods with the highest energy for weight ratio, the lowest GI (long-lasting energy) and things which kept reasonably well without refrigeration; fruit and nuts, peanut butter, Nutella, multigrain bread, cream cheese, tuna, olive oil, sweetened condensed milk, Anzac-type biscuits, fruit cake, pasta, rice, honey and sugar. Fresh food was always a premium and we could only buy as much as we could eat. Leaving Armidale along the Waterfall Way, we thought we were only supposed to do an 80-km half-day, but the demands of the route combined with encroaching tiredness saw us consume a whole one-kilogram fruit cake during that time as well as the usual staple diet. If we continued in this manner, there would have been more than one reason why some of the less understanding people we met would call us fruit cakes!

A section of Ebor Falls, Waterfall Way

We couldn't pass along Waterfall Way without diverting to visit some of the falls. When John Oxley, the first European explorer through the region, stumbled upon them in 1818, he must have been astonished at their scale. Wollomombi Falls, where the Wollomombi and Chandler rivers meet, are Australia's second highest. Due to the dry season, only a trickle cascaded down the 100-metre straight drop, 220 metres in total. The following morning, we diverted to see Ebor Falls, where the Guy Fawkes River drops 115 metres in a number of spectacular stages over columned basalt once laid down by a long-extinct volcano of the same name. Over the millennia streams have gradually eroded down through fractures and weaknesses in the plains. The rolling hills among which these spectacular chasms and waterfalls are set give no indication of their existence.

After we crossed the Great Dividing Range for the third time so far on the expedition, the plateau fell away and the exhilarating descent was some type of instant karma, rewarding the efforts of the last couple of days. The escarpment was hardly level and we twice had to ascend back up into clouded rainforest. There the atmosphere became instantaneously humid and the bitumen wet. We had briefly entered a completely different world, one more reminiscent of the ancient Gondwana supercontinent from which many of the temperate rainforest

Greg about to ascend from Billy's Creek into the rainforest, just north of Tyringham

species are descended. (Formed mostly during the Jurassic Period, Gondwana was one of two supercontinents which resulted from the break up of the Pangaea landmass. Gondwana basically includes the countries of the Southern Hemisphere.) The vines and ferns enshrouded by mist belied most people's image of Australia. I could hear what were probably lyrebirds, busy at work mimicking all sorts of bird calls and sounds of the forest under the protection of the undergrowth. It has been documented that lyrebirds have learned to mimic the sound of a chainsaw. As we rode through the forest, the lyrebirds may have learned to imitate Greg as the surroundings sent him off on another tangent: 'Reminds me of when I was in...' Just before Nymboida the land opened out and we were back down into warmer climes.

As we approached Australia's most easterly point, it was evident that we had arrived in a subtropical climate. After Grafton, we picked up the busy Pacific Highway briefly before diverting on to Woodford Island, an isle in the Clarence River which we had been following. The flatness was such a contrast as we pedalled through fields of towering sugar cane. Vietnam again?...Then Scotland. At MacLean, where we rejoined the Highway No. 1 thoroughfare, nearly every lamp-post was painted with the tartan of a Scottish clan.

Reaching Cape Byron meant we had attained the first goal in my aim to visit all four of the country's major geographical landmarks: east, north, west and south. The intrinsic prize for straining to pedal up to the headland was one of deep satisfaction.

◆　◆　◆

Two weeks out of Canberra it really felt like we had covered a significant amount of territory. On this magnificently warm, clear day we constantly searched the eastern blue horizon for migrating humpback whales which can frequently be seen from the headland. A pod of about thirty dolphins frolicked near the rocky shoreline, surfing the waves and playfully leaping out of the water, showing off to all of us – visitors and locals – watching in awe from our vantage point. The water was so clear we could also spot turtles and schools of silvery fish swimming in the shallows.

Avoiding the main highway and built-up Gold Coast, we left Byron Bay on the Old Bangalow Road, heading west back up into the mountains towards Lismore. Following a high ridge, we were treated to extensive views of the very rich hinterland. Plantations of macadamias, avocadoes, citrus trees and market gardens thrived on the uplands. The chocolate-red coloured soils were once volcanic, and together with surrounding rock formations provide a clue to the dramatic geological history of the whole region.

As the continent moved over a hotspot in the earth's mantle about 23 million years ago, the Tweed volcano erupted through a weakness in the earth's crust.

A pod of wild dolphins surfing the waves at Cape Byron

By the time the eruptions ceased, about three million years later, the centre of the Southern Hemisphere's largest volcano had risen up to a height of over two kilometres. Layers of ash and lava had been deposited over its outward slopes to a diameter of about 100 km, from Cape Byron to Lismore in the south and the Kyogle district in the west. The Tweed volcano eventually collapsed, creating an enormous caldera – bowl-shaped depression – 1000 metres deep and 40 km wide. The remnant volcanic plug, Mt Warning, rises 1100 metres from the centre of the caldera valley.

The Bundjalung people regard Mt Warning as their sacred volcano Wollumbin, a name meaning 'fighting chief of the mountains'. It is a traditional place of cultural law, initiation and spiritual education. When Captain James Cook first sighted the extinct volcano in 1770, he named it Mt Warning as a caution to other seafarers of the numerous treacherous reefs along this coast.

From Lismore we followed a broad, open valley toward Kyogle. The mountains to the north appeared to form an impenetrable barrier which we knew we would have to scale to reach Brisbane. Our path, gradually gaining altitude, converged with the Richmond River, one of the principal streams to be fed from the ranges, just before we headed into Kyogle – or 'place of the plain turkey', according to its original inhabitants. It was tempting to stop there but we needed to push on a little further to have a chance of reaching Brisbane the next day. Timing needed to be exact because we had prearranged to meet with a Channel Ten film crew to shoot a story for their children's program, *Totally Wild*. We were also looking forward to meeting our Russian friend, Yuri, who was expecting us the following evening.

Hugging the course of the upper Richmond River, we persevered to the village of Wiangaree and decided to stop there, satisfied that we were in range of Brisbane. There was no accommodation, so we called in at the lone service station/shop to find out where we could camp. Fortunately, we caught the proprietor as he was closing up. I glimpsed what was stacked on the dusty shelves: a few 'handy' items such as toiletries, tinned food, country music cassettes, locally produced handicrafts, bags of fruit and firewood as well as a freezer full of ice creams. Pride of place on the upper shelves next to some large jars of honey was an extensive collection of preserved snakes. We were assured that they were all local varieties which the proprietor had captured and pickled.

He was a suitably eccentric character who, after giving our request some thought, decided we could pitch our tent out the back of his shop. It started to rain as he escorted us to a site among the empty oil canisters, piles of wood and disused beehives. Taking pity on us, he offered to open up his disused honey factory so we could have some shelter. As we swept away the dead cockroaches and bees from the once sterile floor, the owner revealed snippets of information which enabled us to make some sense of the situation. Since his wife had passed away six months previously he had thrown himself into his passion of making furniture out of recycled red gum which he collected after it had been discarded. He obviously loved collecting things. The back room of his house boasted a magnificent collection of coloured 'antique' Queensland cordial bottles. He was proud of his snake collection too, and as we had to wander among the wood piles to reach the facilities, I tip-toed with extra caution.

It was disappointing but hardly surprising that it started to rain as we set off from Wiangaree; we were heading into the sub-tropical rainforest of the Border Ranges which receives an annual dousing of 1555 mm (62in.). The tepid, soaking dollops were mildly refreshing as we turned off at The Risk and started to climb up the Lions Road.

The Lions Road carves a relatively direct route through the McPherson Ranges and Border Ranges National Park, running alongside the Sydney-Brisbane railway line and Gradys Creek to cross the Range at Richmond Gap. It divides the eroded remains of two huge shield volcanoes, Mt Warning in the east and the Focal Peak volcano in the west. Visibility was poor here. Our path diffused into a grey silhouette of the mountainous wall ahead broken only by the fringing lighter shade of grey of the swirling, moody rain clouds. The conditions forced us to focus on the task at hand. The soggy map showed that the railway line around which our road was entwined made a complete spiral loop above Cougal. This was an ominous sign for us. If the gradient was too steep for trains...? The purpose of the Border Loop Railway was to elevate the track an extra 20 metres in order to reach the kilometre-long tunnel which had been bored through the lip – the caldera rim of the McPherson Range – into Queensland. When a long goods train passes through the spiral, looking like an oversized toy train set, this rare engineering feature becomes a trainspotter's heaven.

Adjacent to the dreaded loop, the road ascended like a celestial stairway through the cloud line. The natural terracing caused by the intermittent volcanic flows in aeons past gave us some respite between the short, intensive bursts of effort. There was no point in stopping to admire the views from the look-out. The highly sought-after hardwoods and hoop pine which were harvested from the state forest and processed in now-abandoned villages like Cougal are protected as national park.

Since leaving Sydney we had encountered discontinuous patches of sub-tropical and temperate rainforest. Forming the Central Eastern Rainforest Reserve, these patches exist like a chain of islands vulnerable in a sea of fire-prone eucalypt forest and agricultural lands. Inscribed on the World Heritage list in 1986, the forests include the most extensive areas of subtropical rainforest in the world, large areas of warm temperate rainforest and nearly all of the Antarctic beech cool temperate rainforest. They are an important example of significant ongoing geological processes, of biological evolution and of biological diversity. Along with the other national parks in the Wollumbin vicinity, the Border Ranges form part of the 'Border Group', which has been singled out as being a particularly rich area with the highest concentration of frog, snake, bird and marsupial species in Australia. Our friend at Wiangaree had preserved a number of these species.

Despite being in the middle of an evolutionary equivalent of Noah's Ark, we saw little of the documented natural diversity as we reached the dank summit. The state border, three kilometres further along, is manned only on the NSW side to regulate the flow of livestock to protect NSW from cattle tick. Needless to say, the guard looked very bored, passing the time on his twenty-four-hour shift by watching old movies on a black-and-white television which was probably older than the road itself (the Lions Road was first pushed through in 1973, sealed in 2002). Buoyant with the prospect of entering our second state, we did not allow the conditions to dampen our spirits.

We left the headwaters of Gradys Creek, crossed a cattle grid and within a few metres entered the headwaters of Running Creek, which we followed all the way down to the valley. After one slip, I took the greasy descent through the clouds carefully. There were no fences and cattle roamed freely, leaving messy deposits of liquid cow pats. Skidding on the dung at 60 km per hour could have spelt an unlikely end to the expedition, as embarrassing as the old slipping-on-a-banana-peel trick. We were now in Queensland, home of the 'banana benders'! We proceeded with caution.

The road to Rathdowney was lined with vast thoroughbred training studs. Even though it was humid after the rains, groundwater was being pumped to irrigate the prized pastures. At Innisfail our quiet road abruptly ended as we picked up the Mt Lindesay Highway which in turn became progressively busier as we neared Brisbane. I phoned Yuri to arrange our rendezvous point in Brisbane. We were looking forward to having him join us for a week's cameo appearance.

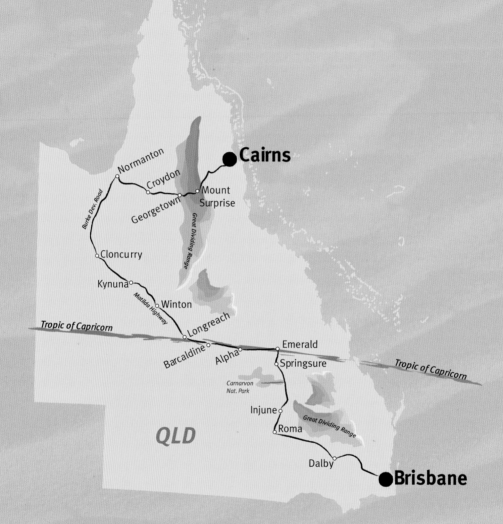

Cairns

Normanton
Croydon
Mount
Surprise
Georgetown
Burke Dev. Road
Great Dividing Range
Cloncurry
Kynuna
Winton
Matilda Highway
Longreach
Tropic of Capricorn
Barcaldine
Alpha
Emerald
Springsure
Tropic of Capricorn
Carnarvon Nat. Park
Injune
Great Dividing Range
Roma
QLD
Dalby
Brisbane

Brisbane to Cairns
3045 kilometres
29 May to 24 June 2004

Sealed road
Unsealed road
(gravel)

| 0 | 100 | 200 | 300 | 400 | 500 | Kilometres |
| 0 | | 100 | 200 | | 300 | Miles |

3

Storylines, straightlines, airlines and oolines
(Brisbane to Cairns)

The first I knew of the existence of Yuri Trusov was when I received a fax from the depths of the Novosibirsk winter of 1993. I had just started to organise the Trans-Siberian Cycle Expedition and had sent out letters to Russian cycling clubs hoping to find Russian cyclists to join me for the journey. Relying on the Russian postal system at that time was optimistic; as with most former Soviet systems, it was extremely inefficient and there was no guarantee of when these letters would reach their destination, if at all. So I was surprised and excited when I read:

> My name is Yuri Trusov, I am 27 years old. I was graduate at Novosibirsk University as biologist and I am currently working in research institute. I speak English but insufficiently good. Your idea is very interesting to me. I am offering to accompany you and to give any help through all your journey (from St Petersburg to Vladivostok).

From our initial communications it was evident that Yuri was intelligent, of free spirit and a self-starter who was motivated to create and make the most of his opportunities. He joined Greg and myself for a total of five weeks, during which time we got to know each other well and, despite our cultural differences, discovered we were very like-minded. Greg and I found Yuri's enthusiasm for life quite intoxicating. He saw beauty in everything and was excited by the finer details of nature. Whenever we had a break from pedalling, if Yuri wasn't making running repairs to his bike, he was disappearing off into the wilds.

Yuri's participation in the Russian expedition was independent of our association with Centre Pole; his motivation for joining us was to improve his English, meet and spend time with Greg and myself, and explore more of his country. He did not want to be paid (the cyclists who represented Centre Pole received a small amount) which was particularly impressive given his meagre salary. He used his own bike for the trip, a worn-out, four-speed Russian racer. The night before we were due to leave Novosibirsk, he was still fashioning two oversized army-issue bags into rear panniers, which to our amazement did the job. He slung some extra heavy duty tools into his bags and what seemed an excessive bundle of spokes.

The fact that we three made it in one piece and remained on schedule was a small miracle. The panniers were so big they unbalanced the bike, whose steering was already extremely suspect due to a loose headset. If we rode side by side to talk, both Greg and I were at times nearly nudged off the road by this friendly, over-width swaying juggernaut.

Like most Russians, Yuri had learned to adapt and cope to survive. While it was annoying that his bike kept breaking down on a regular basis, forcing the team to wait, he was an excellent mechanic and nothing seemed to faze him, even when five spokes popped at one time. After starting out on his three-week journey through the Sayan Mountains carrying forty extra spokes, he arrived in Krasnoyarsk with only one spare spoke! Yuri struggled on some of the longer mountain passes (the Sayans are almost the size of the European Alps), but soon learnt to latch on to the back of a passing truck, hitching a free ride. Things were even trickier when descending some of the massive passes, such as the West Sayan Pass. As his rear brakes rubbed against the wheel rim, and he normally travelled with them disengaged, steep gradients meant he had to first stop and manually engage the brake pads. He would then descend dragging both feet on the gravel road to keep everything under control.

We left Yuri in Krasnoyarsk, where he took the train back home, and headed east, thinking sadly that we probably wouldn't see him again. But he kept our itinerary and decided he would rejoin us for the final two weeks of the expedition. He assumed that we would remain on time, despite the unpredictable trials and tribulations of the Swamp with its 1500 km of suspect and even non-existent tracks. When we arrived, ahead of schedule, in Blagoveschensk at the eastern edge of the Swamp, we checked hopefully at the post office for any sign of Yuri as he had said that he would try to meet us there. He didn't, but on our first day out of Blagoveschensk a bus pulled up in front of us and out jumped Yuri with bike and bags! It requires a fair amount of faith to take a train for four days across Russia on the assumption that Greg and I would arrive on bikes at exactly a nominated time and place. Yuri had received the message we had optimistically left at the post office and caught us up. This time his bags were loaded with such essential items as a two-kilogram pot of homemade jam, dried toast, dried fish and a diving mask and snorkel for a swim in the 'warmer' seas around Vladivostok. He had convinced his workplace that he was going on a two-week field trip, searching for seeds in the far eastern reaches of his country known as Ussuriland.

We pretty much lost contact with Yuri over the following years, but then Greg heard that he had moved to Australia. I tracked him down at the University of Queensland, and we made contact.

The story of Yuri's endeavour to come to Australia for 'a better life' is one of courage. Initially, he left his wife, Svetta, and son, Misha, behind in central Siberia as finding the money for a single ticket to fly to Australia was a challenge in itself. His only vague contact here was a Russian colleague with whom he was to stay for a year in Brisbane. He found work, developing a certain pineapple variety. He then returned to Novosibirsk, completed his doctorate, and was eventually able to bring his family back to Queensland.

Knowing the type of existence Yuri, Svetta and Misha led in Russia, I was interested to learn how they had adapted to Australian life. We waited expectantly for Yuri to meet us at Browns Plains, a busy junction leading towards the city centre. Finally we saw him striding towards us – he had parked his utility on the other side of the busy junction and was looking for us on foot. He hadn't changed very much and still looked fit, even if he was a little heavier, attributable to being ten years older and now living a more prosperous life. As he drove us to his new home, it was a joy but also weird to be able to communicate so easily. Back in Russia, Yuri's English was rudimentary and it took a lot of time and energy to make ourselves understood. Now we could freely express ourselves as our unrestricted conversations explored many new topics.

Yuri and Svetta's home in Novosibirsk

We found our friend revelling in the opportunities of his new life. He was particularly proud of his new house. In Novosibirsk we had stayed in the family's matchbox-sized university apartment which was set in a dreary, poorly maintained series of uniform high-rise buildings. The day we arrived in Novosibirsk, Yuri had cycled for a couple of hours out of town to meet us and escort us back to his home. When we reached the building, Yuri parked his bike and disappeared excitedly up the stairwell to fetch his family. He soon returned very embarrassed – he had taken us to the wrong set of apartments! The design of each block, with their grey concrete and identical quadrangles, was so uniform that even Yuri couldn't identify his own home.

The contrast could not have been greater as we arrived at his recently built house in Karana Downs, a new suburb in the fringe of Brisbane's western sprawl. This time it was my turn to feel a bit bushed as we arrived in the dark, winding our way through a maze of crescents and cul-de-sacs. The concept of buying a block of land and building his own home, unimaginable in his former life, was now a reality. In Australian terms, the family was restricted financially, but they had made the most of their situation and, true to his Russian ingenuity, Yuri had improvised by doing much of the handiwork himself.

Yuri and Svetta at their new home in Brisbane
(photo: G Yeoman)

Svetta and Misha (now sixteen and preferring to be called Michael) had only been in Australia for a couple of years and were not as well-adjusted to their new surroundings. Svetta, a biochemist by profession, had had to struggle to make ends meet back in Russia, while Yuri was seeking out a new life on the other side of the world. Leaving her home, family and culture to come to Australia had been a brave and difficult decision. At the time we re-met she was not confident of her ability to speak English, nor was she qualified to drive. She was lonely and missing her family, but, as before, looked after Greg and myself very well.

During our two-day turn-around in Brisbane, as arranged, we filmed the story of our expedition for the Channel Ten program *Totally Wild* with Year 4 students at the Bulimba State Primary School. This school had been singled out because it has an extensive environmental program. Its latest project was the building of a totally sustainable toilet, of which the young students were very proud.

◆ ◆ ◆

Yuri was to join us for a week for the journey out to the Carnarvon National Park. He would have liked to come for longer but could not afford the time off work. I don't think they would have accepted the idea of a week's field excursion to Carnarvon Gorge to collect seeds. Like last time, he used his own bike, which I was glad to see was a step-up from his Russian model. It was not a great quality machine, however, and it was soon evident that Yuri was going to have to work hard to keep up. As with the previous expedition, he was still fixing things the night before. He had borrowed some panniers from his friend Merrick Ekins, a veteran of many expeditions, who was due to join me on the Canning Stock Route after Greg left. With a little ingenuity he secured the racks effectively to the bike-frame. I was not concerned, though, about his fitness. As he had been regularly cycling to work, about a 60-km round trip over some testing hills, I imagined he would manage.

The route along the Warrego Highway past Ipswich was busy with heavy semi-trailers and unpleasant to travel on until we turned off towards Esk. I was testing out a special undergarment padded with sheep's wool in the hope that it would be the answer to my saddle sores. My mother had bought it for me years ago when I complained of the same problem and, concerned that I would have to endure the tender condition for another nine months, I had thought it worth a try and asked Arnaud to send it to Brisbane. I was conscious that the white padding made my behind look like a rabbit's rear end and hoped no one would shoot me as vermin! The extra padding actually added pressure to the sores and aggravated matters but I persevered for a few days in case the discomfort proved to be short-term. I gave the idea away completely after a week.

We followed the course of the Brisbane River up to Wivenhoe Dam. Greg and I were now aware that we were three and that this changed the group dynamics. The more people in the group, the longer it takes to organise the basics, whether it be getting ready, taking photographs, or stopping for a toilet break. We could only progress as fast as the slowest rider. A benefit was that we were able to share some of the load, including food supplies, between us. This became an issue, however, later on during the day when Yuri tired and fell behind, still carrying all the energy food.

By the time we reached Esk, after roughly 65 km, Yuri had started to struggle and even walked his bike up one of the long hills. The 'good life' had made him

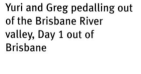

Yuri and Greg pedalling out of the Brisbane River valley, Day 1 out of Brisbane

a bit soft, we thought. The toughest part of the day was yet to come as we climbed steadily through farmland and up into the bush. We lost Yuri early on the climb, but pushed on, presuming he would manage at his own pace.

About halfway up another crossing of the Great Dividing Range, I spotted a koala actually moving up a tree trunk. As they tend to sit around most of the day either sleeping or chewing gum leaves, it was a rare privilege to see a koala climbing in the wild.

Making slower progress than expected, we were still on the road as the sun sank behind the tree line. As we pushed on into the gloom, the light gradually diffused into darkness and the narrow, single-lane strip of tarmac gave way to gravel studded with a minefield of potholes. We proceeded cautiously but when blinded by on-coming traffic, the wisest course was to get off the road completely. By now, Greg and I were worried about Yuri. One driver we stopped to ask said he was miles back. We stopped another car travelling in the opposite direction and the driver agreed to go and collect Yuri and drop him off at the next rest stop near Ravensbourne. Everything seems a lot further in the dark and the temperature of the brisk headwind plummeted as we again ascended. Another half an hour passed and still no sign of our friend. Eventually we arrived at the rest stop and found him waiting there for us. He had passed us in the car but hadn't thought to let us know. It was a relief to find him, even if he wasn't too worried. It had been a tough first day for Yuri.

Koala in the wild

We decided to wind our way along the back roads from Hampton to cut through to the Warrego Highway and on to Dalby. As we headed west the long, rolling hills gradually flattened out into vast, rich, chocolate-coloured plains, the fertile soils providing a hearty medium for arable land use. Although the region has traditionally been a wheat-growing centre, it also now produces cotton, sunflowers, sorghum, millet and barley. Between Jondaryn and Dalby, we found the roadside was littered with balls of raw cotton left over from the recent harvest. The production of cotton has part-replaced wheat as the major crop grown around Dalby and in the Condamine River catchment area which we followed through to Chinchilla and Miles the next day.

The cultivation of cotton in Australia is controversial due to the high water consumption requirements and need for use of chemical pesticides. Even though Australian cotton producers are the world's most efficient when it comes to water consumption (they use 50 per cent less water than the global average), many argue that growing cotton (and rice) has no place in the world's driest habitable continent.

In response to this criticism, farmers have invested heavily in research and technology. Irrigation water is recycled, shorter season varieties have been developed, cultivation methods improved and cotton has been genetically modified, reducing the need for chemical pesticides by half. One cotton bale (227 kg) can produce 215 pairs of jeans, 1217 tee-shirts, or 681 000 cotton-balls. Other cotton products include bank notes, margarine, paper, cooking oil and soap. In other words, we all benefit from the industry, and so efforts to further streamline sustainable practices are paramount, even if prolonged drought may mean the industry is forced to scale down.

Compared with the first night out of Brisbane, where we struggled in the dark and strong winds to erect our tents on sloping ground, the Dalby town campsite, complete with warm showers, gas cookers and campfire, was sheer luxury. It was here we took stock of all the items Yuri had forgotten to pack. He had remembered the basics – tent, sleeping bag and two mats for comfort – but he had no eating utensils, plate or cup and his tool kit comprised of one screwdriver and one spanner. It was useful to have found out about the lack of tools before there were any real problems.

On our way next day, the land was completely flat all the way to Chinchilla and the road dead straight, which was more of a mental than a physical challenge. Looking at the fertile countryside around Chinchilla, the Condamine and the Darling Downs, there is little evidence of the world's greatest plant invasion, that of the prickly pear, which prevailed before 1930. Chinchilla was at the epi-centre of a vast 24-million-hectare infestation and its eventual demise by biological control.

The cactus with its bright yellow flower was introduced from Texas, USA, as a pot plant in about 1839. The first plants appeared in the Condamine region in 1843 and started to become a menace some twenty years later. When plant numbers reached a critical point, the spread became rapid and the situation desperate. Settlers attempted to remove the vermin plants with knives, slashers, hoes, ploughs, a series of mechanical devices and poison, but physically cutting the cacti only served to propagate more plants from the pieces which fell on the ground. About 400 000 hectares (one million acres) per year were overrun with infestations so dense that farmland and bushland became impenetrable and homesteads were abandoned.

In 1911, Queensland government representatives combed the world for a solution to stem the tide. Eventually they discovered one and, in 1925, introduced the species of moth – *Cactoblastis Cactorum Berg* from Argentina. The larvae of this moth specifically devoured the cactus. This biological control method was so successful that the cactus was completely under control within eight years.

The cactoblastis was so important to the local population that they commemorate the insect in eulogistic terms. For example, at Boonarga, a few kilometres from Chinchilla, we passed the Cactoblastis Memorial Hall. At Chinchilla itself, the sign at the entrance welcomed us to the now 'Vital, Friendly Town'.

A general pattern emerged travelling towards Roma and then Carnarvon Gorge. Our route was literally straightforward, so there was little chance of losing anyone. Each day Yuri coped with a little more distance. He would stick with us for a while and then drop back; we would wait at our two-hourly breaks for him to catch up. For the final stretch he elected to hitch and meet us in the town. We couldn't slow down too much because we needed to keep up with the schedule and couldn't afford to lose days this early in the expedition.

From Roma, home to the Southern Hemisphere's largest cattle market and birthplace of the Australian oil and gas industry, we turned north towards Carnarvon National Park. The terrain started to change into open cattle country. The land became much drier, especially after crossing the Great Divide once more, reminding me a little of the vast plains of Montana, USA. The day out of Roma was one of nagging headwind and pushing gradually uphill. By the time we arrived in Injune for a late lunch, we realised we weren't going to get as far as I had planned. We needed to do another 20 km or so to give us a chance to make Carnarvon the following day. There were no obvious places to camp and I was hopeful that the only farm marked on the map, Ridgelands, would appear soon. There was some tension as Greg as usual was becoming grumpy about not finding a campsite and didn't want to set up camp in the dark again. Yuri was fairly relaxed about things and so we rolled on, constantly skirting the bushland for any signs of homesteads or suitable land on which to camp. Our small-scale map did not show sufficient detail for our needs, and in any case, many of the features were inaccurate.

Prickly pears can grow anywhere
(photo: G Yeoman)

Arriving in Roma
(photo: G Yeoman)

Eventually, we found the front gate to Ridgelands and approached the farm buildings about 300 metres off the road. As we had spent the first few weeks travelling through more densely populated east coast regions where there were plenty of official camping facilities, we hadn't been so successful in our attempts to stay with people. I think Greg was disappointed about this aspect of the trip as it hadn't matched the Russian experience.

The three of us together in this situation was like old times and I adopted the same strategy for approaching our prospective hosts. Bill answered the door with the kind of facial expression he may have reserved for unwanted sales callers. I explained who we were and what we were doing and asked whether we could camp and use their water. 'I'll just ask the wife,' he said.

Bill and Margaret kindly offered for us to stay in their home and borrow their kitchen to cook our dinner. I was able to draw on my farming background to ask the type of questions they could relate to and we learnt about local history, their 6000-hectare (15 000 acre) property, recent droughts and the grandchildren. If we had been driving a vehicle instead of cycling, we would not have stopped at Ridgelands as it would have been easy to drive on to Carnarvon Gorge and stay in the camp-ground. These unplanned experiences were like discovering little gems, adding value and depth to my evolving portrait of the country.

Analysing the variety of road kill we came across gave a good indication of the diversity of fauna of the region. We passed a high density of carcasses, mostly eastern grey kangaroos, wallabies, kites, eagles and echidnas. This required a fair amount of breath control as we had to anticipate where the odour would be lurking by taking into account the prevailing wind in relation to the position of the animal. The first wild pig encountered on the expedition was detected by its stench well before we found it. The existence of wild boar was another indication that we were not far off the Tropic of Capricorn. I spotted our first live black snake just in time for us to swerve around it. The involuntary reaction was to take my feet out of the toe-clips and lift them over the handlebars, but even with adrenaline pumping, my inflexible body was incapable of such a contorted position. After that shock, every stick, snapped fan belt and remnant of tyre blowouts was carefully scrutinised for signs of movement.

Yuri and I approaching Carnarvon Gorge
(photo: G Yeoman)

Crossing the boundary of the eastern-most section of the Carnarvon National Park gave us a taste of what was ahead: spectacular views of sandstone cliffs flanked us for several kilometres before they veered off westwards towards the main section of the park. Vegetation took on a more prehistoric character as we passed cycads and different varieties of ferns. On the way out of the valley, the nature and terrain changed abruptly and we were back into the open, Mitchell-grass-covered grazing land.

Although Ludwig Leichhardt led the first European expedition through the region, in 1844, it was Major Thomas Mitchell who named the ranges two years later after the Caernarfon Ranges in Wales. Mitchell grass, so-called in the explorer's honour, is the dominant ground-cover and has proved to be the essential dietary component of the sheep and cattle industries which have flourished in the area.

Having lost Yuri early in the day, we took a lunch break under a shady tree at the entrance to a large property to await him. The owner drove up in his utility buggy with blue heeler dog sitting faithfully under his legs. He took our water-bottles back to the house for a refill and as he returned, to our surprise, Yuri also appeared. We thought he had accepted a lift, but on his final day of cycling he rode the whole 130 km to the campsite. He was obviously getting fitter and he was also excited about arriving at the Carnarvon Gorge. Yuri had travelled there by car before, and was keen to explore.

We kept together for the final 60 km, the last 20 km of which was rough gravel road. Unusually, it was Yuri complaining about the state of the road. It wasn't just that he had grown used to the relative comfort of roads closer to Brisbane – his bike was making worrying twanging sounds because the spokes were too

OUT THERE AND BACK

loose and were bowing under the pressure of hitting corrugations and stones. Remembering how Yuri had snapped some thirty-nine spokes in three weeks in Russia, I feared it would only be a matter of time before one of his wheels capitulated. Despite our concerns, we eventually made it to the Takarakka camping-ground at last light with everything intact, looking forward to a day off the bikes after six days and 750 km since Brisbane.

Walking almost 20 km on our day off was not exactly a rest although we welcomed a different form of exercise. The gorge had such a prehistoric ambience that I half-expected a dinosaur to appear around each corner. We spent hours weaving our way back and forth over Carnarvon Creek among the macrozamias, ferns and stands of spotted gums. The Rock Pool, Moss Garden, Ward's Canyon and the Art Gallery adorned the creek like jewels. The delicate Moss Garden, which nestled in Violet Gorge, one of the many chasms feeding into the main valley, was a particular favourite. A raindrop landing on top of the gorge takes 4000 years to filter through the layers of sandstone before it seeps through the saturated walls to nourish the Moss Garden. After a short, steep climb past Lower Aljon Falls we arrived at the small but beautiful Ward's Canyon. Among its flourishing mosses and ferns is the rare King Fern which has the largest fronds of any fern in the world. The natural enclosure can only sustain fourteen of these ancient plants, their number remaining constant, in balance with their unique habitat.

The Traditional custodians of the gorge have illustrated the importance of the region to their culture by engraving, stencilling and freehand painting over 2000 images onto a 62-metre-long canvas of sandstone at the Art Gallery. This was as far as our tired legs would take us on our 'active recovery' day. As an outside observer trying to make sense of the art, the details of design did not particularly impress me – the majority of the paintwork is applied using very basic stencilling techniques. The rock, however, is a significant religious site. Even touching the rock was a big thing because it was, and still is, sacred. When Aboriginal children laid their hands on the pure sandstone surface to be stencilled, they received power from the rock and were bonding themselves to the site.

The Moss Garden,
Carnarvon Gorge

Carnarvon Gorge was certainly worthy of several days of exploration, but we needed to push on to stick to the schedule. Yuri's journey with us was finished. We said our goodbyes and he headed back to Brisbane after visiting other sections of the national park by vehicle with friends.

◆ ◆ ◆

Away from the gorge we were back into rich pastoral country. The plains were once part of a huge inland sea, its shores forming the sandstone cliffs which are now Carnarvon Gorge. Around Rolleston the tinder-dry grasses made way for paddocks of sorghum, the main summer crop in central Queensland.

By sundown, we were midway between Rolleston and Springsure, still searching for a suitable site to camp. We were hoping to find a farmhouse near the road as we had with Ridgelands. As we paused to assess our options, a massive road train approached from behind and parked in the middle of the road so that any passing vehicle would also have to stop. We declined an offer of a lift, but the driver, who called himself Mr Nixon, told us that if we continued about three kilometres down the road and turned off along a dirt track we would arrive at Jamieson's farm. Mr Nixon had been driving these parts since 1948 and knew everyone in the district. When we located his friends, Knox and Pauline Jamieson, they duly obliged, allowing us to stay on their shed floor (their house was full for the night), and use their facilities.

The squawks of noisy mobs of sulphur-crested cockatoos, which stirred with the first rays of light like a natural alarm clock, woke us early. We joined the Jamieson family for breakfast, an opportune time to learn about the region, and find out what we could about our projected route ahead, the old agricultural town of Springsure, the gem fields around Emerald and Anakie, and about ooline trees. Knox and Pauline loaded us up with homemade biscuits and a dozen eggs, which we requested that they boil to avoid any messy disasters during the day.

As we headed due north to Emerald and the Capricorn Highway, the land seemed to graduate to a new echelon of dryness. A persistent headwind gusted unimpeded across the open, grassy expanses and parched the back of my throat. Despite being set in the middle of rich gemstone country, there are no emeralds in Emerald: the town was named after the lush colour of Emerald Hill Downs. The shire does, however, contain the largest sapphire-producing fields in the world. After 'refuelling' at a service station, we raced the setting sun to Anakie, 'Gateway to the Gem Fields', eventually finding the camping-ground in the dark. We were in time to share a barbecue with a group of hopeful fossickers who were relaxing after a thirsty day of rummaging through the old gem reserves. Fossickers flock to the region from all over the world, driven by the intoxicating excitement of potentially unearthing their own precious stones.

Along the Capricorn Highway, the land was now only supported with low scrub, the monotony broken every so often as we passed clearings with the old diggings left by the sapphire miners. The Drummond Range loomed as the major obstacle for much of the day. Smaller climbs gradually built up like a staircase over the ancient, worn sedimentary layers. My legs were certainly stronger than when we first ventured into the Blue Mountains: the final giant step to the 535-metre summit would have been right on the limit less than a month before.

To the west, the land had been almost totally cleared for grazing. With the Drummonds soon a distant ripple on the horizon behind, we came across a remnant stand of ooline trees. Even a handful of the threatened species was noteworthy. The ooline or scrub myrtle is an ancient tree with its origins in

A lone ooline tree with the Drummond Range in the distance

Gondwana, a relic of a time when Australia was covered by rainforest. Although a different species, it looks like a slender, taller version of the bottle tree, of which we had seen many around Roma and along the Warrego Highway. The wood from the slightly bulbous-looking trunk is extremely dense. The Jamiesons told us that a Springsure artisan who specialises in carving the wood has to allow it to dry for twenty years before he can work an extremely limited supply.

Approaching the railway town of Alpha, the road crossed many dry creek beds which swell into raging torrents after infrequent violent storms which characterise the region's climate. We had left the Central Highlands behind. Alpha, from the Greek word meaning 'beginning', is claimed by locals as the 'beginning of the west'. The town has been destroyed by flood and fire over the years, most recently in 1990 when flood waters drowned the main street under two metres of water. The region is particularly susceptible because we were parallel to, and within a few kilometres of, the Tropic of Capricorn. This transitional zone lies between the tropical north, defined by the Wet and Dry seasons, and the temperate south, which experiences the more familiar summer, autumn, winter and spring. From now – early June, the beginning of the Dry season – I had until October to travel my intended route through Northern Australia and the central deserts. The Wet season, which begins sometime in October, can not only be unbearably hot and humid but the regular storms can make unsealed roads impassable. I was acutely aware of the very heavy schedule that had to be adhered to over the next five months.

Strolling back from dinner at the pub at Alpha, Greg and I were both still ravenously hungry. We noticed the lights were on in the bakery, and when invited in through the back door, we thought this was our lucky night. A bakery to a hungry cyclist is like a lolly shop to a child. The staff were hard at work

Inspecting the 1990 floodline in the main street of Alpha beside Snow's Bakery
(photo: G Yeoman)

preparing the dough for the following day. Tantalising aromas emanated from the ovens and circulated torturously under our noses. It was difficult to concentrate on polite conversation as trays of piping hot sticky buns were retrieved at intervals, baked to perfection. Salivating like rabid dogs, we tried to engineer the conversation towards food and just how much energy we used each day, but somehow the friendly bakers didn't take our hints. Over a mug of tea we learnt plenty about the region and how Mr Snow had built the business, but we failed to elicit even a sample of the produce. Eventually, the work for the evening was finished and we were left to wander back to the campsite with stomachs still grumbling. Needless to say, we were up at the crack of dawn the following morning and straight back down to Snow's Bakery to buy a pack of the 'best sticky caramel buns in the district' for breakfast.

About 10 km before Jericho we crossed the Great Divide once more. It wasn't a particularly difficult climb, just 450 metres, but the landmark was significant. Water which falls on the western side of the divide flows south-west into the Lake Eyre catchment. The water Greg symbolically poured from his water-bottle could have, in theory, followed a course of over 1000 kilometres: via the Barcoo River to Cooper's Creek and the Channel Country, across the Sturt Stony and Strzelecki deserts and finally into Lake Eyre. In actuality, it would have evaporated: water only reaches Lake Eyre after heavy monsoonal Wet season rains and even then 75 per cent evaporates en route. Alternatively, if the water had seeped into the ground and through the layers of sandstone, it would have ended up as an insignificant drop in the Great Artesian Basin, one of the largest artesian groundwater basins in the world. Underlying one-fifth of Australia's land surface, the basin covers an area of over 1.7 million square kilometres and is estimated to hold a volume of 32 500 million Olympic-sized swimming pools. Fed primarily by the run-off from the western slopes of the Great Dividing Range, the aquifers extend under the waterless Simpson Desert and the Lake Eyre depression, north to the Gulf of Carpentaria and to the Tip of Cape York. Under the pressure of gravity, the waters flow through the permeable sandstone layers at a rate of one to five metres per year. The contents of Greg's bottle could theoretically end up surfacing at Dalhousie Springs, a natural outlet maintaining the water pressure equilibrium, on the western edge of the Simpson Desert – in two million years time.

Entering the Cooper's Creek catchment where water flows (if it doesn't evaporate) south-west towards Lake Eyre

On our final stint for the day into Barcaldine, the landscape flattened out and the road verge suddenly acquired tinges of green grass. During the last few kilometres into Barcaldine, or 'Barky' as the locals call it, the pastures became verdant, the late afternoon sunshine enhancing the lush appearance. We were soon to learn that it had not rained significantly for nearly two years. While levels of potable water were alarmingly low, it was the highly mineralised artesian water supply which fed the rich pastures. In some parts of Barcaldine, the sulphurous-smelling groundwater lies only one metre below the surface.

Taking a break between
Barcaldine and Longreach
(photo: G Yeoman)

Barcaldine itself sprang into existence with the arrival of the railway in 1886, connecting the vast sheep-producing plains with the markets and port of Rockhampton. A goods shed was built directly behind a tree where teamsters loaded their wool. This ghost gum, estimated to be between 170 and 200 years old, has been silent witness to much of the town's history. In the early days it served as a meeting place for townsfolk and was known as the Alleluia Tree because the Salvation Army regularly met under its leafy boughs. It also became the meeting place for the increasingly disgruntled Teamsters' Union, the strongest union in that period. During the 1891 Great Shearers' Strike that shook the nation, the striking shearers held their meetings under the tree and the Eureka flag, protesting against poor working conditions and low wages. The strike was the catalyst for the foundation of the Australian Labor Party. The gum has since become an important symbol known as the Tree of Knowledge because of all that has passed beneath its branches. Recently vandals poured thirty litres of poison over the tree's roots, thwarting efforts being made to preserve this important symbol. Fortunately, the shire council had been propagating some 'offspring' from the famous, already ailing icon so that the spirit will live on.

At 'Barky' we also joined the Matilda Highway, a 'touristy' name for a number of highways that link through outback Queensland from the border with NSW to the Gulf of Carpentaria. I chose this longer option not only to avoid the highly populous coastal route but also in order to cycle into the heart and soul of outback Queensland. The highway crosses the paths of many of Australia's great explorers and is the birthplace of a number of Australian legends.

◆　◆　◆

With the water-table so close to the surface, the green plains between Barcaldine and Longreach certainly looked prosperous. The thick mat of humus formed by layer upon layer of grass has provided rich pastures for the sheep and cattle industries. In 1860, Nat Buchanan and William Landsborough recognised the potential of the land around Longreach on the banks of the Thomson River, a reliable permanent water supply. With Edward Cornish they set up a pastoral company leasing half a million hectares which they called Bowen Downs, and stocked it with 350 000 sheep and 35 000 cattle. The town at the western

About to enter the torrid zone – crossing the Tropic of Capricorn for the first time at Longreach

terminus of the Rockhampton railway line received its name from a property outstation probably located on the 'long reach' of the Thomson River.

In Longreach, we visited the Longreach School of Distance Education (LSODE), whose motto is 'Effort Conquers Distance'. One of the teachers showed us around, promising that staff would to follow our progress and involve their classes in some way. The school's 200 students live spread out over an area more than three times the size of England.

As well as being a famous centre for the pastoral industry, Longreach is also the birth place of Qantas – the Queensland and Northern Territory Aerial Service. The Australian icon, now the world's second oldest serving airline, started back in 1920. Funded by local graziers, its first aircraft carried just two passengers in an open cockpit behind the pilot. When Hudson Fysh and Paul McGinniss first set up the air service, they could not have possibly imagined the enormity of both the empire and the lonely Boeing 747 aircraft which is now parked on the tarmac dwarfing the original 1921 hangar. The first service operated by Qantas was the mail run between Charleville (400 km to the south) and Cloncurry, stopping at Longreach, Winton, McKinlay and Cloncurry – our exact route ahead. The first commercial flight by Qantas, in an Avro504K, took off from Longreach on 7 February 1921, taking three hours and ten minutes to reach Winton. As Greg and I crossed the Tropic of Capricorn at 8am, and then the Thomson River with 185 km to make into a gentle headwind before the day was out, I thought how the first Qantas airplane would have managed the distance three times over in the time it was likely to take us. Effort Conquers Distance!

Heads were down and tails were up as we took turns in drafting. As much of the energy required to propel a bicycle forward is used to combat wind resistance, we shared the load by each doing ten minutes in front, taking the brunt of the wind, and ten minutes behind, following in the slipstream – approximately one metre from the wheel of the lead bicycle – to 'rest'. The hours seemed to pass by more quickly that way too. As no one could tell us whether there were any reliable drinking water sources beside the road, we had loaded up with extra water-bags.

A fugitive escaping the Morella CWA hall – going to great lengths to find water

All that was left of the settlement of Morella, 75 km from Longreach, was a railway siding and a corrugated iron CWA hall – all locked up. There used to be more but when the last elderly inhabitant sold her house that was effectively the end of the township. The rainwater tank beside the building looked promising, but there were no accessible outlets outside – all taps were locked inside the hall. We carefully removed the glass louvres from a side window and Greg climbed in armed with all our empty water-bottles. It was obvious from the water clouded with unwanted nutrients that it hadn't rained for a long time.

Like seasoned criminals we carefully replaced the panes of glass and ate lunch on the shaded steps outside. A flock of tiny zebra finches flew about frenetically in the heat, gathering seeds and making the most of any moisture they found, as they need it to digest the grain. The presence of the desert birds was a sure sign that we were on the fringe of the arid zone. With another 100 km to go and the midday temperature starting to soar, their never-ending motion made me feel weak.

Towards the end of the day, Greg noted that if we were in England we would have just traversed the whole country from London to Bristol. We, however, had seen no people, no settlements, no water and no shelter (apart from at Morella) – only plains of Mitchell grass supporting thousands of cattle. According to the proprietor of the Tattersall's Hotel in Winton, these natural grasslands are some of the world's richest and can support one sheep per four acres and one cow per 45 acres (20 hectares).

By the time we had set up in the Winton camping-ground in the dark, we were more than ready for a shower. Like Barcaldine, Winton is also famous for its water supply which thrusts its way to the earth's surface from three artesian bores, all around 1200 metres deep and emerging at a temperature of 83°C. They certainly have a cheap hot water supply there. A short walk from the camping-ground, the Tatts was a convenient place to frequent on our rest day in order to satisfy our enormous appetites. Like cattle on the surrounding plains, the whole day was spent continually grazing. I set up my office on the hotel veranda and caught up with all the administration work.

As with all the towns on the Matilda Highway, Winton boasts a proud history and vies competitively with the other 'nearby' settlements to lure in passing travellers. Winton claims to be the home of Australian bush poetry, a legacy of the fact that it witnessed the first recital of A B 'Banjo' Paterson's *Waltzing Matilda*. Paterson penned the poem early in 1895, while he was staying at Dagworth Station, which lies between Winton and Kynuna. The site claiming to be the inspiration for the legendary story is actually 150 km up the road at the Combo Waterhole near Kynuna. The words were fitted to a Scottish tune, *Bonnie Wood of Craigielea*, to become Australia's unofficial anthem. The first performance of the ballad was reported to be at Winton's North Gregory Hotel on 6 April of the same year.

Although Longreach is accredited as being the 'home' of Qantas, the local saying is that it was conceived in Cloncurry, born in Winton and grew up in Longreach. The first board meeting was held at the Winton Club on 10 February 1921. Far more ancient are the 93-million-year-old fossils of a prehistoric dinosaur stampede at Lark Quarry, another 'local' attraction, 110 km to the south-west – a bit far for a day trip.

◆　◆　◆

All in a day's work. Travelling from Longreach to Winton is the equivalent distance of London to Bristol
(photos: G Yeoman)

Catching up on the administration using my iPAQ hand-sized computer and folding keyboard, my office at the Tattersall's Hotel, Winton

With the prospect of another monstrous 170-km day ahead to reach neighbouring Kynuna, it was an effort to motivate myself to get started after a day off. The temperatures were steadily increasing as we headed north and were now constantly into the low-to-mid 30s. I discovered that if I protected my skin with a long-sleeved tee-shirt and fitted a cap under my helmet, I could reduce the cumulative effect of the intensifying sun.

As we pedalled off, I tried not to think about the number of kilometres we would have amassed by day's end, focusing instead on the beauty of the morning. I absorbed the pure, unadulterated outback air efficiently and in vast volumes. The clarity of the morning light was highlighted by the sharpness of our shadows, which appeared to glide effortlessly across the plains as we pushed along the bitumen. Leaving Winton, our shadows hugged the gutter. During the course of the day, they gradually shortened as the sun moved directly overhead and then steadily elongated, so that by dusk our images stretched across the expanse of the two-laned highway. Our figures eventually fused with the darkness as it encroached from the east.

Many would be uncomfortable with such open spaces, but given where I grew up, I felt quite at home. The region would certainly be hell for an agoraphobic. This day, after about 60 km the monotony of the terrain was broken by a chalky-looking breakaway. These pale orange, sparsely vegetated hills which extended to the west were once rich with opals. The road slowly but surely neared the course of the Diamantina River, the other main contributor to Cooper's Creek, as we passed the turn-off to the Combo Waterhole and on to what is left of Kynuna.

At the time of Banjo Paterson's visit, the town had a population of 450 and was an important outback centre with a Cobb and Co. coach stop and a wool-scouring plant. The Blue Heeler Hotel, built in 1889 as the Kynuna Hotel, is the only building which has any association with the first days of the song *Waltzing Matilda*. Banjo Paterson drank there, and both squatter and swagman had their last drinks there. Folklore has it that Bob MacPherson (owner of Dagworth Station) told Banjo the story of the suicide, in September 1894, of Samuel Hoffmeister beside the Combo Waterhole. Hoffmeister had reportedly been one of the striking shearers involved in the burning down of the Dagworth Woolshed. This story inspired the backbone of the song, Paterson adding flecks of social comment and various poignant events of the time to add interest to his tale. The cryptic element has kept historians busy debating and analysing the lyrics ever since.

A rare notable feature in the countryside, near the opal fields between Winton and Kynuna

As we approached the lively old pub, we could not miss the flashing blue and pink neon image of a blue heeler dog. In modern times the town, with a current population of twenty-two, relies on tourism to see it through. The gaudy sign is designed to round up the passing trade like a true blue heeler, the Australian-bred working dog which has been a faithful participant in outback life over the years. Relaxing with a drink in the cosy timber building, I thought about what the place would have been like during Paterson's time; horse-drawn coaches arriving at the front veranda, the colourful characters who patronised the bar. The bar's walls are decorated with a mass of signatures of visitors, some famous, and we added to the collection. The proprietor, Barbara, explained that when guests find green frogs in the toilet, this is a good sign as it indicates that the surrounding environment is healthy. Not all patrons understood this.

The manager from the roadhouse at Kynuna generously donated some food supplies to help see us to Cloncurry. Just out of Kynuna, the gently undulating terrain signifies the watershed. All water flowing to the south and west of the road ends up in the Diamantina River and the Lake Eyre catchment, while creeks and rivers to the north and east of the 'high' ground empty their waters into the Gulf of Carpentaria.

◆　◆　◆

The town of McKinlay, along with the river which flows through it, was named after the first explorer to the region. John McKinlay led an expedition starting from Blanchwater Station in South Australia in search of Robert O'Hara Burke, William Wills, Charles Gray and John King. The quartet had failed to return from their 1861 expedition – the first south-to-north traverse of the continent. When McKinlay discovered the body of Gray, the first to die on the ill-fated journey, and then learned of the fate of Burke and Wills, he decided to continue north to the Gulf.

Of similar population to Kynuna, McKinlay is more famous because of its Walkabout Creek Pub, which featured in the *Crocodile Dundee* films. Originally known as the Federal McKinlay Hotel, the pub was located at the rear of the town, but after *Crocodile Dundee II*, the building needed renovating and the owner decided to move it to the main road to attract tourists. The local who explained the situation to us said people in the town were rather resentful of the move and felt that the pub had lost its character. The move backfired for the owners because when they came to shoot *Crocodile Dundee III*, the film-makers decided they needed continuity and sent the carpenters to McKinlay twelve weeks prior to reconstruct the pub on the original site. Like other tourists, we could not pass by without a look, but after one peek at the price list, we were happy to eat our lunch in the municipal park.

The land north of McKinlay changed dramatically from grassy plains to bushland pimpled with red anthills. We saw our first camels, a pair of wedge-tailed eagles and flocks of budgerigars. Kites circled overhead with intent waiting for gaps in the traffic to dive in for a feed on the plentiful carrion, mostly wallabies and kangaroos. It definitely felt as though we had entered the north.

The road trains became more imposing and numerous as we climbed the latitudes. I saw what I thought was a 'normal' train with eight carriages just

Learning when to give way on the Burke Development Road. The world's second largest dump truck was being transported to the Gregory Mine; the wheels and tray came on separate vehicles

outside McKinlay – until the front cabin came into view. Built especially to service the Cannington mine about 90 km west of McKinlay, these ships of the highway, up to 53 metres long, deliver ore directly to a siding on the main line to Cloncurry. We became used to them passing us. Most drivers were very considerate and we enjoyed being pulled along by the draught when they were travelling in the same direction. The same draught tended to almost completely stop us, like hitting a wall, when they crossed our path.

Since we had entered Queensland we had been overtaken by a steady stream of caravans and 4WD vehicles being driven by 'the grey army' – mostly couples in early retirement escaping the winter cold of Victoria and NSW. Very often we covered the same amount of territory per day on our bikes as they dawdled from town to town. Pulling off the main road towards Elrose Station in search of a secluded campsite, we stumbled across a group of four couples with their caravans and shared their campfire as the evening temperature dropped. Ray explained that they were proud members of the SKI Club (Spending Kid's Inheritance) and the CRAFT Club (Can't Remember A Flippin' Thing). They were having a fantastic time.

We planned to take a day off in Cloncurry, home of the Royal Flying Doctor Service and the first copper mine in Australia. At breakfast I bumped into a family friend, Alasdair Cooke, who was in town to oversee a feasibility study to redevelop this mine. Copper was discovered in 1867 by Ernest Henry, Cloncurry's founder, and the mine he built, the Great Australia Mine, has functioned intermittently since then. In the operations of their Perth-based company, Exco Resources, Alasdair and his business partner, Steve, are careful to use minimal impact techniques. First, the area is mapped by aerial survey using magnetic equipment, then rather than clearing the vegetation in grids, they use a Global Positioning Satellite (GPS) System to survey the area on foot. Reworking the old mine site and drilling deep with advanced extraction methods means there is little evidence of their activities. This seems to be a very responsible approach to management, far removed from some of the unsightly mining practices I've seen, especially (not only) in developing countries.

Conical termite mounds on station country north of Quamby, Burke Development Road

From Cloncurry we took the Burke Development Road to Normanton. For most of the way the road was just a single lane strip of tarmac, often with rough edges and a precarious drop off to the gravel. Negotiating road trains now meant getting off the road completely and all vehicles, even passing cars, delivered a shower of dust and rocks. It was especially important to hold our breath when being passed by stock trucks as we would usually receive a smattering of manure in the debris. The most unpleasant mutterings, however, were reserved for the few inconsiderate drivers who didn't bother to slow down so that we were struck with rocks at greater speed.

Quamby was once an important centre for a prosperous mining and pastoral community. The pub, originally built as a customs house in 1860, was barely operational. In the days of horse-drawn transport, Cobb and Co. stage coaches would have serviced a thriving community, but now with motorised vehicles the social hub has shifted to Cloncurry about 50 km south. From the outside, it was easy to imagine the pub in its former glory, but internally things were in a sorry state. The owner, who was waiting to sell and retire to the east coast, seemed uninterested in every topic of conversation I tried to introduce. All the same, she allowed us to camp on a patch of grass beside the old accommodation – but there were more dog turds than blades of grass and we bent a few tent pegs as we tried to drive them into the stony ground.

In the morning we could see the full extent of the mess. I concluded that the large green frogs living under the rim of the toilet may not have been an indicator of a healthy environment at Quamby. It certainly wasn't easy to relax knowing what I was sitting on! Goats roamed freely throughout the premises and we kept a watchful eye – we didn't want them gnawing on our tent or any of the equipment. Two horses walked right up to the back door, looking for breakfast. Dogs slept on the dusty foam mattresses in the old hotel rooms and we had to warn them away from our food. In fact, the term 'dog's breakfast' was apt in describing the sad state of Quamby.

Always keen to find out about the path ahead, Greg struck up a conversation with a local who had stopped off for a drink. The most impressive feature on the road to Normanton, we were told, was Bang Bang Jump-Up, where we would have a long, enjoyable downhill run to the Gulf plain. As Bang Bang Jump-Up was a further 200 km away, we thought it either must be very significant or that there was very little between Quamby and that point. After some interesting rugged granite landscapes, the red soils we passed started to change into the grey earth which typifies the floodplains of the Gulf region. The termite mounds gradually became taller and more prominent, taking on the grey shades of the soil, which gave the large stands the appearance of a cemetery. These flat lands had me fantasising about Bang Bang Jump-Up.

One way of luring passing trade. Burke and Wills Roadhouse
(photo: G Yeoman)

Situated about halfway between Cloncurry and Normanton at the crossroads of the Burke Development Road and the Wills Development Road, the Burke and Wills Roadhouse was like an oasis. Up for sale for a reported $1.5 million, it certainly had no competitors, so it must have the potential to return the profits of a small goldmine. Just before we left the roadhouse, we started talking to a couple of army men who said their job was 'internal security'. They travelled the back roads of Queensland meeting people in order to find out what was happening. We gratefully accepted their offer to do a water drop for us and we arranged for them to leave some water beside the first sign for the Flinders River. It was a luxury not to have to carry quite so much water and we took comfort in the fact that we were guaranteed enough to see us through to Normanton.

Bang Bang Jump-Up was like a tsunami in the landscape. We had been cycling with great expectations for a day and a half to reach the top of the rocky escarpment. This is the point where the plateau gives way to the tall savannah grasslands which typify the deadpan-flat Gulf region. In reality, it was just a small rise and after a 30-second descent it was all over – so much for freewheeling down a long drop-off! North of Bang Bang Jump-Up the termite mounds were the most significant rises on the floodplain.

The road seemed to follow parallel to the path of different waterways which we could see demarcated by meandering ribbons of green in the distance. The savannah grasses were often tall enough to impede our view from the saddle. I wouldn't have liked to have been caught as a fire swept across the plains.

At the sign for the Flinders River we stopped to collect the water we had trusted the army men to drop. We found the unmistakable green canteens under camouflage netting, but when Greg reached over to collect them, he discovered that the bottles had been emptied onto the ground and that the bag was filled with litter. This was very baffling as no one would have noticed the water dump from the road. If someone did find the bottles it would have been obvious that someone else was relying on the water. We quizzed the workmen at the Flinders River Bridge who claimed they saw nothing. The whole incident was highly suspect and gave rise to an uneasy feeling as we had depended on the uniformed men. On this occasion we were going to be all right but if this situation had occurred in the desert, we would have been in trouble.

We needed no further persuasion to heed the warning signs, this one at Leichhardt's Lagoon

(photo: G Yeoman)

We decided to camp near the river so we could use its water for washing and cooking. The other main concern was that for the first time we were in crocodile country. We chose a site well away from the water's edge and near another 'grey army' couple. Greg was particularly paranoid about the idea of crocodiles and so I, only slightly braver, cautiously neared the section dammed by the causeway, constantly searching the still waters and the river banks for signs of the prehistoric hunters. My imagination got the better of me and my heart raced as I frantically scooped up just enough water in our collapsible bucket and retreated hastily from the edge of the causeway, spilling some of my cargo in the panic.

Normanton was an easy morning's ride away. Our fertile imaginings about being taken by a crocodile were further fired by a life-sized replica of the largest crocodile ever caught, which was on display outside the shire offices. Shot in 1957 on the Norman River, the monster, known as 'Krys', was 8.63 metres (28ft) long. The sheer bulk of the creature was even more imposing as my whole body could easily fit within its jaws.

The major administrative centre in the region, the second oldest town of the Gulf has a colourful history. The first European to sight the Norman River was Abel Tasman in 1664. Ludwig Leichhardt was the first land-based explorer through the region, half-way into his epic journey from the Darling Downs to Port Essington. In 1867 William Landsborough sailed up the Norman River and chose the site for the settlement of Normanton. The town became an important port, initially to service the cattle industry and then for shipping out the gold that was discovered at Croydon, 150 km to the east. We too used Normanton to re-supply and as a pivotal point before heading east along the Savannah Way towards Cairns, 700 km of gradual uphill.

Travelling north to the Gulf we had been generally blessed with favourable winds, crosswinds at the worst. This was all part of the plan, because in plotting the course of the expedition I knew that if we travelled in an anti-clockwise direction around the country we would benefit from the predominant high pressure system which sits over the centre of the continent, at least during the winter/Dry season. This should ensure mostly tailwinds at least until we headed south into the Tanami Desert. Pushing east from Normanton to Cairns was an annoying glitch in the plan with regard to headwinds. The cross/tailwinds which fanned us up the Burke Development Road now provided energy-sapping resistance all the way to the Atherton Tablelands, just before Cairns.

The lands around the Norman River and Leichhardt Lagoon were as flat as a bowling green and the road arrow-straight as we rode to Croydon parallel with the 110-year-old Gulflander railway line to Croydon. As much of the land can lie under water for long periods during the Wet season, the line was built with submersible sleepers. Our path was flanked with dull bush and grassland which was slightly claustrophobic after the open plains we had just crossed. The bush did, however, provide plenty of cover for wildlife. Spotting kangaroos, wallabies and a variety of birds diverted our attention from the drudgery of the task at hand. There was a notable absence of road trains to intimidate both us and the natural fauna. In fact, we saw more live animals than road kill, a pleasing improvement. The landscape changed just before Croydon, which could not have been more of a contrast to the Croydon that Greg knew in south London.

Old chimney stacks and mining ruins were dotted among the welcome undulations. Georgetown was surrounded by similar-looking gold country, but as the undulations became compressed into the prominent peaks of the Newcastle Range, the quadriceps started to complain again and the extra workload not so well received. These were the first hills we had climbed since the Drummonds.

Before leaving Mt Surprise, we paid a visit to the local primary school. It was virtually impossible to pitch my talk at a level that maintained the attention of all nine students as their ages ranged from six to twelve. The older children, though, listened with interest. Not many city kids would have thought of questions such as 'How long can you hold your breath when you pass the road kill?'

The days seemed to be getting harder, but this may have been because we were in need of a decent rest. Although we had cycled a couple of half-days, we hadn't had a full day out of the saddle since Winton. The gradual climb, along with the battle into the wind, was taking its toll. From Mt Surprise we ascended another 400 metres to reach an altitude of 800 metres. Stopping at the Forty Mile Scrub National Park, we were suddenly surrounded dry rainforest – trees lose their leaves in the Dry season to reduce water loss.

The dry rainforest soon became wet rainforest on the fertile Atherton Tableland. Having had to carry extra water over the previous few weeks, suddenly we were up in the rain clouds, pushing through the mist on Queensland's highest road (1138 metres). With the altitude came the cold. With the proximity to Cairns and more productive lands came an increased population and tourist density. The steepness of the volcanic landscape probably helped save the pockets of rainforest from being clear felled: as a result, the countryside was a patchwork of green pastures and pristine rainforest, treating we cyclists to extensive views and then dropping into dark dense masses of vines, ferns and strangler figs.

Descending the hairpins of the Gillies Highway was the reward for the toil of the previous six days. It was like unwinding and reminded me of some the cycling I had done in the mountains of the Cevennes region in the south of France a couple of years ago. About twenty kilometres later we were back at sea level in the Mulgrave Valley. Sensing we were nearing the end of the first 5000-km stage, I forgot that my legs were exhausted and felt obliged to make the most of the strong tailwind as we sailed passed fields of flowering sugar-cane and into Queensland's northern capital.

Dusk afterglow on Leichhardt's Lagoon

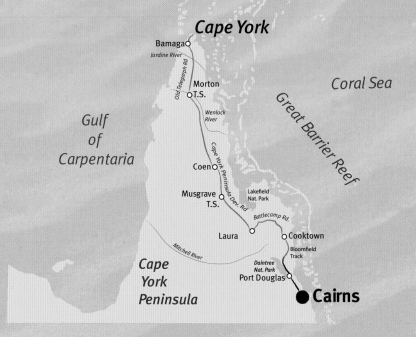

Torres Strait

Cape York

Bamaga

Jardine River

Old Telegraph Rd

Morton
T.S.

Wenlock River

Gulf of Carpentaria

Coral Sea

Great Barrier Reef

Cape York Peninsula Dev. Rd

Coen

Musgrave
T.S.

Lakefield
Nat. Park

Battlecamp Rd.

Mitchell River

Laura

Cooktown

Bloomfield
Track

*Daintree
Nat. Park*

Port Douglas

Cairns

**Cape
York
Peninsula**

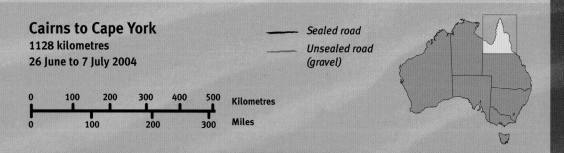

Cairns to Cape York
1128 kilometres
26 June to 7 July 2004

—— Sealed road
—— Unsealed road
(gravel)

| 0 | 100 | 200 | 300 | 400 | 500 | Kilometres |

Miles

| 0 | 100 | 200 | 300 |

4

To the Tip
(Cairns to Cape York)

The fuel tank at Musgrave
Telegraph Station – did we
have enough fuel in our
tanks?
(photo: G Yeoman)

'...And you must watch out for the wild boar. If one attacks you it will try to rip you open with its razor-sharp incisors. If you're attacked, you must let out a high-pitched scream or blow a whistle to put it off.'

My friend's father, whom we met in Cairns, reeled off a long list of hazards and tips on how to avoid them. According to Les, crocodiles, snakes and wild boar were very real dangers, while the rough and sandy roads, the dust and the humidity in the Far North were all going to make our travels uncomfortable.

'The sand flies will eat you alive if the crocs and pigs don't get you first!' Les was now starting to get a bit carried away and couldn't keep his serious face any longer. 'The people can be a bit strange too. Humidity can do strange things; send them troppo.' For the rest of the evening, more little comments and stories crept into the conversation as to the dangers and difficulties that we could encounter between Cairns and the Tip of Cape York. We all had a laugh at the exaggerated tone but knew that underneath lay a serious message.

Our quest to reach 'the Tip', the most northerly point of the Australian mainland, was always going to be a race against time. I had booked our flights back to Cairns and then my Cairns-Perth return way back in Winton as I had to be sure that I could get to Perth in time for the wedding of my younger brother, Tony. Family always comes first. Given Greg's and my experience, on bitumen roads we were adept at making time schedules; the route to the top of the country, however, was far more of an unknown quantity. The gravel roads, by all reports, were going to be impossibly rough; many vehicles, both 4WD and bicycles, succumb to the testing conditions every year. Some twenty to thirty cyclists venture to the Tip every Dry season, embarking on an adventure which is a major trek on its own. Many of them travel as an organised tour group with a support vehicle to carry their equipment. Our route of over 1100 km, which involved negotiating the Bloomfield Track to reach Cooktown, the Battle Camp Road to Laura, the Cape York Peninsula Development Road and the Old Telegraph Road, was the first of the five main 'off road' challenges of the expedition.

We decided to leave a day earlier than planned, foregoing the extra recovery day which our bodies could have done with, to reduce the pressure of time. Our new fat, knobbly-treaded tyres, which we had fitted to combat the sand and corrugations ahead, felt cumbersome and whirred inefficiently over the asphalt streets of Cairns. Greg had also fitted a new suspension seat-post to make his ride more comfortable. I had ordered one too, but unfortunately it had not arrived in time. I was concerned how my backside was going to cope with the bumps, given that I was already on antibiotics for my painful condition which had developed soon after I left Canberra.

It wasn't long before we had left behind the busy streets of the capital of the Far North, passing strings of hotels and backpackers' accommodation, cosmopolitan bars and restaurants, didgeridoo shops, characterless shopping centres and finally the international airport. The port of Cairns is built on a mangrove swamp and mudflats, but north along the Captain Cook Highway the coastline starts to reveal the white sandy beaches for which the region is famous. The half-day ride to Port Douglas was spectacular, although the road, in many places only a few metres from the beach, was busy, mostly with tourist traffic. It must have been a considerable engineering feat to etch such a winding route into cliffs which plummet sheer to the shoreline. I told myself that one day, when I had more time, I would explore the Daintree Mountains, silhouetted in the distance by the sinking afternoon sun.

Cycling through the sugar-cane plantations near Mossman, on the way to the Daintree River
(photo: G Yeoman)

North of Port Douglas we entered a region classified by UNESCO as one of outstanding universal value, cycling along a narrow band of coastal plain predominantly featuring sugar-cane plantations. To the east the Great Barrier Reef extends virtually the length of Queensland over an area greater than that of Italy. To the north and west, the Daintree National Park is a main feature of the Wet Tropics which lie between Townsville and Cooktown and cover an area of approximately 900 000 hectares (approximately two million acres). At the point where we took the ferry across the Daintree River, these two diverse ecosystems converge, the only place on the planet where two World Heritage areas exist side-by-side.

The Great Barrier Reef is the world's most extensive coral reef system and one of the world's richest areas in terms of faunal diversity. Contrary to popular belief, the reef is not a continuous barrier, but a broken maze of coral reefs and coral cays. Visible from space, it includes some 2800 individual reefs, of which a quarter are fringing reefs, varying in size and shape. It also contains extensive areas of seagrass, mangrove, soft-bottom communities and island communities. The Great Barrier Reef provides habitats for diverse forms of marine life, including an estimated 1500 species of fish and more than 300 species of hard, reef-building corals.

Although Australia contains less than one-thousandth of the world's tropical rainforests, the Wet Tropical forests are some of the most significant ecosystems globally. The 135-million-year-old rainforest of the Cape Tribulation section of the Daintree is the most primitive in the world. As the ancient forests receded over the millennia, remnant pockets of the rainforest wilderness remained, containing an almost complete record of the major stages in the evolution of plant life on earth. Of particular importance are the primitive flowering plants – this region has the highest concentration of such families on earth, their great diversity extending over the spectrum of the plant and animal kingdoms. Some 390 species of plants and twenty-five species of animals are rare and threatened.

One of these species, a giant birdwinged butterfly, attracted my attention as we arrived at the summit of the Alexander Range look-out point. Out of breath and glistening with perspiration, we had delved into the lower range of granny gears to cope with the first long, steep incline for some weeks. The vibrant blue, fragile wings fought constantly against the gusting coastal breeze to enable the ultra-light insect to maintain its position. I was astonished and inspired by both the beautiful creature's aerial ability and the incredible view over the mouth of the Daintree River and Schnapper Island just out to sea.

North of the Daintree River, the steep-sloped terrain remained a challenge. Here the rainforest was a dense mass of ferns, vines and towering, straight-trunked trees with massive supporting buttress roots which prevented the midday sun from penetrating through to the ground. Like the plants of the stratified forest, it felt like we too had to compete for the light as we ascended from the gloom of the valleys through mottled shade and finally into direct sunlight.

◆　◆　◆

Being on the tourist run to Cape Tribulation, we benefitted from the associated facilities: tarmac road and convenience shops. On the negative side, from Port Douglas to Cape Tribulation, this gearing toward the tourist dollar has bred an impersonal demeanour. We received few of the friendly waves from passing drivers we had become accustomed to in the outback. Shops and bars were reluctant to provide us for free with the water we needed, insisting we bought bottled water from them instead. Given the vast amounts of fluid we needed to make our way, there is no way we could afford the exorbitant prices they charged the tourists.

Ferns competing for light
(photo: G Yeoman)

Cape Tribulation is the end of the road for the hoards of visitors, many international, who come to chill-out in the largely pristine environment. Suddenly we hit the gravel and immediately had to slalom our way between walkers and potholes. Within a kilometre or so, the hikers petered out and we crossed a dry creek bed. Known as Blockade Creek, this now-innocuous landmark was the site in 1983 of heated protests opposing the construction of the controversial Bloomfield Track.

In the early 1980s, at about the same time that the National Park was gazetted, the Douglas Shire Council proposed building a road to link Cape Tribulation and Bloomfield. Although this road would pass along the coastal fringe of the proposed park, the developers justified its construction by claiming it would benefit tourism, better equip authorities to police a steadily growing drug problem, deter bird trappers and orchid thieves, and provide residents of Cooktown with easier and quicker access to Cairns. Those campaigning against its construction argued that the building of the road would threaten the scientifically important area and that the increased pressure of tourism which would surely follow would put an unsustainable burden on the region.

When in December 1983 bulldozers arrived, many people gathered to physically try to prevent work from proceeding. Protesters set up headquarters at the work-site at Blockade Creek and a long confrontation began. A large contingent of police was sent in. Over the following days protesters climbed or chained themselves to trees or buried themselves in the path of the bulldozers, and many of them were arrested. The confrontation attracted international media attention and the building of the road soon became the major environmental issue in Australia. After some delay, bulldozers began work from both the Cape Tribulation and the Bloomfield ends and the road was pushed through in only three weeks. But the hurriedly built track could not withstand the seasonal deluges of the Wet; it became blocked by resultant landslides, and significant amounts of soil were flushed into the waters of the Great Barrier Reef. The road was repaired the following Dry season, and was officially opened in 1984. The major positive of the blockade was that it brought the Daintree to world attention and the battle was instrumental in leading to World Heritage listing of the area. The road has also benefitted tourism, enabling many people to experience this beautiful region.

Passing the creek, we were now on the Bloomfield Track, notorious not only for its construction but also its ruggedness. We were soon to learn that the lung-busting climbs to reach our first water crossing at Emmagen Creek were merely the warm-up. The hastily constructed road was poorly engineered and laced with rim-threatening boulders and potholes. Our intention was to reach Bloomfield by nightfall, but as we struggled up and down the severe slopes, it was evident we were not going to make it.

There was nothing horizontal about the road at all. Creeks drew a natural line dividing each ascent and descent. Crossing the larger streams required us to stop, remove shoes and socks, and drag and lift the laden bikes across. The climb into the Donovan Range was the steepest extended incline I had ever attempted, the gravel surface adding to the degree of difficulty. At a one-in-five gradient, it was tougher than the Swiss Alps, coastal Turkey or the Sayan Mountains in Siberia, and the Cowie Range, five kilometres further north, was something else.

We climbed a short distance from the dry Melissa Creek, turned a corner and were confronted with what looked like a bloody great wall. The one-in-three (33 per cent) gradient had been concreted to prevent it being washed away every time it rained. I tried to put on maximum power in my lowest gear and zigzag back and forth across the single lane to reduce the gradient but my efforts were futile. Being a little stronger, Greg fared slightly better – a whole five metres further before he too was halted. Pushing was incredibly awkward and involved leaning all my weight on the handlebars so my body was almost parallel with the slope. It was like having to hold a 'plank' position in Pilates for an extended period of time, but with a lot of extra resistance. My steps were stunted as I was not tall enough to stride clear of the front and rear panniers. So acute was the angle of the road that I was forced to walk on my toes, with hands glued to the handlebars as I lifted and drove the bike at the same time. To prevent the bike escaping back down the slope when I paused, I had to apply the brakes.

It was a matter of taking one step at a time. My body and mind were screaming out to stop, but my head remained down. A couple of vehicles roared past with their straining engines complaining almost as much as my body. They were probably in their lowest ratio and first gear as the slope is almost at the limit of a 4WD's capabilities. It would have been tempting to thumb a lift, but that was not the point of the exercise. We had to get there under our own steam – and we were definitely producing plenty of steam at that point!

Defying gravity, we eventually reached the summit. With little daylight left we decided to head for the Woobadda River a few kilometres further on, where we hoped there would be sufficient clear and level ground to pitch the tent.

Descending such steep gravel terrain to the river with a heavy load is particularly treacherous – losing control could be a terminal mistake as we would have ended up careering over the edge of the mountain or wrapped around a tree. We crept down the slope at a snail's pace, not daring to release the pressure on the brakes for even a moment. I was glad we had chosen disc brakes for the expedition as they were extremely efficient in this situation; normal calliper brakes, which pinch on the wheel rims to control the bike speed, tend to become overheated in this situation and as a result are ineffective. There had been times in the past when I was forced to stop to let brake pads cool down before I could not stop at all. The technique for descending on such an angle on the gravel involved leaning the body back, holding as low a position as possible behind the saddle.

By the time we reached the Woobadda River, the most significant stream between Cape Tribulation and the Bloomfield River (about 10 km further on), it was almost dark. There was no clear ground to camp on the south side, leaving us no option but to cross the river in the murkiness. This normally wouldn't be a problem, but Greg was absolutely terrified at the prospect of crocodiles and his fear rubbed off on me, more so in the dark. We parked the bikes and hesitantly entered the water, testing the stream for depth and current to determine a path to haul the bikes across. Fortunately, the water never reached much over knee height as we stumbled over the smooth river stones, and the current was manageable.

Halfway through the return leg of our reconnaissance, Greg froze and grabbed my wrist so tightly my hand would have dropped off had he persisted.

'Is that a croc?'

'Where?'

'Just there, just after those stones.'

At this point my heart skipped a few beats and spurts of adrenaline surged through me, heightening my already anxious state to an amber alarm. By now, Greg was in a state of panic – red alert. This is when you get to find out just how good friends you really are! Was it going to be him or me? Our head torches, batteries running low, emitted an undefined glow as we carefully inspected every stone ahead for movement. It was impossible to make out just how much of the blackness beyond was river and how much was forest. But although the moon had not yet risen and it was pitch dark, I could see where Greg was pointing – to a large, partly submerged body a few metres away in a deeper pool. There was no movement. Was the ultimate hunter stalking us, sizing up its next meal?

'You can't see its eyes...If it was a croc, its eyes would glow in the torch light.' My observation instilled some calm. We contemplated the situation for a few more moments.

'Come on, we can't stand here any longer or we won't be able to see anything at all,' I urged. We stepped cautiously at first, constantly glancing over our right shoulders, but nearing the river bank we scrambled quickly and splashed clumsily in a mad panic. We could not leave the water fast enough.

'Shit! Now we have to cross back again with the bikes.'

'There can't be any crocs or they would have had us by now.' I tried to think objectively to settle the nerves. We dragged and lifted our awkward loads back across the river, remnants of the adrenaline rush fuelling newfound strength for a hasty traverse to the northern bank. On a small patch of ground away from the water's edge and the road, we set up camp.

Everything seemed so tranquil in the morning. Daylight returned our sense of reason: the freshwater stream was 183 metres above sea level and there was

The 33 per cent gradients on the Bloomfield Track were too dangerous to descend mounted on loaded bikes

negligible risk of crocodiles. We pushed on to Bloomfield, first having to descend the Cowie Range. The one-in-three gradient was too steep to negotiate from the saddle, forcing us to walk the bikes cautiously down. Fortunately we arrived at the Bloomfield River causeway at low tide, otherwise it could have been a long wait for the waters to recede. Back at sea level we were definitely in estuarine crocodile territory. Still paranoid after the previous evening, we were careful to keep to the centre of the concrete barrier just in case there was a monster salty ready to explode out of the water and take one of us.

The Traditional custodians of the land reside in the Wujal Wujal Community, formerly known as the Bloomfield River Mission. We paid the community store a visit, which gave Greg the opportunity to top up on treats. The need to indulge in morale-boosting pies, chocolate bars and ice creams was always more pronounced after a tough stint. My budget was too tight to follow suit: I had to ration project funds over nine months and could not afford these simple pleasures.

◆ ◆ ◆

Back on the bikes, the route to Cooktown from Bloomfield improved markedly, apart from a few testing climbs through the Cedar National Park. When we turned on to the bitumen of the Cooktown Development Road, Black Mountain in the distance looked like a giant pile of mining rubble. The natural phenomenon is, in fact, a colossal mound of lichen-covered granite boulders which is said to be decomposing from the inside out. In the spaces between the rounded boulders lie a labyrinth of caves, crevasses, holes and deep drop-offs. Black Mountain has been the subject of legends since the first people gazed on it tens of thousands of years ago. To the Kuku Bidiji and Kuku Yimudji people, the Kalkajaka region, as they call it, is sacred and the source of many Dreamtime tales. In the late 1800s, many of the Welsh and Irish tin miners attracted to the region spun yarns about whole tribes vanishing into the mountain while being pursued by police troopers. Even better are tall stories of entire cattle herds disappearing into one of the small valleys. I could easily imagine someone like my friend's father pulling the leg of a non-local.

We crossed the Annan River and were soon back into civilisation, passing plots of cultivated land before reaching the tidy streets of what for us was the last large town on our trek to the Tip. Locals refer to Cooktown on the Endeavour River as the 'Queen of the North'. Founded in 1873 after the discovery of gold on the Palmer River, inland from Cape Tribulation, the settlement soon became the chief port servicing the rich goldfields. Both Cooktown and the river owe their names to Captain James Cook who in 1770 careened his ship *Endeavour* there for seven weeks, repairing damage incurred on the Great Barrier Reef (at Cape Tribulation). Cyclones and the threat of being bombed during World War II challenged the continued existence of the isolated town. Cooktown was finally connected by road to the rest of Australia in the 1950s, which led to its 'discovery' by tourists and today a population of about 1200 thrives. We just had enough time to catch the shops to prepare for the journey ahead and enjoy the waterfront views over the harbour.

To reach the Cape York Peninsula Development Road from Cooktown we would have to either retrace our route along the bitumen Cooktown Development Road to Lakeland or cut directly across to the Lakefield National Park and on to Laura via the Battle Camp Road. The latter route had been described to us by those who knew it as notoriously rough, but it did cut off a significant distance. A fellow patron of the Cooktown camping-ground told us he had passed an exasperated cyclist who was cursing and swearing at the sandy, corrugated track as he repaired a puncture, saying it was the worst road he had ever pedalled. We opted for this adventurous alternative.

The Battle Camp Road at the base of the Lakefield National Park was all sand and corrugations (photo: G Yeoman)

The first stage along the Endeavour River to the magnificent falls of the same name was a well-maintained gravel road which also serviced the large Hope Vale Community further north. The first part of the Battle Camp Road to Isabella Falls wasn't too bad either and we were starting to wonder what all the fuss was about. Although conditions did gradually deteriorate, our efforts on the Bloomfield Track had prepared us well and I felt strong climbing through the Look Out Range and then the Battle Camp Range. But nothing had prepared us for the road that followed. Descending at a speed greater than I should have been, I had no time to evade its deep corrugations which lay camouflaged by the dappled shade of surrounding woodland. The extended washboard surface was made up of continuous waves with amplitudes of about 15 cm; these acted like speed bumps, which shook loose the panniers and destabilised the bike. Miraculously I managed to stay on and the wheels remained round.

For the remainder of the day we proceeded with greater caution. Once over the ranges and into Lakefield, the road was just a mass of corrugations and sand – it was easy to understand how that cyclist had lost his cool. We picked up his tracks, which snaked all over the road in search of the best path. We'd try the sand for a while, find it extremely heavy-going, and then the more solid corrugated surface would look more appealing. We'd get shaken to pieces for a while and then opt back to the softer alternative. It was sand to corrugations, corrugations to sand all the way to Old Laura.

The Battle Camp Road was appropriately named considering the difficulties we endured. The road, mountain range and nearby station were named after a battle between the first group of diggers, heading for the 1872 gold strike at Palmer River, and a large band of Aboriginals. The road follows the path of an old railway line which joined Cooktown to Laura. Built in 1890 and closed in the 1960s, the line was supposed to join Cooktown to the south, but the system was never completed.

Greg was in a real hurry all day because the final obstacle before reaching the Old Laura homestead was the Laura River. We knew it was possible that there were crocodiles in the Laura River (and Normanby River, which we had crossed earlier) this far inland, although it was unlikely. Greg wanted to avoid crossing in the dark and I had a job keeping pace when he was so anxiously motivated. We made it at dusk, feeding time for crocs, and didn't waste time fording the stream.

Just as we had settled in for the evening a lone cyclist appeared out of the dark. Rob, an American, had sold his bicycle shop to spend a year pedalling through Australia. He had left Cooktown two days previously, passed Old Laura and turned north along the Lakefield Road, but fed up with the unrelenting sand-corrugations-sand conditions, he had decided to turn back after about 20 km and head for Laura and the main road. The following morning, we had a chance to compare experiences and how we were set up to travel. Rob seemed to be carrying a lot of extra equipment. 'Rosella' was loaded like a faithful pack horse and every spare inch of the frame was taken up with water-bottle attachments. He was also dragging a trailer behind him filled with many 'inessential items' which he considered important for making a year of travelling alone more comfortable. We headed off toward Laura together, but pretty soon it was evident that Rob had to work much harder through the sand than we did, and he dropped behind.

We were completely parched by the time we reached Laura and the main road, and in need of sustenance. The little general store served nothing fresh. Stepping through the fly curtain of coloured plastic strips which hung from the door frame was like entering into a time warp. In a scene reminiscent of some of the shops we visited in Russia, all the tins were lined up on the shelves behind the counter and the bill was calculated by hand on a piece of paper before being rung up on the old-fashioned cash register. At least Greg was able to fill up with a mid-morning snack – his usual pie and ice cream – to restore morale for the next onslaught. The ice cream had to be consumed in a hurry, before it melted.

Pedalling along the much busier Cape York Development Road was thirsty work as the humidity level was noticeably higher. The main reason for the frequent traffic was that it was school holidays and many families took the opportunity to race to the most northerly point in the country. Sometimes we

Greg loading up with a morale-boosting snack at Laura

would be passed by a convoy of four or five vehicles travelling way too fast and following blindly in each others' dust clouds. It couldn't have been much fun with no view and being rattled by the constant vibrations of the corrugations. At such speeds, drivers regularly lose control and vehicle casualties are high during the Dry season.

Being a still day, clouds of fine, choking dust hung in the air and formed a thick, red paste when combined with sunburn cream and my sweaty skin. I called this my Northern Australian mudpack, but I doubt whether it has any potential as a beauty product. It was difficult to hold my breath long enough to avoid inhaling the dust. I usually pulled my shirt up over my nose until Greg produced a very useful item called a Buff out of his bags. This seamless knitted fabric tube with breathable and moisture-wicking properties has many uses: as a scarf/neck gaiter, balaclava, hat, bandana and others. We used it primarily as a scarf, but pulling the stretchy material up over the nose filtered out the worst of the dust. The Buff came into its own on the busy dirt roads, especially when we were totally enveloped in clouds of dust for extended periods.

We pushed on past the Hann River and Musgrave roadhouses. Most of the roadhouses were once telegraph stations; now they cater for tourists and a handful of locals. The road follows the route of the old telegraph track virtually the whole way to the Tip. The track was the only link between the isolated telegraph stations and the south.

◆ ◆ ◆

Back in Cairns I had arranged for us to stay at New Bamboo Station with Joan and Ernie Henderson. Their grandchildren are involved with the Cairns School of Distance Education and I had been given their contact details. It was a pleasant surprise to find Joan waiting for us when we arrived at the Musgrave Telegraph Station/Roadhouse. Thursday was mail day – the mail arrives once a week by a special Australia Post flight which lands on the adjacent airstrip – and Joan had driven in to collect it. For a change we had plenty of time and were able to chat to some of the locals. Leaving Musgrave for a rough 20-km ride to New Bamboo, we opted to cycle along the runway as it was much smoother than the road. Rather than any prospect of aircraft landing, we only had to worry about avoiding the cows.

Greg about to be consumed by another choking dust cloud near Hann River

Sporting my Northern Australian mudpack
(photo: G Yeoman)

The Musgrave airstrip proved to be a smoother path for a kilometre or so

Joan and Ernie Henderson,
New Bamboo Station

As we arrived at New Bamboo, Joan and Ernie were waiting to greet us. They showed us into the house – or what eventually was going to be their house – where Ernie had his home brew chilled and waiting for us. They were building at the time and Joan had already mentioned that she hoped we didn't mind roughing it. Their home was being constructed out of corrugated iron but as yet it had no walls, just a roof and concrete floors with all the essential items – refrigerator, stove, cupboards, and basic furniture – exposed. Before the onset of the Wet, they hoped to have walls, to protect them and to keep out the cane toads, which during our stay seemed to monopolise the floor space as we relaxed around the kitchen table. Our hosts could both talk and not even Greg could fit a word in at times. I didn't mind. I was both intrigued and entertained by the conversation.

Joan and Ernie were actually newcomers to the area, having bought the 90 000-hectare (211 000 acre) property three years previously. Prior to this, they were banana farmers in Tully, south of Cairns. The family got out of producing bananas because the industry is being destroyed by buyers, such as large supermarket chains, importing the fruit from overseas and undercutting the Australian market. Ernie explained that it cost them almost twice as much to produce a carton of bananas in Tully than to import varieties from South-east Asia. He said the pineapple and sugar-cane industries were suffering a similar fate.

The station had been run down, let go by the previous owner. Even with the help of their son, it is a bold move for Ernie and Joan to take on the re-development of a station when they had been looking to retire. Among sustainability issues they deal with, is the control of the feral animals. In their first year they culled 270 brumbies which, according to Ernie, had had a devastating effect on the land. Wild horses consume three times as much food as cattle, and wreck fences and water troughs. Wild pigs are a problem too. At the time we met, they were running about 1500 head of cattle, and estimated the sustainable threshold for the property was around 6000 – once they controlled the vermin and developed the infrastructure such as fences and waters.

The flow of home brew seemed to induce a steady stream of local stories about some of the 'feral' characters of the Peninsula. Ernie especially was becoming progressively louder and more animated as the evening wore on. He asked us whether we ever hitched a ride. 'Taking a lift is cheating,' I explained. Ernie agreed: 'If you ride around Australia, then you ride around A-bloody-stralia!'

Joan apologised once again that our home for the night was the old musterers' quarters. We certainly didn't mind. It was a roof over our heads and by the time I hit the dusty foam mattress, I could have slept anywhere. Walking around by torch light, we had to tiptoe carefully so not to squash the toads. The hideous amphibians plodded about clumsily as if they too had been treated to Ernie's keg of beer.

The conversation resumed around the breakfast table the following morning as if we hadn't paused for sleep. Joan generously provided us with a hearty meal to fuel up for the day. We couldn't leave, however, without a tour of her diverse

Receiving advice from Wayne, who hailed from Dixie Outstation

vegetable garden. Any fresh produce had to be home-grown as a round trip to a major centre such as Cooktown was 700-800 km. Obviously a skilled gardener, Joan had good reason to be proud of the fruits of her labour. Her 'Garden of Eden' was lush and stratified like the rainforest we had passed through on the way to Cooktown. We were soon loaded up with passionfruit, tomatoes and other 'goodies', all bursting with the flavour which is often lost during mass production.

Out of New Bamboo, we climbed up the Bamboo Range, crossing the Great Dividing Range for the tenth time. Each traverse was slightly lower than the last and the summit was only 245 metres. The humidity was starting to take its toll and by the time we paused at the top, it looked as though I had been climbing for hours. My clothes were completely saturated.

The road to Coen, the only town on our route before Bamaga (near the Tip), was a particularly testing slog and my handlebar bag-rack snapped without warning due to the relentless corrugations. I twice attempted to repair the frame by splinting some old spokes across the sheered joins, but the rough, temporary job could not withstand the strain.

When the going gets tough, it is best to approach the situation with a sense of humour. Annoyed at the steady flow of 4WD vehicles hurtling past, Greg's comment helped alleviate the rising levels of frustration and tension. A woman, probably with good intentions, gave us what looked like a royal wave from the cocoon of her air-conditioned vehicle, which led Greg to inquire, 'What? Is she drying her nails?' as we were enshrouded in yet another dust cloud.

Hitting the bitumen, we were definitely nearing a 'major centre' complete with regional airport, hotel, motel, garage, a couple of shops, hospital and administration buildings. Although Coen developed after the discovery of gold in 1883, it now exists to provide services for the passing tourist trade in the Dry season and for the handful of surrounding pastoral properties. We arrived there in the nick of time, managing to catch a welder before he finished for the night. Fixing my handlebar bag-rack was a minor job compared to dealing with broken chassis and other major casualties of the route north.

Continuing past Archer River, Wolverton Station and Piccaninny Plain we reached the junction between the Peninsula Development Road and the Telegraph Road. Up until this point the Development Road had been one with the original track, but here it peeled off west to Weipa, the largest town on the

Camping in the 'wild' near Wolverton Station
(photo: G Yeoman)

Early moonrise

Cape York Peninsula, whose port serviced the mining industry of the bauxite-rich region. The original route of the Overland Telegraph Line which continued due north was just a graded track. Thankfully, there was considerably less traffic here and it was not so hacked up by heavy vehicles. The terrain and vegetation changed noticeably, the land appearing greener, termite mounds taller, and the dry, scrubby savannah evolved into woodlands featuring more prominent trees. A higher annual rainfall obviously made a big difference.

At the Wenlock River, one of the major rivers on the peninsula, we were thankful that a bridge had been completed in 2001. Prior to this, travellers relied on a raft built with 44-gallon drums to float their vehicles across when the depth was too great. We paused to read a sign hanging in a tree 14.6 metres above our heads proclaiming that 'Ando', 'Warewolf' and 'Tubby' had been there in a boat when the flooded river had reached to that height. It was difficult to imagine that such a sedate-looking stream could swell into a virtually immeasurable volume.

Just as we were preparing to cross the bridge and head into Moreton Telegraph Station for the midday break, two young boys came sprinting over to catch us and ask whether we would like to join their family for lunch. Making the most of their school holidays, the Walkers from Melbourne were returning from the Tip. Greg and I really appreciated the fresh, gourmet food they shared which we could never carry ourselves and which was unavailable in any of the roadhouses. We tried to be polite and leave some of the salmon paté, avocado and an assortment of goodies from the deli for the rest of the family but maintaining decorum was somewhat of a challenge. With regard to food, nothing on the Peninsula is cheap due to the isolation and lack of competition. Most roadhouses only serve junk food, which is particularly inadequate for hungry cyclists. I never understood why they can't supply something other than unsustaining white bread and plastic, processed cheese. We thanked Brigid and Tim for their kind gesture and promised to stay in touch.

At Bramwell Junction we had to make an important decision – whether to follow the straight Old Telegraph Track or take the bypass road. The track is only 70 km as opposed to the 111-km Southern Bypass, but it merely consists of two deep wheel ruts, is often sandy and corrugated, and contains many river crossings. The bypass road also had poor surfaces, but would probably allow us to travel a little faster. After weighing up the advice of many different travellers, we chose the Old Telegraph Track.

On a good section of the
Old Telegraph Track
(photo: G Yeoman)

Not many kilometres had gone by before I doubted the wisdom of our decision. By this stage, I'd fallen off (for the first time) and skinned my elbow. We could not cycle through some stretches of deep sand and found it quicker to venture cross-country. Confined as we were to following the single wheel track, if the sandy road surface gave away and the wheels sank or slipped, there was no option but to push until we could re-mount on firmer ground.

River crossings were simpler for us than other vehicles. After assessing the shallowest route, I learnt to balance the load on my hip and carry the awkward machine across so that the working parts stayed out of the water as much as possible. If the water was deep and fast flowing, as at Cockatoo Crossing, we took the bags off. Crossing each stream was like drawing a line behind us; we had reached a more northerly rung on the ladder. Even though this was an extremely physical day, we made it through, reaching Eliot Falls campsite battered and bruised. We had come 87 km from Bramwell Junction.

◆ ◆ ◆

At our last river crossing on the Old Telegraph Track – Sam's Crossing – we bumped into our new friends Paul and Mandy and their children. (We had first met them in Coen, and then at Archer River, where they offered to drop us some water further up the track.) When we stopped to chat, I leant my bike up against a tree near the creek bank, and believing it was secure, became engrossed in the conversation. Suddenly, one of their girls exclaimed, 'Look, the bike fell in the water!' My whole bike had tumbled down a rocky ravine, plunged into a deep pool and was being swept rapidly towards a waterfall, kept afloat by the waterproof panniers. Without hesitation Paul dived in and rescued the machine, bags and all, as if he was saving one of his children. The main problem was that my bar-bag was not waterproof and it contained my most valuable items – diary, wallet, iPAQ computer and mobile phone. The main casualty was the phone. Despite becoming soaked, the computer survived, my written diary was readable and my digital camera was well shielded in its own protective case within the rear panniers.

We were unable to continue up the full length of the Old Telegraph Track as this would have involved crossing the crocodile-infested Jardine River, which is not recommended. Instead our plan was to cut back across to the Northern Bypass Road and then use the ferry.

Feeling worse for wear
filling my drinking bottles
from a waterbag on the
Northern Bypass Road
(photo: G Yeoman)

With Cronan O'Meara, Father Tom Mullens and Ben Olsen, Bamaga
(photo: G Yeoman)

Our eighth day from Cooktown continued in this eventful vein. Greg had a heavy fall and hurt his knee when a stick became caught and jammed his front wheel. I came off several times in the sand and our food supplies were dwindling down to nothing. The state of the Northern Bypass Road was terrible and didn't get much better until we reached the last five kilometres of tarmac before Bamaga, 99 km from Eliot Falls.

Arriving virtually in the dark, we found that the service station was closed. Attracted by lights in the church, we decided to take a break there and work out what to do next. Father Tom Mullens and his colleagues, Cronan O'Meara and Ben Olsen, who had arrived that morning from Thursday Island to prepare the new chapel for consecration, greeted us. They kindly offered (much-needed) use of the shower, and tea. That night we slept on the concrete floor with the entire sodden contents of my panniers draped irreverently over the pews to dry. It was fortunate the chapel was not due to be blessed for a few days.

From Bamaga, we had a simple, short ride to the tip of Cape York and plenty of time to enjoy it. As we were to return to Bamaga, we left most of our load behind for the day. Handling the rough but well-formed dirt roads was far easier without the weight. The corrugations of the previous ten days had really taken their toll on my body, though, and I had lost sensation in most of my left hand. Fine motor control was impossible; I could really only grip the handlebar. It was a relief that we were going to reach the Tip within the restricted time-frame – in fact, with a day to spare. As I started to relax, I was overcome with tiredness, which made the 40-km journey a drawn-out affair.

Crab diggings on the tidal shoreline near the Tip
(photo: G Yeoman)

About 25 km from Bamaga we suddenly entered a verdant rainforest, ill-named the Lockerbie Scrub, which was a pleasure I had not expected. The first scientists to focus on what has become perhaps the most studied patch of rainforest in the country were guests of Frank Jardine. With his brother Alexander, Frank Jardine drove a small herd of 250 cattle, together with forty-two horses, from Carpentaria Downs Station to the region, arriving in 1865. He was subsequently employed by the Queensland government as the magistrate for the far northern region. Jardine established several cattle properties, including Lockerbie, and helped found the pearling industry in 1886.

The road ends at a car park beside an abandoned Injinoo Community which could most aptly be described as 'the Tip before the Tip' – rubbish tip, that is. It is hard to understand how this important region could be treated with such disrespect by any Australians. I tried to put the first 'tip' out of my mind as we followed the path through the rainforest to the beach. From there it was an easy scramble over the rocky headland to the very top of mainland Australia.

Made it!

Reaching the most northerly point of my country was a major landmark of the expedition and there was certainly a great feeling of satisfaction at getting there under my own leg power. The first fifty-nine days and almost 6000 km had been eventful and packed with variation as we traversed the latitudes back and forth across the Great Dividing Range. Canberra seemed such a long time ago and yet I still had nearly 20 000 km ahead of me.

We visited Thursday Island and then flew out from Horn Island back to Cairns in time for me to catch the connecting flights to Perth for my brother's wedding the following day. Arnaud was flying across from Melbourne for the event, and my middle sister, Robin, was flying over from California with her family, so I was looking forward to seeing them all, along with my extended family. I had been regularly telephoning Arnaud, but this was the first opportunity to see him since Canberra. The wedding over, the expedition resumed a few days later from Karumba where we picked up the Gulf Track.

Arnhem
Land

Katherine
Mataranka
Roper Bar

Nathan River Road

Stuart Hwy

NT

Booroloola

Gulf
of
Carpentaria

Wollogorang
○Hell's Gate
Doomadgee
Burketown

Karumba

QLD

Burke & Wills
Camp 119
Normanton

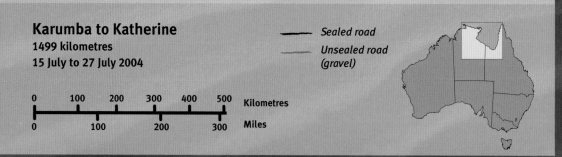

Karumba to Katherine
1499 kilometres
15 July to 27 July 2004

———— *Sealed road*
———— *Unsealed road*
(gravel)

0   100   200   300   400   500   Kilometres

0   100   200   300   Miles

5

The Gulf Track
(Karumba to Katherine)

Greg braving the water's edge for the first time after travelling for more than three weeks in crocodile territory, Little Bynoe River

Our flight from Cairns to Karumba in a cramped eight-seater treated us to a fantastic birds' eye view of the land we had taken six days to traverse in the opposite direction a couple of weeks previously (Normanton to Cairns). After take-off, we cleared the mountains and fertile green tropical Atherton Tableland. As we continued west, the terrain below changed abruptly. It was like a huge iron had been applied to the landscape, flattening the bumps and scorching the savannah grasses. Predominantly dry river beds, including the Mitchell and Gilbert rivers, were lined with narrow ribbons of green, which provided relief from the plains as we followed their course towards the Gulf of Carpentaria. As we approached the coast, the afternoon sun reflected off the sea as it oozed for many kilometres up the tidal waterways, looking like rising mercury through dense thickets of mangroves.

I hoped the rough landing attributable to the corrugated gravel airstrip and the plane receiving a puncture were not ill omens for the task ahead of us. While the thermometer at the airport terminal – a tiny corrugated-iron shed – showed a temperature in the mid-30s, barometer readings would have indicated we were definitely into the Dry season. It was thirsty work putting the bikes back together. Repacking and reloading so everything was balanced and tightly secured was by now a well-rehearsed science. We pushed on into town.

Karumba and environs was the end goal for many of the 'grey army' with whom we shared the Matilda Highway. They were seeking the sun's warmth in this fishermen's paradise, which beats to the pulse of the prawning season and lives and breathes fishing. The tidal mudflats at the mouth of the Norman River are marketed as 'the' place to watch the sunset. We did the tourist thing, including devouring some of the best fish and chips I have ever had, and then set the cameras up on the beach to catch the sun as it sank below the horizon. While it did so, I contemplated what the Gulf Track might have in store for us.

◆　◆　◆

It took time to find rhythm after a week out of the saddle. As usual after extreme exertion and then having a relatively inactive few days, I suffered from a terrible outbreak of cramp-like muscle spasms. I had initially experienced this affliction after my first day of cycling 200 km plus from Bordeaux to Biarritz fifteen years ago. In Russia, the discomfort forced me to cycle out of Novosibirsk on one leg. The spasms are debilitating as the major working muscles are affected – quadriceps, gluteals, hamstrings and, occasionally, lower back. Stopping to stretch and apply self-massage gives temporary relief, but in general I just keep going. By the end of the first day out of Karumba, I had endured a number of bouts, with the pain moving from one muscle group to another. I knew that the following day these muscles would feel like they had run a marathon and then been trampled by a herd of stampeding cattle.

We appreciated the last 80 km of tarmac we would see for a while; it stretched across the floodplain from Karumba to about 4 km south of Normanton. The headwind was strong enough to warrant us sharing the load by doing ten minutes in front and ten behind, flashing past abundant birdlife, such as brolgas and ibis, gathered around the many waterholes scattered throughout the landscape.

Suddenly Greg screeched to a halt. 'Did you see that?' Our cumbersome, laden bikes took some stopping as we had started to find our cycling legs. His reaction was to glimpsing the tail of a mature estuarine crocodile slip into a murky pool. By the time we stopped for a second look from the safety of a built-up bridge, all we could see were a pair of eyes gliding across the surface. Not a ripple disturbed the water as the hunting machine kept us firmly in its sights. It was a stern reminder that we had re-entered dangerous country.

Arriving back in Normanton, we rejoined the line of our route which we had already travelled and took the opportunity to stock up as Burketown was at least two days away. Four kilometres south of Normanton, we turned off on to the gravel and into isolation. We had to be well prepared as we might only see a couple of cars a day.

Our goal for the first day was the Burke and Wills Camp 119, the most northerly campsite of the explorers' ill-fated 1861–62 expedition. About 40 km from Normanton, we arrived at the site, 3 km off the Burketown Road, near the Little Bynoe River. Burke, Wills, King and Gray had used the camp as a base to push north towards the Gulf. Although they never sighted the coastline itself, they decided they had reached their destination when they came to the impenetrable mangroves and observed the rise and fall of the tidal saline water.

As we looked around at the original ring of trees blazed by Burke which have now been marked with plaques, we could hear a power generator through the bushes. Following the sound, we found Muriel and Francis camping on the track which led down to the river. As with many Gulf travellers, Francis was a keen fisherman and we were treated to fresh queen fish caught in the Limmon Bight River further up the track. Muriel had taken helpful notes about the track and conditions which she passed on to me.

Constantly left choking in the dust clouds of inexperienced 4WD drivers as they raced towards the Tip of Cape York under the time pressure of school

An original blazed tree at the Burke and Wills Camp 119, Little Bynoe River

holidays, it was a pleasure for us to meet people like Muriel and Francis. They were typical of the more seasoned connoisseurs of outback travel we encountered on the Gulf Track. Most of such drivers would slow down or even stop for a chat, frequently offering a top up of water or food, which we never refused. There were other benefits to the scarce traffic; firstly, the road was generally well-maintained and in reasonable condition, and, secondly, the amount of wildlife on view increased. Wedge-tailed eagles ruled the route and we were privileged to be able to sneak up as they feasted on road kill.

The cattle station terrain around the Queensland Gulf, a mix of low scrub and open savannah, was almost completely flat. I couldn't help but admire the navigational abilities of the early explorers, with no points of reference to assist them. Ludwig Leichhardt was the first land-based explorer through the region on his way from Brisbane to Port Essington (north of Darwin) in 1845. Leichhardt Falls on the Leichhardt River, 120 km west of Camp 119, are named in his honour (along with Leichhardt Lagoon, 20 km east of Normanton, where we had stopped earlier). We camped there on our second night out from Karumba. All sorts of wildlife used the permanent pools during the Dry season: flocks of noisy galahs and sulphur-crested cockatoos, and extremely bold black-eyed wallabies. It was difficult to imagine that the 12-metre drop at Leichhardt Falls in a big Wet becomes barely a ripple in the face of a raging mass of water. Trees below the falls were just bare sticks, stripped by the power of the rushing water.

Wedge-tailed eagle

Burketown, the main port in the Gulf, is built on a fractionally higher piece of ground than the surrounding marine plain. The rise away from the Albert River was hardly noticeable as we arrived at our important supply stop. This town was once considered the wildest and most unruly in Australia, where nearly everyone carried a gun. Forgetting it was a Saturday afternoon, we headed for the only place open, the Burketown Pub, originally called the Albert Hotel, which according to the sign was 'Australia's Greatest Outback Hotel'. The interior of the social hub of the town possessed many classic outback characteristics including walls of corrugated iron adorned with posters and an array of local memorabilia. The special meal of the day was pastie and chips for $5 – the most nutritional benefit of which would be to soak up more amber fluid. There were all sorts of signs which obviously appealed to the local sense of humour such as 'Beer, helping ugly people to have sex since 1862'. The bar was, of course, the principal meeting place in the town, propping up a menagerie of living relics,

The quieter roads around the Gulf region brought us much closer to the wildlife

although some were not so old. Entering the premises in cycling gear, we drew some bewildered glances, mainly from those who relied on the counter for balance. Our priority was to negotiate for the only store to be opened. We were fortunate to catch the owners and be able to stock up.

The corrugations had destroyed the welds on my bar-bag frame for the second time. I eventually asked Tom White, a travelling handyman and temporary resident at the pub, to fix the frame for the price of a carton of beer – the local currency. The end result certainly looked more rigid than the Coen job but I did not trust the repairs for the long term given the thousands of kilometres of corrugations that lay ahead.

Station sign beside a cattle grid near Burketown
(photo: G Yeoman)

We pushed on to the recently re-opened Tirranna Roadhouse, where we met more locals, and then Doomadgee, a large Indigenous community (population 1200), on the Nicholson River. We ate our usual picnic lunch in the shade of the huge sports hall, one of many impressive but poorly maintained facilities. Physically, the community was a mix of new buildings and derelict shells of homes covered with graffiti. The large police presence (opposite the sports hall) restricted the quantity of alcohol to be brought back into the community to three cartons of beer per car, and the penalty for exceeding the limit was a $75 000 fine. For the next 85 km, all the way to Hell's Gate Roadhouse, a steady flow of thousands of empty beer cans and cartons lined the route. All beer in excess of the quota was consumed outside the settlement and the evidence hurled out of the car windows. The roadside, not the only time we thought this during the expedition, was a complete disgrace.

Hell's Gate lived up to its reputation rather than its name. We were treated by Allan, the proprietor, to as much food as we could eat during our stay. Our appetites were enormous, especially after almost 150 km on the gravel from Tirranna. The following morning we witnessed vivid red and orange glows on the horizon – constantly changing reflections of the sunrise on the escarpment behind the airstrip which gave a clue to how Hell's Gate came by its name. In earlier days, anyone travelling from east to west was escorted by the police based at Nicholson River (now Doomadgee) as far as this point and then left to their own devices. The 'Northern Territory of South Australia' as it was known in the early days of European settlement was a wild place where laws were impossible to enforce. The government of South Australia (SA) gained control of the newly discovered territory in 1863 with ideas of developing colonies in the same way it had done in the south. However by 1911, South Australia decided the venture was all too difficult and handed administration over to the federal government.

◆　◆　◆

We crossed into the Northern Territory (NT) just before Wollogorang Roadhouse/Station, 57 km from Hell's Gate, feeling as though over the last seven weeks we had covered Queensland comprehensively. The reception we received at Wollogorang also lived up to its reputation. Unfortunately, it could not have been more of a contrast. There was little for us to buy, and when we asked for a tomato, the roadhouse manager wouldn't sell one because 'I buy them by the kilo and wouldn't know how much to charge you'. She then thought she might be able to calculate the value by measuring the circumference!

Crossing the Robinson
River; one of sixteen water
crossings on the Gulf Track
(photo: G Yeoman)

As etiquette dictated, we asked whether it was possible to camp further down the road on the station land. As with everything, the answer was negative and, anyway, 'You shouldn't be cycling...' I took a deep breath and tried not to say anything which would inflame the situation. I knew that the property extended as far as the Calvert Road, and assured the woman that we wouldn't camp on Wollogorang. I don't think she could comprehend that we could make it off her family's land by evening on bicycles. On the other hand, as station owners are responsible for what happens on their property, perhaps she was concerned that if something should happen to us, they would be liable in a court of law. As independent cyclists travelling through such an isolated area, we were unlikely to be irresponsible travellers, leaving gates open, starting fires or getting in the way of a cattle muster.

The route through the remainder of their property took us over rugged terrain, whose only blemish was the leaking of green effluent from the Redbank Copper Mine into the surrounding creeks. Stunning white trunks of river red gums and ghost gums contrasted against the almost purple backdrop of the ranges. We struggled on a further 60 km along the rough and at times steep road and made it to our destination as the sun set and my energy levels petered out.

The quality of the Gulf road in the Northern Territory was significantly poorer. There were also ten water crossings between Wollogorang and Borroloola which slowed us down. Our water crossing drill had been well rehearsed on our Cape York adventure: remove shoes, put on sandals, check the route, drag and lift the bike across – trying to keep the working parts out of the water where possible – clean and dry feet before replacing shoes and socks.

Water lilies, Snake Lagoon
(photo: G Yeoman)

Keeping up the standards at the Borroloola Pub

Students at the Nunngurrie Homeland School, Ryan's Bend Outstation, near Borroloola

The Robinson River Station country – Garawa Aboriginal Land – was still smouldering as we passed through a number of 'cool' burns. Using fire is an important part of Aboriginal land management and typically occurs in the earlier half of the Dry season. There was no one tending the fires which seemed to slowly swallow up the undergrowth. If the wind strengthened, fanning the flames out of control, they would be left to consume everything in their path.

Vegetation changed as we moved north. The low lying, more swampy areas were characterised by pandanus and cycads. We spotted a sign saying 'Camping – 5 kms' pointing towards Greenbank Station just before our intended destination, the Foelsh River. We were already exhausted, but after a quick check of our original intended site, we decided to head for the camping-ground and potentially a shower. The final five kilometres really finished both of us and we were pretty shaky by the time we turned down a sandy track to Snake Lagoon.

The small Aboriginal station was run by Dave and his family. Dave had only erected the camping signs two weeks prior and we were his first cyclists. He had recently mown an area of grass near the lagoon and sectioned it off with a few stones for markers. We were invited to the house to meet the family and shared some damper and hot water for tea, which kept us going until we could cook our own 'pasta Mediterranean'. As we were so limited in what we could buy and carry, our camping meals offered little variety and required a combination of imagination and culinary ingenuity. Our special recipe included spaghetti (as much as we could fit in the pot), sardines, a knob of Philadelphia cream cheese (which seemed to last a long time without refrigeration), olive oil, garlic and a squeeze of lemon.

Serving Dave's new campsite was a corrugated iron ablution block. The facilities wouldn't receive too many stars, but that chilly night they were worth all the stars in the brilliant, clear sky. (By now we were used to sharing the flushing toilet with frogs.) The light of a frosty morning revealed the beauty of our surroundings as mist rose from Snake Lagoon, which was covered by a carpet of water-lilies and teeming with bird life. We bade farewell to Dave, who didn't charge us, and headed for Borroloola, 'place of paperbarks', 80 km away.

Borroloola was supposed to be a quick pit-stop; a few emails, telephone calls, stock up on supplies and head off. But by the time we crossed the McArthur River and into town, we realised we needed the afternoon off. It was during this 'down' time that we met Piet, a primary school teacher on his first year out, who suggested we visit his class later in the day. We agreed, and I subsequently gave a short talk to the students. During our time at the school, Greg and I gained an insight into some of the problems involved in educating

children of mixed abilities, many of whom receive little support from parents who are themselves illiterate. Piet invited us back to his flat to stay the night. As an elite swimmer and triathlete, he was frustrated at being sent, on his first posting, to Borroloola, where there is no pool and few sporting facilities. We ate that evening at the pub with some of his teacher colleagues. One of them, Malcolm, invited us to drop in on his special school the following day.

Ghost gums at Batten Creek

Visiting the Nunngurrie Homeland School at Ryan's Bend was as much an education for us as the children. The twelve students, nine from the Pluto family alone, are collected each morning by Malcolm, who drives them 30 km to the outstation for lessons. I gave another talk to this interested and well-behaved class, who bombarded me with questions. Showing the pupils the map was a real eye-opener. While they would have been experts in local knowledge, a journey to Darwin was difficult for them to comprehend, let alone the fact that we had cycled all the way from Canberra. Later, we watched the children in the playground. They were such a happy group with amazing nurturing instincts, the older ones looking after the younger. We rattled off down the rough, stony track feeling as if we were the ones who had learnt the most.

We camped that night at Batten Creek, 85 km from Borroloola, a wonderful place to pitch the tent, close to mature paperbarks and a feature stand of white-trunked river gums. The Nathan River Road that followed was the roughest part of the Gulf track: hilly in parts, the 97 km between Batten Creek and Butterfly Spring involved six water crossings, but enduring the bumps and sand was really worth it. We followed parallel with one escarpment for about 25 km and then up and over another ridge into a broad, ancient valley whose creeks were lined with flowering grevilleas, hakea and wattles.

Butterfly Spring is a stunning place, especially in the evening light. A small waterfall (small in the Dry season) cascades about 20 metres down the rock face into a large pool. It was a great place to cool off and have a soap-less wash, especially with the whole spring to myself. Our energy needs were extremely high and we felt insatiably hungry at times. In addition to its natural attractions, Butterfly Spring will also be remembered as the place we devoured a whole large jar of peanut butter, the highest calorie food, spoonful by spoonful. Obviously there was no talk during this feat!

◆　◆　◆

Typical Nathan River Road
(photo: G Yeoman)

Freshening up at Tollgate
Spring, near Roper Bar

As we headed north, the humidity steadily increased and with it our fluid requirements. Unable to find enough water by our usual means, the ceramic water filter – designed to remove all bacteria and unwanted nasties from normally undrinkable water and which we carried for such an occasion – came into its own here. However, due to our paranoia about crocodiles, obtaining the water from the river's edge remained a traumatic chore.

Crocodile fears were renewed at the Little Towns River crossing. Trudging through the muddy water while trying to manage the loaded bikes was particularly awkward. Greg was most of the way across and I was just entering the river when we heard something drop into a dark green pool nearby. This sent my heart racing and I immediately entered into fight or flight mode, picking up the load with virtually one hand, my feet barely touching the water as I scrambled to the safety of the opposite bank in a mad panic. In retrospect, it was probably just a harmless freshwater crocodile, but we didn't hang around to find out.

When searching for our final campsite before Roper Bar, we stumbled across Lomarieum Lagoon, covered with water-lilies, tucked in behind the St Vidgeon homestead ruins. We were now definitely into saltwater crocodile territory – we were told that a four-metre reptile had been seen the previous day. Needless to say we camped well away from the water's edge, assuming that any crocodile would first attack the occupants of the lone caravan parked by the bank of the lagoon. Their little dog would have been a tasty entrée.

A single-lane strip of tarmac was a welcome sight 40 km west of Roper Bar. From there it was a straightforward ride along the Roper Highway past Elsey Station – of *We of the Never Never* fame – to Mataranka. Hitting the Stuart Highway just before Mataranka was a rude shock. Suddenly we were hassled by the drivers of huge road trains who seemed impatient about sharing the road with anything smaller or slower than themselves. The absence of a significant hard shoulder meant we were at times squeezed out and dangerously forced on to the loose gravel. Cyclists are a common sight on the main north-south highway as it is a popular challenge for many overseas cyclists to pedal from Darwin to Alice Springs.

Back at the start of the Gulf Track, Muriel had given us the contact details of her nephew, Garry Riggs, who manages Mataranka Station, just north of the town. I had arranged for us to call there. We were certainly ready for a break after nearly 1400 km and eleven rough days without a full day off.

Mataranka Station is a teaching station owned by Charles Darwin University. Garry, Michelle and their four children live on the 170 000-hectare (400 000 acre) station where Garry is a fulltime lecturer. Five years previously the Riggs had bought Lakefield Station when a larger property was sub-divided. Adjoining the Mataranka property, Lakefield Station, of similar size, had to be developed from scratch as it had no infrastructure. Michelle and Garry have relished the challenge, especially as it enables them to put into practice many of the techniques they have trialled and developed at the university station.

Garry has developed an effective fire management strategy which involves cool-burning half of each paddock one year, the other half the following year. Bi-annual burning optimises soil quality (heavily depleted if the country is burned every year) while it reduces the risk of the wild fires which devastate everything in their path – animals, people and infrastructure. The controlled fires encourage new growth and regeneration of the natural vegetation, which is also a better quality of stock feed, and minimise the loss of wildlife. Animals simply move across the fire break to the section not being burnt.

Like a water feature in an enormous garden, Lake Buggan is positioned at the far end of Lakefield Station, 35 km from the new homestead. Michelle drove us to see the lake, a significant wetland, 8 km in circumference and home to nineteen species of waterbird. To protect the lake, the whole area had to be fenced off and the watering points repositioned well away from the water's edge. Without this strategy, cattle would deplete the water quality and contribute to soil erosion as their hooves churned the muddy banks of the lake each time they entered the water to drink.

Greg and I spent our 'rest day' with Michelle and her oldest daughter, twelve-year-old Tahlia, at Lakefield. As Michelle was busy working on the house (still under construction), and tending to the stock, Tahlia enthusiastically showed us around. She was highly aware of the various station projects and her environment, at one stage demonstrating how she thought the undesirable cane toad should be treated. Bare-footed, she lined up a mature unsuspecting toad, took a few measured steps back and charged it like a raging bull, repeatedly kicking it ferociously. I am sure there was a degree of showmanship there, but the message was clear. She picked up the now-disfigured vermin amphibian and proceeded to describe its anatomy, including the location of its poison sack, whose venom is lethal to native wildlife.

Tahlia Riggs with the unlucky cane toad

The cane toad menace, spreading west from the Queensland canefields, where it was first introduced, has been responsible for threatening many endemic Australian species. Some species, such as birds of prey, have learned to adapt to the problem by flipping the toads on to their backs before killing them, thus avoiding the deadly toxin. This most serious scourge of northern Australia is spreading like wildfire. In the last couple of years, the toads have been discovered across the Western Australian border in the east Kimberley region.

We said our goodbyes to the Riggs family early the following morning before setting off for a simple day's ride on the Stuart Highway up to Katherine. I was looking forward to my tour of the Top End where our plan was to link some of the best known attractions, including the Nitmiluk, Kakadu and Litchfield national parks.

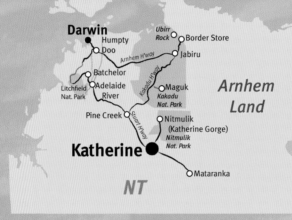

Darwin
Humpty
Doo
Batchelor
Litchfield
Nat. Park
Adelaide
River
Pine Creek
Ubirr
Rock
Border Store
Jabiru
Arnhem H'way
Kakadu H'way
Maguk
Kakadu
Nat. Park
Arnhem
Land
Nitmulik
(Katherine Gorge)
Nitmulik
Nat. Park
Katherine
Mataranka
NT
Stuart H'way

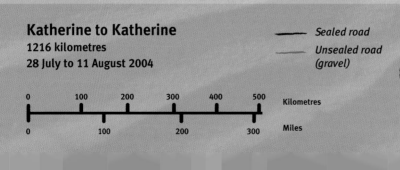

Katherine to Katherine
1216 kilometres
28 July to 11 August 2004

Sealed road

Unsealed road
(gravel)

| 0 | 100 | 200 | 300 | 400 | 500 | Kilometres |

| 0 | | 100 | | 200 | | 300 | Miles |

6

To the Top
(Katherine to Katherine)

> Coming up from the river, the Katherine Settlement appeared to consist solely of the 'Pub', which, by the way, seemed to be hanging on to its own verandah posts for support. We found an elongated, three-room building, nestling under deep verandahs, and half-hidden beneath a grove of lofty scarlet flowering poinsettias.

In her much-loved account of station life in *We of the Never Never*, author Jeannie Gunn recollected thus her first contact with the town of Katherine in 1908.

Throughout its 'European' history, Katherine has often been referred to as the 'Crossroads of the North'. For untold generations before that, the region was an inter-tribal meeting place for the Aboriginal people. Traditional lands of the Jawoyan, Walpiri, Dagaman and Wardiman tribes from the desert and the tropics converged here, and consequently the river and nearby Nitmiluk (Katherine Gorge) were favoured places for gatherings.

The region lies in a meteorological transition zone – not as humid as the far north of the Northern Territory but far wetter than the deserts to the south. The Dry season, as we were experiencing, is tinder dry, but the monsoonal rains do not hold back during the Wet. Between November and March, Katherine averages 960 mm of rain (significantly higher than the annual average rainfall received in Melbourne or Perth) and has a history of flooding. In 1988 rains from Cyclone Les caused the Australia Day Flood when the Katherine River rose

21 metres, devastating the community. Crocodiles washed in with the current patrolled the main street, making the clean up very tricky (and giving a whole new dimension to the term 'streetwise').

John McDouall Stuart named the Katherine River (after the daughter of his sponsor, James Chambers) during an expedition to determine a route for the overland telegraph line, which eventually linked southern Australia to Europe. Since Jeannie Gunn's time the settlement has expanded to become the third largest town in the NT, serving the pastoral industry, the Indigenous community and a steady flow of tourists. After a simple ride through the scrub country from Mataranka, Katherine seemed like a bustling metropolis. We even had traffic lights to deal with – the only ones along the 1500-km Stuart Highway linking Darwin and Alice Springs. As Katherine lies at the junction of two major highways, we also used it as a gateway, stocking up on supplies as we first entered the tropical Top End and then again before heading off towards the Tanami Desert.

What we didn't realise was that Katherine is also Australia's didgeridoo capital, as it lies in the centre of a corridor which grows the prime timber used in making the ancient instruments. Coco's Backpackers, where were stayed, must have been the didgeridoo epicentre of Katherine. Travellers flocked here from all over the world to hone their circular breathing skills, grooving with the resident world champion didgeridoo player – from Belgium. Pulsating drones loud enough to register on the Richter scale meandered through the night, sounding like a herd of flatulent Brahmans. Sleep was an elusive escape.

The name Nitmiluk is the Traditional Jawoyan owners' word for Cicada Dreaming. Set at the time of the Creation of the thirteen sandstone canyons, the Cicada Dreaming is one of the area's most important Dreamtime stories. It is interesting that in isolated ancient cultures around the world, the humble cicada has evoked similar mythology. (The Australian variety, incidentally, are the loudest insects in the world.) The Jawoyan people's Dreamtime story, like ancient Greek and Chinese legends, depicts the cicada as a symbol of resurrection, rebirth and immortality. I wonder whether the thousands of Chinese immigrants who settled in this part of the world to work as mining labourers and later on the Pine Creek-Darwin railway ever drew the ancient connection? We pedalled with the tide of tourist buses and vans out to Nitmiluk on a day trip to get a better idea of the region. The highlight of this 'active recovery' day was paddling a canoe up the first couple of towering gorges, giving the upper body a workout it was not used to.

Doing 150 km in a day on good roads no longer seemed so difficult. We simply broke the day up into manageable sections punctuated by plenty of high calorie snacks. Heading north to Pine Creek and then east on the Kakadu Highway, we rode separately for most of the day...sometimes we both needed some space, and there was no shortage of that. Spending such long hours in the saddle and in view of the rising humidity, we were mindful of our increasing fluid requirements. We each consumed about eight 750-ml bottles of water on the road and more at water stops. With temperatures in the mid-30s and the radiant heat from the road much greater, an added problem was that the drinking water warmed up and was not very thirst quenching.

◆ ◆ ◆

Kakadu National Park was one on Australia's first jewels to be inscribed as a UNESCO World Heritage site in 1981, for both its outstanding natural and cultural universal values. The Kakadu and Arnhem highways, the busy bitumen artery roads of Kakadu, make access simple for tourist buses and vehicles, even in the Wet, when some of the region receives an average of 1600 mm of rain. The Kakadu Highway provides a window to explore the stone country of the southern hills. The area is in a transition zone, still relatively dry, like the Nitmiluk region. Its hills provide the catchment area for the South Alligator River, the main waterway running through the heart of Kakadu. The Arnhem Highway crosses vistas of the internationally important wetlands – the floodplains stretching north to the mangrove-lined coast.

It requires a major effort to tour Kakadu by bicycle. To actually see anything much at all we needed to venture down the unsealed side tracks, which were often sandy and corrugated, requiring the expenditure of a lot of extra time and energy. We couldn't afford the time to visit all the renowned gorges and waterfalls which are some distance off the Kakadu Highway. To see Jim Jim Falls (of *Crocodile Dundee* fame), for example, would have required a whole day to get there and back, and as with all the major waterfalls in Kakadu, it was not running in the Dry.

Our compromise was to visit Maguk, also known as Barramundi Falls – a simple, but rough, 24-km round trip. We weren't disappointed. To view the gorge we locked up the bikes and walked for about a kilometre through the monsoonal forest along the sandy Barramundi Creek. The lower pools were a stunning natural tropical aquarium, their emerald green water, impossibly clear, harbouring schools of colourful fish. The track continued over rocks, culminating in a short scramble to the top of the cliff. Here the views were awe inspiring, especially looking down on the main plunge pool at least 50 metres below. At the top of the falls were a series of deep circular rock pools, where we took a dip. During the Wet, these mini-plunge pools would be extinguished as torrents of water crashed over them with unimaginable power before being channelled between the rock wall and boulders and then cascading over the sheer drop. Although it is technically possible to find estuarine crocodiles in these gorges, rangers have a comprehensive trapping program which makes visits safe (we hoped). From the sandstone overhang we spotted the large resident freshwater crocodile swimming in the bottle-green waters below. On the way back to our bush campsite, we filled our extra water-bags from Barramundi Creek, whose water was pure enough to drink without filtering.

Red Kurrajong flower, near Maguk

On leaving Maguk, Greg's rear pannier rack, which was supposed to be of the highest quality, snapped at the join where it attached to the bicycle frame and the loose parts began to rub against the tyre. This was a nasty surprise but at least it had happened a few days from Darwin, where we were on sealed roads and not in the middle of the desert. Greg cleverly manufactured a temporary repair by moulding a couple of spare spokes to attach the rack to the frame. The load was rearranged to reduce the pressure on the broken rack.

Not far from Jabiru, we met a couple of cyclists, Maggie and Jan from Dresden, Germany, who had taken fourteen months to travel 22 000 km on their tandem across Russia (where we had been eleven years before) and down through China. They were excited about finishing their personal odyssey in Darwin. We compared the experiences of our adventures. Russia had been the highlight of their journey due to the overwhelming friendliness of the people, especially the Siberians. They had elected to take the train across the Siberian Swamp as their set-up, a tandem with a two-wheeled trailer, was not as versatile as ours, making rough tracks and water crossings a problem. With two pairs of legs to drive the rear wheel, however, tandems are more efficient on tarmac.

In Australia, the couple had struggled with the isolation and huge distances

Crocodile tail, East
Alligator River, Kakadu

up the west coast from Perth. The Gibb River Road in the Kimberley, which is about on par with the Gulf Track for ruggedness, had been one of the most testing parts of their whole journey. It also made me realise just how long and intense the GRACE Expedition was. I was still on track to do 25 000 km in nine-and-a-half months of which over 7000 km was on rough gravel roads.

We rode with Maggie and Jan for a while, pausing at the main waterways to spot crocodiles. Despite us being armed with telephoto lenses and safely on a built-up bridge, the sight of a primeval beast was enough to send shudders up my spine. Each billabong was usually ruled by the dominant king of the food chain. The first salty I spotted was sunning itself on a river bank with its mouth open as if it was permanently yawning. This is the way these relics of prehistory cool down their peanut-sized brains.

From Jabiru we took an extra day to cycle out to the East Alligator River, which forms the border between Kakadu and Arnhem Land, in order to explore the cultural landscape. Ubirr Rock, the first port of call, is perhaps the centrepiece of the regional art sites concentrated along the Arnhem Land escarpment. The X-ray-style paintings at the principal gallery depict mainly the animals and activities most important to Aboriginal culture – food, hunting and Dreaming figures. One of the focal reasons for the World Heritage listing, these detailed paintings illustrate an 'outstanding record' of human interaction with the environment over at least 25 000 years. It is believed that Aborigines may have inhabited this land for between 40 000 and 60 000 years.

View from the Nadab
Lookout, Ubirr Rock, across
the wetlands where buffalo
once roamed in their
thousands

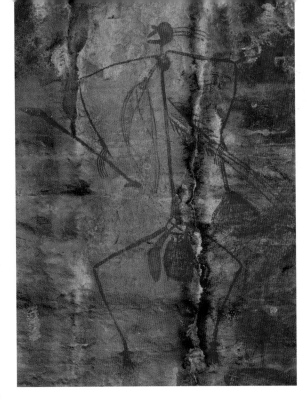

While crocs keep their mouths open as a form of prehistoric cerebral temperature control, our open mouths were a reaction to needing to cool down our highly evolved brains after the sensory overload! The Nadab Lookout on top of the rock presented unrivalled, jaw-dropping views for 360 degrees, encapsulating what Kakadu is all about. To the north and west were stunning scenes across the wetlands, home to a diverse variety of birdlife. Over 400 000 buffalo, introduced from Java, used to roam the wetlands before they were strenuously culled in the 1950s to protect the natural environment. To the east and south lay the rugged escarpment of Arnhem Land, and woodlands harbouring records of thousands of years of mankind's habitation and spiritual and cultural interaction with the natural landscape.

Referring to his Kakadu homeland, Brian Baruwei of the Wurrkbarbar Clan (one of a number of groups from the Kakadu region) said after he was elected chairman of Kakadu Board of Management in 1992, 'If you respect the land, then you will feel the land. Your experience will then be one that you cannot get anywhere else in the world.' I aspired to be infused with this attitude so I could take it far beyond the boundaries of Kakadu National Park, throughout the GRACE Expedition and further on.

This painting of Mabuyu at Ubirr Rock reminds Traditional owners to tell a story which warns against stealing

Back-tracking was something I always loathed as it felt like a waste of time. Venturing over the same 45 km in the late afternoon on the way back from experiencing Ubirr and cruising down the East Alligator River on the Arnhem Land border, however, was a pleasure. We saw the land in a new light, and couldn't help stopping to photograph everything from the stunning rock formations to minute details, including dragonflies with raffia-like wings, yellow kapok flowers, orchids and grevillea.

Opposite the remnant sandstone outlier we had paused to explore was a swampy woodland bristling with signs set back from the built-up bitumen strip. From among the melaleucas they warned trespassers to 'Keep out' and that this was 'Private land'. Passing through part of the Jabiluka mining lease, admiring the craggy Jabiluka Hill and Jabiluka Outlier, we had unknowingly paused at some of the most hotly disputed land in the country. At the foot of the Arnhem Plateau lies an area of high mineral concentration, specifically uranium and gold. The Jabiluka uranium deposit is located along the floodplain of the Magella Creek, a tributary of the East Alligator River. Together with the adjacent Ranger uranium mining lease to the south, the Jabiluka lease forms an economic island worth billions of dollars set in the midst of one of Australia's priceless natural regions. Australia contains some 40 per cent of the world's known uranium stores and the Ranger Mine is the world's third largest. It was built in the same year that Kakadu was declared a national park; Jabiluka was pegged in the early 1970s. Out of all this has evolved a situation as complex as Kakadu's ecological web. The duel between conservationists and the Traditional owners in one corner and the uranium mining industry in the other has been characterised by passionate bouts of non-violent protests.

Dragonfly

Kapok flower and fruit: minute details of the Jabiluka bush
(photo: G Yeoman)

Massive open-cut mining operations may put an ugly scar in the landscape but it is the pollution that we can't see infiltrating the water cycle that is more of

Passing the Jabiluka
Outlier
(photo: G Yeoman)

a concern here, affecting all those who live in the region. Four months before we stayed in Jabiru, the town built to service the uranium mining community, the East Jabiru water supply and Magella Creek were significantly contaminated after an incorrect connection of water pipes. There have been at least 120 recorded 'minor' accidents since 1981. In a region of high rainfall, radioactive tailings dams are at risk of flooding. The problem of what to do with spent nuclear fuel which takes thousands of years to 'cool' is the biggest argument against using uranium to supply electricity. Australia's principal uranium customers include the USA, Japan and the European Union. Uranium is sold strictly for electrical power generation only, and the Australian government issues assurances that safeguards are in place to guarantee this. Australia is a party to the Nuclear Non-Proliferation Treaty as a non-nuclear weapons state.

The Mirrar people are the legal title holders to the area surrounding and including the Ranger and Jabiluka mineral leases, and they steadfastly oppose the proposal to develop the Jabiluka Uranium Mine. The Mirrar argue that mining and its associated social, economic and political impacts are the single greatest threat to their living tradition, and that an additional mine will push their culture past the point of cultural exhaustion to 'genocidal decay'. Mining royalties, which have totalled over $200 million since 1980, have been divided up by the government and distributed among the Aboriginal groups of the Northern Territory. Money, however, does not offset the importance of the land for the Mirrar and their long-term physical and spiritual health. Mining of the Jabiluka lease will not proceed without agreement from the Mirrar people and after passionate protests in 1998, the exploratory excavations were backfilled. Ranger is due to scale down production in 2008.

We returned to our Jabiru campsite to find that Maggie and Jan had thoughtfully placed a pile of supplies for us under the flysheet. Even after 22 000 km, excited to be shortly finishing their journey in Darwin, they had been motivated to do this for us. Their kindness allowed us to make an early start the next day. Mutual respect.

Travelling along the Arnhem Highway, we could have entered a different country. Greg was probably thinking of Vietnam again. An elegant pair of jabirus, Australia's only stork, tiptoed through the reeds as if walking on a tightrope. Startled by our presence, they struggled to take to the air, labouring like B52 bombers. We were crossing the vast floodplain of the South Alligator River, about 50 km south of where it empties into Van Diemen Gulf. The wetlands provide an abundant diet for the sixty or so species of wading birds; not only jabirus but magpie geese, different types of heron, and pelicans. The Traditional owners call the lush wetlands the 'supermarkets of Kakadu' as they use them for their bounty of goodies. Despite being protected within

Pig hunters weighing one of the night's catch

the national park, these freshwater wetlands are under threat as sea levels rise, washing salt over the land. Global warming accelerates the rise in sea level, meaning that the natural levees that act as a barrier between Kakadu's freshwater and saltwater systems – in places only 20 cm high – will be breached, leading to a significant loss of these lily-carpeted waterways that sustain the Aboriginal owners and wildlife and attract more than 165 000 annual visitors.

On leaving the Northern Territory's most famous park, I considered a theoretical future dilemma. Despite being internationally recognised and protected for all its values, the uranium mining issue versus global warming remains a double-edged sword. Hypothetically, if some of the world's richest uranium reserves were exploited to the full, the need for burning fossil fuels for energy would be reduced and therefore ease the effects of global warming. Kakadu and its inhabitants could potentially either suffer the consequences of uranium mining and its string of calamities, or face its freshwater landscape being flooded with salt water from global warming.

Loading the last sow

Just out of Bark Hut Inn, near Mary River, we met a couple of pig hunters on their morning collection rounds. Initially, they seemed guarded about their profession, probably thinking that we would be shocked at the blood and guts, but when we explained the purpose of the expedition, they opened up and allowed me to photograph their night's work. Eradicating feral pigs in the north of Australia is an important sustainability issue as they are a dangerous pest, causing environmental damage to the bush. The meat is exported to Germany, usually for about one dollar per kilogram, where it is made into sausages. Each pig weighs about 60 kg and the hunters usually trap five or six a night using their highly trained team of pig dogs. Led by a cocky Jack Russell which sniffs out the ferals' scent, the pig dogs work to round up and bring each wild animal down. They are fitted with a Kevlar yoke around their necks to protect their vital organs from being slit open by the razor-sharp incisors of their quarry.

Top tee-shirt

The men told us that, although they make a reasonable living, their business would be far more profitable if they were allowed to venture inside the Kakadu boundary. The park boundary fence has the effect of keeping vermin in and the system for catching pigs in Kakadu is not effective, according to the hunters. They farewelled us after they winched the last sow, still alive, onto to the back of the ute. They were off to Humpty Doo (40 km from Darwin) to give a live demonstration at a pig hunting workshop of how to prepare the animal for export.

◆　◆　◆

Back in 1898, Banjo Paterson said that Darwin broke everybody who ever touched the town. He cited the unbearable heat, no water during the Dry, and flooding rains in the Wet. Crops failed and termites devoured any wooden structure. It was extraordinary that anybody chose to live there. In its 135-year existence, the resilient frontier settlement has been blown away by three cyclones and was bombed by the Japanese during World War II. Between February 1942 and October 1943, the Japanese launched more than sixty air raids on Darwin; 300 bombs were dropped and 243 people killed during the first attack. It was not until the Americans sent reinforcements in April 1942 that the Japanese started to endure heavy losses.

We were interested to see the place for ourselves. From about Humpty Doo, as we got closer to the city, the bush gave away to market gardens, plantations of blossoming mango trees, and general signs of civilisation. The final push along the Stuart Highway was a tantalisingly cruel slog: a hot gusting headwind, rolling hills, heavy traffic invading 'our' space and polluting 'our' air. An uninspiring chain of light industrial developments flanked the roadside. We'd been going hard since Karumba with only one complete day out of the saddle and in dire need of a break in this northern city. We had done 8000 km since leaving Canberra.

When I was growing up, the two things I associated with Darwin were Cyclone Tracy and the Darwin Stubby. I was very young when Tracy, Australia's worst natural disaster, struck Darwin residents as they slept early on Christmas morning, 1974. The cyclone had been tracked a few days prior to Christmas as it gained intensity over the Arafura Sea. By Christmas Eve, it had passed the western tip of Bathurst Island to the north-west of Darwin, and was assessed as posing no threat. Then, as cunning and sinister as the crocs which haunt the local waterways, the storm turned and accelerated, honing in on the town in the dead of night. Between midnight and 7am on Christmas Day, the cyclone passed directly over Darwin, battering the unsuspecting inhabitants and their property. Its wind speed was recorded at 217 km per hour before the gauge broke; unofficial estimates place it as high as 300 km per hour. The town was flattened (around 90 per cent of homes, mostly prefabricated fibro buildings, were destroyed) and seventy-one people were killed. The first television scenes showed heart-rending symbols of the Christmas festivities, presents and decorations, strewn among the wreckage.

Darwin's heat, isolation and hardships have created an ideal climate for high alcohol consumption. It was said at the time that, just before Cyclone Tracy, Darwin held the world record for beer drinking. Even *The Guinness Book of Records* made special mention of Darwin's super-human level of in-take. The people of Darwin used to imbibe a whopping 194.6 litres of beer per person annually, and that included women and children. Drinking became such an integral part of their culture that Darwinians created their very own two-litre beer bottle – the Darwin Stubby. A stubby, usually 375 ml, is meant to be a handy drinking size, so downing two litres would have saved a few trips to the esky/fridge!

In the thirty years since Cyclone Tracy, the town has changed beyond recognition. The pre-Tracy rows of drab transportable asbestos residences which housed a population of about 48 000 – made up of Australians of Chinese, European and Aboriginal extraction – have been replaced by suburbs of more sturdy bricks and mortar. The blend of today's population of 110 000 has diversified a great deal over the intervening decades. This is reflected in the cosmopolitan array of restaurants that now grace the city centre: they include

Thai, Japanese, Mexican, Turkish, Indian, Swiss, Chinese, Italian, Greek and, of course, Australian.

Business opportunities are only limited by imagination and retain a frontier flavour. We were fortunate to stay with Steve McNamee, a friend of Alasdair Cooke's. Steve once worked as a New York stockbroker and it appeared as though these skills, along with intrinsic local knowledge, were coming in handy as he kept an eye out for good investments and new ventures. I barely left Steve's office, which became home for three days. There was a complex web of administration and personal tasks to work through, and preparations to make. I made phone calls, wrote countless emails, tried to sort out my website and who was taking care of it, and organised the next stages into the deserts: supplies, equipment, contacting places we planned to visit, personnel, drumming up more sponsorship. I updated existing sponsors on our progress, burnt CDs of our digital pictures, posted things we didn't need to carry into the desert, and so on.

Greg servicing the bikes in Darwin

Greg was able to have his rack re-welded and had new brackets made to attach it to the bike. With typical outback ingenuity, the brackets were built to last – the bike-frame would snap before these new additions broke. Greg also serviced the bikes and replaced all the working parts, generously supplied by SRAM, one of the sponsors, in readiness for the rough(er) stuff. We almost forgot to see any of Darwin.

Off again, we retraced our path back down the Stuart Highway, the bikes gliding effortlessly over the bitumen as we passed the Arnhem Highway junction, turning west towards Berry Springs. Our destination was the Litchfield National Park which was recommended by just about everyone who had been there. It wasn't long before we had left civilisation and the perfumed scent of the mango flowers behind. The transition was complete as we turned on to the gravel towards Finniss River and Wangi Falls. The moment we hit the deep corrugations – perhaps a little hard – my brand-new handlebar bag flew off, the front panniers flapped loose and the extra water-bottle cage which Greg had fitted to the cross-bar broke. The honeymoon was over. I secured the water-bottle and cage with a spare toe-strap and more zip ties, and tied the bags more securely with luggage straps, which seemed to do the trick.

About 30 km along the rough road, we stopped for a breather at what was, until six years ago, the Finniss River Store. There didn't seem to be anyone around and so we knocked on the door as we thought this was a good opportunity to replenish our water supplies. We found out quite a lot about the area as we chatted to Jim, who lived there with his family. Just near here, a boy had been taken by a croc in the previous Wet season, making national news. The croc had killed the boy, carried his body back to its lair to rot and then bailed his terrified companion up a tree for a day and a half before he was rescued. We filled up from the rainwater tank and headed for Wangi Falls.

Litchfield's attractions are far more accessible than Kakadu's. A new section of bitumen made the going easier as we scaled a steep jump-up at the crumbling fringe of the dominant Tabletop Range. Litchfield is understandably a popular tourist destination. Also unlike Kakadu, the spring-fed waterfalls cascade over the sandstone plateau all year round. We arrived at Wangi Falls early the following morning, just as the fruit bats, which hang upside down from the

The work of piping termites
(photo: G Yeoman)

upper branches in the monsoonal rainforest surrounding the twin waterfalls, were noisily settling in for their daily slumber. The plunge pool is enclosed by a cliff and rainforest which made the atmosphere so humid that it could be sliced with a knife. Even the video camera seized up – a protection mechanism preventing moisture entering the machine.

Further along at Tolmer Falls, we could only look down from a purpose-built platform as the attraction was closed off to protect two species of rare bats. The water was as clear and green as a glass bottle and the hierarchy of palms, cycads, pandanus, vines and ferns reflected the mid-morning rays so well the leaves could have been polished like house plants. At the melaleuca-lined Tabletop Swamp, which lies in a depression on the plateau, we stood quietly to watch little flashes of colour dart about: tiny blue-winged dragonflies, rainbow lorikeets, sulphur-crested cockatoos and plenty more.

Perhaps the most outstanding phenomena were the collection of magnetic termite mounds which stand like headstones aligned above a grey soil plain. Following architectural information passed on genetically, termites build the mounds on a north/south compass bearing to minimise exposure of the outer walls to the sun's rays, therefore keeping their skyscraper homes cool. As the sun passes from east to west, only the thinnest edge of the mounds are exposed to direct light. During the day the termites migrate to the coolest section of their abodes.

We had now seen all four main types of termite mound throughout the north. Termite colonies which build cathedral mounds can exist for about a hundred years as long as the single queen termite survives. Once she is gone, her whole empire is finished and the mound, sometimes up to five metres tall, will return to the earth. Conical mounds appear mostly on floodplains. Piping termites eat out trees, houses, fences and destroy anything wooden.

Pockets of the Litchfield bushland could also be considered as park features. All the way to the park boundary near Batchelor, the bush had been managed with regular cool burns to control the ground fuel and help with the germination of many native species. Groves of zamia palms with charred trunks sprouted new growth, appearing like lime-green feather dusters.

◆　◆　◆

Zamia palms rejuvenated after a 'cool' burn

From Adelaide River, we decided, on the recommendation of a pair of motor cyclists we had met, to take the scenic route to Hayes Creek. It added an extra 20 km to our day but we thought an opportunity to avoid the busy highway should not be missed. With little traffic, the road had the feel of a country lane – we could have been in the south of France – as it wound its way along a creek valley and over rolling hills with lines of escarpments and rocky outcrops. To entertain our minds, Greg introduced a game whereby we had to go through the alphabet, in turn naming bands and singers starting with a particular letter. Greg would start with A – Abba, me B – Beatles, Greg C – Coldplay and so on. The first round was fairly straightforward, but by the time we entered the third round, some of the names were extremely obscure – I am sure Greg was making up some of those heavy metal bands! We managed to string the game out for a good portion of the time.

The game also helped to lighten the atmosphere between us. The tension building was centred on the trailer Greg had ordered from Germany. He had decided he wanted a trailer to help carry the extra supplies and water we needed to take into the remote desert regions ahead. I felt we didn't need one, believing that we could manage with what we had, and that an extra piece of unfamiliar equipment was just another item that could break down. I was also concerned with how it would travel in the sand. The expedition budget was extremely tight and I didn't want to pay for a trailer out of GRACE funds. The model Greg had chosen, a single-wheeled 'Monoporter', was not available in Australia and had

Making fire the Traditional way

to be brought in from Germany. He was supposed to collect it in Darwin, but due to a customs technicality it was still sitting with FedEx in Sydney. After a long-winded negotiation, Greg arranged for it to be delivered to Katherine. When he phoned from Hayes Creek to check that it had arrived, he found out that it had been delivered to Darwin. An hour of heated phone calls later, he eventually arranged to have it sent to Katherine by local courier.

By the time we left Hayes Creek, Greg was in such a state that he promptly bought two chocolate bars and an ice-cream as comfort food. We kept a fairly lively pace all the way to Emerald Springs, and although it had slowed by the time we checked in at the Lazy Lizard campsite at Pine Creek, he was still a man of few words.

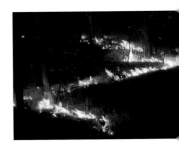

Fire front of a 'cool' burn near Pine Creek

Back-tracking to Katherine was a thankless task into a hot, niggling headwind. It was useful to have a familiar base at Coco's Backpackers. There I collected a satellite phone, an essential safety item in the desert, organised by Alasdair Cooke. Katherine was the last major supply point for some time, although we knew for sure that we could find basic supplies at Victoria River Downs Station, Lajamanu, Rabbit Flat and probably Suplejack Downs Station. After yet more drama, the trailer was finally delivered and Greg chilled – even with the constant drone of European didgeridoo enthusiasts. Now he just had to assemble the trailer. Somehow it all came together in time to set off toward the Tanami Desert without losing a day.

Approaching the fire front on the Stuart Highway in the late afternoon
(photo: G Yeoman)

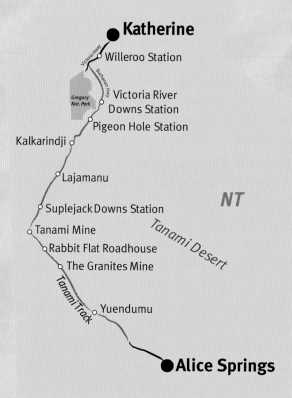

Katherine

Willeroo Station

Victoria River
Downs Station

Pigeon Hole Station

Gregory Nat. Park

Kalkarindji

Lajamanu

Suplejack Downs Station

Tanami Mine

Rabbit Flat Roadhouse

The Granites Mine

Yuendumu

Tanami Track

Tanami Desert

NT

Alice Springs

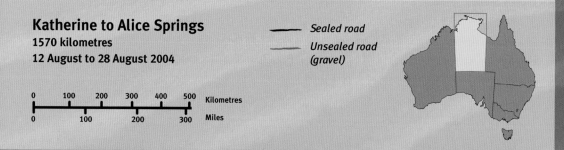

Katherine to Alice Springs
1570 kilometres
12 August to 28 August 2004

—— Sealed road
—— Unsealed road
(gravel)

| 0 | 100 | 200 | 300 | 400 | 500 | Kilometres |

| 0 | | 100 | | 200 | | 300 | Miles |

7

Into the Tanami
(Katherine to Alice Springs)

Trying to appreciate the rugged beauty of Jasper Gorge while enduring a bone-rattling ride to Victoria River Downs Station
(photo: G Yeoman)

Trailer in tow, we departed Katherine for the second time, loaded to the hilt with provisions. We knew most items would be difficult to find in the remote regions down the track. The single wheel 'Monoporter' trailer fitted into the rear axle of Greg's bike and rolled along efficiently, tracking the bicycle line perfectly. It took a while for Greg to get used to manoeuvring the extended length of his vehicle, a human-powered road train. It certainly had a much bigger turning circle than the bike alone. Progress on the tarmac was virtually unhindered, but I was worried how the combination would fare for resistance and balance when we hit the sand and corrugations on the desert roads. The only downside initially was a monotonous squeak emanating from somewhere within the axle joint, which may have confused the local bird life as it rhythmically pierced the warm, Dry season atmosphere. There was little to divert my attention from the annoying, high-pitched, screeching sound, as the first 100 km west of Katherine was through the nondescript savannah woodland which lined the Victoria Highway, void of extensive views.

This suddenly changed as we reached the edge of a plateau. Descending a jump-up, we were confronted by a vast ocean of sclerophyllous green, studded by the distant remnant buttes of the Victoria River catchment. Most of the land towards the horizon was part of Willeroo Station, owned by the Sultan of Brunei, and our destination for the first day out of Katherine. I had telephoned in advance from Coco's to set up our stay. Jim, the manager, was expecting us and we joined him and the jackeroos for a beer and chat after their long day of mustering. Both parties could certainly justify hard-earned thirsts. As some of the musterers were camping out overnight, we were fortunate in being able to stay in their quarters and were generously given free rein of the kitchen.

The station extended as far as the boundary with the Gregory National Park towards which we squeaked our way the following morning. The park was named in honour of another of Australia's greatest explorers, Augustus Gregory, one of whose many feats was to lead the first European land-based expedition to explore the Victoria River region in 1855–56. The Victoria River with its eight tributaries is the largest river system in the Northern Territory and one of Australia's mightiest. During the Wet, it can rise 17 metres above its normal level in places.

Gregory and his team made many new discoveries in the world of botany, including the boab tree (*Adansonia gregorii*) which was named after him. The Australian boab, with its huge swollen trunk, is closely related to the African baobab (*Adansonia digitata*). It has been suggested that seeds from the tree were washed into the sea off the coast of Madagascar and carried across the Indian Ocean to the Kimberley coast of north-west Australia; birds then continued the boab's eastwards expansion, carrying seeds across northern Australia. Despite similarities, the boab is not related to the ooline or bottle trees we saw in Queensland.

Interestingly, Aboriginal and African legends about the boab tree have a remarkable similarity. In essence they say: when God created the boab, it was to be the most beautiful tree in the universe, bearing the juiciest fruits. But when the tree grew and produced fruit which had a bad odour and tasted vile, God became so angry that this tree would not conform to His wishes that he pulled it out of the ground and slammed it upside-down into the earth. This is why the boab looks as though its roots are above the ground, struggling for survival.

The Victoria Highway carved its way through spectacular layered sandstone formations. Spinifex, lime green and sprouting after an unseasonal 100-mm boost of rain, clung on to all those parts of the scree slopes which weren't bare rocks. Flowering yellow kapok trees contrasted against wine-coloured, iron-based cliffs.

Greg with his new trailer at the Victoria River crossing

OUT THERE AND BACK

We paused to appreciate glimpses of the spectacular Victoria River Gorge just before the roadhouse. At the end of the day we were to turn off the highway and onto the gravel. We had attempted to obtain information about water supplies on the route ahead, as the Victoria River Inn was the last obvious reliable information and water stop, but it was unclear what would be available. Greg had even contacted the ranger from the Gregory National Park, but did not receive any guarantee of drinking water. We loaded up at the inn, labouring out of the valley weighed down with an extra 12 litres of water each to last the next day and a half.

Most cyclists would barely acknowledge the junction with the Buchanan Highway, a well-graded gravel road heading south, but for us it was significant, a geographical landmark for the expedition. Travellers tend to stick to the tarmac and head towards Kununurra if they are circumnavigating the country. The turn-off marked the start of a 5500-km triangular loop through isolated desert tracks, traversing the Tanami Desert, to the Red Centre, then along the Great Central Road and the Gunbarrel Highway. If all went according to plan, I then proposed to cycle with the aid of a support vehicle up the Canning Stock Route. The schedule was tight because I had to return to Halls Creek in the eastern Kimberley before the onset of the Wet season – usually in late October – and it was already mid-August. We bumped off from our high point near Kuwang Lookout, descending the stony road for a few kilometres before finding an old gravel pit secluded from the track, where we pitched the tent.

The Buchanan Highway is named after perhaps Australia's most famous stockman, Nat Buchanan, and is a clue to our next destination, 110 km to the south. Through his explorations which opened up huge tracts of land in the Northern Territory and the Kimberley, Buchanan helped settle more new country than any other person in Australia's history. His most famous exploit was to lead a team of seventy drovers to move 20 000 head of cattle from Central Queensland to Glencoe and Daly River stations south of Darwin in 1880, a feat still unequalled by any other drover in the world. In 1883, he pioneered new tracks from Queensland to the Kimberley, where he took up Wave Hill Station in partnership with his brother. He also helped his son pioneer Flora Valley and Gordon Downs stations near Halls Creek in 1887. His mates often called him 'Old Bluey' because of his red hair and fair Irish complexion, which he shaded with a battered green umbrella.

Our destination was Victoria River Downs (VRD) Station, perhaps Australia's most famous cattle station – so well known that Greg recalled learning about it at school in England. VRD is the centrepiece of Heytesbury Beef, owned by the Holmes à Court family. I had contacted Catherine, a friend from my university hockey tour of Great Britain, and she kindly arranged for us to stay there. Acquired in 1989 by her father, the late Robert Holmes à Court, VRD is part of the company's 33 000 square kilometre (eight million acre) territory, which encompasses eight stations including Nat Buchanan's Flora Valley. Wave Hill is a neighbouring property.

Despite not being a well-documented tourist route, the Buchanan Highway through Jasper Gorge and the heart of the Victoria River catchment would rate in my top ten riding days for consistently awe-inspiring scenery. The broad valley gradually narrowed over about 40 km, until the road drew in to hug the path of Jasper Creek, sandwiched between two jagged cliffs. Reflecting the rugged surrounds, the state of the road surface inflicted lasting physical impressions on particular body parts and equipment. At Jasper Gorge, the palm-fringed permanent waterhole was a subtropical oasis which provided welcome respite

Passing by remnant buttes
south of Jasper Gorge on
the Buchanan Highway

from the heat of the day. South of the gorge, loose stones played havoc with our wheels as we climbed out of the valley. Pushing past Kidman Springs towards the end of the day, we were entering productive station land. The alluvial black-soiled plains formed originally by Cambrian basalt can support up to ten cows per square kilometre – a pastoralists' idea of heaven.

◆   ◆   ◆

Arriving at the well-maintained VRD settlement seemed like heaven after a long week pedalling almost 900 km since Darwin. With a population of around seventy, the station headquarters is virtually a small town, complete with its own post office, shop and weather station. Even the lawns are a manicured green. We cycled past the airstrip and the busy Helimuster Company headquarters, where pilots were arriving back in the last light after a long day of cattle mustering. Looking for Maureen and Jim Coulthard, who had kindly offered to have us to stay, took us past houses which were set just back from the banks of the Wickham River. As general manager, Jim is the big boss of the 'Big Run', the name most commonly given to VRD in the Top End, and Maureen is in charge of employee recruitment. We had managed to get our wires crossed when making arrangements; I had mentioned the right day but the wrong date, and subsequently they were away when we arrived. Eventually we found Karen Brosnan, who took care of us and gave us the use of their visitors' quarters. Her husband, John, is the Centre Camp manager. It was great to be able to relax with them over a bottle of Vasse Felix at dinner, a valued company perk. (Vasse Felix winery is another Heytesbury company.)

As usual after a long stint, we wandered around in a daze for much of the following morning. After Karen had taken the meteorological readings – which she does five times per day – she drove us out past the airstrip and the old hospital, to the Centre Camp stock-yards. There John was working with a team of seven jackeroos and jillaroos, drafting and loading the Brahman cattle. The scale of it all was astounding. Six three-trailer road trains lined up in a row, each vehicle approximately 50 metres long; the queue that extended over 300 metres contained 372 wheels (sixty-two wheels per vehicle). Eighty per cent of the stock were being sent out to the rich flood plains to be fattened and 20 per cent of the heaviest (350 kg) beasts were being sold off to Indonesia. VRD/Heytesbury Beef have led the way in developing their own South-east Asian markets.

Jim and Maureen returned later in the afternoon with their friends Elspeth and Roy. They invited us for afternoon tea, and later, dinner which rounded off the most civilised day we were likely to experience for some time. Maureen had been following our journey by regularly checking the website.

We were able to find out important details about our proposed route of cutting across from Lajamanu to the Tanami Track – a track, known locally as the Suplejack Road, about which we had previously been unable to discover any information. It was vital to know where we could find food and water supplies, and to be able to calculate accurately what we needed and what we could carry. Key in finding out about the Suplejack Road was to talk to Letty and Bill Cook at Suplejack Downs Station, the only habitation on the 240-km stretch. When I rang her, Letty sounded most enthusiastic about our proposed visit and told us that their cattle road trains were able to negotiate the road, even with the sand. This was enough assurance for us to commit to travelling the route.

I next called Bruce Ferrands of the famous Rabbit Flat Roadhouse for any further information he could give us. I had been warned by several people who had driven to Australia's most isolated roadhouse that I might not get a friendly reception. Bruce and his wife, Jacqui, only open for business four days per week, from Friday through to Monday. Anyone showing up on Tuesdays, Wednesdays or Thursdays will not be served under any circumstances, no matter who they are or what they require. With this in mind, I dialled the number. But I needn't have worried: when I explained what we were doing, Bruce proved helpful and enthusiastic and, in the end, I had a job putting down the phone. Before I did, he told me how to get in contact Newmont Mines. These two major installations – the Tanami Mine and The Granites – are about 100 km apart, straddling Rabbit Flat and positioned conveniently to fit in with our daily schedule. I called the Tanami installation and they didn't hesitate to accommodate us.

Satisfied that the following week was under control, we now had to pay attention to the following day. Jim gave us permission to travel along their private tracks to Pigeon Hole Station, explaining the route with detailed maps and loaning us a two-way radio as an extra precaution. It was only just over 70 km through but we were assured that the going would be slow. Maureen took me over to the shop to stock up for the next couple of days and then generously wouldn't let me pay.

Thinking that the route to Pigeon Hole, even if a bit rough, would be only a half-day ride, we were in no hurry to leave the comfort of the VRD Centre Camp. As the day started to heat up we at last farewelled our friends and headed off back past the airstrip, through a pair of rusty gates and across the shallow pools in the sandy Wickham River bed. The deep sand on the track was testing for a few kilometres, but then the land opened out into vast plains with more ancient escarpments. A sense of freedom enveloped me as we crossed land which few cyclists would have had the opportunity to tackle. The usual red soil abruptly changed to a monotone grey. Coarse grey stones combined with corrugations were camouflaged by the alluvial dirt of the floodplains so the track lived up to its notorious reputation, belying its initial, tamer appearance.

Police Hole Yards provided some welcome shade for a lunch break and was also the end of the more moderate track. For the final 30 km of the day, we navigated our way along fences and through cattle-yards over the roughest track of the whole journey to date. It was all large, awkward-sized stones, some

'Don't mess': a jillaroo at work, VRD. At times I may as well have been sitting on one of these! (electric cattle prodder)

Riding spurs, VRD
(photo: G Yeoman)

'What an earth are you doing?' Brahman cattle, VRD

Obtaining water from a stock trough, Pigeon Hole Station
(photo: G Yeoman)

embedded into the ground, others loose. In the face of adversity, Greg remained in touch with his sense of humour. This time he made jokes about wanting to divert down an even rougher track so that he could boast about visiting Gregory's Remarkable Pillar – a prominent landmark named after Augustus Gregory, a few kilometres west of Pigeon Hole. We arrived at the homestead just after sundown, later than expected. I felt like a boxer suffering from brain shake. Chaffing was so bad I walked like an apprentice jillaroo after her first day of mustering. Greg was no longer making gags about remarkable pillars!

Pigeon Hole Station has been chosen by Heytesbury Beef as the company's site for research into sustainable grazing practices in the Victoria River District. Working with Meat and Livestock Australia (MLA) and supported by a number of institutions, the five-year project is developing grazing and infrastructure guidelines which aim to improve economic performance while maintaining the condition of the land and minimising impacts on biodiversity.

The Pigeon Hole Project focuses on finding out what specific rates of pasture use are sustainable in larger paddocks (20–50 km square), and what paddock design (size and number of watering points) cost-effectively reduces uneven pasture use and provides for a sustainable balance of pasture use and productivity. The project is also researching what impact the rate of pasture use has on biodiversity and the impact of different-sized 'conservation' areas on the preservation of biodiversity within the commercially managed property. It is an important investment of time and money, with benefits which will hopefully flow on to the natural and grazing environments. For example, the project has revealed more about the world's smallest marsupial – the long-tailed planigale – which lives in the cracks of the black-soiled grasslands. Weighing about three grams, this ferocious little carnivore, related to the Tasmanian devil, has been assessed as being more abundant in areas of Pigeon Hole which are lightly grazed.

Sonya and Russell Teece, who manage Pigeon Hole, were most hospitable although life for them, especially at this time of year, was non-stop. Along with all the usual mustering work, they had visitors, students and a young family to take care of. We left the following morning well fed and watered, ready for another 30-km battering before arriving at the main road. Crossing the Victoria

Crossing the Victoria River upstream, Pigeon Hole Station
(photo: G Yeoman)

River so far upstream and in the Dry was a tame affair. Greg made it all the way across, pedalling through the shallow pools and maintaining balance over the loose boulders. I almost made it until a rock sent me off course and, annoyingly, into a deeper section and an unwanted foot-bath.

Pigeon Hole was my last opportunity to contact various people. I was able to speak to Arnaud and give exact dates of our arrival in Alice Springs, so he could book flights. I was already very much looking forward to seeing him. From this distance I also continued to coordinate those who had offered help with the website and promoting the educational side of the project. I was becoming, however, more and more frustrated because some of the volunteers (with my strict budget I couldn't afford to employ anyone) were not doing as they had promised and in the time-frame required. When I had left for Canberra, everything was in place, but now at Day 100 into the journey, I was still having to ask why things had not been done. In addition, technical difficulties with the website meant that the educational information was not being posted.

By this point, I was feeling very let down. Thankfully, my brother, Tony, stepped in to help with the website where he could and my sister, Jane, helped with some educational promotion. Simone, a good friend, promised to assist with promotion in Western Australia. I knew I could definitely rely on family and friends to contribute.

Kelly Bore; last water for a day and a half

I was also thinking ahead for when Greg left the expedition in Wiluna. Merrick Ekins, whom I had briefly met in Brisbane, had committed to cover the Canning Stock Route. He had also said he would sort out a support vehicle, which was a great relief. As Merrick was a veteran of many expeditions, I was comfortable that he knew what he was getting himself into. But suddenly he had become hesitant, seemingly put off by others who claimed the trek would be impossible, especially in the heat, as we would be heading north into the 'build-up' to the Wet. I didn't know Merrick very well, but I was becoming less confident that he was switched on with regard to the crucial timing of it all.

I pondered over all these frustrations while we rested in the shade at Whylong Bore. Most of the shade had been monopolised by the Brahman herd which stared inquisitively, as if thinking, 'What on earth are you doing?', when we set up the shadecloth for a picnic table on a rare patch of cowpat-free ground. Maureen's home-grown tomatoes were appreciated, especially as Greg had somehow managed to prevent them from being damaged while riding over the rough terrain.

According to Russell from Pigeon Hole, Kelly Bore, which is a part of Samford Station (another Heytesbury property), was the final reliable watering point before Lajamanu, unless we diverted to Kalkarinji. Here we filled everything; all the bottles, five four-litre bags and even more in reserve. The increasing daily temperatures meant we used more water than before. We repacked our loads, putting one heavy water-bag in each front pannier and generally stacking the weight as close as possible to the centre of gravity of the bikes. The trailer was used to carry the lighter bulky items which were awkward to fit into the three-dimensional jigsaw puzzle. On rough roads, the trailer was only recommended to carry 15 kg, whereas it could carry 25 kg on tarmac. Moving the extra weight was exhausting, especially on the climbs.

The road to Lajamanu was well maintained and we were generally able to avoid the worst patches of sand and corrugations by taking most of the gravel surface to snake around the bad bits. Apart from a few snapshot views through the bush from an ancient jump-up, the scenery was unremarkable. A closer study of the flora on our breaks, however, revealed an incredibly diverse display

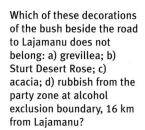

Which of these decorations of the bush beside the road to Lajamanu does not belong: a) grevillea; b) Sturt Desert Rose; c) acacia; d) rubbish from the party zone at alcohol exclusion boundary, 16 km from Lajamanu?

of colour and textures. We were definitely entering a drier habitat which hosted a range of varieties of flowering plants. Different types of grevillea, yellow and purple Sturt Desert Roses, acacias of all sorts and delicate everlastings with papery petals studded the bush like Christmas decorations.

By contrast, the scene changed 16 km from the townsite – the limit of the alcohol-free zone. It was disappointing to see the roadside and surrounding bushland littered with a sea of green – Victoria Bitter cans. The 'party' zone was a continuum of cans and rubbish. Locals simply relocate their gatherings to a legal area away from the town, but nothing seems to be done about cleaning the mess.

Arriving in Lajamanu, I hadn't realised that it was a closed community and that we required permits to stay. I had contacted the Northern and Central land councils in advance to ask whether I needed to seek permission and had sent them a copy of our route, but was told we were unrestricted. The town is administered almost solely by non-Aboriginal staff who liaise with the community elders. It was the white Australians who seemed most concerned, one person telling us we had to leave the town and camp three kilometres outside. Having just loaded up with stocks from the very well-equipped community store, we were not very keen to turn around and back-track. The local people did not seem perturbed by our presence; many, in fact, were extremely interested in what we were doing and asked plenty of questions. Overall, I felt there was a mutual respect – that we chose to travel in a way which was so closely connected with the land conformed to the essence of their cultural values.

We eventually discovered that we could stay in the 'Long House' and I was able to negotiate a reasonable rate at the council offices. It was an uncomfortable feeling, staying in a kind of 'us and them' atmosphere. I felt alienated in my own country, and while I respect Indigenous culture, I don't feel that segregation helps any situation. It was the attitude of some of the administrators which was more of a concern to me rather than the locals.

Lajamanu was formed in 1949 when it was decided to move Walpiri people from Yuendumu to what was formerly known as Hooker Creek Station. On the first three attempts, people left and returned to their own communities, walking directly across the desert. Lajamanu is a very strongly Traditional community, where the English language is secondary. Traditional customs are still practised and dominate the thinking of the community. In general, it is not in the nature of Aboriginal culture to directly say 'No' to people, which may at times explain why non-Aboriginal staff are often left to enforce the rules. This may have been the case in our situation.

I confirmed with Letty from Suplejack Downs that we would be there in two days. Before setting out, I revisited the Lajamanu store for some extra supplies. Here, I struck up a conversation with Jim, the store manager, who was most knowledgeable about the road ahead. We definitely had between 40 and 50 km of sand to contend with. Jim also mentioned that there could be more Aboriginal people than usual using the road, for two reasons. Firstly, there was a funeral taking place the following day. It was to be a Traditional burial for a well-respected woman from Lajamanu. As the community still relates very much to Yuendumu and other Walpiri communities, people would be arriving from hundreds of kilometres away to pay their respects. The second reason for the potential influx of traffic was that it would be 'royalties' day in two days time. Anyone other than the Traditional owners has to pay royalties as a form of rent to use the land. Newmont Mines, for example, pays for the use of the mining land. People would be driving all the way from Yuendumu and Balgo to collect their cheques.

We set off with 36 kg of extra water and a full complement of food to weigh us down. Greg had dismantled the wheel-joint of his trailer and greased everything in an attempt to get rid of the infuriating squeak which mysteriously continued to haunt us. His efforts were in vain as the high-pitched screech, like nails scratching on a blackboard, restarted just as we crossed over Hooker Creek and out of town. A strong tailwind behaved like a true friend, nursing us along in our time of need on the patchy road. Some exposed, wind-swept sections were reasonably solid, hard-packed grit, and despite heavy corrugations, we made faster progress overall than we had planned. Very often we were challenged by deep sand drifts which had settled over the road. These were tackled with as much momentum as possible and usually very little control. Steering the heavy front wheels was near impossible, as they were channelled along depressions made by vehicles: the best chance of keeping balance and staying upright was to keep spinning the pedals rapidly in a low gear, adding power in deeper sand. Yanking feet out of the toe-clips was often the reflex action. However, this meant immediate loss of momentum and certain stoppage, usually culminating with a rolling dive into the sand. We gave each other marks out of ten for style and degree of difficulty for every tumble. There was definitely no poise or grace involved: it was a matter of making the right decision as to when to try to push through and when to abandon ship. Once stopped, the bike needed to be wheeled to more solid ground before restarting, a process which sapped a lot of energy.

I was amazed at how well Greg was managing with the trailer in tow. At times it acted like a rudder, steadying the ship, while at other times I am sure the added dimension was a hindrance to handle. All things considered, we were moving along pretty smartly, covering nearly 20 km in about seventy-five minutes. The trailer had mysteriously stopped squeaking, as it tended to do from time to time for no rhyme or reason, so we were enjoying the peace.

It was too good to last. All of a sudden I heard a 'clunk', followed by, 'Bollocks! Stop!' I thought Greg must have fallen off again. I struggled to control my bike as it was misbehaving like a stubborn mule. I looked around and was relieved to see Greg was in one piece. The trailer, however, was not. The wheel had fallen off after the axle bolt had become detached and dropped off somewhere in the previous 20 km of sand. Finding a needle in a haystack would have been given better odds.

Greg was enveloped by a wave of deep anger, his frustration so intense that he was lost for words, which was disconcerting because he was seldom silent. Our first, most obvious option was to search for the rogue bolt. The bikes looked like beached whales when we laid them on their sides so they rested on the bulging panniers in the precious shade, and we set off to search on foot. Greg then cycled back slowly for about five kilometres. No success.

Jim and Joe to the rescue

The next option was to try and temporarily fix the axle joint by improvising with a replacement bolt. The best Greg could come up with was to remove the skewer bolt from the steering unit (head set). It almost fitted, and we could have fashioned a washer from one of the empty beer cans littering the side of the road. But this may not have been a good move, as it would have weakened his machine and we were facing about 1000 km of rough road ahead. The remaining option was to cycle back to Lajamanu, which would mean virtually losing a day by the time we pushed in the sand and into a serious headwind. Although it would be difficult to make the extra day up, we were beginning to think this was going to be our most sensible approach. Then I remembered that there were some 'local' telephone numbers printed on my 'Desert Tracks' map, and promptly found a number for the Lajamanu service station. It was an opportune time to test the satellite phone. I explained our situation and what we needed to the service station, and half an hour later the cavalry was on its way with an assortment of spare parts.

The 'rescue party' consisted of Jim, the store manager whom I had notified of our movements earlier that morning, and Joe, a community elder. Jim said that he didn't hesitate to help us out because we had been well prepared and responsible enough to tell them where we were heading. He hauled a massive 20-litre container of nuts, bolts and washers off the back of the ute. Joe, an expert tracker, was very keen to help and was sure that he would be able find the missing bolt. Confident that Joe would be successful, Jim threw him the keys. Joe drove slowly back towards Lajamanu with his head out of the window, employing all his Traditional skills in the search.

Soon the contents of the container were scattered over the ever-useful piece of shadecloth and Jim and Greg combed the collection for the appropriate pieces. Success eventually prevailed as they found a screw of the right thread, length and width and a solid nut and washer to match. At this point, Joe returned minus the missing bolt. The outcome was even better than the original because, thankfully, the trailer no longer squeaked. Jim and Joe topped up our water-bottles before heading back to town and we pushed on towards Suplejack Downs Station.

About 50 km from Lajamanu, a second drama for the day unfolded as we continued to slide around and tumble in the sand. When I depressed my left pedal I could hear and feel a faint grinding sensation, reminiscent of the state of the cartilage in my right knee after I had been running around a real tennis court. I couldn't see anything wrong and deduced that a few grains of sand had probably entered the pedal unit. I was just at an 'abandon ship' part of a fall, desperately trying to extract my foot out of the toe-clip, when the whole pedal fell off, exposing the single spindle. This was serious as we were not carrying spare pedals. While in theory it would be possible to cycle just pushing the axle of the pedal, this would be extremely uncomfortable and inefficient.

It was an unusual breakdown. Greg pulled the pedal apart to find that I had shredded the bearing casing and the tiny ball bearings were floating around loose. The only option this time was a 'bodge' job. Greg located a washer which fitted in the pedal barrel to keep the spacing, and put everything back together.

Approaching a jump-up on to a higher plain at the end of the sandy section
(photo: G Yeoman)

The effect was a bit loose but seemed to hold together. The question was – how long would it last?

The road improved as we approached and climbed a jump-up on to a higher plain (known as down land). There we made better pace through monotonous bush, trying to make up for lost time as the dark orange sun kissed the horizon. It took a while to spot a campsite – a recent clearing in the tufty scrub out of sight from the track. Despite all the hold ups, we made sufficient distance and so did not lose a day.

◆　◆　◆

I hadn't known what to expect of the Tanami. Apart from the basic information provided by the map, I had been unable to find out anything much at all about this region during my research for the trip. The reality was that its terrain was not as many would imagine a desert to be, even though we were officially travelling through lands receiving an average rainfall of less than 250 mm per annum – and unreliable and infrequent at that. The dominant vegetation is stunted mulga scrub, which is perfectly adapted to survive on meagre amounts of moisture and which, along with the spinifex, stabilises the sand and prevents it from blowing away. It is all very different from the naked dunes of the Sahara or Gobi deserts. Another noteworthy feature of this desert is its red, rocky outcrops. They may have been dwarfed by some of the more spectacular, large-scale scenery to the north or towards the MacDonnell Ranges hundreds of kilometres to the south, but on this open, fairly flat terrain, they definitely stand out.

Even with the absence of boundary fences, it was still obvious when we entered station land. There were no boundary fences because the property is completely surrounded by desert, which is Indigenous-owned land. Cattle never stray too far from their water supply so it is relatively simple to maintain control without the expense of constructing fences. The first signal that we had arrived at the Suplejack Downs Station border was hitting the deep furrows across the road, tracks made by cattle. The next signal were water-pipes that converged with these trails and disappeared off into the bush. Just before we stopped for lunch, we came across our first vehicle for the day. It was Bill Cook doing the water rounds, checking that all the bores were in order. Knowing we wouldn't be far away, he had been keeping an eye out for us. He gave us directions for a shortcut to the homestead which he said might be a bit rough but should be quicker. Heard that one before!

Our lunch break was taken under rare shade on some desolate-looking country next to a cairn marking the boundary between the Katherine and Alice Springs shires. We were about midway between the two towns, roughly 800 km from both. Other than a few trees beside the dry bed of Wilson Creek, we were surrounded by open ground with tinder-dry sparse spinifex cover. The midday mirage shimmered over the barren gibber plain, giving a lone burnt-out shell of a car the appearance of floating.

I had allowed extra time to pedal the Suplejack Road because we did not know what to expect of the track quality. As no one cycles these parts, we have learnt from experience not to completely rely on information from drivers. Their 4WDs can skim over corrugations at great speed, and they don't have to physically struggle through softer parts. On the other hand, sudden dips, potholes, larger rocks and bulldust concern them more than they do us. As we had progressed faster than I expected even with the mechanical problems, we could relax (relatively speaking) as for once we didn't have to race the setting sun to arrive at our destination.

Sixteen kilometres further along the track we arrived at the creek and bore which matched Bill's description. They would have been difficult to miss in any case because Bill had mentioned that there was a dead cow opposite the turn-off. We became victims of the south-easterly wind direction as surging whiffs of the putrid odour were inescapable.

It was immediately evident why the cattle trucks avoided this shortcut. The two wheel ruts that were just deep sand around the bore graduated to hard-baked clay disguised under thick deposits of bulldust – dust as fine as talcum powder which settles into potholes and depressions. Previous warnings about bulldust had never been a concern for us as it was easy to spot at our speed. Here, however, I had no idea what lay under the surface. It was basically a blind run, the powder so fine that it felt cool and wet as it splashed over my legs like a liquid. We took our time and still arrived at the homestead by mid-afternoon. Bill had contacted Letty on the two-way radio and she and her niece Kylie were waiting to greet us.

Letty and Bill Cook, Suplejack Downs Station

After a quick wash, we were soon relaxing over afternoon tea. How this family-run property, named after the native suplejack tree, came to be and its scale of operations is quite a contrast to what we had witnessed at Victoria River Downs. Letty grew up on the property, which is approximately 400 000 hectares (one million acres). Her father was a drover working the Tanami Track, and when he first arrived in the area in 1963, the region was classified as 'vacant land'. He sank a few bores and received his first cattle as payment for his droving work. There was absolutely no infrastructure at the time, and everything had to be built from scratch to develop what is now Australia's most geographically isolated cattle station. Suplejack Downs Station closely vies for this distinction with Tanami Downs. Formerly known as Mongrel Downs, the Tanami Downs homestead is situated about 50 km south-west of Rabbit Flat on the Tanami Track.

Letty's family lived in a tent for a year before they built a one-roomed shed – home for the next fourteen years. As the land gradually developed they applied for its tenure. It wasn't until the pastoral lease, after many years of negotiation, was finally granted in 1977 that they allowed themselves the comfort of a house. It is not easy to obtain building materials and expertise when you are about 800 km from Alice Springs, 750 km from Katherine and 550 km from Halls Creek. Mostly it was a case of doing things themselves and improvising with whatever was available.

Letty drives the corrugated Tanami Track to Alice Springs every two or three months to do the shopping. During the Wet, the Cooks have to be prepared for being cut off for longer periods of time, during which they manage by producing much of their own fresh food. As one might imagine, beef and home-grown vegetables are on the menu most of the time.

Modern communication technology has dramatically improved the family's contact with the outside world. In particular, being connected to the internet enables them to keep in touch with friends, watch cattle market prices or attend to business matters (although receiving technical assistance remains a problem). We were even able to watch the Athens Olympics on their television thanks to satellites. Being connected to the telephone was a relatively recent advance, along with UHF radio for school lessons.

Letty was a 'full bottle' on sustainable land management. She explained that in the Northern Territory the Pastoral Land Board systematically evaluates grazing areas, taking photographs of the exact representative plots of land at the same time of year on a regular basis. The measurements are analysed and the board has the power to ban stock from areas which are overgrazed. Being located on the periphery of the Tanami, the marginal land is particularly fragile, making the need for grazing control even more paramount. Letty produced the Pastoral Land Monitoring File documenting the research, proudly showing how Suplejack remained well within the sustainable grazing levels. The station uses less than 10 per cent of the palatable vegetation for its 10–12 000 head of cattle. Greg found it astonishing that there could be a variation of 2000 cattle – a mix of short horns and Brahman, whose numbers were unable to be confirmed.

While we were there, Bill and Letty had seven stockmen working from dawn to dusk. They used horses to walk the stock for dipping to rid them of the health-threatening tick, parasites which are a curse of Northern Australian regions. Walking the cattle with horses is a less stressful way of moving the animals than using helicopters, even if it is slower. The stockmen arrived back at the homestead exhausted and ready for some home brew. As usually happened with locals, they were astonished to learn of what we had achieved so far and questioned our plans to cycle the Gunbarrel and particularly the Canning Stock Route. At the least, our presence provided some novel entertainment as fourteen of us sat around the long table for dinner.

The musterers left before the crack of dawn next morning. While we packed and prepared ourselves for the road, Bill made use of the daylight by doing odd jobs near the homestead. He was waiting around to see us off. For her part, Letty was keen to try riding my bike to feel what the weight was like. Greg had serviced the gears and other working parts, and in doing so had left my bike in its lowest gear. Being much shorter than me meant that Letty could barely reach the pedals. When she rolled off down a slope, there was little control and she screamed with laughter as she wobbled all over the place. She couldn't work out how to change gears which were set to a ratio suitable to climb a steep hill, so she probably didn't get much idea of the usual effort required to ride, except in handling the weight. The bike nearly toppled over when she finally found the brakes and came to a sudden halt.

Lunch on the road; making the most of the shade
(photo: G Yeoman)

We were loaded up with home-cured corned beef, a loaf of home-made bread, rice and dates. After goodbyes, we set off along Suplejack's main front entrance which was far smoother than the track we had arrived on. Back on the main track we negotiated all the usual nemeses – sand patches, corrugations, loose stones and wash-outs. The morning was spent pedalling through a completely exposed, vast landscape. In the heat of the day we had to push on for many extra kilometres to find a tree which provided at least some shade for us to enjoy our special lunch hamper.

As we laid out the shadecloth, our usual table, some geologists from Cobar, NSW, stopped for a chat and topped up our water-bottles. Then, as we were about to leave, another vehicle approached. As it drew near I could see it meandering all over the road. The four intoxicated Aboriginals inside were driving from Balgo at the northern end of the Tanami Track to Lajamanu to collect their royalties. Their car was in a sorry state of disrepair, scratched, dented and covered in red dust; its engine roared more like a souped-up V8 than a beaten-up, old, cream-coloured Torana. There was obviously a hole in the muffler, the radiator grill was missing and the bonnet did not close properly. An external fan was fitted in front of the radiator to prevent it overheating. It was astonishing to think the occupants were attempting a 900-km return journey across the desert in such an ailing machine. But even in their drunken state, they still stopped to see if we were all right and to offer water and beer. Being fully loaded we didn't need either and after a comical chat, they roared off, stirring clouds of dust which lingered in their wake.

We passed the abandoned Piccaninny Outstation and continued towards the Tanami Track junction. The huge mill installation at the Tanami Mine near the junction ahead was visible from about 12 km away. We turned off the road, passing the 'Strictly No Admittance' signs and keeping an eye out for the huge mining trucks. Drivers would not have been expecting to see two bicycles on their pristinely maintained private roads. We found the temporary settlement, which consisted of rows of 'dongas' – basic, transportable sleeping accommodation. To our amazement, everyone knew we were coming and the VIP treatment we enjoyed, including joining in the Saturday night barbecue, was both welcome and rather surreal in the middle of the desert.

Gold was discovered at the Tanami site in 1900 and over the next thirty years small amounts were extracted from alluvial deposits and quartz veins. Following an agreement with the Traditional owners, modern mining commenced in 1983. The world's largest producer of gold, the Newmont Mining Corporation, leases 60 000 hectares of mining tenements, including the Tanami site and the larger Granites installation, 100 km to the south. At the Tanami Mine, ore was transported 40 km via a private road from the open-cut pit at Groundrush to the mill and main camp where we stayed. Mining began at Groundrush in 2001 and the operation was due to be decommissioned three months after we left.

◆　◆　◆

The Tanami Track started out as an important stock route for the station owners of central Australia. Once considered a horror track, it has been relatively tamed by road trains and goldmines and is now an important arterial route between Alice Springs and the Kimberley. The road is as wide as a major highway, but that is where the similarity ends. Corrugations are compacted deep beneath the surface; even after a grader knocks the tops off the bumps, the washboard effect recurs straight away. Drivers despair at the monotonous shaking which has notoriously caused roof racks to wear through car roofs, exhausts to fall off and many machines to rattle to pieces.

Rabbit Flat, the world's most isolated roadhouse to which I had earlier made the phone call, has only ever been owned by Bruce and Jacqui Ferrands. The couple arrived in 1961 and built everything from scratch. Given the isolation and the fact that there isn't anything much around, this was a major feat. We didn't know what to expect as we arrived at what is now a shady oasis. Jacqui is French, and an artist, and the roadhouse would not have looked out of place in the south of France. Out the back flourished fruit trees and vegetables, all grown by Jacqui.

The kiosk section was protected by security mesh. I rang the bell and Jacqui appeared, displaying little interest. We bought some token drinks as everything was so expensive. Feeling disappointed at her lack of reaction, we rested in the

Bruce Ferrands, Rabbit Flat Roadhouse

shade outside. When we were ready to leave, I rang the bell again. This time Bruce appeared and I handed him one of the expedition postcards. (I had had special cards printed to give as mementoes of the expedition.) After a short conversation over the counter, he invited us into his home for tea and biscuits. He talked while we ate and listened. The only way we could get a word in was to speak over the top of the monologue, but squeezing a word in usually only prompted a new topic of discussion. Bruce had an opinion on everything, insisting he was well informed as he now had television! The topics he covered included religion, politics, war, Aboriginals and environmentalists. I didn't dare challenge the Rabbit Flat view of the world as Bruce – a man of feral hairstyle who had allegedly pointed a shotgun on someone who was out of line – freely expressed his ideas. Considering his more than forty years of 'desert island' existence, I understood how he had drawn some of his conclusions. Over the years, Bruce and Jacqui have had to deal with all sorts of challenges and strange and interesting visitors with no security. Being on bicycles we were certainly non-threatening and definitely broke down barriers at Rabbit Flat.

We didn't leave for The Granites until mid-afternoon and after we had devoured a packet of Hydro Creams. (These were a treat, as we couldn't carry cream-filled biscuits or chocolates because they melted very quickly.) The surrounding plains we encountered were indeed flat, their monotony relieved only by the odd proliferation of termite mounds in the shape of mud huts. With 37 km to go, my ailing pedal gave up and dropped off. The washer Greg had inserted 300 km earlier had disintegrated and worn away part of the barrel of the pedal in the process. We could not find anything to repair the problem. Fortunately Denise, the environment officer from The Granites Mine, whom we had met at the barbecue the previous night, chose that moment to show up. She had driven out with a colleague to give us accurate instructions for finding the mining settlement, as taking the wrong road could have been hazardous. The women could not find anything in their toolbox to fit my pedal and started to inspect the LandCruiser for the right-sized washer. A couple of washers extracted from under the bonnet and the back tray of their utility did not do the job but eventually they found one which did. As it was connected to the fuel tank, they proceeded to saw off the part with a hacksaw blade. This whole process would have looked highly suspicious to anyone passing! Our friends

Losing another race with the setting sun – still nearly two hours to go before reaching The Granites Mine
(photo: G Yeoman)

OUT THERE AND BACK

planned to work on some good reasons to explain to the company engineers why their vehicle was falling apart.

The state of the Tanami Track, especially the section we had to endure to reach The Granites, was certainly a believable alibi. We were shaken to bits, making slower progress than expected. As the sun set, we still had about fifteen kilometres to go. On the horizon, the floodlights of The Granites mill, which operates around the clock, acted as our lighthouse beacon for the final hour. An hour seems a very long time when you are riding in the dark. Our torch lights were useless and there was little moonlight to illuminate our path, and no white lines to follow. We rode virtually blind, relying on senses other than sight. With no points of reference apart from the lights in the distance, spatial awareness and balance were affected. My sense of hearing became far more acute, attuned to the sound of the wheels rolling over the gravel, the loaded bikes rattling over the corrugations, and the distant noise of the mill machinery which drifted unchecked over the empty plain. The gentle evening breeze could be heard rustling through the spinifex, rapidly chilling my moist skin once the sun had disappeared. We had to keep moving to stay warm. Nearer The Granites, the road – frequented by heavy vehicles – was well maintained and watered several times a day to settle the dust. It was a relief to roll over the smoother surface, and to smell the moisture rising from the damp ground.

Near the settlement, a dingo, obviously accustomed to human activity, kept guard from a safe distance. Dingoes, which here rely on scavenging spoils from the community, have far more highly evolved senses of hearing and smell than humans in order to make their nocturnal activities efficient.

The Granites goldmine was a pit-stop, both in the general sense and that it was an opportunity to explore the Callie Pit. At 760 metres and becoming deeper, it is one of Australia's deepest underground mines. The next day Denise arranged a special tour of the mine situated at Dead Bullock Soak, 40 km by private asphalt haul road from The Granites mill site. After the trials and tribulations of reaching our location, it felt bizarre being driven along a smooth, sealed road across the treeless, featureless Tanami Desert, 500 km north of Alice Springs. Even more unbelievable was the size of the road train which crossed our path. It was the world's longest, transporting the high grade ore from pit to mill and trailing seven wagons. Carrying an average payload of 275 tonnes, the 93-metre monster has an extra engine between the third and fourth carriages to propel the three rear wagons.

Wiring up the Callie Mine with 70 tonnes of the explosive ammonium nitrate

After an hour's crash induction course – we were versed on emergency procedures and the mining processes used – we were driven down the terraces encircling the open cut section and into the deep black hole. To geologists, what lies beneath the surface of the Tanami is not so featureless. They would have been ecstatic at the discovery of the high grade ore at the Callie Mine, which returns six grams per tonne of rock. The compulsory protective clothing only felt appropriate when we left the comfort of the vehicle to meet some of the engineers at work. They were busy filling and wiring up stopes (side vents drilled through low grade deposits leading into the high grade reservoirs) with 70 tonnes of ammonium nitrate in readiness to blast out 250 000 tonnes of rock. To put that into perspective, four tonnes of the same type of explosive was used in the Bali bombing in 2002 and one tonne was used in the bombing in Oklahoma City in 1995. The scale of the operation was enormous. We descended to the bottom of the hole to watch the diamond drillers in action. Three days later, the base of the mine would be blasted much deeper and the infrastructure of the whole underground mine would then need to be rebuilt.

Inspecting the Tanami's giant termite mounds

Two hours later, we finally exited the dusty, oxygen-starved tunnel, reacting like startled rabbits as we were exposed to the raw sunlight. The contrast between the claustrophobic conditions of the mine and the vast plains was profound. I felt released, and had a sudden urge to expand my lungs with as much of the pure dry desert air as possible.

On the return journey, Denise enlightened us about her work as an environment officer. Overall, her job was to reduce the mining footprint both during the operational life of the mine and even more so after the mine is decommissioned. While the mine is being worked, particular attention is paid to the management of three aspects: cyanide used in the extraction process, surface and underground water supplies, and threatened species. Cyanide is so lethal, it only requires a teaspoon of solution with two per cent of the element to kill a human. Recycled processed water ponds contain a cyanide solution that poses a significant risk to migratory birds and other wildlife. Groundwater supplies are also susceptible to contamination via seepage of water from tailings facilities at The Granites and surrounding areas. Once the mining process is complete, the land must be returned to nature to the stipulations of the Traditional owners; the infrastructure removed, land re-sculptured to blend in with its surroundings and the natural flora and fauna re-introduced. Positions as environment officers have multiplied over recent years as the need for such overseeing has (not before time) become an essential part of the mining process.

◆　◆　◆

We set out from The Granites the next day with renewed energy and a revamped pedal, thanks to the engineering department. Denise had loaded us with extra supplies from the kitchen to see us through to Alice Springs. After a couple of kilometres, the road returned to its usual condition and we were violently shaken without respite. Most of the terrain bisected by the Tanami Track appears to be very long, slow undulations which in aeons past may have been far more pronounced. Somehow, it always seemed as though we were pushing uphill, but we may just have been trying to catch up with the horizon. Did passing a receiver mast mean we had reached a high point? In any case, there was no point in becoming excited about a long downhill phase as the corrugations took away the opportunity to freewheel. Despite the horrifically rough roads, over the two days after The Granites, we managed 260 km, a serious effort. By the time we reached the major Aboriginal community of Yuendumu, my knee was not the only body part complaining.

It was early evening by the time we rolled under an archway welcoming us to Yuendumu (population 1300) and into town. As at Lajamanu, it felt as though we were intruding into a different world, one we knew little about. The streets were lined with junk discarded by the community's inhabitants – old washing machines, refrigerators, sheets of corrugated iron and rusting car parts all abandoned on the verge of the road. By contrast, the people looked happy: children played, laughing infectiously, and adults seemed content sitting outside, soaking up the last rays of the sun. Some were just watching the world go by, others interacted or listened to music on their ghetto-blasters. A number acknowledged us with baffled expressions but all responded to our friendly waves with welcoming smiles. There were no street signs and we were conscious that we should not be wandering aimlessly. As the council offices were closed by now, we stopped to ask for directions to the white people's accommodation. Mr Wood, an older gentleman, was only too happy to assist after the usual questions ('Where have you come from? Where are you going? How far do you cycle each day?...').

We shared the accommodation with a group of health care workers from Alice Springs. They were developing a program for women's health in the community and from them we gained an insight into the major health issues confronting Aboriginal women. Without a doubt, the major concern was violence. There are very few families, even in an alcohol-free community, that are not struggling with the debilitating effects of trauma, despair and damage resulting from their experiences with physical, mental and spiritual violence.

We learned that in Yuendumu and many other Indigenous communities, alarming levels of domestic and sexual violence, particularly against women and children, is commonplace. The reasons for the behaviour are complex and vary from one group to another. The root cause stems from layers of pain built up over the generations which have never healed. Forced removal from their places of birth, loss of identity and sense of purpose, for example, can breed anger and grief and also boredom and loss of self-esteem. A health education worker explained that for the perpetrators the violence was an issue of possession. Under their punitive cultural laws, victims of violence are sworn to secrecy for fear of retribution. They would be punished if they landed the offenders in trouble with the law outside of their community. Their children are growing up in such a violent cultural environment that many know no other way and are likely to repeat the cycle if their society does not help take responsibility for such actions.

The past cannot be changed or brought back, so I find it heartening when self-motivated communities actively seek to resolve their own issues. The women of Yuendumu had, with the guidance of outsiders, already built a safe haven from domestic violence. It is a place they use as respite and protection when their home situation becomes dangerous. The healthcare worker explained that the refuge is not abused as just another house; the women use it for its intended purpose.

Nowhere to go on the never-ending corrugations
(photo: G Yeoman)

The Walpiri people are known as being very wilful and keen to own their problems and solutions. Had we cycled into Yuendumu fifteen years ago, the scene would have been very different and potentially volatile. About 10 per cent of the community and half of its children were then addicted to sniffing petrol. Children and teenagers were dying as a result of horrific burns or violence, or developing mental illness and permanent brain damage from lead toxicity. There were more kids sniffing petrol in the school grounds at night than attending classes during the day.

Pooling their financial resources and using mining royalties, the elders approached local language groups and gained permission to access Traditional land at Mount Theo, an isolated outstation about 150 km to the north of Yuendumu. The petrol sniffers were rounded up and relocated there in order to undergo the Traditional brand of rehabilitation. Walpiri culture was taught through story telling, bushcraft and bush medicine, while boys and girls were split up for cultural mentoring in women's and men's business. Those not cured by the first 'treatment' would again be returned to the outstation for another stint, double the length of the first session.

The system was extremely successful and the youth culture changed from being sniffing-dominated to one dominated by other activities. The community never asked for funding for the program's conception, or for the first few years of its operation, which meant it was run purely on the motivation of the people to fix the problem. Due to the foresight and innovative efforts of the Yuendumu

10 000 km done; 'around the clock' on my odometer for the first time near Alice Springs
(photo: G Yeoman)

A blue-tongued skink in the middle on the Tanami Road

elders, the younger generation of the largest community in Central Australia (with the exception of Alice Springs) has a better future and a better understanding of their identity. There is still a long way to go.

Back on the bikes, south of Yuendumu we encountered gradually more frequent traffic. Just before Tilmouth Well Roadhouse we were taunted with a couple of short bitumen strips which broke up the bone-rattling surface. Finally, after a couple more rough stints, we hit the tarmac south of Tilmouth, and it was plain sailing as the road turned eastwards to run parallel with the spectacular West MacDonnell Ranges. The fertile floodplain which flanked the range was a carpeted green meadow that appeared out of character with the desert country we had just crossed. As we neared Alice Springs, my pace quickened and Greg had a job keeping up with me. I was desperate to arrive in time to meet Arnaud when he arrived off the plane, so that we didn't waste a minute together.

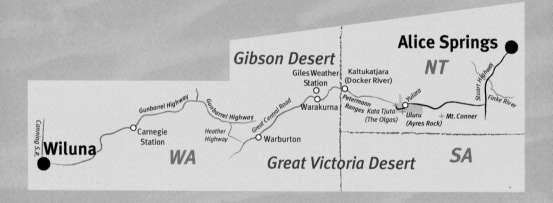

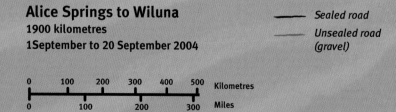

Alice Springs to Wiluna
1900 kilometres
1September to 20 September 2004

———— Sealed road
———— Unsealed road
(gravel)

Scale:
0 100 200 300 400 500 **Kilometres**
0 100 200 300 **Miles**

8

Across the Red Centre
(Alice Springs to Wiluna)

Delicate flowers of
the central deserts

Leaving Alice Springs was extremely difficult. Arnaud and I had spent three wonderful days together, not letting the other out of our sight. I kept stalling as I packed my panniers. Arnaud helped me fit on a new set of pedals, which I hoped would see out the whole expedition.

Saying goodbye was made harder because I still had about 15 000 km to go and the next two stages – across the Red Centre to Wiluna via the Kaltukatjara (Docker River) Road, the Great Central Road and the notorious Gunbarrel Highway, then up the Canning Stock Route – were going to be the most difficult of the expedition. I felt numb as we set off and, to make matters worse, the tailwind switched to a headwind once we passed through The Gap and out of town.

The first 460 km on the bitumen roads which connect Alice Springs to Australia's most identifiable natural features, Uluru and Kata Tjuta, were relatively straightforward compared with what we knew was to follow. Pushing along the smooth Stuart Highway, the rugged MacDonnell Ranges to the north, was a physical luxury. Mentally, it meant I didn't have to concentrate so much to avoid the bumps and could spend more time dwelling on my emotional state. But I did notice that the recent rains had rejuvenated the land, and turned it into a canvas of colour. Wild flowers created a carpet of pink, purple, yellow and white; closer inspection during our breaks enabled us to appreciate their delicate features.

Reaching the Finke River for our first night out of The Alice was particularly satisfying. We pushed and dragged our gear along the sandy banks of the world's oldest river away out of view of the busy highway and set up camp. The mightiest waterway in central Australia germinates high up in the West MacDonnell Ranges, gradually carving a path through intervening rocks before disappearing into the sands of the Simpson Desert, 690 km from its source. For several thousand years the ancient stream has been flowing from the same bed; and from the evidence of the rocks, in ages past it carried a lot more water than today. Indigenous cultures have long used the bed as a highway as, somewhat more recently, did the first European explorers such as John McDouall Stuart and Ernest Giles. I thought about all this by a permanent-looking pool where I had wandered at dusk in the hope of spotting wildlife. It was good to keep my mind busy as the day had been a personal ordeal. Soon the last of the sun's rays were replaced by a magnificent full moon.

The following morning we awoke to a snap-frozen tent. The conditions echoed our brittle emotional states. Tea and rice pudding helped us thaw out our bodies, but as we recorded one of our daily joint video reports, our feelings poured out. Greg was also missing his partner, Lucy, and my low spirits had made him feel worse. He had only three weeks to go before he finished his part of the expedition, but often the final stages of a long trek are the most difficult. When the task seems daunting, it is best to take things stage by stage, so the frost having melted in the sun, we pushed our bikes back to the modern highway, photographing the ancient natural highway before moving on.

Arriving at Erlunda Roadhouse at the turn-off from the Stuart Highway to the Lasseter Highway felt almost surreal. The roadhouse catered so well for the tourist trade, it reminded me more of a services stop in Europe. However, when we elected to sit outside in order to keep an eye on our bikes, the countless flies that hung around us and our food soon put paid to that illusion.

Tourist buses are about as common as flies on the Lasseter Highway as they race out from Alice Springs to catch the sunset on Uluru. Many passengers fall asleep on their 900-km round day trip, meaning much of their 'outback adventure tour' must be wasted. They may get to view the Rock at the best time of day, but their recollection of the experience would surely be like looking at a postcard. Gazing at us through the tinted windows of their air-conditioned prisons-on-wheels, they probably thought we were nuts. We would wave back, thinking the same thing about them.

The tarmac sliced through the desert landscape, bisecting sand dune after sand dune. Bombing along at 24 km per hour, we felt obliged to make the most of a tailwind. The bitumen was only there to cater for the tourist dollar and in a couple of days we wouldn't be doing much free-wheeling through the sand.

About 40 km from Curtin Springs Station, Mt Conner rose on the south-west horizon. The massive butte is 28 km in circumference and three times the size of Uluru. Sea shells have been found on top of the plateau, showing that the whole Red Centre was once under the sea. The giant tor is not accessible as it sits on private land so we had to appreciate its glow at sunset from Curtin Springs.

Most importantly at Curtin Springs, we followed up on the progress of our permit application to travel through Ngaanyatjarra Land across the Western Australian border. Our application, complete with supporting UNESCO letter, had to be circulated to all twelve tribal elders. We needed seven positive responses to allow us to travel through to Warburton unsupported. By the following morning we had received a fax granting us permission, a huge relief considering our limited time-frame, even if we were restricted as to where we could camp. We left for Yulara in good spirits, quite excited that Uluru would soon be appearing above the sand ridges. I wondered what impact the great Rock, an important symbol to all Australians, Indigenous and non-Indigenous, would have on me.

Finke River – the world's oldest river was also an ancient highway

Keeping an expectant eye out for the national icon, I almost ran over a thorny devil, and then Greg almost crashed into me as I slammed on the brakes and took evasive action without warning. Any vehicle would have flattened the little chameleon lizard whose spiky skin takes on the colour of blue metal so that it blends in perfectly with the road. These diminutive creatures need all the protection – their evil appearance must help here – they can get because their slow, jerky movements are no challenge for their usual predators, such as birds of prey. We had plenty of time to stop and record our own encounter. The thorny devil lives solely off tiny black ants, each licking up some 5000 per day. Later on during my journey, I would have been happy to carry a pet thorny devil to let loose in my rest breaks and give me some respite from intruding hordes of those highly annoying little insects.

About 30 km from Yulara we caught our first glimpse of Uluru and Kata Tjuta. The latter is a further 45 km away but almost double the height. Through the distant heat haze, the great tors were initially a powder blue colour, but as we gradually drew nearer, Uluru changed progressively to mauve then to a stronger purple and by the time we arrived at Yulara, the sandstone monolith was a striking warm orange.

Yulara is a purpose-built tourist resort town, 18 km north of Uluru. It seemed sterile and characterless to us, but is necessarily so in order to cope with thousands of tourists who visit daily either via road or the international airport nearby. Yulara is certainly not attractive, but at least the tourist industry is managed to protect national heritage. We took the opportunity to stock up on supplies in the well-equipped general store; thanks to the demands of international visitors, we were able to find some of the slightly more exotic supplies to maintain morale. The decent bread was a treat: usually we had to make do with unsatisfying processed, sliced, white loaves, the only option in many isolated areas. Couscous was another preferred dinner ingredient when we could get it. Not only did it give longer-lasting energy, but it requires little water to prepare and just enough fuel to boil the cup or so of water – another important consideration.

As we progressed towards Uluru the next morning, the scale and the beauty of the sandstone lump made a heartfelt impact on me. I kept noticing different aspects, somewhat like zooming in on a digital photograph to view the finer details. We cycled the 11 km around the circumference, studying every weathered angle, dwarfed by the sacred site, which rises 348 metres above the plain.

The great Rock at close range: scenes from cycling around the base of Uluru

♦   ♦   ♦

Three great tors

Mount Conner from Curtin
Springs Station

Uluru
(photo: G Yeoman)

Kata Tjuta

OUT THERE AND BACK

Anangu, the Indigenous people of the landscape, divide the year into five separate seasons which are demarcated by changes in weather and the availability of different types of food. It being 5 September, by their reckoning we should have been experiencing the Piriyakutu/Piriya-Piriya season which begins around August/September. This is when the Piriya comes – a warm, steady wind from the north and west. The weather we experienced while cycling around the Rock was more typical of the previous Wari season. Characteristic of late May, June and July, the Wari season is the cold time when there is nyinnga (frost) and kulyarkulyarpa (mist or dew). I had never imagined that we would be cycling around Uluru wearing our waterproofs to keep out the wind chill from a cold southerly breeze and sporadic showers. While the weather was typical of the Wari season, the presence here of edible honey grevillea and numerous other flowering plants was more typical of the Piriyakutu season.

As Australia's most recognisable icon, it had been important to include Uluru in the itinerary and it was definitely worth the time and effort to do so. Like most special places on the expedition it really warranted a longer visit but as I only had nine months to complete the journey rather than nine years, we had to push on to Kata Tjuta, formerly known as the Olgas, 50 km to the west.

Travelling along my final black strip of bitumen for 3500 km (apart from the town sites of Warburton and Wiluna) I felt like I was on a tourist-run conveyer belt. During the two or so hours we took to pedal to the giant domes, we encountered scores of vehicles of all shapes and sizes; large tour coaches, smaller 4WD bus 'adventure tours' and private vehicles circulated between the great sites like a production line. Many passed us on the way in and on the way out.

As we moved away from Uluru, I kept looking over my shoulder to glimpse Australia's heart from a different angle. Approaching Kata Tjuta, it was easy to understand why the local Pitjantjatjara name means 'many heads'. As the sun finally peeked out from behind the gloomy clouds, we again experienced a full spectrum of colours on the rocks, from dark blue-grey to mauve through to burnt orange. Drawing nearer, we could start to make out the finer details. Vertical striations ran down the steep-sided domes like chocolate topping, cutting through the horizontal sedimentary layers. Small pockets of spinifex and stunted shrubs clung from their precarious positions on top of the flatter surfaces. The magnitude of the thirty-six beehive-shaped mounds was evident as they gradually filled our field of vision. At 546 metres above the plain and 1066 metres above sea level, the tallest is almost 200 metres higher than Uluru, now a lone, distant figure on the horizon.

One of Kata Tjuta's 'many heads'
(photo: G Yeoman)

We had even less time to appreciate this second feature of the UNESCO World Heritage site because we had to cycle beyond the boundary of the national park to camp. On a slightly hurried walk up the Valley of the Winds, I could appreciate the obvious differences in the texture of the rock faces between the 'many heads'. The surface of Uluru appeared so smooth that, after a deluge, it looks like an oversized water slide. A closer inspection of the Kata Tjuta rocks revealed rough sedimentary layers – actually made of a conglomerate (gravel consisting of pebbles, cobbles and boulders cemented by sand and mud) – which appear to be crumbling in little chunks. As on Mt Conner, sea shells have been found on these domes.

Turning west off the 'civilised road' on to the Docker River Road dramatically changed the ambience of our short ride beyond the park boundary: suddenly we were really struggling through sand patches and rattled by corrugations and loose stones. The road was much narrower than the Tanami Track. There was no chance of being able to glance casually over my shoulder to admire the glow of

Heading into isolation: a camel on the Docker River (Kaltukatjara) Road

the setting sun on Kata Tjuta. All concentration was focused on the road and searching for an appropriate place to camp.

We followed an overgrown side track for a few hundred metres and chose a site nestled in the mulga scrub. Although the ground surface of this bush terrain appeared hard, knocking in tent pegs was almost effortless. The absence of hoofed animals or vehicles meant the topsoil remained in its natural state. A thin crust caused by moisture reduces the effects of erosion; without the cover of vegetation, the powdery sand would otherwise be blown away and the topsoil with it. In the morning light, I was able to appreciate the delicate flowers which subtly studded the gnarled, smoky grey-green scrub and red earth.

The east section of the Docker River Road had been graded, which was good for cars but not for bikes. The grading may have knocked the tops off the corrugations, but it had also loosened the sand and rocks and filled the potholes. The surface appeared reasonable, but the going was very heavy. At times it felt as though the road was playing Russian roulette with our wheels as we blindly fell into sand-filled potholes or hit hidden obstacles.

It was evident from the many camel tracks that were now starting to appear that these hardy animals preferred to walk along the cleared road surface rather than in the bush. Noting that most of their tracks were concentrated down the side of the road, in the solid, undisturbed gutters, we followed suit. If we built up enough momentum we found we could skim over the thin crust formed on the gutters by overnight moisture. This fine balancing act was risky at times because, again with no warning, we would hit disguised soft patches at speed and end up flying off, hopefully into the sandy border for a soft landing.

Moving forward was therefore a choice between travelling slowly on the corrugations and being shaken to pieces or humming along at speeds of up to 20 km per hour beside the gutter with the associated risk of falling off and incurring an injury. Mostly we took our chances and sped along on the angled option.

◆ ◆ ◆

Reaching Irving Creek, midway between Kata Tjuta and Kaltukatjara/Docker River, was an important historical milestone. In January 1931, Harold Lasseter, while searching for his mythical reef of gold which he believed to be located in a region west of Giles Weather Station, became stranded when his camels bolted, leaving him with very little water at the hottest part of the year. He took refuge in a cave for twenty-five days, waiting to be found, then decided to attempt to walk to Mount Olga, 140 km away, where he hoped to met up with his search party. Carrying with him only three pints (1.7 litres) of water, he made it as far as Irving Creek, 55 km away, before he succumbed to dehydration and died.

Pumping water at the Irving Creek bore
(photo: G Yeoman)

By phoning the Docker River Community in advance, we had found out that there was a bore with a hand pump at Irving Creek; sunk somewhere near Lasseter's final resting place, by last reports it contained potable water. Following instructions, we took a rarely used track to the north after crossing the dry creek bed. The overgrown path ran parallel to the creek, and a couple of kilometres along we spotted the rusty pump tucked away behind the scrub. We dug out all our empty water containers and I started pumping. For quite a few minutes there was little resistance as the pump merely sucked up air. We were just starting to become worried when I finally felt some weight and heard gurgling sounds and up came a mix of air and water – the bore must have been very deep down. The combination of excitement and relief was akin to fishing all day and finally luring a bite. If I stopped pumping, it would be like letting the fish off the hook. The water I drew initially was an undrinkable red-brown colour – probably a cocktail of dirt and rust.

Pumping the water involved a complete upper body workout and was extremely tiring. We couldn't stop or we would lose the siphon and have to start again, so we took it in turns to work the pump lever while we topped up our supplies in relay fashion. With everything refilled, we resumed the struggle, whisked back to the main road with an almost gale-force north-westerly at our backs.

Searching for the Irving Creek bore
(photo: G Yeoman)

In the late afternoon the winds whipped up into a storm and the clouds closed in. Under a magnificent double rainbow we cycled a further twenty kilometres, looking for a campsite and feeling very vulnerable as there was a distinct absence of shelter. The landscape was completely open, with no clumps of scrub at all, and we needed to be screened from the road – a basic safety precaution. As usual, Greg got uptight when a campsite took some finding. I always believed that something would show up sooner or later.

Our map showed a private track leading to the abandoned Little Puta Puta Community somewhere on the southern side of the road. Just as the heavens opened we found the overgrown junction, and pushed our bikes a couple of hundred metres, the heavy, messy clay caking up the tyres. Our search for a patch of bare ground, void of spinifex, was unsuccessful. Eventually we opted for a spot of gardening, clearing a small area downwind of a lone bush, our only shelter, and set up camp.

During an uncomfortable night, the wind swung around to the south-west and I awoke to a howling gale threatening to blow everything away. The fly sheet flapped violently and I unzipped the door just in time to catch it before it flew off into the Never Never. The tent pegs didn't make much of an anchor in the poor, gutless sand so we got out of our warm sleeping bags and shoved every tent peg and guy rope we had into the ground, then laid all our bags over them, in the hope that everything would be held in place.

The morning dawned calm and chilly and, fortunately, everything was intact. I donned a number of layers of clothing as the usual breakfast was prepared. The rice pudding took on a dirty brown colour due to the sediment in the Irving Creek bore water – it tasted all right, but I added extra sugar just to be sure. The tall spinifex plants formed a warm micro-climate and sheltered us from the fresh south-westerly breeze as we ate. Like sentinel meerkats keeping guard over savannah grasslands, our heads constantly bobbed up above the grass level to admire the Petermann Ranges to the south. First thing in the morning, however, we did not feel as alert as these creatures are.

Progress to Lasseter's Cave was swift as we took our chances on the soft shoulder. I gradually learnt to recognise the disguised soft patches, but I didn't always get it right and the graded sand banks beside the gutter often cushioned my landing. To passing motorists it must have appeared as though we were racing to nowhere. We each took a side of the road; one would take the lead with a good run and then come to grief which allowed the other to catch up and overtake.

With only four to five hours of pedalling planned for the day, we had time up our sleeves to explore Lasseter's Cave and its surroundings. The cave sits in a craggy rock face overlooking the dry bed of the Hull River, near to the Tjunti Community. I tried to imagine what the hopeless situation would have been like for Lasseter, sitting day after day in a three-by-seven metre (approximate) shelter as supplies gradually diminished, waiting in the vain hope that a search party may have been dispatched from the direction of Mt Olga.

In the circumstances and in the height of summer, Lasseter probably did not appreciate the beauty of his environs. We admired majestic river gums sprouting out from the river sand and clothed with two-toned bark. The fibrous, brown, outer layer

'Lasseter's view' of the Hull River from inside the cave where he took refuge for twenty-five days
(photo: G Yeoman)

curled up and exfoliated away piece by piece, revealing a finer layer of similar colour which then shed to leave a bare white skin to reflect the sun's fierce rays. As I pedalled across the heart of the country's red centre and further, it felt as though my understanding and appreciation for this beautiful but unforgiving environment was advancing to a deeper level. Like the river gums with their protective bark, waxy, moisture-conserving leaves and deep water-drawing roots, we needed to adapt to make the most of it all.

Bark shedding from river gums growing in the bed of the Hull River

During the final 40 km into Docker River, we were treated to some inspiring scenery, an unexpected highlight of the whole expedition. The road divided a broad ancient floodplain through the Petermann Ranges, and the palette of colours it displayed was easily as impressive as that of more famous relatives to the east. Weeping desert oaks were a prevalent feature of the landscape, and in some places it looked as if someone other than Mother Nature had planted the perfect avenue of them which lined the route. Groves of ghost gums contrasted against the red-purple backdrop. We couldn't help ourselves from making several photograph stops. Suddenly we realised the time and had to make a mad dash to the Kaltukatjara Community to catch the store for supplies.

We arrived just after closing time. The Kaltukatjara Community consists of a transient population of about 350 and is administered by thirty-one non-Indigenous staff. As with other communities, there was broken glass everywhere and plenty of puncture-threatening shrapnel to avoid. Greg had phoned ahead to let Richard, the manager, know we were coming and to find out about potential water and food availability. He had already been helpful in assisting us to find the Irving Road bore. We slipped in through the back door of the store and restocked for the next three days to Warburton. As usual, we took the opportunity to make phone calls home and organise things in advance. We learnt a lot about the community during our conversations with Richard, who hailed from Ipswich in the UK. He had come to value the gentle nature and spirit

A grove of desert oaks beside the Petermann Range

of the local Pitjantjatjara people but he was also disheartened by the (alleged) reported misdirection of funds, in this case from the Central Land Council. We heard how a convoy of vehicles containing government officials had arrived recently – unannounced – looking for places to spend the huge budget the Council had been allocated. Richard told us that they had no substantial plans and no long-term goals, and that there appeared to be no active strategy to transfer skills and knowledge to the Indigenous people.

The officials had money and needed to spend it so they could justify receiving the same benefits the following year. As a result, funds were lavished on cosmetic facilities which weren't needed and had no chance of being maintained. To Richard, this band-aid approach was very frustrating when education and health issues were in so much need of attention. In his opinion, there needed to be a more coordinated plan to facilitate self-determination within the community.

We shared the Docker River bush campsite, two kilometres west of the community, with two very interesting women from Sydney. Mary and Judith were spending their retirement years searching for, discovering and cataloguing Indigenous art. They had already been on the road for four months, and when we met them they were returning from the Burrup Peninsula (near Dampier, Western Australia). They were passionate about their subject, still excited about their visit to the site of the greatest density, subject style and diversity of Indigenous art in the world, which I was also planning to visit. Much of the Burrup artwork including 100 000 petroglyphs (rock engravings) at some five hundred sites is yet to be documented. Each year, the pair travels somewhere new to search for art. I really admire their adventurous spirit and hope I have the same enthusiasm for life when I am of retiring age.

Bush tucker: a desert tomato, or *kampurarrpa* to the local Pitjantjatjara people

◆　◆　◆

Eight kilometres from the campsite, we crossed into Western Australia (WA) on the Great Central Road. The amount of time I would be spending in WA, and distance covered, I had calculated as being proportional to the size of the state: around 9000 km and three-and-a-half months in an area bigger than Western Europe. The population of WA, however, is just under two million (1.4 million in Perth and the rest dispersed over the biggest Australian state), in contrast with about 350 million people in Europe.

Judging by the graveyard of abandoned vehicles scattered by the roadside, we weren't the only ones to struggle with the first 50 km of the Great Central Road, which took about four hours for us to tame. The Petermann Ranges veered away to the south-west and an equally spectacular desert range – the Scherwin Mural Crescent – dominated the horizon to the north.

The tough going played havoc with our energy levels. Energy 'bonks' were becoming a regular occurrence so we decided to break the day into slightly shorter sessions and more regular food stops. The persistent cold southerly breeze also increased resistance and contributed to the depleting energy levels. As we were moving more slowly than expected, we decided that it was too late to drop in to the Giles Weather Station that day. Instead, we camped at the nearby Warakurna Roadhouse and postponed our prearranged visit to mainland Australia's most isolated meteorological station until the following morning.

Everything happens for a reason. Also staying at the campsite were the returning members of a successful 4WD expedition to retrace the path of the virtually non-existent Callawa Track. Seventy-two flat tyres and a cracked chassis had tested participants travelling in eight vehicles to the limit. Only three vehicles had made it as far as Warakurna on their way home. The Callawa Track was constructed in 1963, linking the Canning Stock Route with Marble Bar in the Pilbara, but was rarely used and had not been touched for twenty years. We gatecrashed the friendly gathering, who remained tethered to the warmth of their campfire. This was an opportunity to make new friends, and to learn more about our path ahead. We were careful to note the location of reliable watering points and road conditions. A number of the expedition members had years of experience travelling in the region, although not, of course, by bicycle.

Meeting this group was of particular significance for us. A prominent member of the party was Connie Sue Beadell, daughter of Len Beadell. Generally considered as Australia's last great explorer, Len Beadell spent his lifetime surveying, mapping and creating access to a vast portion of the Australian Outback. In 1947, he was assigned an enormous task by the Australian government: to locate and survey the site for a rocket-testing range in northern South Australia which would stretch across the west of Australia almost to the Indian Ocean. The base for the range was a town later named Woomera. As a surveyor, Len was responsible for the initial town survey and launch sites. In the years to follow, he led a gang of roadmakers that created over 6500 km of access roads for scientific observers of various weapons tests. In completing the Callawa Track, Connie Sue had succeeded in travelling every kilometre built by her father.

The Gunbarrel Highway, which we were soon to experience, is the best known of the road network covering the centre line of fire north-west across Australia, from the Woomera Rocket Range to Eighty Mile Beach between Broome and Port Hedland. The network was created to provide access to the more than two-and-a-half million square kilometres of uninhabited desert wilderness. The tracks enabled a ground survey to be carried out to determine the curvature of the earth in that area. Instruments to trace the missiles could then be placed by scientists with exact knowledge of their positions in relation to the launch pads. During the Cold War years of the 1950s, the atomic bomb test sites at Emu Plains and Maralinga in South Australia were also located and laid out by Len Beadell. In all, an astounding quarter of the Australian continent was opened up by Len Beadell and his team. The legacy of the defence program is that the roads are still there for the adventurous to enjoy.

We pushed up the hill to the Giles Weather Station to catch the complimentary tour which starts daily at 8.30am. On our arrival we discovered that the staff were expecting us the previous evening and had arranged for us to stay.

The site of the Giles Weather Station was also selected by Beadell in 1955 to provide vital weather data for Woomera, Maralinga and Emu, first transmitting weather observations by radio on 2 August 1956. Today it is the only staffed weather station in an area of about 2.5 million square kilometres; its location near the core of the sub-tropical jet stream gives it a central role in forecasting and climate measurement over most of eastern and south-eastern Australia, particularly for rain and assessment of severe storms. It is also used for 'local' weather forecasts for places such as Uluru and Alice Springs, or for aircraft operations to Aboriginal communities. As well, Giles provides useful meteorological data in a remote region to the west and north-west of most major population centres of Australia. This data is vital for global and local computer models, and for forecasting, and is particularly useful for international air flights.

Nigel from the Giles Weather Station releasing a weather balloon to measure atmospheric conditions

An instrument which measures daylight at the Giles outdoor laboratory

After a fascinating tour of the station, the manager, Godfrey, asked us back for morning tea in the staff quarters, where four people live at a time during their six-month tours of duty. This was a chance to make contact with Merrick to ensure everything was on track for him and a support vehicle to join me at Wiluna for the start of the Canning Stock Route in two weeks time. Deep down I had been concerned about Merrick's level of commitment. All the same, I felt disappointment when he informed me that he was unable to take part, due to work commitments. Fortunately, he had made contact with Don Walker, an experienced 4WD enthusiast, who had agreed in principle to be the support, so this gave me some peace of mind. I just had to get my head around the concept that I was now going to be cycling alone over the longest, most testing track in Australia. I tried to contact Don without success, and had to be content with waiting until I reached Warburton, still two days away, to sort out the details.

We were eager to hear Giles' analysis of the four-day forecast so we would know what to expect. Heading off towards Warburton, we were satisfied that the prediction had been accurate and were pleased to have a cross-tailwind. About an hour later, we should have phoned the station to correct its forecast. Even with all their knowledge and technology, staff had failed to predict the cross-headwinds which hindered our movements for the next two days. My mind, however, was mostly elsewhere, deliberating the finer points of organisation for the attempt on the Canning Stock Route.

Leaving the hills around Warakurna behind, the open, fairly featureless plains did little to divert these thoughts. The only variation in vegetation came as we passed through thickets of mulga scrub. Greg took to sampling some bush tucker by sucking the honey grevillea flowers to supplement lunch. It would have taken a long time to get a substantial nutritional benefit from the natural sugars! We needed all our energy as the final 230-km stretch to Warburton in very strong winds really knocked us around. After ten days straight, we were showing definite signs of being tired and run-down, not the optimum way of approaching the Gunbarrel Highway, the most difficult challenge of the journey so far. Taking a break in Warburton would allow me to sort out all the usual administration – plus plan Greg's departure from Wiluna, negotiate Don's part in the proceeding leg, allow us to resupply – and have a physical rest.

Despite the fact we had crossed into a new time zone, we decided to stay on Northern Territory time to make the most of the daylight. This meant we arrived in Warburton during office hours and in time to meet the CEO of the shire and arrange use of the council's plush new offices the following day (Saturday). With a population of about 500, Warburton is one of the larger, alcohol-free communities, and on initial appearances looked better kept than some of the others we had visited. Warburton is the headquarters of the Ngaanyatjarra Shire which has a total area of nearly 160 000 square kilometres and a population of 1500, many of whom are scattered among ten minor communities and smaller outstations. It is the shire that we had most trouble gaining permission to travel through, allegedly because of safety concerns.

The Warburton Community started out as a United Aboriginal Mission in 1934 after William Wade had observed Traditional gathering places in several waterholes in the bed of Elder Creek. Wade brought his family out from Laverton (350 km north of Kalgoorlie) and set up a mission station. Originally he chose a site at the Old Well near the meeting places, then relocated the following year to the present town position, five kilometres from Elder Creek.

Initially a trading post and an orphanage were established, but gradually many parents came to leave their children in the care of the missionaries who

Desert weevil (size of a 20-cent piece)

OUT THERE AND BACK

provided an opportunity to attend school. By the early 1960s the Aboriginal parents had decided to care for their children themselves and the mission dormitories were closed, although the school continued. By the mid-1960s, when Aboriginals were moved from the land which was used as the Woomera Rocket Range, the Warburton population expanded to about 500. To relieve the pressure of this increased population, the Docker River Community, where we had visited three days earlier, was developed. In 1973, an Aboriginal Council was formed and incorporated at Warburton and the community took over the administration from the United Aboriginal Mission. Many people returned to Warburton, attracted by the prospect of self-determination, employment opportunities and housing.

It appears that, as with other communities, Warburton is striving to find the best way forward for its people, searching for its place in a Western-dominated world. The issues its residents wrestle with are complex and there are no simple answers. Alarming rates of domestic violence, poor health, illiteracy and vandalism are examples of the problems facing community leaders, symptoms of the past and evidence that there is a long way to go. Cultural-specific initiatives such as those adopted by the Yuendumu elders are testimony to how problems can be solved with the right motivation. To an outside observer, it is obvious that literacy, and participation in sport and Indigenous cultural pursuits such as art, music and dance, are essential for improving motivation and self-image.

I found that when travelling through outback Australia it was impossible not to be affected by visits to Aboriginal communities. It was like opening a can of worms. The more I saw, the more questions I asked and the more complex I realised the various situations are. They raise more questions than answers, but I came to feel that the most important underlying principle is that we all, Aboriginal and non-Aboriginal, must be prepared to understand, compromise and work together to go forward.

◆　◆　◆

It took us quite some time to prepare for our own next move forward, creating enough storage space in my panniers for five days worth of food. Just to be on the safe side, I had catered for a little extra. If the Gunbarrel Highway took more than six days, we would be in trouble and have to rely on the hope that a vehicle would pass. Between us we were carrying 33 litres of water, which would last for two-and-a-half days if we used it frugally. We also carried two extra 10-litre plastic, collapsible water-bags, in case we needed to carry more later on.

We had asked many people about where the reliable water sources were along the way but it was debatable as to whether we had received accurate information. Travellers now use the well-maintained Great Central Road if they need to drive through to Laverton in the WA goldfields and beyond. Anyone taking their 4WD across the original route carries enough water with them, so they don't need to rely on the desert water supply as we did. Our travels to date had shown us that the amount and quality of water in the few bores indicated on our maps varied with the rise and fall of the water-table and the state of repair of each bore. Some water sources we came across weren't shown on our map and some that were marked had dried up.

One person's verbal information on occasions contradicted another's. To find out what we wanted to know we resorted to using techniques we developed back in the Siberian Swamp. To validate the information received we would also ask the informant when they had last travelled the track, what time of year it was and whether they had actually tested the water. What we discovered was that there weren't going to be many opportunities to replenish our water stores during the next stage. Another concern was that all the known sources were located in the eastern half of the 500 km between Warburton and Carnegie.

On advice from the experienced adventurers we had met at Warakurna, I bought a length of rope in the Warburton community store. It was suggested we carry 30–40 metres of rope and an empty baked bean tin to retrieve water from one or two of the bores. Beans were on the menu the first night out from Warburton.

We needed to be self-sufficient and endeavoured to be well prepared. We very much wanted to avoid using the satellite phone to summon help and as it was late in the season, passing vehicles could not be relied on for assistance. An important and logical precaution was to tell people at either end of our plans and timing. Carnegie knew to expect us in five days. At Warburton, the manager, Kevin, knew to mention to anyone travelling the Gunbarrel to look out for us. In the light of prior failures, particularly of mad Japanese cyclists attempting to cross the Gunbarrel totally ill-prepared in mid-summer, locals tended to be sceptical about our plans. They told us of one fellow who was found dying of thirst, sitting in a pool of water he wouldn't drink because it was 'a bit brown'.

Heading off, our bikes were so heavy that their normally rigid aluminium frames flexed as we manoeuvred them. The first section of the journey down to Steptoe's Turnoff wasn't too bad and the weight of our load seemed to iron out the corrugations somewhat.

Surveying the landscape at Steptoe's Turnoff

A few kilometres out of Warburton, we passed the turn-off to the southern section of the Connie Sue Highway, marked by a rusty 44-gallon drum. The track was part of Len Beadell's network, named after his daughter whom we had just met. We soon had a mind-numbing 360-degree view of nothing. Coming from England where hilly fertile landscapes are heavily populated and on a much smaller, even claustrophobic scale, Greg felt as if he was on another planet. With nothing in the landscape to stimulate the thought processes, the mind tends to wander, and if we were not careful to keep it busy with an interesting train of thought, we were likely to suffer a terrible affliction – annoying songs would get stuck in our heads, choruses revolving as if played on a scratched vinyl record. Unfortunately for Greg, passing the Connie Sue Highway started up Buddy Holly's *Peggy Sue*, which continued to haunt him for most of the Gunbarrel. (Apologies to any Buddy Holly fans.) Not wishing to suffer alone, he attempted to infect me with lines from similarly annoying songs.

At Steptoe's Turnoff, we headed north on to the Heather Highway, named after the daughter of David and Margaret Hewitt, whom we had also met back at Warakurna. The first 48 km of the road was fairly well maintained as it served the Tjirrkarli Community. We paused at the junction for a snack break and to absorb the sensation of being surrounded by space. Leaving the relative safety of the Great Central Road, we were buoyed by a 'Grader Ahead' sign but there was no evidence of the grader's work as we traversed large, semi-permanent sand ridges. It was obvious that the sizeable ridges had been stable for a long time as they were bound by rocks and mature, stunted vegetation.

A third of the way along the 'good' section, we caught the grader and stopped to lunch with Darren, the driver, and his partner, Natasha. They probably knew many of the outback roads better than most as Darren was employed to maintain them. It was going to take three to four weeks to grade the 100-km stretch from Steptoe's Turnoff to the community.

Darren stoked up their smouldering campfire to boil water for tea. Their bush kettle, or billy, was fashioned from an old, blackened tin that had once held Sunshine brand dried milk. The handle was an extra-long piece of wire. A rudimentary frame had been built over the fire-place to hang the billy above the flames. Once the water boiled, Darren simply threw in a handful of tea leaves which were scalded before he removed the billy from the fire with a stick to let the tea brew for a few minutes. This, Darren declared, was the only way to make proper billy tea. This scene was symbolic of the simple lifestyle the young couple had chosen. They seemed happy living in a caravan, moving from one road camp to another with few of the mod cons we take for granted and only a puppy for extra company. Natasha topped up our water-bottles and we moved on.

The ancient sand ridges made a roller-coaster of our path. It was tempting to get up speed on the descents, but the brief pleasure of wind in our faces and ease of free-wheeling was balanced by first hitting the bumps, usually halfway down, and then the sand which had washed into the depressions. We had to be careful not to let things go past a point of no return or our journey could end in disaster.

Each hill formed a blind crest. Fortunately, being out in the elements meant we could hear everything coming. As usual, we used the whole road to find the best pathway. Luckily on the alert on one crest, I just managed to scramble back across to the left as we met a convoy of 4WD vehicles head on. The occupants were a group of Polish adventurers partway through their 'Strzelecki Traces Expedition'. They had just conquered the Gunbarrel and were optimistic about our chances of succeeding. The general consensus was that it was very rough but there wasn't much sand.

Boiling the billy
(photo: G Yeoman)

I was a little puzzled as to why the Poles were crossing the western and central deserts when Paul Edmund Strzelecki spent four important years of his life exploring south-eastern Australia. The Count, as he was often called because his name was too difficult for Australians to pronounce, is most famous for discovering and naming in 1840 Mt Kosciuszko (Australia's highest peak) after a Polish general. He published his many geological and scientific discoveries, observations and theories on agricultural potential in a 460-page tome imaginatively entitled *Physical Description of New South Wales*. I learnt that the Count claimed to be the first to discover gold in Victoria but was asked to keep it secret by Governor Gipps, for fear of the anarchy that would surely break out at news of a gold strike (which is what did happen when a gold discovery was broadcast in the early 1850s). In honour of Strzelecki's work, a number of famous explorers in subsequent years named various features after him, such as the Strzelecki Desert, Ranges, National Park, Regional Reserve, Track and even a koala.

A main purpose of the Poles' expedition was to link these sites, but that didn't explain why they were on the Heather Highway. The reason turned out to be that they had arranged to meet with members of the Polish-Australian community across the country and relate the spirit of Strzelecki to the large number of fellow-countrymen and women who had adopted Australia as their home, especially as refugees after World War II. One of their intentions was to nominate Strzelecki as a patron of the Polish-Australian community.

I could relate to this particular purpose of their expedition because my home town, Northam, still has a significant Polish population. A refugee camp was stationed there after 1945, processing thousands of displaced persons. They were my best customers for my cow and sheep manure loads, and I remember my father being treated on occasions to a tipple of fine Polish whiskey.

◆   ◆   ◆

Our map stipulated that the northern section of the Heather Highway was 'very corrugated'. This was an ominous sign as none of the roads we had travelled prior to this carried such a label. The second section of the Heather Highway and the first section of the Gunbarrel were the only roads on the map to carry this warning.

The reason for the warnings was immediately evident as we turned north on to the second half of the Heather Highway. The word 'highway' is highly misleading and probably should be renamed as the 'only way'. We followed the two wheel tracks of 4WDs, which were indeed heavily corrugated; in addition to our own discomfort, traversing the washboard-like path put worrying stress on the equipment. Bananas and tomatoes had to be especially well packed.

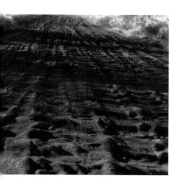

The 'only way' through. A typical Gunbarrel surface

Initially our route followed an ancient sand ridge which was rough but solid. All concentration was on the few metres ahead of the front wheel, in order to avoid rocks and constantly search for smoother ground. Occasionally there was a gap between the spinifex and the wheel rut and I would try to stay on this line as long as possible, making faster and more comfortable progress. But I would usually slip into the deeper tyre track which would draw me into the bumps like a magnet. On the higher ground, there was often more than one option. In order to avoid the shocking condition of the official track, 4WD vehicles had ventured into the spinifex and created new paths. This is frowned upon by those concerned with the environmental impact, but as I didn't think two bicycle tracks would make any difference, we took advantage of even a slight improvement in surface.

Descending from the higher ground introduced us to the surface we quickly learned to dread the most. A fine type of shale washed off the plains causing a deep, structure-less layer of grit. Powered vehicles sculptured the grit into severe corrugations and the track into deep channels. Our laden bikes sank into the surface and even though our balloon-like tyres were the right choice, we struggled to find traction. It was like pushing through a heavy type of sand. The weight on the bikes made a huge difference to our workload: had we been travelling with the aid of a support vehicle and suspension, we would have been able to skim over much of this type of surface. As it was, many patches of lower ground were simply unable to be cycled over and we could only hope there wasn't too much of this type of surface on the Gunbarrel or we would fall behind schedule and run out of supplies.

The original Gunbarrel joined Victory River Downs Station near the Stuart Highway (south of where we turned off along the Lasseter Highway to Uluru) and then passed through Giles Weather Station to Carnegie Station, 1500 km west. Carnegie was chosen to be the western terminus because it was the most easterly station in central Western Australia already linked to the Western Australian road system. We were unable to obtain permission to cycle unsupported along the 'Old Gunbarrel' section from Giles past the Rawlinson Ranges, then north of Warburton to the T-junction where we joined the route.

Arriving at the Gunbarrel was exciting as we had been gearing ourselves up for the challenge for so long. For Greg, it would be the finale to his journey. Many of those who had driven the Gunbarrel looked upon our attempt to cross the Gibson Desert with guarded respect. Although we felt we had prepared well, we would have preferred to have more knowledge of reliable water sources before setting out on this phase. We paused to photograph the sign at the T-junction with the Heather Highway which pointed to Wiluna, 720 km to the west.

Len Beadell's brief for construction of the great road network was to keep the roads as straight as possible to minimise the fuel needed to travel them. With this in mind, he named his team of seven men the Gunbarrel Road Construction Party (GRCP) after the design of the roads they were to survey and build. In honour of the GRCP, Beadell named the first link between Central Australia and the West the Gunbarrel Highway. Once surveyed, a signal was given for Doug Stoneham, the bulldozer driver, to head straight for the next surveyed point. The grader then followed, covering each section of road five times. The GRCP usually covered eight kilometres a day.

We were attempting to cover about 80 km a day, give or take, depending on the most appropriate-looking camping locations on our map. By all reports, the Gunbarrel had rarely been touched by maintenance vehicles and no grader had serviced the straight orange strip for at least twenty or thirty years. Even if the going was worse than expected, we could keep chipping away at the task from dawn to dusk to make the desired distance. We followed the track which had been scraped through the scrub as straight its name suggests. The only diversions were to avoid the regular washouts or shockingly surfaced sections. Our first short-term goal was Beadell Tree, eleven kilometres from the turn-off.

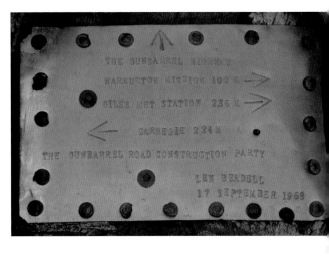

As the desert is unable to support much more than the usual stunted scrub, the mature bloodwood tree provides a notable landmark. The Beadell Tree was used as one of the survey markers. We leant our bikes against its trunk and studied the original aluminium plaque while taking advantage of rare shade. The GRCP had passed through on 17 September 1958.

Plaque nailed to Len Beadell's tree

Our research revealed there was a bore about 500 metres south-west of the road. Reports received from our different sources suggested we would find water of debatable quality, somewhere between good and barely drinkable. We followed the obvious path back into the bush and found the hand pump. At this stage we weren't desperate, but needed to keep on top of the situation because water supplies ahead would be scarce. So we unloaded all our bottles and bags and Greg started pumping – without reward. At that moment I heard the sound of vehicles. Sensing an opportunity, I leapt on my bike and raced back to Beadell Tree at the junction, hoping to catch the occupants as they stopped to investigate the historical landmark. It was just as well I did hurry as they weren't planning to visit the bore. One of the vehicles had punctured a fuel tank on the Heather Highway and so the travellers, from Queensland, were forced to keep moving fairly swiftly. After establishing that they could give us water, I cycled back to fetch Greg. He had been pumping continuously for ten minutes with no result.

Not only were we able to replenish the 33 litres, but even more importantly we arranged for the Queenslanders to drop water for us at Geraldton Bore, our intended destination two days down the track. We tested the first of the 10-litre bags we carried spare for such a situation and found it to leak. This was extremely frustrating as it had virtually never been used. Our new friends took the other bag and another 1.5-litre water-bottle and promised to leave them at the bore. If all went to plan, this would relieve some of the worries about having enough water for the last couple of days out from Carnegie Station.

The track quality deteriorated into deep sand away from Beadell Tree. Although there were sand ridges drawn in on the map, this was worse than we had imagined. The Polish people, who had just driven over this section when we met them, didn't think it was too bad or went on for very long. They, however, were not cycling with an extra 50 kg that forced the two thin wheels to sink further into the sand. There were plenty of times on the expedition when I had little directional control of the bike, but on the Gunbarrel there was just a single track to ride on and nothing else. An attempt to find better ground often resulted in crashing against the encroaching spinifex; thankfully, my panniers would mostly protect my legs from being spiked and scratched.

Occasionally I risked becoming too friendly with the sharp spines. At one point I misjudged the compactness of the ground and landed fair on top of a spinifex bush. The sand had given way without warning, and I had no chance to free my feet from the toe-clips. Fortunately for Greg, he was too far ahead of me to hear the verbal abuse I heaped on that hummock of spiky grass which had made me an instant human pin cushion. Needles had pierced my clothing and skin, including a splinter embedded in my lip; I was fortunate not to receive anything in my eyes. It was often difficult to remove the whole of the spines, as the tip would snap off and remain beneath the skin, leaving it prone to infection.

Reunited and exasperated, Greg and I ate lunch under the shade of a stunted mulga bush, sitting on a sand bank on the edge of the track. Dragging our wheels over the sand and especially up the dunes was exhausting. It was evident that we would not make our goal – Camp Beadell – and we were concerned about the prospect of falling behind schedule. The days were warming up too, and in addition to the problem of slow progress, we were consuming more water than usual.

Back in the saddle, heads were down most of the time. Greg explained later that it was just as well that I was far enough behind not to hear the unmentionable expletives flowing past his lips. The Poles weren't popular as their description of the route had given false expectations. Pushing the loaded bikes was particularly awkward because trying to keep the wheels on the firmest part of the ruts meant we had to step on the soft bank, which was like walking through dry beach sand. Leaning across and down to push on the handlebars caused constant backache, and my steps were stunted as stride length was restricted by the front and rear panniers. Greg being taller was able to lean over further and walk more freely, but this probably put more pressure on his back. As soon as the road appeared rideable, we would try to pedal, as any form of cycling was quicker than walking. Getting started, though, was extremely difficult. Even if the surface looked like an improvement, the corrugations threw us off balance.

The next short-term target was Thryptomene Hill, first discovered by David Carnegie in 1897. Being so engrossed in our struggle, we barely noticed it as any more than a giant sand dune. Such an unremarkable blimp on the landscape would not normally have been noteworthy, but out on the edge of the Gibson Desert a feature like a decent tree, or a slight rise above the plain, was recorded by those who first explored the country. Thryptomene Hill also signified that we didn't have too much sand dune country to go.

Our map showed that there was a bore marked at the edge of the sandy country which no one had mentioned and so we had assumed it to be dry. Greg noticed water in its drip tray and pumped experimentally; after two pumps, out gushed water – brackish, but we drank it anyway, and collected some for cooking. No matter how much I gulped down, though, the high mineral content seemed to induce a greater thirst and the tepid temperature also meant it was not very satisfying. Off the sand, we found ourselves traversing a flat plain and

Struggling in the sand near Thryptomene Hill
(photo: G Yeoman)

Making bricks of damper
(photo: G Yeoman)

Exhausted at the end to
Day 2 on the Gunbarrel
with only 60 km done; slow
going in a tedious 'kitty
litter' section

back into the shale. Pushing on for another few kilometres, we decided to be
content with stopping 28 km short of our original goal. Going any further would
have compromised our ability to recover for the following day. We had only
managed 60 km in a full day.

I built a camp fire which provided warmth as the temperature plummeted
with the setting sun. The embers were also vital, as I now had to cook damper
each night. I combined flour, water, olive oil and salt in the smaller cooking pot,
divided the dough into even portions and nestled them over the glowing coals.
It was a perfect opportunity to write my diary in the warmth as the damper
roasted. Having only practised making this Aussie staple once before, back in
Kakadu, my first attempt on the Gunbarrel to replace our daily bread resembled
the rocks we encountered the following day!

◆　◆　◆

We woke next morning to the chilling howls of dingoes in the distance. Then I
noticed a camel approaching, Normally this wouldn't be a concern, but as the
bellowing beast drew nearer, we identified it as a young, in-season male
behaving erratically and frothing at the mouth. We kept very still as it passed
without noticing us. Knowing that bull camels when in-season aren't selective
about their affections, we laid low to avoid being humped by a randy, hormone-
drunk dromedary.

Optimistic dreams that we would wake to find a smooth, solid track were
immediately dashed. We started our third day from Warburton as we had
finished the previous one: pushing on the corrugated mess of tiny pebbles. We
had planned to reach Geraldton Bore by the end of the third day, but because of
the previous day of slow progress, we realised that achieving 120 km in one day
on the Gunbarrel was an unrealistic goal, unless conditions dramatically changed.
At least we were able to pause to appreciate a sweeping panoramic view from
Notabilis Hill, which we climbed with less effort than the previous mound. Our
first destination was Camp Beadell, where we had hoped to stay the previous
night. It took about two-and-a-half hours to cover 28 km as we were violently
shaken about on a continuous washboard surface, brushing past spinifex and
ducking and weaving around bushes which infringed on our path.

Preparing the bean tin to try to scoop up water from the Camp Beadell bore

Again, we were unsure what the state of the bore and water quality would be. We were pleased to discover that the capped PVC-cased bore had been tested only six days prior. The good news was the water quality was high. The bad news was the water level was 57 metres down.

Fortunately I had bought 50 metres of nylon rope, rather than the 30 metres which had been suggested, and with our washing line attached, it was just long enough to reach, with a bit of a stretch. Greg's scouting prowess came in useful as he attached the bean tin. We put a small stone in the bottom and lowered the container down the shaft. Even with the weight in the tin, we failed to scoop up any water. The next technique was to punch a small hole in the base of the tin. The problem with this, we found, was that we couldn't withdraw the tin back up the 57-metre shaft in time to garner more water than would fill an egg-cup. We needed about eight litres.

Greg remembered he had a bag made of water-resistant material, the circumference of which appeared to be no greater than the bore casing. Placing a few stones in the bag, he lowered it down and could hear it filling. Retrieving it was another matter. The bag had expanded with the weight of the water to a circumference greater than the bore hole and became lodged in the pipe. As we tried to hoist it up, the snug fit had caused a vacuum between the water level and the bag.

The struggle was akin to playing tug-o-war. Greg did most of the lifting and I acted as an anchor with the rope wrapped around my waist and hands a couple of times. As Greg hauled the rope up vertically one or two feet at a time, I took a step backwards. The nylon rope stretched to an eventual length much greater than 50 metres, and cut into our hands; our cycle gloves came in handy in protecting us from rope burns. By the time we finally succeeded in retrieving the bag, I had ended up way back in the bush. The outcome of this exhausting half-hour of heaving was that we collected about two litres of water.

While water of this quality was valuable, we decided we had expended time and energy which could have been better spent moving forwards as our food supplies were now limited. Although we had water at Geraldton Bore awaiting us, our information suggested there was another unmarked bore with brackish water – good enough for cooking – before Everard Junction.

We pushed on with Mount Beadell in our sights. To our delight, the road was solid and very rocky in places. The uneven rocks and washouts are treacherous for 4WD vehicles but anything solid was better for our more versatile set-up. We ate lunch at the base of Mt Beadell, the most prominent land feature between Warburton and Carnegie. Len Beadell obviously thought this hill was remarkable as it prompted one of the few serious kinks in his road design. The achievements of the 'Last Great Explorer' are honoured here by a cairn and replica theodolite. Lunch included tinned tuna, a tomato and damper. The bricks of damper took some chewing, but were very sustaining.

We made relatively good progress on the rocky sections – fall-out from the ancient crumbling range. This raised our expectations of reaching Everard Junction, 56 km from Mt Beadell, by nightfall. Our plans soon altered as we descended to the plains and were confronted by more soft grit. Partway along a particularly bad section we met a convoy of five 4WD vehicles whose occupants hailed from the Geraldton 4WD Club. This was a welcome opportunity to replenish supplies and obtain accurate information about the track ahead. Travelling from the west, the party had met with the Queenslanders we had encountered earlier who verified that they had placed our water supply at Geraldton Bore. We also found out that we had plenty more of this terrible road to negotiate, and spent the remainder of the day pushing and pedalling through more of the same, keeping an eye out for the bore which was supposed to be on our right-hand side. It never materialised, leading us to believe it was probably the hand pump we had found unexpectedly near Thryptomene Hill. We did note a sign informing us that we had crossed into the Gibson Desert Nature Reserve, but didn't notice any difference in the landscape.

Shadows cast by the spinifex in the low, early evening light made it difficult to see the darkened track. But camped that night on a disused, washed-out section of road, 15 km short of our destination, we were awed by one of the most spectacular sunsets of the journey so far. On the domestic and personal hygiene front we didn't have much to do – our water conservation mode meant no washing, cleaning cooking pots or even spitting after cleaning our teeth. Another advantage of cooking couscous, other than water conservation, was that dishes were easy to clean. We used dry sand to 'clean' the pots because it is abrasive and absorbs moisture. As I sat by the fire, cooking the damper, I attempted to operate on the infected splinters of spinifex embedded under my skin. Another problem was that my finger knuckles had become chapped in the hot, dry atmosphere. One had opened up, becoming raw and cracked – plasters didn't stay on long enough to provide protection for it to heal.

The reason for being extremely frugal with water usage was that the only guaranteed water we had was the eleven and-a-half litres dropped at Geraldton

Sunset, Day 3 campsite near the southern boundary of the Gibson Desert Nature Reserve

Bore to get us the 250 km to Carnegie. In the worst case scenario, if we didn't meet any vehicles, we only had about 35 litres for three days of thirsty work.

Our various discomforts and concerns about having enough water and food pale into insignificance in comparison with the experiences of Ernest Giles, during his first attempt to cross the centre of the continent in 1874. With his companion, Alf Gibson, and four horses he set off west of the Petermann Ranges on a line similar to the first stage of the Old Gunbarrel Highway, passing through the Rawlinson Range to Lake Christopher and then due west. A chain of mishaps led to the explorers becoming drastically short of water and food. They reached a location which nowadays would be approximately on the eastern edge of the Gibson Nature Reserve, about 130 km north-east of our present position, and were forced to make a hard decision.

> The hills to the west (which Giles named the Alfred and Marie Range) were twenty-five to thirty miles away, and it was with extreme regret I was compelled to relinquish a farther attempt to reach them. Oh, how ardently I longed for a camel! How ardently I gazed upon this scene! At this moment I would even my jewel eternal have sold for power to span the gulf that lay between! But it could not be, situated as I was; compelled to retreat – of course with the intention of coming again with a larger supply of water – now the sooner I retreated the better.

With a pint of water and only one horse left between them, Giles sent Gibson ahead on horseback to safety and to raise the alarm. That was the last he saw of his mate, and Giles named the desert in honour of his lost companion. Travelling mostly by moonlight, Giles described his solo struggle on foot through the spinifex.

> ...My arms, legs and thighs, both before and behind, were so punctured with spines, it was agony only to exist; the slightest movement and in went more spines, where they broke off in the clothes and the flesh, causing the whole body that was punctured to gather into minute pustules, which were continually growing and bursting. My clothes, especially inside my trousers, were a perfect mass of prickly points.

A man of immense fortitude, Giles miraculously made it back to the waterhole known as the Circus and drank to his heart's content. He had long since finished his last strips of smoked horse meat and, having relieved his thirst, was overcome with burning hunger. Starving and footsore, he crawled away from the waterhole and heard a faint squeak.

> ...and looking about I saw, and immediately caught, a small dying wallaby, whose marsupial mother had evidently thrown it away from her pouch. It only weighed about two ounces, and was scarcely furnished yet with fur. The instant I saw it, like an eagle I pounced upon it and ate it, living, raw, dying – fur, skin, bones, skull and all. The delicious taste of that creature I shall never forget. I only wished I had its mother and father to serve in the same way.

The tiny wallaby tipped the balance from death to life and Giles made it a further 30 km back to safety, nine days after he had last seen Gibson. The following year he successfully traversed the continent south of his first attempt in a region he called the Great Victoria Desert.

Mt Everard, part of the Browne Range, provided more rocky sections which would have given any skilled mountain biker much pleasure. (I would never consider myself in this category.) Then it was back to the shale surface which Greg aptly described as 'kitty litter'. Mostly I could stay upright on it and turn the pedals, but not without a fight.

Everard Junction is where the Gary Highway meets its southern end, making a T-junction with the Gunbarrel. Nearly 200 km north of Everard Junction, the Gary Highway meets the Talawana Track at Windy Corner. The Talawana Track runs parallel with the Gunbarrel, forming part of the Canning Stock Route (between Wells 22 and 24) and then continues all the way to Newman in the Pilbara region. Everard Junction consists of an old Beadell marker set in tyres and a lectern containing a visitors' book. We recorded our passing and left one of our postcards for future travellers to read. Many of them, I am sure, will wonder how we managed to get there as their vehicles were shaken to pieces.

At our first break of the day, it was time to delve into a family pack of fruit and nuts which I had been carrying since Katherine. We were reminded of the incident on the day we left The Granites goldmine, when a can of WD-40 lubricant had leaked through one of my panniers. We had one kilogram of tainted fruit and nuts to work our way through. At least the nasty flavour stopped us from devouring our energy food too quickly.

The piste greeting us at the beginning of Day 4, just south of Mt Everard

From Everard Junction, we had a further 32 km to go to reach to our water supply at Geraldton Bore. The party we had met the previous day had mentioned they had heard our second 10-litre waterbag had leaked, so we just had to hope our benefactors had been able to fix it. Surely they wouldn't leave us with nothing. We certainly could not afford a situation such as we had experienced back at the Flinders River. I tried to ration my water intake a little, but was conscious that water requirements were greater in the warmer weather we were experiencing, and that not drinking enough would compromise my health. Conditions remained defiant and we required two rest/food stops to sustain us along the way. On the second break we tore open my second attempt at damper and poured the now molten peanut butter over the dough. Although I had managed to burn the base, this effort was certainly an improvement on the previous doorstops.

We were relieved to arrive at Geraldton Bore, optimistic that our friends hadn't left us high and dry. Locating the water was like a treasure hunt. We found a note addressed to the 'Pushbike People, 14/9/2004' attached to the bore casing – identical to the type of structure at Camp Beadell. The note read:

Dear Kate and Greg, Sorry but 10 Ltr container got a hole in it. Left you 25 Ltrs to refill your containers. If you stand in front of the bore sign and walk straight ahead in a westerly direction you will find. Have a good trip.
Regards, The Convoy.

Excited and relieved at the news, I promptly headed off in a direction 90 degrees to the west, until Greg corrected me. The sturdy plastic container had been hidden under a bush. We drank as much as we could without making ourselves sick and topped up all our water vessels. In all, we used two-thirds of the container and left the remainder under a shady tree with a dated note for someone else to use if they were desperate. It would have been all too easy to get comfortable here as it was a great campsite, but we needed to move on. We conceded that we required a sixth day to reach Carnegie, and we had to keep going to make it before our food ran out.

Fixing a puncture under the shade of the lone bloodwood tree blazed as a marker on the western edge of the Gibson Desert Nature Reserve
(photo: G Yeoman)

As we left Geraldton Bore, I noticed a slow puncture and pushed on a few hundred metres to change the tube under the sparse shade of a lonely, dying tree. As it turned out, the old bloodwood on the western edge of the Gibson Desert Nature Reserve was another of the special landmarks chosen by Beadell. The original plaque, as had happened to many, had been stolen but an Australian Geographic Society expedition, which included Connie Sue Beadell, had replaced the original blaze and plaque a couple of years previously.

The unbending road could be viewed as far as the horizon, the rusty-coloured line the sole disruption to the open, golden plains in the late afternoon. We only managed a further 20 km after the long break. So weary by the time we had selected a bush campsite after another turbulent day of being thrown around and falling off numerous times to become entangled in more spinifex, I wished the WD-40 lubricant could have seeped through to my aching joints. My knees refused to bend as they had been overworked absorbing all the shocks. At least we could now afford enough water for the simple pleasure of a wash. My washing technique had become so efficient that I used less than a quarter of a drink bottle to clean the most important parts. We were a long way from a Russian *banya*.

Having a good time on the Gunbarrel
(photos: G Yeoman)

A few kilometres into the next day and we hit the Wiluna Shire boundary, about 500 km east of the town. To our delight, reports of the track being graded

were true. Although the surface still deteriorated into bad patches, we were generally able to move at a reasonable pace.

At our first break, we were caught up by two 4WD vehicles. Denise and Bill, Yvonne and Wally hailed from the Riverina region in South Australia. They had travelled the Old Gunbarrel section and reported that the surface was easily as good as the part we had travelled, if not better. It turned out the couples had been following our tracks for days, amazed that we travelled almost as quickly as they had. They had read our entry in the visitors' book at Everard Junction and seen our note at Geraldton Bore. Denise and Yvonne noticed the state of my finger and were able to do some running repairs on it, as well as dig out the spinifex spikes. The fresh, home-grown oranges they donated to our cause were a luxury. After this welcome encounter, we swapped contact details and resumed our struggle. They promised to let Carnegie Station know that we were going to arrive a day late and not to be concerned.

A rare encounter with passing traffic
(photo: G Yeoman)

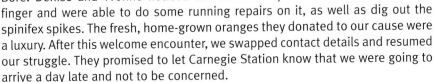

The dried, fragmented mud of the Mungilli Claypan glistened in the heat haze under the midday sun. The barren, fractured surface of the ephemeral wetland resembled shattered windscreen glass, making it was hard to imagine how this nature reserve springs into life at any sign of rain. In fact, the area can become impassable and has the potential to consume vehicles like quicksand.

While the name The Oval evokes images of the hallowed, manicured turf of the famous London venue of the same name, the Oval nestled in the corner of the land belonging to the Mungilli outstation on the Gunbarrel Highway, near the Mungilli Claypan, couldn't have been more of a contrast. The term 'the ashes' at this Oval could have only referred to the remnants of Indigenous fire management. The four randomly pointing rusty goal posts which still stood at the far end are testimony that the favoured game of the locals is Australian Rules football rather than cricket. This Oval was void of any activity except for a willy willy which funnelled dust skywards moving like a random gas molecule over the bare ground. Gaining strength, it swept by the shell of a burnt out car before dissipating in the scrub.

Dried mud on the Mungilli Claypan

Despite moving back into sand dune territory, we generally pedalled at a more satisfying speed and nearly clocked a century. It was just as well that we were in range of Carnegie Station on the sixth day as we had run our food stores down to nothing. Rationing out the last few biscuits, we had just enough to make it without chomping into live wallabies! On the positive side, this meant that our loads were significantly lighter.

Suddenly we had arrived back in station country. Cattle trails formed little gullies across the road where they followed a well-worn path in single file. Hitting one bump too many caused my back wheel to pop a spoke. I couldn't complain as it was my first broken spoke after nearly 12 000 km. I spent my lunch break under a shady tree by Watertree Bore, the most easterly water source on Carnegie Station, trying to fix the problem. Greg was the mechanical expert but soon I would be on my own and have to deal with all breakdowns. While I had changed spokes before, I had never dealt with the added obstacle of disc brakes. The disc was located in a position that prevented the loose spoke from being threaded through the spoke hub and up into the rim where it screws into a nipple. As we weren't carrying the special key required to remove the disc, it was a matter of bending the replacement spoke a few times in order to thread it through the gaps, in the process weakening the tensile strength of the wire. Once the spoke was replaced, it was essential to true the wheel, so there was less than a millimetre of deviation in the rim, otherwise the chances of another spoke going were too great. I wasn't very confident that the temporary job would last as it did all the way to Wiluna.

Spotting a windmill head spinning in the breeze above the level of the bush was the first indication that we had made it to the homestead, the most easterly outpost in central Western Australia. Warburton was 500 km to the east and Wiluna 350 km or three days ride to the west. We had conquered the worst of it! A shower was high on the list of priorities, although there was barely time to relax, what with punctured tubes to repair, telephoning, cooking, writing, and organising to restock with enough basic provisions to get to Wiluna.

Greg had made contact with Wongawol Station 130 km away and this became the goal of the next challenging day's ride. The season had suddenly changed as temperatures regularly reached at least 35°C in the shade and the nights had lost their chill. Just as the road started to improve, after Niminga Well at the turn-off to Glenayle Station and an alternative way on to the Canning Stock Route (which joins in at Well 9), the headwind sprang into opposition. The bore signifies the boundary between Carnegie Station and the one-million-hectare (2.4 million acre) Wongawol Station, which we would travel through for the next 200 km.

Throats were dry as we arrived at Mingol Camp, an outstation belonging to Wongawol, set beside a stunning oasis. The steep-sided banks of the clear green billabong were fringed with weeping river gums and the waterhole was noisy with squawking galahs, sulphur-crested cockatoos and twenty-eight (Port Lincoln) parrots. Turtles resided in the cool waters. I removed my shoes, balanced on the buttress of a tree root, dangled my feet into the revitalising water, washed my face and then splashed more water over most of my body. At least there were no concerns about crocodiles. Near the water's edge was a real micro-environment, but once I had climbed back up the bank and ventured a few metres away, any moisture was immediately evaporated by the dry north-easterly wind. Back on the road, we kept our heads down as we were knocked about by unfriendly gusts. Skirting the northern edge of salt-encrusted barren Lake Carnegie, we were totally exposed, and appreciated the occasional protection of clumps of scrub.

The intense midday sun had been affecting us badly in recent days. One sign of this was that we needed significantly more water. Our routine changed to incorporate an hour-and-a-half of rest during the heat of the day. After lunch, we both lay on the shadecloth which doubled as a tablecloth and closed our eyes for a brief siesta.

The last few kilometres into Wongawol in a growing dusk were basically a blind run. The diffused glow from my head torch meant it was impossible to distinguish obstacles and potholes. Earlier we had lost time: it was my turn to snap the bracket connecting the rear rack to the bike-frame, as Greg had done in Kakadu. We just kept pedalling towards a light in the distance.

At the homestead we were welcomed by John and Laurie Snell and joined them for a well-earned beer. I was interested to find out whether we were related, given that they shared their surname with my great-great-uncle and we were arriving into his territory. We ascertained that any relationship must be

Spencer Snell confronting a distressed cow, Wongawol Station

very distant. John, Laurie and their adult son, Spencer, live on their farm near Waroona, south of Perth. They travel over 1000 km up to Wongawol for about six weeks annually for mustering. The cattle are sorted and some are sent to the rich pastures and feed lots of their Waroona property to be prepared for market.

The Snell family's hospitality was very much appreciated. As I lay in my first bed since Alice Springs, my stomach so full of lasagne and trifle that my heart and lungs felt like they had been displaced upwards, I contemplated what we had just achieved and what was ahead of me. The good company and food and a bed temporarily numbed memories of the hardships of the previous eighteen days, however I was anxious about the transition ahead – Greg leaving and Don, my support driver for the Canning Stock Route, arriving. I had never met Don and hoped he would arrive on time with all the provisions.

Our aim on Greg's penultimate day was to at least reach the edge of the Snell's property. Our legs were completely worn-out as we traversed the Princess Ranges and we were glad to have a break at the cattle-yards by Wongawol Creek. Spencer and the jackeroos were working the yards – drafting, tagging and sorting the mixed mob. Some were off to greener pastures and a milder climate while others were sent back out to the bush.

All elements seemed to be against our flailing bodies. We battled on a chopped-up road, into the wind, through monotonous bushland and in consistent heat. We decided to stop early at Leaman's Bore on the edge of the Snell's property, 102 km from the Wongawol homestead, to relax and enjoy Greg's last night under the stars. Camping near a water source meant we didn't need to carry extra water further down the track for cooking and washing.

We chose a site a short distance away from the water trough so we didn't impede animal access. It was a case of avoiding the redback spiders while splashing breathtakingly cold water straight from the pipe over my body. I could hear kangaroos bounding towards the nearby trough as I walked back to the tent in the dark. After Greg's last meal of packet pasta bulked up with extra pasta, he lay back to appreciate the clear, star-filled, southern night sky one more time.

The final lunch – sardines, wilted carrot and dry bread – was difficult to swallow
(photo: G Yeoman)

The most memorable part of the final day's journey into Wiluna was lunch, but not for the right reasons. All we had left was a can of sardines, which we mushed up and spread on dried-up slices of bread with slices of old, wilting carrot. Void of moisture and taste, the result was an effort to swallow. Our siesta was interrupted when the occupants of two heavy vehicles – one truck carrying water, the other drilling equipment – stopped to talk. The men were returning from exploratory drilling near the Canning Stock Route. The vehicles were reaching the route by travelling along the superior roads of Glenayle Station and entering the track at Well 9. As usual, the men couldn't comprehend what we were doing. Our detailed experiences and close connection with the land through which we had cycled were on another level; our approaches were very different.

We paused to celebrate the start of the five-kilometre strip of tarmac. It felt as though someone had rolled out the red carpet to signify our arrival into Wiluna and civilisation. Greg celebrated the end of his rough journey by lying on the bitumen. We polished off the last of the tainted fruit and nuts and rolled on into the outback town. After four months on the road, we had again managed to arrive exactly on time.

Wiluna, the most northern of the WA goldfield towns, has a long and colourful history. The site was discovered by explorer and surveyor Lawrence Wells in 1892, and developed after the discovery of gold at Lake Way in 1896; it also served as a centre for pastoralism. By the mid-1930s, the population had grown to over 9000 people. At its peak, the town had a regular railway service to Perth, four hotels and many other amenities and facilities.

These days Wiluna, gateway to both the Gunbarrel Highway and the Canning Stock Route, retains little of its heyday glory. Most of the buildings of the gold rush era did not survive when the mines closed, and by the 1960s the

Civilisation: arriving at the Club Hotel, Wiluna
(photo: G Yeoman)

OUT THERE AND BACK

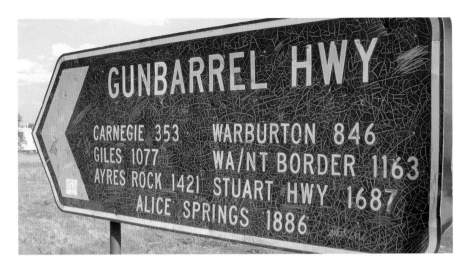

A very long way from Alice Springs
(photo: G Yeoman)

population had dropped to about ninety. Although goldmining restarted in 1981, the mining community now exists self-sufficiently from the town. In recent years, the population of the town of Wiluna has stabilised at about 300, including a large Indigenous population. Three times as many men as women live there.

The sign 'Welcome to Paradise' greeted us as we arrived outside The Club Hotel in a pleasantly exhausted state. Owned by Kerrie and Ken Johnstone, the hotel is the only architectural remnant of the gold rush era. We were fortunate that Kerrie, the shire president, and Ken generously sponsored our stay as it was important to have a comfortable and secure base for the two days I had to turn around and prepare for the toughest physical challenge of the journey. Greg admitted he was exhausted, but he was also ecstatic about finishing and the prospect of seeing Lucy in a few days. As with the Russian expedition ten years before, we had maintained a strong friendship and a successful cycling partnership. We had worked as a team through thick and thin, had shared the load evenly and compromised when there was a difference of opinion. We had rarely argued because we shared common goals and understood each other's strengths and weaknesses.

As paying for Greg's flight to Perth proved to be beyond the expedition budget, I had arranged with my mother that she would drive up from Northam with her friend to collect Greg and then deliver him to Perth on time for his connecting flight to Melbourne, and eventually around the world and back to England. Mum's round trip of over 2000 km in two days was a massive effort which I appreciated very much.

Zombie-like after our twenty-day stint on the bikes, we were content to let Kerrie drive us around to see the area, visiting Lake Way, the recently abandoned Desert Gold citrus and melon orchard and the racecourse. We returned to the hotel to find Mum and her friend, Liz, relaxing on the lawn, exhausted after a marathon day on the road. Mum was keen to see what kind of condition I was in after 12 005 km of cycling. I think she imagined me to be much more gaunt than I was. In fact, apart from being very tired, I was in pretty good shape. I needed to be to have my best chance of completing the challenge that lay ahead.

Greg and I said our farewells, and the three of them headed off early the next morning, leaving me on my own. Don Walker, the driver of the support vehicle, was to join me that evening in readiness for setting out on the Canning Stock Route the following day.

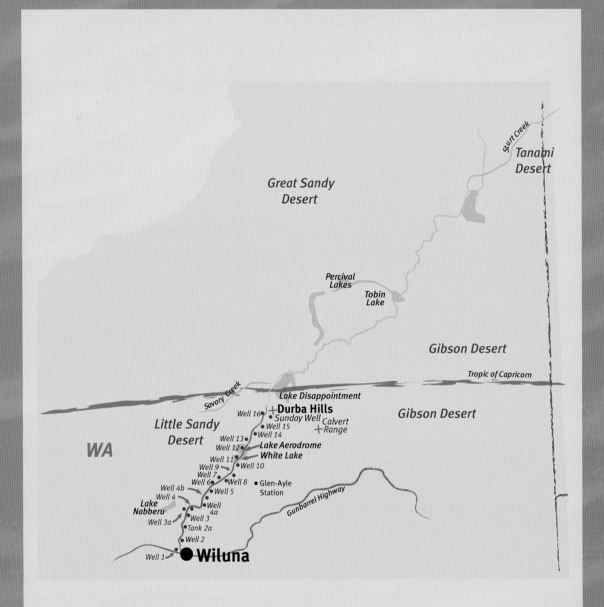

Tanami Desert

Sturt Creek

Great Sandy Desert

Percival Lakes

Tobin Lake

Gibson Desert

Tropic of Capricorn

Savory Creek

Lake Disappointment

Durba Hills
Well 16
Sunday Well
Well 15   Calvert
Well 14   Range

Little Sandy Desert

WA

Well 13
Well 12
Well 11
Well 9
Well 7
Well 6
Well 4b
Well 4

Lake Aerodrome
White Lake
Well 10

Gibson Desert

Well 8
Well 5
Glen-Ayle Station

Lake Nabberu

Well 4a
Well 3
Well 3a   Tank 2a
Well 2

Gunbarrel Highway

Well 1   **● Wiluna**

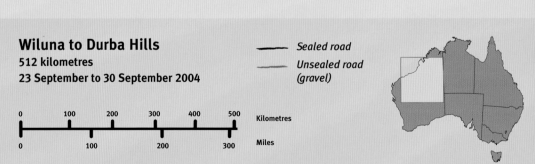

Wiluna to Durba Hills
512 kilometres
23 September to 30 September 2004

—— Sealed road
—— Unsealed road (gravel)

| 0 | 100 | 200 | 300 | 400 | 500 | Kilometres |

| 0 | | 100 | | 200 | | 300 | Miles |

9

Corrugations, sand and rocks
The Canning Stock Route, Week 1

Ancient ridges gave some respite from the sand near The Granites

Wiluna to the Durba Hills

My body was showing definite signs of fatigue. I could have done with an extra recovery day. My distinctly swollen legs looked unattractive and elephantoid – an indication that my system hadn't caught up with itself; the 'floating' feeling as I struggled to catch up on all the administration work was another sign I badly needed a break. All the same, details of the previous section from Warburton to Wiluna had to be documented for the website diary and 4000 words were eventually uploaded. I updated my press release and sent it to my friend Simone, who was helping with the publicity in Western Australia, made further calls attempting to sort out the technical problems with the website, and sent off an application for further funding for the last few months of the expedition. I also sorted out my bike and equipment for the journey ahead.

The Canning Stock Route (CSR) snakes its way from Wiluna to Billiluna Station in the south-east Kimberley, traversing four deserts as it does so. It could be perceived as a spiritual backbone in the history of Australia's exploration, when European pioneers' only hope of survival in the region was to merge their brave, stoic Victorian principles with Aboriginal knowledge and bushcraft.

William Snell's story, like the history of the Canning Stock Route – its construction, maintenance and inspiring characters who worked it – exemplifies the essence of the pioneering spirit. My great-great-uncle was one of the many optimists who explored the unknown, and to whom the Australian nation is indebted for its subsequent development and prosperity. My motivation in attempting to complete the 2000-km route between Wiluna and Halls Creek by bicycle stems from these strands – the personal, the historical and the physical – and it is therefore appropriate to entwine them within the story of my experiences.

The idea of constructing a stock route from Wiluna to the Kimberley was born in the late nineteenth century, when pastoralists from east Kimberley stations such as Flora Valley, Sturt Creek and Billiluna needed to find a way to transport their stock to market. While the west Kimberley had been settled by people arriving by sea (at Beagle Bay and near Derby), the east Kimberley was opened up by single men and by families who brought their cattle overland from Queensland and NSW. Nat Buchanan performed a second, unrivalled feat, perhaps even more arduous than his famous drive of 20 000 cattle across to Glencoe and Daly River stations in the Northern Territory, when he drove 4000 head of cattle from Richmond in Queensland to the Ord River Station. The Durack family followed, bringing their cattle to settle on Lissadell and Argyle Downs stations also in the fertile Ord River valley in 1885. The MacDonalds brought their cattle to Fossil Downs Station near Fitzroy Crossing the next year.

Halls Creek became the major centre in the east Kimberley when the first gold discovery in WA was made there in 1885. After a time the gold prospectors moved south to the Coolgardie and Kalgoorlie strikes, but by then a strong market had developed for Kimberley cattle, and Halls Creek came to be seen as an ideal starting point for a stock route south. Along with their city backers, pastoralists of the region put pressure on the government to establish a route along which cattle could be sent economically to the prosperous south, to the booming economy in the goldfields and to railheads, whence they could be sent on and sold at greater profit.

In 1896, two separate expeditions set off in search of a possible overland route: the Calvert Scientific Exploring Expedition, led by Lawrence Wells, and a self-funded expedition led by David Carnegie. Both parties met with life-threatening ordeals, and men lost their lives. The conclusion to which Wells and Carnegie independently came was that it would be impossible to transport cattle overland as the 'none but useless country', in Carnegie's words, would not support stock.

Facing ruin, the east Kimberley cattlemen lobbied intensely for further investigation. As a result, in 1906, Alfred Canning, a veteran surveyor of many tough expeditions, was appointed to lead an expedition organised for the purpose of exploring the country between Lake Way, near Wiluna, and Sturt Creek, near Halls Creek, to determine a practical route for cattle.

On 7 May 1906, Canning's survey team of eight men, twenty-three camels and two ponies set out from the booming mining town of Day Dawn (now a ghost town) for Wiluna. Canning was well aware of the tragedies and findings of the previous two expeditions when the team began its fourteen-month survey from Wiluna on 29 May. The first traverse to Halls Creek took twenty-four weeks, crossing the previous expedition routes of John Forrest at Weld Spring (1874), Giles near what is now Well 15 (1876) and Warburton near Well 47 (1873). A telegram sent to Perth announced the party's safe arrival in Halls Creek on 30 October. The return journey started out the following February after the Wet. Arriving back in Perth, Canning reported that it would be possible to establish a stock route with fair feed and good water from fifty-two wells and watering points. The survey had been a success and received a standing ovation when the results were tabled in state parliament.

Having surveyed the Wiluna-Kimberley Stock Route, Alfred Canning was the logical choice to lead the well-sinking and construction expedition that followed. With first-hand experience of the isolated, unforgiving territory in which the team would have to work, Canning was able to plan the logistics. On a far grander scale than the survey expedition, he estimated he would need seventy camels to carry equipment, materials and a twelve-month food supply (this would need to be replenished for the return journey in the second year). Apart from shooting some game, Canning's team relied little on natural 'bush tucker' resources. Two camel-drawn wagons could be used until the sand dune country started in earnest just before Goodwin Soak (Well 11). After this point, the pack camels would have to carry everything. Food for thirty-one men included 1460 kg of meat, the same weight of flour, 1090 kg of sugar, 142 kg of tea and a herd of 400 goats used for milk and meat. Equipment included 100 tonnes of building materials, survey gear, well-sinking tools, camera and darkroom equipment, three camp kitchens, a medicine chest, veterinary and blacksmith's kits, and dynamite.

The construction team, whom Canning and his deputy, Hubert Trotman, individually interviewed, included a geologist, bore experts, well-sinkers and builders, carpenters, cooks, camel men, a saddler and a blacksmith. The expedition started out from Day Dawn on 17 March 1908 and arrived at Wiluna two weeks later. By the time it had reached Flora Valley Station in July 1909, thirty-one wells had been sunk, an average of one well every eighteen days. After a month of rest, the group headed south again to construct the remainder of the watering points. The final twenty wells left for the return journey tended to be more difficult to build as many were in treeless locations and so the timber needed for their construction had to be transported over long distances.

When Tom Cole first overlanded 310 cattle in 1910, he claimed, 'This is the best Stock Route in Australia. Cows often have calves and all arrive in good condition.' The Canning Stock Route, however, was never used to the extent that the Kimberley pastoralists' lobby had predicted. Market forces changed and the WA government decided to build a meatworks at Wyndham (north-east Kimberley), which opened a few years later and reduced the need for transporting cattle overland.

Two years later, after Tom Cole had brought another 300 bullocks along the Canning to Wiluna, he stated: 'On the route there are now long stages of poor country which must be hurried over. A small party should always travel ahead of the mob to avoid the disaster of two consecutive wells being unfit for use.' In January 1914, Edward Kidson reported that between Wells 5 and 51 there was much dingo damage. By 1917, Michael O'Connor observed that wells were showing damage and dry rot; ropes had rotted and buckets rusted. Aboriginals had also damaged many of the wells. Travelling the route was dangerous too, as a number of drovers and explorers had been speared by Aboriginals. Overall, the condition of the stock route wells was depreciating rapidly.

The station which used the route the most was Billiluna, as lessee Robert Falconer transported stock to his Carnegie Station (the supply point for Greg and myself at the end of the isolated stretch along the Gunbarrel Highway), east of Wiluna. Falconer put together a petition with neighbouring stations Ruby Plains, Beaudesert, Lower Sturt and Lamboo, and lobbied the government to repair the wells.

In March 1928, cabinet agreed to reopen the Canning Stock Route. Before accepting the job of doing so, William Snell was emphatic that the country through which the CSR passed was unsuitable to drive stock on. He referred to the sand hill, spinifex-covered terrain and the limited water supplies then found at the wells. Based on his extensive experience travelling across the land, Snell suggested an alternate route to the east of Canning's path. After considering this option, the government decided to go with its original investment and Snell was employed to lead a reconditioning party of ten men to do the job.

At the time Snell was appointed to recommission the first 500 miles of the CSR in 1929, he was considered by many, including the Undersecretary of Works and Labour in the WA parliament, as the 'finest bushman in Western Australia'. Snell's curriculum vitae boasted some impressive credentials. To adapt, survive and succeed as he did, he was clearly a 'jack of all trades' – explorer, pastoralist, miner, businessman, orator and politician.

Born in Hamilton, Victoria, in 1872, Snell left school at the age of twelve. Working under the shire engineer of Hamilton, he gained valuable experience as an engineering contractor building roads and bridges. At the age of twenty he arrived in Fremantle, bringing with him a road-contracting plant and horses. With no call for his work there or in Perth, he joined the gold rush in Coolgardie. Following closely in the tracks of the pioneer prospector Paddy Hannan, he was one of the first on the scene at 'Hannan's Find' (Kalgoorlie) and a number of other gold rushes in the region. During this period, Snell experienced some life-threatening hardships, on one expedition he found himself alone with a dying mate whom he had to bury with his bare hands and a spoon in rock-hard ground. Snell was later discovered near the grave unconscious through dehydration.

After further varied experiences he realised that it was more profitable to cart machinery and stores than look for gold and so he opened a store in Menzies (240 km north of Kalgoorlie) in 1897, just before his epic trans-Nullarbor cycle adventure. Returning with his new bride, he moved to the new town of Leonora, 100 km further north, to start up a venture called WA Snell and Co. Styled as a 'General Merchandisers and Importers', this was run in partnership with an Afghan camel business. Up to three camel trains would deliver goods to and from the store at any one time. Dealing in mining requisites, drapery, groceries and alcohol, Snell became a successful businessman and a popular character. At the age of twenty-eight, he was elected Leonora's first mayor.

Seven years later, the Snell family, which now included four young children, left the comfort of 'civilisation' at Leonora and travelled to the Pilbara region in the north-west to eke out a living from a new challenge. Initially Snell developed a successful camel transport business, then he diversified into procuring mining and pastoral leases. His mining leases mostly produced copper and lead on a small scale and made little, if any, profit.

His pastoral leases proved to be a more stable financial option. Snell's first pastoral lease of 63 000 hectares (150 000 acres) was taken up in 1914 in the Ophthalmia Range, which included Mt Whaleback, now mined by BHP Billiton. If only he had known he was sitting on one of the world's largest reservoirs of iron ore! The opportunity to acquire this land arose when it was relinquished by Daisy Bates, an eccentric, self-taught anthropologist and journalist who decided to devote her life henceforth to the full-time study of the Indigenous people. Her observations are a priceless record of Aboriginal culture at the time of the first contact with Europeans.

In 1922, Snell took out his first pastoral lease in the Lake Nabberu district and by the time he was commissioned to recondition the stock route, he had worked a number of leases in the region. This contributed to the suitability of his appointment with regard to local knowledge, bush skills and understanding the requirements of droving cattle, even though Snell – as mentioned earlier – regularly preferred his trusty bicycle as his form of transport. He would pedal up to 100 miles (162 km) a day and always resorted to his push-bike when out to reconnoitre.

Snell's commissioning brief specified that each well was to be made capable of watering 300 cattle and each alternate well was to be fitted with a windlass, bucket and rope. There was to be no police protection as Snell believed their presence might antagonise the Aboriginals and endanger the party. Three camel wagons, six camel drays along with thirty-five camels, eight horses and three dogs, plus supplies, food and equipment for twelve months were soon gathered and on their way to Weld Spring, Well 9. The plan was to use Weld Spring as the first base, initially working back toward Wiluna to Well 1 before pushing north.

◆　◆　◆

Sophisticated technology and communications have developed since those pioneering days – navigation, for example, is easier now with GPS and a track to follow – but the existence of corrugations caused by motorised transport is a modern-day problem. The desert conditions, however, remain unchanged, and are as hostile as ever. People die out there every year. Locals were not encouraging about my plans even after I described what I had already accomplished and demonstrated that I was well prepared, doubting that I would succeed for three reasons. Firstly, it was late in the season and I would be heading into the teeth of the 'build up' to the Kimberley Wet. I could expect constant extreme temperatures, in excess of 40°C, with increasing humidity and chances of cloud bursts up north if the season broke early. Secondly, the track was in extremely poor condition due to the amount of traffic it carried over the season. I could expect to encounter few vehicles now that the season was finished, increasing the level of isolation. Thirdly, I was travelling in the wrong direction. The prevailing winds which sculpt the sand ridges originate from the north-west. This meant I would need to travel up the steep side of each dune, with the potential for more headwinds than tailwinds. (Cattle were driven from north to south and therefore up the gentler gradient of each sand dune.) I had chosen to travel the route in the same direction as it was surveyed, built and reconditioned and therefore in numerical order of the wells. The route had to fit in with the overall itinerary for the expedition.

Well aware of these issues, I had been preparing my mind throughout the expedition to approach this section with everything I had. I understood the general scepticism mixed with disbelief that greeted my plans, especially since the locals are the first to be called on when someone is in trouble and in need of being rescued, often at great expense and potential risk to the rescuer. I didn't believe that I was taking any unrealistic chances and was looking forward to getting stuck into the challenge. I knew that I would be travelling late in the season, but as I had to begin the whole expedition from Canberra later than I had initially planned, I had no choice – it was now or never. The other two successful attempts of cycling the Canning Stock Route that I knew of hadn't done it two days after completing four months and over 12 000 km and so were able to time their expeditions to take place at a more sensible, cooler part of the year. They had also chosen to cycle from north to south.

It was somewhat of a relief to meet Don Walker in person when he arrived at Wiluna in the evening. It had been a long 1000-km drive from Perth. We had only spoken over the phone, initially when I was in Warburton two weeks earlier after Merrick pulled out. I had to invest complete faith in Don's commitment. We'd had a long discussion about the logistics, including timing, equipment and supplies. Don had shown complete trust in me, committing a month of his time and expertise free of charge and purchasing all the supplies out of his own pocket. I was to reimburse him for expenses at the conclusion of the Canning Stock Route.

We got to know each other better over a beer. A mechanical engineer by profession, Don was developing his own side business called Canning Expeditions, using his two 4WD vehicles to lead select groups up the Canning Stock Route. He had travelled the route a number of times over the previous few years, and given this and his mechanical expertise, experience and knowledge, I felt fortunate to have found someone of his calibre to support this part of my expedition.

For some time, Don had been suffering from a mysterious allergy problem which had affected his health. Not through lack of trying, specialists had not been able to diagnose the cause. This affliction had prevented him from travelling up the Stock Route during the season. In agreeing to help me, Don believed he was fit enough for the task; most of all, he was excited to be travelling through the land he was passionate about but had been denied the opportunity to visit during the Dry season. Travelling responsibly along the Stock Route includes registering with the Wiluna and Halls Creek police. We completed a form detailing our plans, including intended date of arrival, personal and vehicle details, and certifying that we had prepared adequately. It must have been strange for the police to read, under 'Vehicle Details', that these were a Toyota LandCruiser and a bicycle! There were no records of any other cycle expeditions successfully completing the Wiluna to Halls Creek route (or at least to Billiluna Station). No one at either end knew of any other attempts. Given that little gets past these small communities, and especially given the renowned tracking abilities of the Indigenous locals, it was reasonable to assume that, if successful, I would be the first woman to complete such a ride and the first cyclist to complete it from south to north.

Don had phoned ahead to the Kunawarritji Community on the Kidson Track to order fuel, this being the only habitation near the Stock Route, four kilometres from Well 33 and about 1000 km north of Wiluna. Even though his vehicle was equipped with extensive long-range fuel tanks, their capacity would only take him a little over halfway. All drivers of the isolated track have to pre-order fuel at Kunawarritji or arrange for it to be dropped at Well 23 on the Talawana Track. If ordered six weeks in advance during the Dry season, a 200-litre drum can be dumped by the proprietors of the Capricorn Roadhouse, Newman.

The research I had done, and discussions with those who had driven the Stock Route in 2004, indicated that we should allow four weeks for the journey. I estimated that if all went exceptionally well, it would take twenty-four days, and I added a few extra days to allow for unknown quantities. As with previous sections of the expedition, I never took information from drivers as gospel, as they are affected by different problems from someone who has to use leg power, balance and a strong heart to progress. I predicted that the biggest unknown was the quality of the track between the sand ridges. It was impossible to ascertain whether I would be able to pedal over the terrain or whether I'd have to dismount and walk with the bike. Don assured me he had catered for enough food for four weeks and a bit extra. I hoped he had allowed for the vast quantities I was likely to consume. With unpredictable track conditions and knowing that I would have to cope with extreme heat, there was little leeway if I was to complete the whole of the route on two wheels.

Wiluna to The Granites – Tank 2A

Distance – 82 km

Distance from Wiluna – 82 km

Total distance – 12116 km

A myriad of thoughts flitted through my mind as I devoured Ken's generous breakfast at the Club Hotel in Wiluna. I packed the calories in as if it was my last supper. Before leaving, I took the opportunity to make a few final calls as this was my last chance for a few weeks to speak on a land line. I called Arnaud and also my mother, to wish her happy birthday. I would be able to use the satellite phone to 'check in', but as it was incredibly expensive, I planned to make only short calls once a week unless there was an emergency.

Departing from the 'Welcome to Paradise' sign, I headed north, keen not to lose too much time. The day was already warming up, as were my legs which had benefitted from two days off, although they had not fully recovered. The dreaded muscle spasms returned, and I had no choice but to cycle through the pain.

The first 38 km was a properly maintained gravel road servicing the Kutkabubba Community and Cunyu Station. To reach Well 1 I had to turn off the main track 4 km from Wiluna and venture 3 km west along a Gunbarrel Highway-like corrugated track, where it was impossible to avoid the corrugations on the firm surface. Kerrie and her grand-daughter followed, rattling along in their ute, as did Don in his laden 4WD.

Starting at Well 1 seems obvious, but most drivers, including Don, usually leave it out, preferring to head straight for the turn-off from the station road near Well 2 to the rough 4WD track. This they consider the Canning Stock Route 'proper'. I felt that Well 1 was an important landmark and the most appropriate place for an official start.

The last of an estimated thirty-one mobs of cattle were driven down the Stock Route in 1959. Since then, the condition of the watering points has deteriorated and about three-quarters of the wells, including Well 1, are now derelict and unfit for use by stock let alone humans. Only a handful of wells have been restored to supply drinkable water.

At Well 1 with Don Walker: one clean shirt, one dirty shirt

The limited reliable water and food supplies were the main reasons I needed to travel with a support vehicle. With up to 400 km between supplies of good water, it was impossible to carry a week's needs through the heat, especially over deep sand. We could carry 120 litres or six days worth in the vehicle and planned to replenish supplies at Wells 15, 26, 33, 46 and 49. The next time we could buy food would be at the Kunawarritji Community, 1000 km from Wiluna.

Well 1, sunk to a depth of 45 feet (13.5 metres) according to Snell's journal, was built to supply good water for stock as they were kept there for extended periods of time before heading off to market, or new pastures if they were more fortunate. I wandered around the well and the water tanks, situated by Cockarra Creek, which were now in disrepair. The stagnant water which half-filled the wooden shaft appeared more like a murky black soup. The head of the windmill and the decapitated base of the Southern Cross frame lay rusting on the ground nearby, and the two galvanised iron water tanks sat empty and decaying on their concrete bases.

Back on the well-graded road, my bike felt a bit like a racehorse. I positively flew over the dirt at more than 20 km an hour. Minus all the bags, I slammed into all the road imperfections harder than before and my wheels were tossed around at the even slightest bump or stone. Perhaps my bike was more like a bucking bronco – and this was the good road! Apart from a few essential items, everything else was in the vehicle. It almost felt like I was cheating.

In the single rear pannier I carried my camera, basic tool kit, spare tubes, pump, snack food, extra water bottles, map and a two-way radio. The plan was that we would meet up for breaks and obviously to camp, but most of the time I would be alone, out of sight. The two-way radio was an important piece of equipment as long as we were within range. For the radio to work we had to be within 12 km as the crow flies.

It was vital that we tested all our equipment and practised communicating on the first day so we could work as a team when things became more demanding. I had to get used to cycling on my own. In general, I quite liked the feeling of being free to move at my own pace. Although Greg and I were relatively equal in ability, we both had had to compromise. Where strength was a major factor – up steep inclines or pushing the heavy bikes through deep sand on the Gunbarrel – Greg was generally stronger. I was usually better at sustaining a steady pace, especially over the longer days. Now it was totally up to me. I had to listen to my body and adapt my work rate accordingly. At this point it was all positive. I wondered if this would change later on when the notoriously soft sand ridges kicked in and I would have to rely on self-motivational techniques to keep moving forward.

It didn't seem to take long to carve a path through the scrubland to the turn-off to the track. We paused for lunch under the valued shade of the mulga bushes, the wattle *Acacia aneura* which had provided protection through most of the semi-arid country Greg and I had already travelled. The mulga leaves were a valuable source of protein for stock while the timber was used by Canning and Snell to build some of the wells. I passed pockets of everlasting flowers which formed carpets of brilliant yellow with splashes of pink and white.

The track was sign-posted as the Canning Stock Route Heritage Trail. Next to this was a warning stating that the track is recommended for 4WD vehicles only, that there is no water, fuel or services between Wiluna and Halls Creek, a distance of over 1900 km in length, and that motorists are advised to obtain adequate supplies and spares before venturing on this road. No mention of bicycles.

Stony, clay-based ground near Well 2 supports a stunning array of wildflowers

OUT THERE AND BACK

Travelling with a support vehicle proved an utter luxury compared with having to carry everything on the bike. Previously Greg and I had to make do with sitting on a piece of shadecloth or a log for lunch, whereas Don pulled out two folding chairs. In catering for the journey, Don's plan was to carry as much fresh food as would keep. He decided to bring a freezer rather than a refrigerator. The vehicle could only power one appliance and we could carry more major food items in a freezer over the four weeks, especially meat, which would be important for recovery and maintaining strength over the time. I enjoyed the deluxe avocado, tomato and cheese sandwiches followed by yoghurt, appreciating the fact that our sustenance would soon cease to be so varied and fancy.

The Canning Stock Route is not an official gazetted road, and therefore most of it has never seen a grader. Canning's original survey tabled a tract of land about eight kilometres wide. The broad band which connected the fifty-two watering points was wide enough to allow stock to graze on the limited vegetation.

While a few vehicles had made it as far as Well 11 as early as 1929, the entire CSR was not conquered by vehicle until as late as 1968. Surveyors Russ Wenholz, Dave Chudleigh and Noel Kealley had to arrange for three fuel dumps along the way to supply their heavily laden Land Rovers. They averaged 75 km a day at 6.5 km per hour, covering 2600 km in thirty-four days. It was five years before another vehicle traversed the entire route. In 1980, a visitors' book was placed at Well 26 and over one hundred people signed it the following year. Since then, numbers have steadily increased to at least one thousand annually – there may be many more, as some travellers do not register their intentions at Wiluna or Halls Creek as they should. The tyres of their 4WDs have formed the track, as drivers have searched for the best path through the different types of terrain.

At this point, just before Well 2, the track simplified to merely two wheel ruts. Occasionally it diversified into extra options where vehicles had searched for alternative routes to avoid becoming bogged after rain, which turns the ground to the consistency of putty. The first eight kilometres wound through the bush on gravelly conglomerate and clay. I made good progress and at that stage was planning to reach Well 3 by the end of Day 1.

A typical section of poor track between Well 2 and Water 2a, The Granites

Well 2 was in ruins and overshadowed by the newer windmill and water tank. We took a few minutes to check it out. Graffiti on the tank announced that 'Jesus is coming – so look busy!' Beyond the well and without warning, the protected scrubland petered out into a plain of endless sand supporting only sparse vegetation cover. This was bad news for me as the track quality disintegrated with it into loose sand and corrugations. Any minor straight stretch of about 20 metres or more would present me with a washboard surface. This was smooth on the bends, but speeding vehicles had sprayed sand outwards as they accelerated away from the turns and caused ruts with soft banks 30-40 cm deep. Had I been carrying a full load as before, I would have had to walk sections of the track as the wheels would have sunk too far.

Don appeared quite exasperated when we stopped for a breather. He had never known this section of the track to be so rough and cut up. I hadn't imagined that I would have to struggle so much at this early stage. There had obviously been an unsustainable number of vehicles over the track during the season, many of the drivers unaware of the damage they caused by travelling too fast. As the track is not maintained in any way, this is not only dangerous, as they may not have time to react to unforseen obstacles or bulldust, but it is also the cause of the horrific corrugations which are no good for drivers or cyclists.

Don was worried that the track condition would damage his shock absorbers before he reached Halls Creek. The only shock absorbers I possessed were the fat tyres I had chosen to combat sand and corrugations, and either my knees or backside. Shock absorbers would have significantly smoothed my ride on unsealed tracks (they are a hindrance on tarmac). They certainly would have been part of my equipment had I been solely cycling the Canning Stock Route. Here it was only Day 1, and already I was longing for anything that would make my task more comfortable.

Travelling was slower than expected and, due to my late start, I realised by mid-afternoon that reaching Well 3 that day was an unrealistic goal. I adjusted the target to Tank 2A. In the late afternoon, just before my destination, I spotted a wild cat wandering along the track. If I'd had a gun, I would not have hesitated to shoot the vermin animal. Feral cats are responsible for killing more native animals than any other vermin, causing great damage to many of Australia's endemic species. Being down-wind of the black feline, I was able to creep up to within about 10 metres before the animal, which is a larger version of a domestic cat, sensed my presence and darted off through the spinifex and bushes. In earlier days, pastoralists were unable to keep dogs because large numbers of poison baits had been laid to control the fox and dingo populations. Many chose to keep cats instead, the descendants of which roam wild in alarming numbers.

Don drove on ahead to start setting up camp at Tank 2A. The Granites was the last watering point to be constructed by Canning in 1910. The storage tank was blasted out of solid granite rock and at one time had a capacity of 40 000 litres. Transporting the dynamite had been a task to be handled with kid gloves. Reaching the final well with the volatile explosive intact was testimony to good management and a little luck. The quietest camel drew the short straw (which, if the plan went wrong, could have been the straw that broke the camel's back), and carried the dynamite at the tail end of the train. At each camp the explosive was placed in a hole in the ground and covered with branches to keep it cool.

After they had finished Tank 2A, the construction team wearily returned to Wiluna after two seasons on the job. The Canning Stock Route was ready for use, completed at a cost of 22 000 pounds. Today, a crumbling stone fence partially protects the water source which is now half-caved in. Mosquitoes revelled over the stagnant pool as the sun melted into the horizon. We camped a good distance away from the water-hole so animals could get to the tank to drink overnight.

Compared with the lightweight model I had been carrying up until then, the heavy-duty canvas tent I was to use for the duration of the CSR was palatial. Don showed me how to erect it, the single extendable pole pushing up the centre so I could actually stand up in it. I would have had room to swing that wild cat! The self-inflating mattress was also far more luxurious than I was used to. Don insisted that very soon I would need all the comfort I could get. All these little luxuries, which most would not appreciate as much as I did in these circumstances, were to help maintain morale further down the track. Dinner was steak, potatoes and fresh salad with mini-pavlovas, cream, strawberries and kiwi fruit for sweets. It was not going to last, but it was a civilised celebration of our first night on the Canning Stock Route.

Acacia pods such as these at Well 3 would have provided stock with a valuable source of protein

Day 2, Friday 24 September
The Granites to Well 4A
Distance – 100 km
Distance from Wiluna – 182 km
Total distance – 12 216 km

Daily temperatures were now consistently in the mid-to-high 30s, averaging about 37°C (100°Fahrenheit on the old scale). I dragged myself away from the comfortable mattress at 5.45am and pedalled off about an hour and a half later. I had planned to get away earlier, but being the first morning on the road, we hadn't developed a routine. I never like to be hurried first thing in the morning. It always takes time to prepare for the day. The plan was to get breakfast organised, pack my personal belongings, eat and go, leaving Don to pack up camp, load and prepare his vehicle. He could afford to take his time whereas I had a sense of urgency to make best use of the daylight, especially in the relative cool.

Don had remembered the section of track to Well 3 as being good quality; this report, together with the solid surface for the first four kilometres through the scrub, buoyed my expectations for what was to come. As I moved away from the protection of the trees, it was therefore disheartening to find the soft plains return and with them a track quality similar to the section between Wells 2 and 2A. As on the Gunbarrel, occasional ancient sand ridges which had compacted over thousands of years rose above the plain, providing a brief respite.

Of the 31 km to Well 3, approximately 21 km were bad. My average speed had dropped from about 22 km per hour on the maintained gravel road to 13.9 km per hour. While this gives an indication of the relative decrease in track standard, it doesn't, however, give an idea of the amount of extra energy used to maintain balance and push through the sand. Tank 2A to Well 3 took two hours and fifteen minutes.

The benefit of travelling so slowly was that I could identify various animal tracks, which became more frequent as I approached Well 3 and the more productive land around the dry creek bed. Within a few kilometres I identified emu, cat, goanna, snake, small lizard and various bird tracks. The colourful display of flowers was similarly diverse. Large red kangaroos darted in front of me as I approached the turn-off to the well. A flock of white cockatoos, twenty-eight parrots and pink and grey galahs squawked noisily from their perches in the towering river red gums, announcing my presence.

Well 3 sits beside the banks of Sweeney Creek, named after James Sweeney, farrier on John Forrest's 1874 expedition from Perth to Adelaide via a northerly route. Water was drawn from a depth of 23 feet (about 7 metres) but the well only yielded about 4000 gallons (18 000 litres) per day. In 1929, the water quality was classed as excellent.

The well was restored by the Foothills 4WD Club of Western Australia, which in 1998 had made two trips to complete its refurbishment. The members had done a good job, fixing a pair of trapdoors over the top and building a protective fence around the shaft. But even after restoration, the quality of the stagnant water was questionable and certainly smelt unfit to drink. When I opened the lid, I disturbed hundreds of small brown frogs, which normally lived on the ledges of the horizontal wooden planks which lined the walls. They darted chaotically at the shock of the bright light, many belly flopping into the water below. The segmented metal troughing had broken and would need some further work if it were to hold water again.

About 22 km further east along Sweeney Creek was William Snell's Bridleface Outcamp. Between 1927 and 1938, he leased 123 000 hectares in the region, now a part of Cunyu Station, south and east of Lake Nabberu which I was soon to cross. During this time, Wiluna was at its peak, producing 1000 tonnes of gold-bearing ore per day and employing over one thousand men to work in the mines. Snell would take his cattle from his Bridleface lease to his own slaughter-yards just out of Wiluna. There cattle would be fattened on mulga for a couple of weeks before reaching his own butcher shop in Wiluna.

I waited at the well for Don as I thought he said he would catch me up within a couple of hours. I tried the two-way but there was no response. I couldn't afford to wait any longer or I would have no chance of reaching Windich Spring, my intended destination. Clear of the tall timber which may have impeded my reception, I attempted to call him at repeated intervals. The track followed a ruined fence line to White Well and then on to Corners Well; these were station wells with plenty of water flowing from their windmill bores into large tanks and finally overflowing into adjacent troughs. Cattle milled around without a care in the world. I had become accustomed to their reaction to me: fixating stares could have been either in utter disbelief or just that their minds had drawn a complete blank.

I was beginning to think I should turn back to look for Don. What if he had fallen off the roof of his vehicle while loading it? I thought I should at least aim to reach Well 3A for lunch and make a decision then. We had two satellite phones and an E-PIRB (emergency position indicating radio beacon) if required, but all were in the 4WD. I was feeling vulnerable. At least we were still in station country and I could manage to get some sort of help. In another day and a half we would be in the Little Sandy Desert where there would be no option.

Soon I heard a vehicle approaching from behind. It was not Don, but Murray. We had met Murray on Day 1 at the turn-off to the CSR. He was travelling in the opposite direction, heading back to Wiluna to refuel and prepare for driving the full length of the track. Murray said it was his fault that Don was late as he had spent a couple of hours in conversation with him, trying to extract as much information about the CSR as he could. He was amazed at what I was attempting and would have talked on all day, but time was crucial for me and I was keen to get on with it, now that I knew that Don was all right. My water was getting low so I was appreciative of a top up from Murray. We wished each other luck before he motored off ahead of me.

I reached Well 3A by midday and still no Don. By now I was becoming annoyed because he obviously didn't realise that I had been out on my own for nearly five hours and that I might be worried by his non-appearance. I also needed water and was more than ready for food.

Well 3A, also called Government Well, was built by Snell to supplement the small water yields of Wells 3 and 4. The southern end of the CSR was also used to drive sheep on occasions and the extra well made this easier. In keeping with his commissioning brief, the wells constructed by Snell were smaller in dimension than Canning's originals. Later, when he tried to deepen Well 3A to improve the low yielding flow, the water turned salty. The date of 1929 was written on the inside of one of the galvanised trough sections; each of these sections had been transported there balanced on the back of a camel. Judging by the state of the disjointed segments, the trough had not held water for a very long time.

As I wandered around the ruins, it was evident that the water was certainly fit for wildlife. The presence of desert finches is always a sure sign of water. They chirped constantly as they nipped in and out of the well through tiny cracks between the termite-eaten boards which covered the shaft. Zebra finches are grain-eating birds and rely on a constant water supply to metabolise the grains. The fact that they are present in huge numbers is an indication that the season has been good. They mostly live off spinifex seeds and breed when water and seeds are plentiful. Birds which rely on insects and small animals for sustenance receive sufficient moisture from their prey not to have to rely solely on watering points.

I still couldn't reach Don on the two-way radio, and was considering heading off when I noticed a puncture in my rear wheel. Removing the wheel to repair the tube was far less hassle than before as I didn't have to unload all the bags from my bike. Just as I was finishing pumping the tyre, I heard the vehicle. It was a great relief. At the same time, I was annoyed, but I refrained from losing my temper: we had to work as a team and creating avoidable tension would be counter-productive. I calmly told Don how I felt about being left for five hours when I thought he was going to catch me up after two. He needed to understand what was required. I could survive for longer periods of time on my own as long as I was prepared with enough food and water. It was important we developed clear communications before I hit the sand dunes.

From Well 3A, the track had recently been realigned through privately owned Cunyu Station land, missing Well 4, in order to minimise track damage. In wet conditions, the section crossing the narrowest part of Lake Nabberu becomes impassable. Lake Nabberu is a series of salt lakes running east to west for about 45 km. Canning's original route crossed the centre, and to make it easier to navigate in wet conditions, he laid mulga logs in the mud. This became known as the 'Corduroyed Crossing'. Snell also encountered difficulties after eight-and-a-half inches (212 mm) of rain in the region and adopted the same technique, building a corduroy of logs across the narrowest part of the lake to transport the heavy well-drilling plant.

The realigned track wound a path through the chain of lakes, generally running parallel to the Frere Range. The 36 km between Well 3A and Snell Pass, which crosses the Frere Range, were a stunning kaleidoscope of colours and textures. The soft, corrugated orange sand of the track was a stark contrast to a mass of purple flowers, which must bloom at the mere sniff of moisture in the

Desert finches at Well 3a, Government Well

Pushing hard through Cunyu Station country between Well 3a and Lake Nabberu

atmosphere. A thick blanket of dry spinifex could have been mistaken for a prosperous field of meadow hay, were I still in Russia. Thickets of mulga bushes covered the better ground, adding a layer of grey-green, while gnarled skeletons of trees became more prevalent near the lakes' shores. We paused at one of the small satellite salt lakes. I could only squint at the shimmering, white, salty lake bed. Behind the lake was the low backdrop of the ancient Frere Range, its red-orange earth emitting a fiery glow, which penetrated the sparse vegetation even in the mid-afternoon.

Don travelled much more closely to me during the afternoon session. I handed him my camera, both to encourage him to capture a record and to prevent the camera from being shaken to pieces. Overcoming an energy-sapping struggle through deep sand around the top of the lake, where it was a battle to keep the wheels turning, I descended to lake bed level. There the continuously stony surface was unavoidable and the constant pounding was particularly hard on my forearms. My tendons felt as though they were being shaken away from their bony insertions. The painful problem, particularly on my left arm, gradually worsened during the course of the afternoon to a point where I was struggling to hold on to the handlebars. I tried to steer with one hand, alternating left with right in order to rest the other for a few seconds. In normal cycling conditions, it would be easy to steer with one hand, but out here, controlling the bike most of the time required a vice-like grip with both hands and intense concentration to navigate the smoothest and safest path.

Day 2 was an unlucky day as far as punctures go. My fourth puncture occurred near Pharis Bore at the base of Snell Pass and 24 km from Windich Spring. Apart from the annoyance factor, it also meant losing time. Again I realised that I was going to fall short of my planned destination, although not by too much as Well 4A is only 7 km away from Windich Spring.

Climbing Snell Pass I was more concerned with avoiding all the wash-away gullies than the tame ascent. I made up some time on the descent and then over the firm, dry claypans all the way to Kennedy Creek. Arriving at Well 4A, my

Date engraved on the whip pole – 30.3.29

Well 4a built by Snell; a spiritual place for me

odometer clicked over the 100-km mark. I was satisfied with that and wondered whether it would be the only time I clocked a century on the CSR. I was concerned at the state of my forearms as they were painful even to touch, let alone hold on to the handlebars. The muscles, in constant spasm, had ceased to work and I had to prise my left hand off the handlebars by physically peeling each finger away individually in order to release my grip.

Well 4A is one of the more interesting wells en route, especially in relation to my personal family history, and it became a spiritual experience for me. Snell built Wells 4A and 4B to break the long 64-km gap between Wells 4 and 5. Drover Tom Cole had reported losing cattle between the wells due to the distance. When Well 4A was built, the region was in flood, making its construction more laborious. Snell's party fashioned the trunk of an existing tree, which had naturally grown at an angle, as the whip pole. While the remaining woodwork is in ruin, the water supply remains good. Inscribed on the whip pole is the date of its construction: 30.3.29.

The process of 'whipping' was a method used to raise water from the well by camel or horse power. The animal was harnessed by a wire rope, the other end of which was attached to a 90-litre canvas bucket. The rope passed under a pulley on the ground and then over another pulley mounted on the whip pole positioned directly over the well. While one stockman walked the animal back and forth, raising and lowering the bucket, another stockman would pour the water into a chute which led to the trough from which the cattle would drink. Each animal would drink about 50 litres initially and then return for more later on. Given that most herds comprised of between 300 and 800 cattle, the job took many back-breaking hours. This labour-intensive process would be carried out in shifts by the drovers until all the animals were watered and content. Other team members would have to control the thirsty beasts so that they didn't stampede the trough in a frenzied rush for water.

Even though that night I could have been content sleeping on a bed of nails, I was really appreciative of my chair, more fresh food and a comfortable bed.

Day 3, Saturday 25 September
Well 4A to Well 8
Distance – 92 km
Distance from Wiluna – 274 km
Total distance – 12 308 km

Windich Spring; the tranquil oasis was a good place to mend punctures

I managed to get away a little earlier this time so I could spend some time at Windich Spring, seven kilometres from Well 4A. Windich is an old corroboree ground; its native name, 'Koojeela', means 'permanent water'. John Forrest discovered the spring during his 1874 expedition and he named it after Tommy Windich, an Aboriginal who accompanied him on his three expeditions. Situated on Kennedy Creek, the limestone pool can reach about a kilometre in length and 10 metres deep and is a haven for wildlife and stock. It used to be much deeper, but silted up after heavy cyclonic rains in 1965. I wandered along the shoreline among the majestic river red gums. Protected by steep banks, the still waters provided the medium for a perfect mirror image of the surroundings, broken occasionally by a bird landing or a puff of wind. I caused a few ripples of my own as I took the opportunity to mend a punctured tube which I had received en route to the spring. Mindful of yesterday's experiences and keen to develop a better communication system, I radioed to Don that I was on my way.

As I approached Well 4B, I heard and then spotted a number of large red kangaroos darting through the mulga scrub and then an emu with three chicks following in single file, fleeing my presence. I didn't bother stopping at the completely ruined Well 4B, and set off for Well 5, making good distance through the station scrubland. The more curves built into the track, the slower the average speed of the vehicles, which negates most of the corrugation problems. Well 5, 800 metres off the track, was Canning's deepest well. Building it had involved blasting 70 cubic metres of rock weighing 110 tonnes to a depth of 104 feet (32 metres), and then excavating it by hand. The well had been restored four months earlier by Granite Peak Station and the Chamberlain Tractor Company. Don managed to catch me up as I was leaving so I was able to refill all my bottles and have a snack before the nineteen kilometres to Pierre Spring, Well 6, and lunch.

The route to Pierre Spring was not so straightforward. About seven kilometres from the Well 5 turn-off I came to the top of a rise with vast views. Open plains, with only sparse vegetation cover, stretched as far as I could see. Mt Salvado, the Ingebong Hills and a few lesser rises broke the monotony. Descending the gravel track to the plain, I was surprised to be confronted by my first sand dune, an obstacle I hadn't been expecting this soon. Don had mentioned that the ground might go a bit soft but I hadn't realised it would become fly-away beach sand. In the heat of the day it was particularly fluid, filling any spaces in my shoes when I was forced to push. A vile 40-degree wind gusted from a north-westerly direction, singeing the back of my throat. The worst of the sand drifts only lasted about three kilometres, and I spent much of that time cursing them, worrying about what lay ahead. This experience proved a wake-up call; although totally draining, it showed me that I needed to improve my attitude to avoid slipping into such negativity again, as this only intensified and prolonged the mental torment.

Looking down the deepest well on the CSR – Well No 5

When John Forrest discovered the spring, the underground steam which flows north to Mt Salvado actually presented an unlimited water supply at ground level. He named the oasis after another Aboriginal helper, Tommy Pierre. Set amid a lone cluster of river red gums, Pierre Spring (Well 6) is a popular overnight stop for drivers, especially as it supplies high quality water only 3.5 metres down. It was one of the first wells to be restored by the Geraldton 4WD Club in 1991, some members of which Greg and I met back on the Gunbarrel. With an unsustainable number of campers, human waste had started to contaminate the pristine water supply. During our lunch stop I was pleased to note a new Enviro-Loo had recently been installed, which naturally breaks down human waste to nothing.

On Don's recommendation we visited Ingebong Hills, five kilometres further on. Rare, fading examples of Indigenous art adorned the overhangs. Don knew where to look and led me over an obstacle course of huge boulders which lay at the base of the cliff. As a skilled rock climber, he seemed to negotiate the course with ease wearing just a pair of thongs (flip flops) as footwear, making me feel comparatively clumsy. The weathering pattern of the rock formations was unusual, reminding me of flattened orange Mediterranean roof tiles. After climbing through a narrow chasm to reach the summit, we were rewarded with sweeping 360-degree views. Way below, the CSR track was merely an insignificant pencil-line scratched through the desert – easy to rub out.

There were more nasty surprises during the afternoon stint as the track at times traversed along the ridges of more small dunes. Long stretches also presented me with soft waves of corrugations. I could pedal for short sections but it was a fine line between pedalling and having to walk. Fortunately, conditions improved by Well 7, the shaft of which had caved in. The single track gave birth to a multitude of options around the shady well site. It was difficult to ascertain which was the correct path forward. I wasn't keen on wasting energy by following a station track in the wrong direction.

Unusual rock formations of the Ingebong Hills

Again I had to adjust my plan slightly, as I had been slowed by the extensive sand trap. Well 8 was only eight kilometres short of Canning Bore and I was content with that. While Well 8 was derelict, there was a windmill bore nearby to supply the station cattle. Driving in the tent pegs that night was quite an effort. The ground was packed hard, perhaps due to the hooves of introduced animals. The land has been stocked for many years now and cattle spend much of their existence milling around the water source.

Day 4, Sunday 26 September
Well 8 to Lake Aerodrome
Distance – 85 km
Distance from Wiluna – 359 km
Total distance – 12 393 km

I was gradually refining my morning routine and was on the road by 6.45am after my usual huge bowl of muesli and four slices of toast and honey. The mornings had lost their chill, a sure sign that the season was changing, but at this stage the early hours were a comfortable temperature. The first three days on the CSR had been personally inspiring, delivering so much variation in scenery, wildlife and history. I was eager to see what Day 4 would bring.

My body took a real pummelling over the next 26 km to Weld Spring, Well 9. With its 'kitty litter' surface and unrelenting corrugations, the track was reminiscent of the Gunbarrel Highway. It exacerbated the numbness I had developed in both hands, mostly from the excessive vibrations from Day 2. I still made good ground as I averaged 15 km per hour. Weld Spring, now a part of the Ward family's Glenayle Station and the last outpost before the Little Sandy and Gibson deserts, is one of the most historically important wells on the stock route.

Weld Spring was named in honour of the then governor of Western Australia, Aloysius Weld, by John Forrest on his epic journey from the Indian Ocean to the Overland Telegraph Line in South Australia. Forrest, who later became premier of Western Australia and the first Australian-born member of the House of Lords, led the expedition party. The group included his brother, Alexander, who was second in command, two other white men – James Sweeney and James Kennedy – and two Aboriginals, the afore-mentioned Tommy Windich and Tommy Pierre. Some thirty-two years before Canning surveyed the region, Forrest recorded and named many landmarks between Wells 3 and 9 in honour of his expedition party members and eminent persons.

The party discovered the spring on 2 June 1874 and remained there for eighteen days. On the afternoon of 13 June they were attacked by a group of some 40-60 Aboriginals who swarmed down from the hill which overlooks the waterhole, in Forrest's words, '...all plumed up and armed with spears and shields'. The men were forced to discharge their firearms in defence and at least two Aboriginals were wounded. The Aboriginals retreated and the following day the Forrest party hurriedly erected a stone hut near the water to protect them from a potential shower of spears should they be raided again. The explorers were not attacked again and a week later moved east into the Gibson Desert.

Well 9 had the highest yield of all the wells on the CSR at 31 000 gallons (141 000 litres) a day, according to Snell's measurements in 1929. His reconditioning party set up its base camp not far from the remains of John Forrest's barricade and next to a corkwood tree with the initials 'JF' blazed into it. They used the camp for the first few months as they worked back towards Well 1 before moving north.

Weld Spring also witnessed the final chapter in Snell's life. In 1938 he took out his final pastoral lease of 31 000 acres (13 000 hectares) on Gum Creek just north and west of Weld Spring and including Weld Spring itself. During Snell's time reconditioning the stock route, he recorded that there were huge areas of native potatoes, or coolyate, in the region, 'enough', he said, 'to feed 300 Aborigines'. In memory of this, he called his last lease Coolya, although it was officially registered as Bridleface. It was here on 8 November 1942 that at the age of seventy-two he passed away, in the presence of his faithful Aboriginal helper and two dogs. His companion ran all the way to Granite Peak Station and poked his head around the shearing shed to relay the message to a shed full of shearers. The news was eventually passed on to police headquarters. George Nicholson, the policeman sent to recover Snell's body, found his remains near a carrara bush, close to his humpy near Weld Spring. As his body had been part eaten by dogs there was no way of determining his cause of death. Nicholson collected Snell's few possessions, which included a single five-pound note, books, saddle bags and harness. His cattle were rounded up and sold off. The police found several medical books within this collection. Although Snell had only received four years of formal education, he had a disciplined mind. He was deeply motivated by the joy of learning and continued his education throughout his life.

In his later years, Snell had refused to pay the lease fees on any of his Bridleface or Nabberu holdings, maintaining that 'The bloody Government's not getting any of my money. I've got my own bank. My banks are out here in the bush and when I need money I know where to go.' He buried his money and stores in 100-gallon (455-litre) tanks underneath the ground. To prevent the Aboriginals from finding the tanks, he would run a mob of cattle over the top to wipe out all the traces. The Lands Department gave up trying to recover its dues, the Accounts Department placing his case in the 'too hard' basket. I don't think anyone would get away with such tax evasion techniques these days. Nobody has ever found the money buried by William Snell in his 'own bank'.

It was a privilege to arrive at Weld Spring, rolling in quietly without disturbing the animals. The area surrounding the station waters – windmill, tanks and trough – was mostly bare ground; where there was shade, many cattle lazed around, unfussed by my arrival. Three emus appeared from nowhere and seemed content to just wander. I couldn't believe it – usually wild emus would disappear as soon as they sensed I was there. I pulled out my camera, and hurriedly fixed on my telephoto lens. They kept their distance but continued to hover as if checking me out, allowing me to snap away.

I moved the bike up against the ruined walls of the Forrest fortress and had a wander around myself, trying to imagine the historical events just described. The hut's stone walls were originally ten by nine feet and seven feet high

Three emus wandering around Weld Spring

Forrest's stone hut built to protect his party from Aboriginal attack in 1874; Weld Spring, Well 9

(approximately 3 metres square and 2 metres high) and the roof was thatched with boughs. The scene was so tranquil, it was difficult to imagine dozens of Aboriginals attacking the campsite from over the nearby hill, hurling spears at the explorers as they traded fire in defence. I left the Weld Spring site alone. It took Don about four hours to catch up with me.

Just away from Well 9, the track joined a decent station road, which to my amazement had been graded recently. This road passes through Glenayle Station and meets the Gunbarrel Highway about 150 km to the south-east at Niminga Well, 30 km west of Carnegie Station. Many drivers use Glenayle's private roads as a short-cut to reach the CSR from the Gunbarrel.

The graded station road initially made my ride much more comfortable but it didn't last long, soon petering out into the usual 4WD track. This was a mess. In widening the track for heavy machinery to pass, the grader had driven its blade over it once in each direction. Everything apart from mature trees had been scraped level, and I had to stop regularly and remove uprooted bushes and branches from my path. The two wheel ruts of the original track were indefinable, as sand and shrapnel filled the depressions. On the positive side, the grader had knocked the tops off the corrugations. On the negative side, I was unable to determine which parts of the track were solid and which parts would give way. It was here that I faced the deepest bulldust I encountered for the whole expedition. At my pace I had time to distinguish where the depressions were – disguised under the 'talcum powder' dust – but I had no way of telling their depth. The dust particles felt cool and wet – they were somewhat refreshing, as they 'splashed' over my lower legs. Needless to say, dipping into the dust wasn't very good for the working parts of my bike.

As I rode on, it was a lottery as to what was hidden in the sand. I came adrift many times. The most annoying problem, however, was running over hidden stumps and branches which resulted in punctures. The middle strip between the wheel ruts, which was usually covered with small bushes, had been scraped bare. I was regularly lured on to the smoother, more solid surface and the promise of making up some distance. Giving in to this temptation proved a hindrance because by the time I stopped to repair punctures caused by the spikes of the snapped-off bushes, I lost much more time.

Just before Well 10 I met my second vehicle for the CSR section. Two women from Fitzroy Crossing were spending their holiday doing the 'big triangle': the CSR, Gunbarrel Highway and Tanami Track. They were covering my route in reverse in much less time. They too had had a long conversation with Murray, who was not that far ahead of us at this stage, and had learnt of my attempt. Central to their discussion following this encounter was how long they thought it would take me to pedal the CSR. Considering their own struggle to pass through the sea of sand, their estimate was that it would take me at least two months.

As it turned out, the Peak Drilling Company, which Greg and I had encountered on the second last day of the Gunbarrel, was responsible for grading the track all the way to where they were drilling for nickel – just south of Well 15 – in order to allow their heavy machinery access. We estimated the road work was less than three weeks old. I explained that, overall, from Well 9 I had made better progress than before. The women weren't so sure that this would last when I reached the dunes.

Remaining woodwork of the trough section of Goodwin Soak, Well 11

Well 10 was built at the transition between the dense scrub and more barren landscape where mature trees thinned out and the vegetation gradually appeared to diffuse into drifting sands. Drovers called Well 10 the Lucky Well because it marked the end of the worst sand country as they reached pastoral lands. Although it once provided good quality water, the well itself, which I investigated while waiting for Don to arrive, was not in good shape. The whip pole had fallen and the woodwork had rotted with the aid of termites.

I had done nearly 50 km for the day up until Well 10 and it was only about 10.30am. Don had warned me that things might start getting a bit soft before I reached the next well only 15 km away, but I hadn't mentally prepared for the drastic change of terrain. Suddenly I was cursing the sands of the Little Sandy Desert. It didn't matter that the dunes weren't very high as it was the loose, bottomless sand which slowed me down. The women from Fitzroy Crossing had told me that the grader had made a terrible mess of the track and they were right; it had evened out the surface by pushing the sand into the wheel tracks. Where the grader had missed small sections, it was slightly easier because I could find fractionally firmer surfaces to guide my wheels over. There may have been corrugations but at least I could get some traction, even if it was minimal.

I was temporarily relieved to reach Goodwin Soak, Well 11. Pushing over the previous eight kilometres, especially as the temperature soared, heightened the degree of difficulty. The temperature radiating off the sand was much hotter. Below my knees my legs were covered in a paste formed by the red dust which glued to my sweaty skin.

Goodwin Soak, positioned on a samphire flat near the edge of White Lake, originally had a high yielding water supply drawn from just 3.5 metres under the surface. Named after the manager of the Western Australian Bank in Wiluna – a particularly important position during the time of the gold rush – it didn't take much to flood the shaft and for the water supply to turn salty. The succulent samphire bushes had enveloped the woodwork of the well.

Until 1969, Well 11 was the limit of any vehicle transport from the south. In February 1929, seven of Snell's team of ten men were transported to Well 9 in Mr Green's motor truck to link up with Snell and his advance party. In the same year, Harry Paine and A Allsop, surveyors with the WA Department of Lands and Surveys, reached Well 11 in two four-cylinder Chevrolets while surveying proposed pastoral leases. Robert Falconer (owner of Carnegie Station) and his sons frequently drove the route up to Wells 9, 10 or 11 to meet mobs coming down from Billiluna, their Kimberley station. Until 1947, they would bring out fresh supplies in their 1915 Rolls-Royce Silver Ghost, using sand mats to negotiate the small dunes between Wells 10 and 11.

During World War II, sending cattle by sea south from the Kimberley was a great risk, and interest revived in using the CSR as a safer route. In late 1941, the Army attempted a reconnaissance in four trucks, three with 4WD, from Wiluna to Halls Creek but they only made it as far Goodwin Soak because of flooding around White Lake.

In fact, right up until the first successful vehicle traverse of the CSR, the humble camel was by far and away the most efficient form of transport. Camels were the hardcore beasts, invaluable to Canning, Snell and all who chose to live in and develop Australia's arid regions. Everything about the camel physiology is specifically adapted to conserve moisture, from the ability to recycle their tear-drops to the completely dry, pebble-like droppings which are expelled at the other end of the animal. A camel can go up to three weeks without water if it is trained to do so. It has an immensely resilient constitution and can live off vegetation with minimal nutritional value, such as spinifex and mulga. Camels can carry a load of up to one tonne on level ground and half that when the going is soft or more rugged. A camel wagon transport system could travel almost anywhere as camels are expert at climbing sand ridges – they crawl on their front knees and push with their extended back legs. (That is why Giles, on his failed first attempt to traverse the Gibson Desert, so 'ardently longed for a camel'.)

I arrived at Goodwin Soak to find Don talking to a couple of geologists who

Into the Little Sandy Desert, Day 4. A grader had made a mess of the track

OUT THERE AND BACK

had been analysing land near Lake Disappointment further north. Two cars in one day – the place was becoming crowded! They too were annoyed about the state of the graded track. They agreed with Don that it completely destroyed the character of the CSR and made driving conditions more treacherous. Try cycling! The track could never be improved by merely pushing a grader through sand and the maintenance of any road would be a never-ending task. Hostile weather conditions and thunderstorms would either bury it under sand drifts or wash it all away.

We used the vehicle and a lone desert oak for shade at our lunch break, moving our chairs several times to keep in the shadows as the sun tracked slowly west. The desert oak was another signal that we were now in sand ridge country; its shelter, though wispy, was welcome as it filtered out much of the intensity of the early afternoon sun.

I only managed 22 km in the afternoon session, in about three-and-a-half hours. It was completely exhausting and I may as well have been cycling on dry beach sand. There was no telling what my wheels were going to hit next and when I fell off it was difficult to restart as getting any grip at all was a challenge. I realised I needed to develop a better technique to cope with the situation. So I learnt to keep my gear selection low and only use the bottom three on the gear block, even if I could see a better section ahead. A 'good patch' invariably wouldn't last and I would become bogged, unable to restart in the wrong gear. Small gears and a fast, even cadence allowed me to more or less 'skim' over the surface, minimising the pressure of each individual leg drive and therefore the chance of the back wheel spinning. That was the theory, anyway.

On the edge of the desert and between two salt lakes, the ridges appeared to lie chaotically in random directions rather than the more uniform ridges I was expecting. The track wriggled around, along and over the ridges – it was like navigating an exasperating maze. And this was only the start of the sand: there was about 1400 km of the stuff to go.

We were never going to reach Well 12 by nightfall as I had optimistically thought after doing 63 km by lunch. Lake Aerodrome was the new target. Another of Snell's briefs was to locate possible sites for air strips every fifty miles (80 km) or so. Given the terrain, this was not a practical instruction, as the area had to be about 500 yards by 500 yards (455 metres square) and firm enough for a car to travel at 35 miles (56 km) an hour. The only landing ground Snell chose and named was Lake Aerodrome. No air strip was constructed there, however, because although the lake appeared to be suitably level and dry, it was often moist beneath the salt-encrusted surface. I reached the crest of a large dune at sunset, the brilliant white salt lake to the north-west. It was a special sight but Don appeared upset. To make the passage for the drilling equipment easier, the grader had excavated the top off the ridge as if it were making a cutting for a major road, thus reducing the impact of what Don remembered as one of his favourite views on the whole stock route. But I was happy because we were nearing the end of the day. We followed the track a few kilometres further, skirting the edge of the lake. Sand had drifted across the claypan road...there is always a sting in the tail. Eventually we found a narrow strip to set up camp: we couldn't use the lake as it was damp underfoot and, in any case, using the lake surface would scar it for many years.

I took extra time to brush the chain and gears as they had been dipped in bulldust. While Don prepared the evening meals most nights, I attended to the bike, cleaning off the grit and adding some 'dry lube'. No bike is built for the type of constant wear and tear I put it through for extended periods.

A deep red sun rose over the lake, rapidly burning away the morning clouds. I started off on the track, but found it covered with sand spilling from the dunes. I opted instead for the crackling, salt-encrusted lake, following the tracks of the heavy drilling equipment which had already scarred the moist surface. If I hit soft mud, I would merely pick up my bike and walk a few metres. When Don followed later he rightly stayed on the track, the sand being much easier for his vehicle to negotiate. Travelling over the salt would not only have contributed seriously to indefinite scarring, but also put him at risk of getting hopelessly bogged.

From there I hit the sand ridges head on, reaching Well 12 some 5.5 km later. The previous day I had virtually run up the dunes with a real spring in my step. I would then stride down the slope, mindful that I had to move forward at a good pace or the journey would take too long. This time I experimented by mounting the saddle and pushing off strongly so I could slip my foot into the pedal and 'surf' with the sand down the dune. As long as I could stay on, it was quite effective – even fun. At the base of each slope, however, I would encounter a prominent wave of sand caused by vehicles overdoing the power for their ascent. Occasionally, the roller-coaster was large enough to send me airborne, and I was sometimes able to reach speeds of up to 25 km per hour.

Well 12, the shaft of which had been restored, is set among an isolated stand of shady desert oaks. The 500-metre diversion road had not been graded, making my approach both rougher and slightly faster. There were no secrets or short-cuts to reaching Well 13 and lunch; it was simply a long, 27-km slog. The terrain sloped gently, providing a constant resistance rather than being punctuated by regularly spaced sand dunes. I could pedal most of the way, although I could barely manage to turn the cogs. My average speed was only eight kilometres per hour, an alarmingly low figure that was becoming the median speed over the sand-based country. It was simply head down and only think about reaching the next well rather than how far I still had to go. The best analogy I can come up with for the effort required to cycle this bloody 'sand pit' is to go down to the gym and crank the exercise bike up to maximum resistance. When you stop pedalling, the wheel stops turning immediately. It is impossible to gain any momentum and you are completely exhausted after a few minutes. Then try this for eight hours a day while also having to keep balance, losing power each time the wheel spins out. My arms ached and hands were still numb from gripping the handlebars. Moving forward took intense concentration.

Well 13 was another dry, ruined well, two kilometres off the track. The surrounding trees, which provided welcome shade for us, would have also provided the timber for the construction and reconditioning of the well. Snell noted that the surrounding country was poor, providing little stock feed.

The route to Well 14 was more of the same. Focusing on the 10 metres in front of me gave little opportunity to study my surroundings, which were basically sand and spinifex with the occasional bush. There was also the odd 'spear tree' which has a fine white trunk and sparse foliage. I presumed that a denser foliage would increase wind resistance, causing the flimsy-looking trunk to snap or

Delicate desert flora adapted to exist in the sand

blow over. The springy trunks were prized by Aboriginals for fashioning spears as the wood has a high tensile strength and is ideal for making these weapons. The shaft of the spear would be further streamlined by a process of heating to facilitate the removal of the bark, and then straightened by applying pressure with both hands and feet while the shaft was still supple from the heat.

Nearer to Well 14, the land quality improved slightly, signalled by the presence of a greater diversity of vegetation, including purple Sturt Desert Roses beside the track. There was little left of the well itself, positioned on a flat between two sand ridges. When Dr W J Peasley passed through here in 1977 in search of The Last of the Nomads, he found artefacts – numerous pulleys, steel bars and other debris – left by early expeditions and from them deduced that Well 14 must have been used as a depot by either Canning or Snell. On a gum tree about 200 metres from the well a blaze indicated that one of the renowned drovers, Ben Taylor, had come down the stock route and reached the well on 2 July 1939. Near the tree Peasley discovered a fragment of a perfume bottle. He recognised the well-known name still visible on the label – it was one that was popular in the 1930s and 1940s – and postulated that the most likely owner was probably Eileen Lanagan. She was the first woman to travel the stock route, accompanying her drover husband, George, from Billiluna to Carnegie stations with 800 head of cattle over four-and-a-half months. Another potential owner could have been a drover who was carrying a gift back from the wealthy goldfields or even Perth for his lady friend or mother.

It would have taken a fair splash of perfume to mask the rigours of my toil. A storm was imminent and mindful that a downpour could threaten our progress by turning any clay-based zones into a quagmire, I made a hasty inspection of the ruined well, paused for a snack and then pushed on. Well 15, where we planned to replenish our water supply, was 25 km away and I had just two hours of daylight left. Given the state of the track and my slow pace, there was little chance of making the distance, but I was going to get as close as I could.

I seemed to make faster headway after that, partly because the graded track improved slightly and partly because I was anxious about the thunderstorm brewing in the east. Bolts of forked and sheet lightning contrasted spectacularly with the menacing dark grey clouds. In the west, the late afternoon sun cast a golden glow over the spinifex plains in the foreground.

Chased by a storm, just before Well 14

Each huge droplet of rain made a separate mark as it was absorbed into the parched earth until the spots gradually joined up. Some of the moisture evaporated immediately as the raindrops fused with the hot sand. I could see the resultant steam rise from the track ahead and the atmosphere of this natural sauna filled with scents of 'earthen wet hay' and a hint of eucalyptus. I pushed on – these were only a couple of isolated showers on the fringe of the main thunderstorm – not minding the warm droplets rinsing the dust off my skin. The biggest annoyance was the thin topping of mud that stuck hopelessly to my tyres, at times totally caking up my wheels and making them impossible to turn. I was forced to stop regularly to manually scrape it off. If I could get enough speed up, the 'dry' mud would spin off, flicking dollops everywhere.

Don and I kept in radio contact. We had decided that once I reached a certain point I would stop, load my bike on to the vehicle and drive the last few kilometres to Well 15 so we could set up camp. This would make it more convenient for Don when he came to draw the water the following day. The next morning he would drive me back to the point I had reached, so that I could resume cycling and not break the continuous line of my attempt.

About five kilometres before my intended finish point, the heavens really opened. Thunder and lightning closed in and it felt like they were chasing me. There was no shelter; I was completely exposed. The scale of the scene made me feel insignificant and powerless, with no choice but to race for my destination as fast as I could. Up until then I had been feeling exhausted from the day's efforts but the adrenaline roused by the situation made me immediately forget this and run my body into overdrive. The ground had by now become completely saturated and the mud too wet to stick to my tyres. I was soaked through to the bone but not too cold as long as I kept moving. Don headed back to find me, but by that stage I had found a second wind. I continued on an extra three kilometres further than I had planned until the storm subsided. By this stage there was barely enough light to see the track, across which I drew a line, marking it with a stick and a couple of rocks.

It felt strange sitting in the vehicle to drive the 5.7 kms to Well 15. There was no struggle, the 4WD making light work of any rough road. It all felt very cosy. By the same token there was not the same sense of achievement or connection with the ground we were covering.

I was pleased with my efforts. I had been on the road from 7am to 6pm, and it had taken nearly nine hours of pedalling and pushing to cover 72 km at an average of 8.5 km per hour. Cycling over this type of terrain was a totally different league to anything I had done before, each pedal stroke taking so much more strength and energy. I could afford to relax slightly because I had planned two 'half days' and then a full day off in order to visit and appreciate the Calvert Range and the Durba Hills.

Day 6, Tuesday 28 September
Well 15 to the Calvert Range
Distance – 51 km

Distance from Wiluna – 482 km

Total distance – 12 516 km

Well 15 was restored in 1998 and Don was accustomed to relying on it as a water source. A simple plaque positioned near the well marked the death of Joseph

Edward Wilkins, who in September 1936 was speared by natives 24 km east of the well at Boonjinji native soak. His remains were recovered and interred in the Wiluna cemetery.

In the morning I was delivered back to where I stopped the previous night. The storm had settled the dust and cleared the air. I ensured that I started behind the line I had drawn – it would be very unsatisfactory to miss even the smallest section of track. I started out with less of a sense of urgency than usual, knowing that I only had to cover about 50 km to reach the turn-off to the Calvert Range.

After a kilometre, the graded road finished; the heavy vehicle tracks peeled off to the east toward the drilling site. With that episode complete, I now faced severe corrugations over a fairly flat straight stage, which ran more or less parallel with the line of the ridges. There was no escape; I could only choose the right or the left wheel track. The anatomy of a single wheel track in cross-section would show a V, the consistently corrugated sand filling in the shape. No matter how hard I tried, I could not prevent my wheels from slipping into the centre of the depression, so I was forced to ride over the deepest, softest part of the track.

A few kilometres after passing Don, who was hard at work refilling our water containers, the dunes returned at a higher frequency than ever before. Eighteen kilometres north of Well 15, I paused at the wreckage of a small handcart parked under a tree. Murray Rankin's trolley remains as a monument to the first failed attempt to walk the CSR in 1974. Rankin returned to achieve his mission two years later, making it to Wiluna with one companion after some two-and-a-half months on the track.

Walking is actually a good way of appreciating the CSR; there would be no concerns with corrugations or being channelled into the softest part of the track. It would be more efficient to march through the sand than pedal two narrow wheels. I could only move about 25 per cent faster on average over the sand than walkers do, and cycling requires far more energy.

Parking my bike near Murray Rankin's trolley, I explored the diverse vegetation between the dunes. There were spectacular white grevilleas, yellow flowering acacias, fine powder-blue pincushions, and all sorts of desert plants with delicate foliage which I couldn't identify. The view at lunch resembled the yellow plains Greg and I travelled through along the Gunbarrel Highway.

Back on the track, I spotted all sorts of lizards between Wells 15 and 16. Larger goannas and monitors lay across the route, basking in the heat and unthreatened by my presence. By contrast, little dragon and 'tartar' lizards darted in and out of the spinifex, playing 'chicken' with deftly timed late runs in front of my advancing wheels. I clocked these tiny creatures scurrying in short bursts at about twenty kilometres an hour, the 'tartar' appearing to stop and wave, hence their name. Thorny devils were also abundant, although slightly less numerous at the end of a busy season of passing 4WDs as drivers would rarely see them and the devils were unable to react to oncoming vehicles. I stopped a few times and carried my bike around so as not to disturb them. I saw a number of squashed devils on the track in this section, their little bodies ironed out with four legs pointing outwards in a star position.

Riding 50 km normally wouldn't be a big deal but the conditions and terrain prolonged my struggle through the heat of the day until about 3pm. Camels made my path more arduous – they prefer to use the clear track where possible rather than stepping through the spinifex, and in doing so, churn up the surface. Camel tracks, especially near the turn-off to Well 16, prevented me from surfing down the sand ridges.

White grevillea

A perentie lizard (approximately 1.5 metres long) taking to a desert oak for safety

Lesser used track near Sunday Well

At the junction with the Calvert Range track, we secured the bike to the roof of the LandCruiser and I put my feet up as Don drove the 40-km diversion off the stock route to the Calvert Range. It was a bonus to take advantage of the vehicle and make the most of a rest break. The ranges were named by Lawrence Wells after the sponsor of the 1896 Calvert Scientific Exploring Expedition which Wells led. Albert Calvert financed the fateful expedition from Geraldton to the Kimberley to search for minerals, find a stock route and carry out a scientific survey.

Important Aboriginal painting and engraving sites located within gorges of the Calvert Range have raised new prospects for understanding both the nature and deep antiquity of Aboriginal peoples' occupation of the Western Desert. The weathering sandstone range has probably acted as a meeting place for Indigenous people for tens of thousands of years. One of the most interesting carvings to be found at the Calvert Range is a depiction of a thylacine (Tasmanian tiger) dated at 26 000 years old. The thylacine has been extinct on the mainland for 4000 years.

The major point of interest en route was the now-defunct Sunday Well. In 1906, during Canning's survey, the party had become desperate for water. An Aboriginal guide pointed them towards a native soak and they started digging. Working by candlelight, they struck water at 2am the following morning after sinking a shaft three metres deep. As it was a Sunday, Canning named the well Sunday Well.

Approaching the Calvert Range

Even though the track was far superior to the quality of the CSR due to the less frequent traffic, a vehicle can only average about 25 km per hour in the high dune country. Between the sand ridges, it was more reminiscent of the Canning of five years back when Don first travelled it. The journey took about two hours (with a couple of photo stops) and as we arrived at the table-topped range, the late afternoon sun lent the sandstone a spectacular deep red glow. I climbed the boulders to gain a private vantage point from which to enjoy the sunset.

Day 7, Wednesday 29 September
Calvert Range to Durba Spring
Distance – 30 km
Distance from Wiluna – 512 km
Total distance – 12 546 km

I awoke next morning to find myself in the middle of a natural amphitheatre of rust-coloured rock and majestic ghost gums. Flies, which become active with the first morning rays, buzzed menacingly outside the sanctuary of my tent, ready to cause maximum annoyance as soon as I unzipped the door. It was incentive enough to prolong my lie-in for a few more minutes. I soon got going, however, as I was keen to explore the rocky ravines before the worst of the heat.

An ancient mortar and pestle, Calvert Range

Don led me south around the base of the range for a 20-minute walk, before following a dry creek bed up into a gorge which housed a high concentration of Indigenous artwork. He left me to it. I trod as tentatively as a thorny devil over the rocks, fully expecting at any moment to accost a snake out sunning itself, drawing energy from the rocks. I had no desire to disturb anything.

Artwork, Calvert Range

Judging by the diverse collection of paintings and petroglyphs, the rocks have witnessed thousands of years of Indigenous habitation. A dingo, serpents, kangaroos, various animals, shields and corroboree pictures adorn the rock faces. Pictures exposed to constant sunlight and the erosive elements have generally faded away but those protected beneath overhangs, in crevasses and caves have retained their definition and colour intensity. In the shade of a gallery overhang I saw a well-used stone 'work bench' complete with depressions and smooth grinding stones, an ancient version of a mortar and pestle which was used to grind and mix painting materials. To maximise the longevity of the paintings, the ochre pigments would be combined with emu fat or witchetty grub as a base. The predominant colours were red and white with the occasional use of yellow ochres.

On our return journey, I noted how skilled Don was as a driver. He was patient over the rough track, always mindful of the style of driving required to preserve both the condition of the track and his vehicle. Traversing each dune involved gauging just the right amount of power at the base so it would barely carry the vehicle over the crest. Many approaches required a run up but on some occasions we didn't have enough power to reach the top of the ridge, so Don had to reverse back down the slope for a second attempt. Too much power, on the other hand, caused the formation of the large waves at the base of the dunes, dangerous for drivers and for me on the descents. Since the start of the sand ridge country Don had reduced his tyre pressure (as had I on my bike) to allow for maximum traction over the sand.

Stepping out of the vehicle to prepare to set off from the Calvert Range turn-off at the southern end of the Durba Hills was like entering a furnace, the harsh conditions seeming even more extreme after I had been taking it easy in the 4WD. As I headed off, Don reassured me that the 30-km ride to Durba Spring on the north-east side of the range would be mostly rocky. Rocks may be difficult

Canning's Cairn and the Durba Hills

for drivers, but I had been longing for a rocky surface over the last few days; anything solid was welcome. The first five kilometres were sandy and slow going, but after that conditions improved, a combination of rocks and sand drifts.

Canning's Cairn, a two-metre pile of stones set on the south-western spur of the Durba Hills, was erected on his first survey expedition in 1906. I hadn't realised there was an easier route as I scrambled up the edge of the 62-metre cliff to get a closer look at the historic trig point. Snell had christened these hills The Rockies. The sweeping views were spectacular, but their small scale and the nature of their beauty is in stark contrast with their American namesake. To the north and west were endless waves of sand ridges, apart from the lone Diebel Hills. To the east and south lay the crumbling cliffs of the Durbas, pockets of green near to the base of the range indicating areas that were watered by run-off from the slopes.

I crossed a couple of dry ephemeral creeks and was surprised to find a patch of flowering Sturt Desert Peas. I had expected to see more of these beautiful native plants during the expedition, but this was the only wild spray I saw the whole way. On the way to our campsite, Don stopped to collect firewood, mainly needed to burn our rubbish; the idea was to reduce our refuse down to very little and dispose of any residue such as cans later on. My last few kilometres became a drawn-out affair as I hit impossible sections of sand washed off from the slopes. It was a race to reach my destination before the steadily encroaching darkness. Landing fair on top of a large hummock of spinifex virtually in slow motion had me cursing out loud. I couldn't waste time picking out the spines – they had to wait until I arrived at last light.

Sturt Desert Pea

Crossing over a dry stony creek, I could just make out the stunning campsite, considered by many to be one of Australia's finest natural venues. The oasis, with its clear running spring water, huge white gum trees up to 24 metres high and luxuriant permanent couch-grass cover, had been a popular camping place for drovers during the heyday of the stock route. A few date palms thrived beside the permanent water, most likely grown from seeds left by the Afghan cameleers who accompanied the drovers. The site was also an important meeting place for the Aboriginal people who recorded their presence and indicated the site's spiritual significance on the sandstone walls. When Canning's party came through in 1906, they found a large cache of spears and, concerned for their safety, confiscated them. The high cliffs flanking the mouth of the gorge would have made a perfect vantage point for an attack.

During the dry season, the site is rarely free of campers as they usually plan to spend a rest day after a week out from Wiluna. I too had taken a week to cycle there from Wiluna and was physically exhausted, but very satisfied with my achievement. At the first opportunity I used the satellite phone to call Arnaud and 'check in'. I felt so far away with so far to go.

Day 8, Thursday 29 September
Durba Spring
Rest day
Distance from Wiluna – 512 km
Total distance – 12 546 km

Somehow the eggs had made it through a week of corrugations without being broken. We didn't think they would last too much longer, so I whipped up a massive pancake batter. It was sheer luxury to have access to decent cooking facilities, compared with the lightweight, multi-fuel burning stove and small pot which usually restricted the menu. I ate so well I had to have a lie-down before spending a leisurely hour exploring the spectacular gorge on foot.

The remainder of the day passed in slow motion as I caught up on the diary, washed clothes and serviced the bike for another week of abuse. Don made his first loaf of bread in the camp oven. Fresh supplies were running out rapidly as we entered our second week.

Durba Spring and Gorge – a quiet day of rest

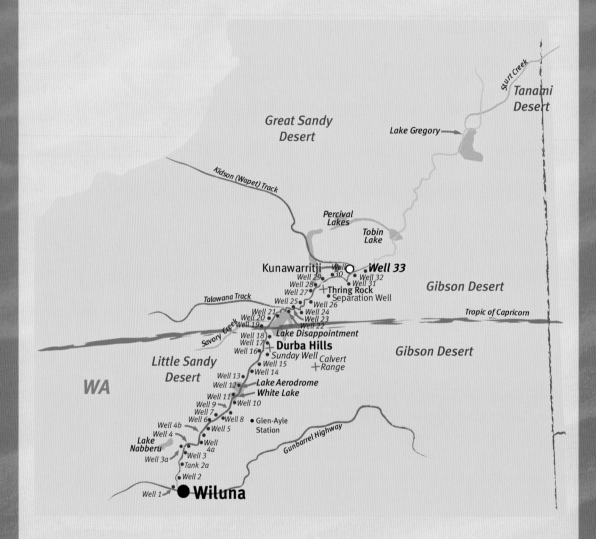

Great Sandy Desert

Tanami Desert

Sturt Creek

Lake Gregory

Kidson (Wapet) Track

Percival Lakes

Tobin Lake

Kunawarritji   Well 30   **Well 33**

Well 29   Well 32

Well 28   Well 31

Well 27   **Thring Rock**

Talawana Track   Well 25   Well 26   Separation Well

Gibson Desert

Well 21   Well 24

Well 20   Well 23

Well 19   Well 22

Savory Creek   Well 18   **Lake Disappointment**

Tropic of Capricorn

Well 17   **Durba Hills**

Well 16   Sunday Well   Calvert Range

Little Sandy Desert

Well 15

Well 13   Well 14

WA

Well 12   **Lake Aerodrome**

Well 11   **White Lake**

Well 9   Well 10

Well 7

Well 6   Well 8   Glen-Ayle Station

Well 4b   Well 5

Well 4

Lake Nabberu   Well 4a   *Gunbarrel Highway*

Well 3

Well 3a   Tank 2a

Well 2

Well 1   ● **Wiluna**

Gibson Desert

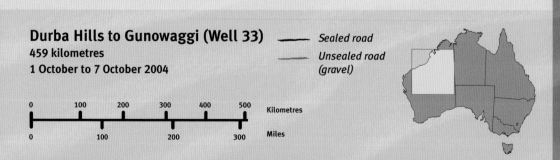

Durba Hills to Gunowaggi (Well 33)

459 kilometres
1 October to 7 October 2004

—— Sealed road
—— Unsealed road (gravel)

| 0 | 100 | 200 | 300 | 400 | 500 | Kilometres |

| 0 | 100 | 200 | 300 | Miles |

10

The grit between my teeth
Canning Stock Route, Week 2

Preparing to 'surf' with the sand down a dune (Little Sandy Desert)

Durba Hills to Gunowaggi (Well 33)

Day 9, Friday 1 October
Durba Spring to Kunanaggi (Well 19) + 3 km
Distance – 63 km
Distance from Wiluna – 575 km
Total distance – 12 609 km

I could not leave the Durba Hills without visiting Killagurra Gorge and Well 17, which I had passed hurriedly on the way to Durba Spring in the half-light. Canning had fashioned a watering point from the natural spring in Killagurra by clearing timber and rocks, and making a trough paved with stones. When Snell arrived at Killagurra Spring on 5 August 1929, he found Canning's original well site had dried up so he built an additional well out of solid rock, also using timber and stone. Over recent seasons, violent rain storms had caused torrential flooding, dislodging some massive boulders and sending them hurtling down the gorge as if they were pebbles. Although the freak weather had changed some of the prominent landmarks and buried Well 17, the flash flooding had fortunately not destroyed the main attraction we had detoured to see. The Indigenous paintings, which indicate the importance and sacred nature of the gorge, were stuck fast to the protected rock face.

Mythical figures at
Killagurra Gorge

Analyses of what the illustrations represent vary greatly. In the cave section, Snell had recorded with his Kodak 'Brownie' camera the Wanambi motif (a mythical water snake) and an illustration of Juno the devil. If an Aboriginal transgressed tribal law, the 'evildoer' would be taken into the cave and shown Juno. If the person didn't die of fright, he/she would be hit on the head.

Some have suggested the paintings in the main gallery may depict an early exchange between the native peoples and Dutch explorers, the first Europeans to discover the Western Australian coast. As their ships sailed towards the Dutch East Indies (Indonesia) to trade spices, the predominant trade winds caused many to become wrecked on the treacherous coastline. Another interpretation is that the figures depict aliens landing on Lake Disappointment about 40 km to the north. The region was given a wide berth by the desert people. One of the principal figures could also be Ngangooloo, the evil man who lives under the surface of the vast salty expanse. He remains in his lair beneath the lake's surface during cold or windy weather and ventures forth on calm, warm days to roam the land, devouring any Aboriginal people he might encounter.

I was tempted to stay longer in this fascinating place, but daily temperatures over the previous couple of days had topped the 40°C mark and by 8am the sun already had an inhospitable sting away from the shade of the surviving majestic white gums. The 34 km between Wells 17 and 18 were considered by the drovers, and now many drivers, as the most difficult to traverse of the whole CSR. The sand ridges are not the highest en route, but the sand has the softest consistency. I had already noticed that, as the day heated up, the sand became more fluid. In the early morning, even miniscule amounts of moisture in the air can contribute to forming a fine crust on the surface. Drivers would not be aware of this crust, but to me it made a significant difference. It meant I was able to cycle up a greater portion of each sand dune and it was fractionally easier to get started in the relative cool. As the temperature increased, the further my wheels sank into the desert sands.

Starting late proved a bad idea. Although I had been concerned about this section, I didn't notice that the sand was any softer than usual; it was simply all soft and my average speed remained at eight kilometres an hour. The most punishing element, however, was the temperature and the lack of any shade. The radiant temperature reflecting off the sand was much hotter than the ambient air temperature. I couldn't take an exact reading but, reportedly, when the ambient temperature is 40°C or more, the sand can reach about 60°C. Whatever the temperature was, the sand was burning my feet. My water requirements were greater than usual and seemed to be increasing exponentially. As soon as I took a swig, it felt as though the moisture leaked straight out again through the pores in my skin.

Don seemed to be taking an eternity to catch up with me. I couldn't reach him on the two-way, so he must have been more than 12 km back and therefore out of range. I needed to tell him that my water supplies were low. Concerned, I rationed my drinks to just a sip at the crest of each ridge. We finally made contact 27 km from the Killagurra turn-off; he was still 15 km back and the intermittent reception made communication difficult. Relieved that he was on his way, as I had only about 100 ml of water left, I pushed on and finished my last drop with 5 km to go before reaching Well 18. Don was still struggling through the soft sand; it was really affecting his vehicle, so that he couldn't travel much faster than me. With only 4 km to go, and no shade where I was, I decided it was best to head for the well – at 8 km per hour, that meant another half-hour ride. I became obsessed with reaching the water. As my body heated to beyond its normal temperature range, this was all I thought about.

By the time Don caught up to me, 200 metres before Well 18, I was displaying obvious signs of heat stress. My heart was racing, my skin had turned pink, I had stopped sweating and felt extremely hot, and my throat was raw. Most alarmingly, with my state of homeostasis under threat, my cooling system was not functioning effectively and as a result I wasn't thinking clearly – I should have crawled under a bush and waited instead of pushing on. It wouldn't have been very comfortable sharing the partial shade with the ants and other creepy-crawlies, but the shelter and rest would have helped conserve moisture.

Don sat me down in the shade and I gradually re-hydrated with several bottles of water. After about fifteen minutes, I felt much better and we wandered over to the newly restored well, where hundreds of small brown frogs leapt from the walls to escape the light when Don lifted the trapdoor. I didn't stay long, adamant that, unless I did a few more kilometres before lunch, I would fall too far short of my morning target. It was evident that I hadn't fully recovered from my ordeal because I started to feel light-headed as I rode. Images of an endless stream of small brown frogs leaping into the water flashed at me – in slow motion. After a further 6 km, I almost blacked out before deciding to take an extended lunch break.

Small brown frogs down the shaft of Well 18

When I picked up the track again, the soft, impossible ground continued a further 10 km toward the south-western tip of Lake Disappointment and then dog-legged away toward Kunanaggi, or Well 19, the Lonely Well. Four kilometres before Kunanaggi, I crossed the Tropic of Capricorn for the third time on the expedition. I was back on a similar latitude to Alice Springs and Longreach.

In perceiving that the real highlight of the afternoon was traversing the intermittent claypans, I was really clutching at straws. Between the sand ridges, the satellite salt pans of Lake Disappointment were a delight as I skimmed over their surface, which had been deeply gouged out by 4WDs fighting to avoid becoming hopelessly marooned after rain. It usually took about thirty seconds to cross each claypan before I'd have another set of dunes to labour over.

Well 19 was little more than a depression on the edge of a samphire flat. Bees swarmed above the small puddle, drinking the stagnant slime. Snell had classed the water quality from this low-yielding well as 'good', but decided not to sink it any deeper for fear of turning the water supply saline and unusable, learning from his mistake at Well 3A.

I waited for Don to catch up to me and drive on ahead to choose a campsite among a stand of desert oaks. That evening, my appetite was suppressed but I knew I had to force myself to eat to keep up my strength. I fell asleep sitting upright in my chair. This was not a good start for Week 2 of the CSR.

Day 10, Saturday 2 October
Kunanaggi (Well 19) +3 km to Well 21 turn-off
Distance – 59 km
Distance from Wiluna – 634 km
Total distance – 12 668 km

Determined to beat the heat, I made an effort to start even earlier. But I was tired and, for the first time, I felt my spirit wane. My muscles were shaky and completely drained of energy, and my heart raced with each minor effort. Yesterday's dehydrated state had caused extreme stress to my cells and they had not recovered.

The first twenty kilometres to Savory Creek was utterly soul destroying. The sand dunes weren't particularly high, but they ran haphazardly in different directions and the track wriggled through them like a seemingly never-ending maze, often traversing diagonally over the ridges, which meant long, slow inclines in hopeless sand. I couldn't summon the power needed to pedal under these conditions, and restarting after losing balance was near impossible. Walking was almost as fast, and required far less energy. My average speed to Savory Creek was just 6.6 km an hour.

The severity of the conditions, combined with my exhausted state, led me to lose control of my emotions. As I trudged up the dunes, thoroughly feeling ground down, tears started to flow, like the summer storm I had endured three days earlier. A few sporadic drops evolved into a torrential downpour. The hot, dry sands instantaneously absorbed my salty trail, as if the desert refused to tolerate such a show of weakness, fragility, vulnerability.

Giving way completely, I sat down as if on strike. I had to think the whole situation through, remind myself of why I was doing this, of the level of satisfaction I would gain from achieving my goals. The CSR was the most important part of the expedition, and I always knew it was going to test my limits. I had at least another 1000 km of sand ridges to go. I had never given up on anything before and I reminded myself of how much I would regret throwing in the towel after only ten days and about one-third of the journey. I couldn't bear to give my doubters any satisfaction.

Psyching myself into a fixated, almost robotic, state, I took several deep breaths and pushed off again. I wasn't going to get there sitting on my bum! Every step forward was a step in the right direction and a step closer to my target. I set very short-term goals, such as reaching a small bush or a desert oak beside the track twenty or fifty metres ahead, then gradually raised my sights to reach the next sand ridge. Making each manageable target was a small success – I was getting there. I needed to see my situation with 'new eyes', so I made a conscious effort to look for the beauty in my surroundings and appreciate that few people ever create such opportunities. It also helped if I diverted my mind away from the task at hand, so I searched for favourite songs and positive

Crossing the highly saline Savory Creek, the main stream which flows into Lake Disappointment

thoughts – I had transformed the desperate situation into a *Beautiful Day*. By the time I neared Savory Creek three hours later, I was feeling much better. I carved my way through the sand in an hypnotic fashion, with a new inner strength, no longer paralysed by the emotional or physical pain which had forced me to question what I was doing.

Don was surprised to catch up to me so soon on a samphire flat just before the creek. The terrain had been little obstacle for his vehicle and he had found this section much easier than the conditions between Wells 17 and 18. He couldn't have imagined the journey I had been through during the previous three hours.

Savory Creek is the most notorious hazard for vehicles on the CSR. This time the saline creek was low, so the crossing, which Don treated with respect, was straightforward. He took care to first walk a path across to ensure his vehicle would not hit any deep soft patches – with no buddy 4WD to act as an anchor to winch the vehicle from a bog, he had to exercise extreme caution. Although I relied on the 4WD to carry supplies, with potentially so many facets that could break down, it was the weak link in my journey. Don is a great mechanic, but if something failed drastically, we were extremely vulnerable. For me, Savory Creek was no different from any other water crossing I had done on the journey so far and, as there was no threat of crocodiles, I simply picked up the bike and walked across. The fine black mud which squelched between my toes was a reminder of how treacherous this obstacle is after rain.

Cycling along the dry, clay-based banks of the creek towards its confluence with Lake Disappointment was a short-lived joy. Savory Creek is the principal stream supplying concentrated brine to the lake. From the Ophthalmia Range (near the mining town of Newman), it traverses hundreds of kilometres over the entire Little Sandy Desert. I am amazed that any water at all reaches Lake Disappointment before evaporating.

Lake Disappointment, whose great white expanse covers an area of approximately 64 km from north to south and 48 km from east to west, was named in 1897 by explorer Frank Hann. Noticing that many waterways headed

Lake Disappointment in the heat of the day

east from the Ophthalmia Range, Hann was searching for an inland sea surrounded by fertile land. The name he gave what he found – a lake which only holds water after heavy rain, and is perfectly flat except for an occasional island of sand – echoes his sentiments. Our arrival coincided with the hottest part of the day and lunch break. After yesterday's experience, I decided to extend my rest period; there was nothing to be gained by flogging myself in such conditions – definitely unsustainable. Our down time provided the opportunity to walk out onto the lake's surface, which was surprisingly moist underfoot. A massive mirage hung over the lake, like a giant blanket of steam, and the islands appeared to hover above the shimmering expanse like extra-terrestrial ships. If Greg was with me it would have definitely reminded him of his visit to Antarctica. It was comforting to imagine the freezing landscapes of that cold desert when it was 43°C in the shade. I am certain the reverse idea has warmed the hearts of many polar explorers. Here the red dunes made a dramatic contrast with the whiteness of the lake and the stunted salt bushes which stabilised its shores in the foreground, the brightness of my surroundings forcing me to squint continuously.

The temperature had dropped five degrees by the time I set off at 2.45 for the afternoon session. Normally I would have cursed the warm resistance of the prevailing north westerly, but this time I didn't mind. The high evaporation rate of the breeze synchronised with the flow rate of my perspiration – an effective air conditioner. I was able to break the 28 km down into four short sections corresponding to minor landmarks on my map: 5 km to the Well 20 turn-off, 5 km to the north-western tip of the lake, then 8 km and 10 km to reach the next important track junction. Thankfully, the path was broken by more small claypans which fringe the Lake Disappointment shoreline. In the transition zone between the salt pans and the high dunes, the track followed parallel to the ridgelines, encouraging drivers to muscle over the sand, leaving me another battle with shocking corrugations.

We camped at the junction leading to Well 21 and 22. As it was twilight, Don decided to camp on the track, the only reasonably flat surface. There was no chance of any vehicles passing in the night and we would be off at first light the following morning. Having done just 59 km after starting at 6.30am, it was the longest day so far for the shortest distance.

Day 11, Sunday 3 October
Well 21 turn-off to Curara Soaks (Well 24)
Distance – 82 km
Distance from Wiluna – 716 km
Total distance – 12 750 km

From our campsite, I had to make a choice between following the route over some of the highest sand ridges of the whole CSR (which was slightly more interesting, according to Don) and pass by Wells 21 and 22 (both derelict) or taking the more north-westerly option, which ran between and over the lower dunes closer to the McKay Range. I didn't feel compelled to pass by every water point and chose the latter, which was seven kilometres shorter. I set off with high hopes of an improved surface.

Within the first few dunes I spotted a mature 1.5-metre snake, probably a deadly King Brown. Instantly stopping in my tracks, I waited silently until I saw the tail slither into the spinifex, well away from where I had to pass. During the course of the morning, I also saw a few tiddlers, most likely juvenile King Browns, about half a metre in length. There was nothing like spotting one of the world's most venomous snakes at close range to start an adrenaline rush. It reminded me that if I had to drag my bike up a dune, I should step down the middle of the track rather than on the outside of the wheel furrow as there was no telling what could be lurking in the spinifex.

Sunrise near Lake Disappointment/Well 22 turn-off – the promise of another scorcher

An inquisitive Gould's goanna – one of the more beautiful animals of the spinifex country

The slightly better surface did mean I could pedal at a more tolerable speed – between 12 and 13 km per hour – but I paid the usual high price and was shaken to bits. The furrows were partially overgrown and as I could not deviate from the line I was forced to crash through the undergrowth. When Don caught up with me for the mid-morning top-up, he was exasperated with the track condition. The ceaseless corrugations caused his heavy duty shock absorbers to overheat and he had to stop repeatedly to let them cool down.

Georgia Bore, the late morning target, is positioned at the junction of the CSR and the Talawana Track. With Newman roughly 400 km to the west, it is one of a few entry/exit points to the Canning. The Talawana Track and the CSR become one from Georgia Bore to the Windy Corner turn-off, just north of Curara Soaks – Well 24.

Georgia Bore was not an original watering point, being installed more recently by a mining exploration company, but it does supply reasonable water. Don decided it was time for a decent wash and bravely offered to wash my cycle shirt. Normally this garment would get a rinse every two or three days but it hadn't had a wash since Durba Spring and was so salt-encrusted from perspiration that, when I took it off, it retained the form of my body.

Leaving Don to enjoy his ablutions, I headed off to put in a few more kilometres before lunch, excited at the thought that the Talawana Track was an official road and therefore had seen a grader. It might have been in better condition had the grader driven through shortly before I came along, but by now it was the end of the season and the track was inescapably soft and hopelessly corrugated, worse for me than before Georgia Bore. This was completely disheartening – the CSR was presenting one mean trick after another. A vicious north-westerly constantly sculpted the vast open land, Mother Nature's own construction site. Coarse grit, propelled like horizontal sleet, stung as it sand-blasted my exposed skin – so much for the romantic notion that cycling allowed one to 'merge harmoniously with the natural momentum of the landscape'. I had told Don I would do about half an hour more and then stop in the shade, which he had assured me would be there. But there was no shelter.

After he eventually caught up, and still nothing in sight an hour or so later, we decided to improvise and create our own shade. There are not too many places in the world where a vehicle can be parked across the width of a road and the driver can be confident that no vehicles will pass. We parked at this angle to protect us from the shifting sands and early afternoon sun, Don attaching a small tarpaulin to the roof rack and pegging the other side to the ground, forming a small canopy. We sat under our little square shelter, shuffling our chairs to move with the shade.

With all the fresh food now gone, the lunch menu had become very bland. Don's bread was good when it was fresh, but difficult to swallow after a couple of days and with a parched throat. Sardines, cream cheese and other bits and pieces which came out of tins and jars were generally on offer.

When Snell arrived at Well 23 on 21 October 1929, he found it completely destroyed with no fence or trough. As was the case with many of the wells in the region and further north, Aboriginals, refusing to use the windlass, had filled it in with sand, attempting to raise the water level. The surface timber had been taken for firewood – a scarce commodity in the region. Snell fashioned 'native' rope ladders and showed the locals how to use them, hoping his innovation would prolong the life of his workmanship. In 1962, Len Beadell reconditioned the well when he constructed the Talawana Track as part of his road network servicing the Woomera Rocket Range. We found Well 23 was just another ruined site with undrinkable mineralised water; it warranted only a quick visit as I needed to make haste to reach Curara Soaks by dark.

Just as I was admiring the late afternoon light on the McKay Range, I was stopped dead in my tracks by another King Brown about seven metres in front of me. Once again, my heart leapt and then I froze, hoping that I was still harmoniously merging with the surroundings. The olive-green reptile was as long as the track was wide. I kept my eyes peeled on the verge for any other surprises. I could barely make out the track by the time I pushed through deep, demoralising sand to arrive at the turn-off to Curara Soaks.

Day 12, Monday 4 October
Curara Soaks (Well 24) to Canning's 1907 Camp
Distance – 58 km

Distance from Wiluna – 774 km

Total distance – 12 808 km

The sign pointing to Windy Corner, positioned where the Talawana Track leaves the CSR

There wasn't much left of Well 24, but in the early morning I was able to appreciate the site at the base of a small rocky hill. Don had insisted before retiring the previous evening that we pack everything away as dingoes frequented the water-hole and were known to demolish anything they could find with a scent – not only food but clothing. The whiff emanating from my cycle shoes, shirt or shorts would have been like Chanel No. 5 to a dingo! Fortunately, everything remained untouched overnight.

I was still feeling extremely tired and motivation to leave camp was so low that I stalled my departure until 7am. I had made good distance yesterday, but had pushed for too long in the heat. The Talawana Track was far heavier going than expected, and my exhaustion had accumulated over the past three days.

Colours of the sand dunes near Well 25

I still had four days to go to reach Well 33 and the Kunawarritji Community, if I continued at the current pace. I tried to focus on the fact that when this day was over I was more than halfway through the week – halfway to my next rest day.

The surface was more tolerable after the turn-off to Windy Corner where the Talawana Track veered off to the east. I pedalled across a vast, treeless plain, over a few claypans and a rocky ridge before heading west toward Well 25. A lone camel was grazing on the plain, and I prayed it wasn't another young bull on heat. More wildlife appeared in the shape of a third King Brown in two days slipping out from behind a spinifex bush. Again, I managed to pull up just in time to avoid disturbing the sinister-looking creature. This one was sepia brown, whereas the previous two were olive-green, even though they were the same variety.

While part of the fence, trough and framework of Well 25 are still intact, the well itself was silted up and dry. Snell decided not to attempt to repair Wells 25 through to 29 inclusive as they had all been completely destroyed by Aboriginals, there was no

Ruins of Canning's work at Well 25

wood in the vicinity, and his supplies of iron work, such as troughing and iron doors, were low. He decided that the most effective use of resources would be to install the remaining iron work into wells he could completely restore to working order.

The skeletal remains of Well 25 would have been the work of Canning's 1930 reconditioning party. At the age of seventy, Canning had been commissioned to restore the remainder of the wells after Snell had completed his part of the job. He restored Wells 25 through to 29 and then all those north of Well 35. To refurbish the treeless sites, desert oaks had to be cut and hauled by camel over long distances. Canning's third and final expedition over the route that bears his name showed immense fortitude – he walked for most of the 16 months it took to carry out the work.

After crossing a larger claypan, the track made a right-angle turn north, leaving me to take some of the highest dunes of the CSR head on. The uniformly high ridges were about 14–15 metres tall and further apart, about 600 metres

High dunes between Wells 25 and 26 (Tiwa)

OUT THERE AND BACK

as the crow flies. The track between the peaks was slightly firmer, although marred by the usual appalling corrugations. At the summit of each ridge all I could see was wave after wave of sand all the way to the horizon although, somehow, this terrain felt less claustrophobic and easier to deal with mentally. Progress seemed to be 'cleaner' than toiling through a tangle of lower dunes. The high dunes, however, can be more difficult for drivers, who need long, measured, run-ups to power up the ridges.

I pushed on through the heat of the day to reach Well 26, hot sand oozing into the spaces in my shoes and moulding around my feet, slowly roasting them as if they were part of a Maori *hangi*.

Well 26 or Tiwa meant that I was halfway through the fifty-two watering points. Even if I hadn't reached the mid-point in distance, psychologically this was an important landmark. The well, which provides high quality water, was restored in 1983 by a group of volunteers from Perth to mark the seventy-fifth anniversary of the stock route. The windlass, whip pole, buckets, troughing and timberwork are all reproductions of the equipment used in 1908, although jarrah was sensibly imported for the timberwork. Don and I were relying on Tiwa's supply: it was our seventh day since Well 15 and we were on our last 20-litre container. We had used the water from Durba Spring and Georgia Bore for cooking and washing only, which had strung out our dwindling stocks.

With barely a skerrick of vegetation substantial enough to make shade, it is difficult to imagine how there could be such an abundant artesian water supply here. The reason is that under the Great Sandy and Gibson deserts, and beneath a total about 40 per cent of the surface area of WA, lie geological aquifers capable of storing and providing significant quantities of water. The groundwater occupies the pores or crevices in sandstone, sand and gravel. During his original survey, and aided by local Aboriginals, Canning identified the sites of native soaks and as a result was able to tap into the three major aquifers – the Canning Basin, the Officer Basin and the Savory groundwater region – where they are relatively shallow. The deepest bore at Well 5 is 32 metres (105 ft) while Well 17 at Killagurra was merely 2.5 metres (before it was washed away). Most waters are between 7 and 20 metres. Well 26 is just seven metres deep.

Tiwa – the first well to be restored in 1983. This shows the typical anatomy of a well: trough (foreground), protected shaft, windlass and whip pole with a pulley

Don worked hard to replenish our 120-litre water supply. The water was collected using the heavy duty iron bucket, which was raised and lowered using the windlass attached by a wire rope. He was careful to partially filter each container by pouring the water through an old tee-shirt. I packed the gear away, at the same time collecting a few rogue empty beer cans. It was extremely disappointing to find that some people don't revere the fragile land they are travelling through enough to bother taking their rubbish away with them. I had imagined that those who are adventurous enough to travel the CSR would have more respect. I also used the break to check over my bike and sign the visitors' book. Heeding the state of my body and mind, I decided to have a shorter day and altered my target destination to Canning's 1907 Camp, only 15 km away, situated beside a dry tree-lined creek which runs off the nearby Slate Range.

Day 13, Tuesday 5 October
Canning's 1907 Camp to Well 28 + 17 km
Distance – 66 km
Distance from Wiluna – 840 km
Total distance – 12 874 km

Once away from the Slate Range, it was back into the high dunes. I adopted a similar riding style as yesterday, as the ridges ran perfectly parallel and were evenly spaced. But rather than each mound being a simple wave shape, they had evolved and reinvented themselves into dual-headed – or even triple-headed – monsters. I was able to build a fair amount of momentum on descent, reaching speeds of 30 km an hour before slamming into the natural speed bumps at the foot of the sand hill. Brakes are ineffectual in loose sand.

From the summit of each ridge, the land below appeared relatively flat, but in cross-section the terrain took on the profile of a salad bowl: steep sides and then a long, slow curve before reaching a short base. Small thickets of tea-tree scrub accumulated on the flat, giving me brief protection from the wind and enforcing bends in the track which provided slight respite from the violent shaking.

Hidden sticks and groundcover growing in the centre of the track were the source of many punctures which were unpleasant to repair in the prevailing conditions. I always tried to repair the inner tubes on the spot and kept at least two spares in my bag. By now, the inner tubes were starting to sport more patches than there was original rubber! The extra activity of mending punctures and repeatedly having to pump enough air into my fat tyres added to my energy expenditure.

A flock of noisy desert finches darting amongst the tea-trees at Well 27 were strong evidence that there was water in the derelict shaft. The water was just seven metres down. Fifteen kilometres north of Well 27 I reached the turn-off to Separation Well. The soak, 34 km to the east of the track, was discovered by Lawrence Wells during the fateful 1896 Calvert expedition, when his party searched for land suitable for building a stock route. Separation Well was so named because it was there on the edge of the Great Sandy Desert that Wells divided his men into two small groups in order to cover more ground. They planned to meet up at Joanna Spring, 305 km to the north. The principal group failed to find the spring, mainly because during his 1873 expedition Peter Egerton Warburton had incorrectly recorded its position, marking it 24 km too far west. They did make it to the Fitzroy River – barely – but failed to notice any pre-arranged smoke signals that the second group, Charles Wells (Lawrence's cousin) and George Jones, may have been sending. Jones and Wells never reached their destination and, tragically, died of thirst only 22 km from Joanna Spring. The following year, a search party led by Lawrence Wells, discovered their mummified bodies, along with a notebook, partially buried in the sand.

When I set off from Canning's Camp the next morning I felt much better than I had the previous three, but by the midday break after 46 km I was parched and not feeling too lively. My body was not recovering from the strain and I again felt badly heat affected. Don constructed shade once more, selecting a site on top of a sand dune so we could make the most of any breeze, and despite the persistent flies and ants we attempted to have a siesta under the moving shade. The sand, which had been storing the sun's warmth during the morning, now radiated heat from below. It was difficult to relax as beads of perspiration dripped constantly, and were readily absorbed into the anhydrous sand.

Not feeling any more rested, I recommenced riding in the early afternoon and continued as far as I could until dark. The fine sand granules seemed to be working their way into everything – I even had grit between my teeth. There was no obvious campsite during the last hour of light so we had to improvise by clearing two small level patches just big enough for the tents. Shovelling sand was not what I had in mind at the end of another day on the CSR.

A typical view from a sand ridge of my path ahead. The piste here was a mess, sculpted into wave shapes (larger at the bottom) by vehicles powering up the dune

Day 14, Wednesday 6 October
Well 28 + 17 km to Nurgurga Soak
Distance – 70 km

Distance from Wiluna – 910 km

Total distance – 12 944 km

It was warm even at 6am, as I ate my milky rice fortified with large dollops of Nutella (I had discovered that this combination gave the longest lasting energy). The track did a seemingly pointless diversion, passing the remains of Well 29 before looping back to Thring Rock. Fall-out from the crumbling landmark presented me with a memorable 5-km section from the dry well to the lone rock. Scrambling up the remnant sandstone outcrop, I was rewarded with extensive views, Thring Rock standing out like an island in the sea of sand which stretched beyond the horizon. The only variation of terrain was the shimmering white expanse of Lake Auld to the west which, along with Thring Rock, had been named by Lawrence Wells. It was apparent why Canning's camels had had to cart desert oak more than 200 km from the south to construct Well 29. I basked on the rocks like a lizard absorbing the morning rays. I really didn't need to absorb any more heat, but the rest helped me re-energise for another stint on the soft stuff.

Progress to lunch was typical of what I had been able to manage of recent times: about five-and-a-half hours of cycling for 45 km at about 8.5 km per hour. I was looking forward to reaching the bloodwood forest surrounding Well 30 – Dunda Jinnda – which had once supplied excellent water. Don was correct in

Don about to catch me for the morning break (about 9.30am) as I left Thring Rock

describing the forest as more of a woodland, but it was easy to see how, after travelling so far through barren sands, the early explorers must have felt like they were in a dense thicket. We rested in the shade of the mature bloodwoods, which grow above a bed of limestone harbouring enough water to support the deeper rooted trees.

Passing the remains of Dunda Jinnda, I set off for the Nurgurga native soak. I had 25 km to do in about two-and-a-half hours, which was always going to be a race to beat the sunset. The forest ended abruptly, opening out into a flat limestone plain where the track surface was a combination of white limestone boulders embedded in the usual red sand. Drivers have to steer cautiously for fear of hitting the rocks concealed beneath the sand but I was able to cycle strongly, developing enough momentum to plough through the intermittent sand drifts. With a friendly tail-wind inducing a second wind, and the sand ridges ironed out for the time being, I positively flew along at 15 km per an hour. A herd of camels grazed the open ground.

As I neared my destination it all became horribly soft again, and the second wind was balanced out by an equal and opposite reaction. In the final three kilometres, I was hit by an energy 'bonk' and broke into a cold sweat, feeling very shaky. Unable to get any traction to push off in the deep sand, I was forced to traipse over the soft ground, dragging my bike despondently, like a child towing a broken toy. I really wasn't feeling too well, was insatiably thirsty and had shooting pains across my lower abdomen. I was pleased, though, to have come far enough to ensure that by the following day I would make Well 33, the goal of my second week.

Day 15, Thursday 7 October
Nurgurga Soak to Gunowaggi (Well 33)
Distance – 61 km

Distance From Wiluna – 971 km

Total distance – 13 005 km

I wished I could have taken my day off a day early. Next morning, I was exhausted, my appetite was poor and my spirits were low. My lower abdomen was sore and I was worried about the cause. To make matters worse, I knew I would be starting off as I had finished the previous day – pushing through gutless sand.

The first section was continuously soft, as though someone had tipped the entire contents of a sand dune over the track – another bloody sandpit. To add insult to injury, I ended up landing in spinifex bushes more than once and was starting to feel like a pin cushion. After seven kilometres I had a choice, either to continue straight ahead or detour to Well 31, which would be more interesting but add a further three kilometres to my journey. I chose the latter on Don's recommendation. This proved to be a good decision because the track was of a superior quality.

In 1929, Snell found that Canning's well had been completely destroyed and decided to build a new one at Wullowla, a native well nearby. When Canning came through the following year, he rebuilt his original Well 31, set among a shady stand of mature trees. Between there and Well 32, it was depressingly soft and flat all the way, a fierce side-wind adding to the degree of difficulty and often forcing me off balance in my weakened state. I preferred to travel over dunes rather than the sandy flat because it broke the monotony and provided some form of shelter. Well 32 was totally exposed on the spinifex flats with no effective shade, just a couple of tea-trees. Gunowaggi could not come soon enough.

The arrow-straight track had been graded twenty kilometres before the Kunawarritji Community, which for me merely stirred up the sand and had no effect on the corrugations. For vehicles to make any progress along the track means going either very fast or at snail's pace. Although it is a dangerous practice, at high speed they can skim over the tops of the bumps and not incur too much discomfort. Because of the speed at which vehicles attack this section, it only takes a few days for its washboard surface to be restored. I obviously had no option about speed and arrived at the crossroads of the CSR and the Wapet (Kidson) Track with numb hands and knees aching from doubling up as shock absorbers.

A vandalised red telephone box was a surreal sight at the barren junction. Four kilometres to the west, the Kunawarritji Community is the only habitation between Wiluna and Billiluna Station at the northern end of the stock route. The Wapet Track was built to service oil exploration in the south of the Great Sandy Desert in the 1960s. It connects the CSR with the Great Northern Highway, halfway between Broome and Port Hedland, at a point over 600 km to the north-west. The road going towards the community appeared smooth and well-maintained – a bit like the first 40 km of the CSR. If I hadn't been completely spent, I would have been tempted to pedal it just to be reminded of how it was to cycle on a proper road. We would visit the following day, but in the meantime I still had a further four kilometres of bone-rattling to reach Well 33.

Reaching my goal for the week, I felt immensely satisfied. As expected, Week 2 had been much more of a slog than Week 1, but despite all the trials and tribulations, each day had been an adventure and my sense of achievement at having attained each landmark, whether it be a well or a point of interest, was strong. At the same time, I was concerned about my health. That evening I was in a fair amount of discomfort and noticed that my pee was a strange colour – it could well have been blood. I had worked myself into a state, worried that this could thwart my chances of conquering the stock route. Talking to Arnaud over the satellite phone instilled some calm. We decided that it was most likely a urinary tract infection which could be caused by the dehydration, but I didn't know for sure. Hopefully I would be able to consult a community doctor the following day.

Don had his own concerns about his health, and our situation. He had found the first two weeks extremely tough. The heat had really knocked him around and stirred up his allergy problems. Each day he repeatedly made comments such as 'It's all too hard', 'It's far too hot', 'I'm too tired'. (To be fair, he had also put a lot of effort into boosting my morale, particularly during the first week.) It was difficult for me to hear these statements, but I did not let the negativity dent my own determination. Don was also very disappointed about the state of the track. He had never known it to be so rough and he was concerned about the depreciation of his vehicle. It was obvious that he wanted out. If I had said the word at this point he would have been gone in a flash.

I said nothing about giving up myself. I wasn't going through all this effort for naught. I had got this far, nearly 1000 km over the harshest long-distance track in the world, and I wanted to finish the job if at all possible. I would have been devastated if my support had given up: we were a team and we needed the support of each other. A day of recuperation could make all the difference.

A saltpan on the edge of Lake Disappointment

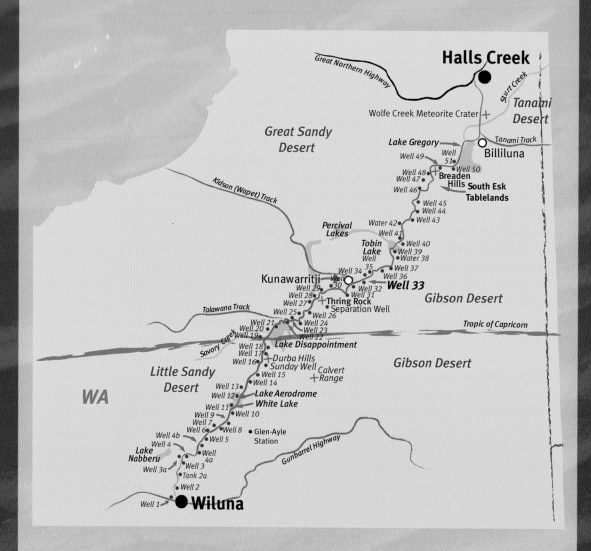

Halls Creek

Great Northern Highway

Tanami Desert

Wolfe Creek Meteorite Crater

Great Sandy Desert

Lake Gregory

Well 49

Well 51

Biliiluna

Tanami Track

Well 48
Well 47
Well 46

Breaden Hills

South Esk Tablelands

Well 50

Kidson (Wapet) Track

Well 45
Well 44
Well 43

Water 42
Well 41

Percival Lakes

Tobin Lake
Well 35

Well 40
Well 39
Water 38
Well 37

Well 34

Kunawarritji

Well 30

Well 36

Well 33

Gibson Desert

Well 29
Well 28
Well 27

Well 32
Well 31

Thring Rock
Separation Well

Talawana Track

Well 25

Well 26

Tropic of Capricorn

Well 21
Well 20
Well 19

Well 24
Well 23
Well 22

Savory Creek

Lake Disappointment

Well 18
Well 17
Well 16

Durba Hills
Sunday Well

Calvert Range

Gibson Desert

Little Sandy Desert

Well 13
Well 12

Well 15
Well 14

WA

Well 11
Well 9
Well 7
Well 6

Well 10

Lake Aerodrome
White Lake

Well 8

Glen-Ayle Station

Well 4b
Well 4

Lake Nabberu

Well 4a

Well 3a

Well 3

Tank 2a

Gunbarrel Highway

Well 2

Well 1

Wiluna

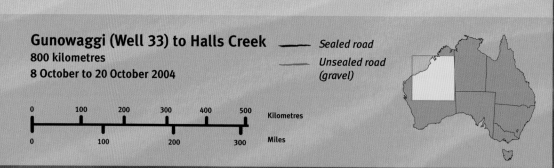

Gunowaggi (Well 33) to Halls Creek
800 kilometres
8 October to 20 October 2004

Sealed road

Unsealed road (gravel)

| 0 | 100 | 200 | 300 | 400 | 500 | Kilometres |

| 0 | 100 | 200 | 300 | Miles |

11

The trouble with spinifex
Canning Stock Route, Weeks 3 and 4

Sunlight on a spinifex plain

Gunowaggi (Well 33) to Halls Creek

Day 16, Friday 8 October
Gunowaggi (Well 33)/Kunawarritji Community
Rest day
Distance from Wiluna – 971 km
Total distance – 13 005 km

Although fresh supplies were very limited at the community store at Gunnowaggi we were able to stock up on the basics and enough fuel to see us through to Billiluna. We visited the community nurse later that evening. To my relief, my problem was treatable with a course of antibiotics, and Don was able to get some medication for his allergy problem. The diagnosis lifted my spirits and I was ready for whatever the track had to throw at me.

It has been suggested that the initials CSR should also stand for Corrugations, Sand and Rocks. This was certainly a fitting description of the track between Wiluna and Gunowaggi and, according to Don, that wasn't going to change. I just wished there were a greater percentage of rocks. A more accurate initial would be CSr! Don warned that I could expect worse conditions on the northern section of the stock route; the sand ridges there would be even more arduous and the maximum temperatures would remain above the 40-degree mark.

The 'S' could also stand for spinifex. This most hardy and versatile of plants exists in the most desolate of places and in the poorest of sand, an essential part of the desert ecosystem, stabilising shifting sands and providing shelter for wildlife. The nature of the spiky grass symbolises the 'pole to pole spectrum' of personalities of the desert. In the earliest of morning light and the last of the afternoon's rays, open plains of spinifex appear as charming as golden acres of oats. Wispy seed heads shimmer in the gentle breezes, enticing the traveller with idyllic images of prosperity and calmness. Up close and personal, however, it reveals its unsavoury side. The needles, which are really just tightly rolled leaves adapted to minimise moisture loss, scratch and puncture anything that leaks – tyres and skin, for example. Even camels avoid walking through spinifex if there is a spine-free option, such as a track or samphire flat. The trouble with spinifex is that the spines are barbed with micro-filaments that snap off under the skin; the fine splinters cause pain and often result in infection. Riding through the Gibson, Little and Great Sandy deserts, being pierced and scratched daily was par for the course. Like spinifex, the extreme aspects of the desert were working their way under my skin and the scars would remain long after the scratches healed.

Day 17, Saturday 9 October
Gunowaggi (Well 33) to near Bungabinni Native Well
Distance – 60 km
Distance from Wiluna – 1031 km
Total distance – 13 065 km

I adjusted my routine to make the most of the cooler mornings, setting my alarm for 4am and preparing for the day in the dark. The plan was to start pedalling at around 5.30 and keep going with only small breaks until midday. Then we would set up camp and rest through the afternoon. That would still give me six or seven hours of cycling.

I felt much stronger and refreshed after my pit-stop, and full of anticipation for the adventure ahead. The track continued to bisect the flat spinifex plain as straight as the Gunbarrel. In the early morning light, the golden country was showing its enchanting side. The track was not. Don was adamant that this

Minjoo, Well 35; the northern limit of Snell's work. Many of the wells of the northern end of the stock route have been regularly flooded and the water has turned salty

section was interspersed by many firm, stony segments and I kept scanning wishfully ahead for some good gravel. But there was absolutely no respite from the soft corrugations, apart from two 100-metre sections just before Minjoo (Well 35), 40 km and four-and-a-half hours from our camp.

Well 35 had been constructed on a tea-tree-covered claypan. During the previous few Wet seasons, it had been totally flooded but the water had subsided, leaving a coating of salt and other mineral crystals on the muddy ground and low vegetation. The site looked a mess, with rusted and decaying fragments of the old well scattered through the bush. The stagnant pools were attractive to wildlife and desert finches sounded the amber alert, ever-busy flocks darting through the tea-trees in formation. There is always safety in numbers, and our presence certainly stimulated their nervous reaction.

Minjoo was the limit of Snell's expedition. With all the iron work used up and the Wet season upon them, Snell decided to return south with his eight-strong party still physically and mentally fit. They had reconditioned thirty-three wells and built five new ones. The plan was to recommence the job after the Wet with a full complement of supplies and fresh men. Heading south, they buried food and equipment in tanks at various well sites along the way for easy accessibility for the return journey. It was a sad homecoming for Snell – in his absence, his only son, William, had died of a burst appendix in the Wiluna Hospital, aged twenty-four. Canning returned to finish the job the following year.

Well 35 is also the junction point for the Callawa Track. I couldn't see any signs of the 4WD expedition which had come through less than two months before. It wouldn't have taken long for their tracks to become overgrown, although a more skilled tracker would have probably picked them out.

By 10am, the heat was particularly ferocious. I wasn't looking forward to venturing away from the shade of Minjoo's tea-trees and desert oaks. Over the previous few weeks when temperatures had been extreme, my drinking water had heated, becoming a less effective coolant. A technique I decided to trial was to wet a pair of socks and fit them over my drinking bottles on the theory that the evaporating moisture would have a cooling effect on the water, making it a more palatable temperature to drink.

The first ten kilometres north of Minjoo was less used and overgrown with spinifex. Spindly strands taller than I was and top-heavy with seed heads drooped over the path so that I struggled to see what lay ahead. I moved faster on the undisturbed track, continually brushed by the grasses. Grass seeds lodged in my clothes and particularly in the socks which covered the water bottles. The faster I travelled the cooler my water – the new technique was extremely effective. It didn't take long for the socks to dry as the middle of the day approached and I developed a technique of dribbling a few squirts of the remaining hot water from an uninsulated bottle into the wool socks without wasting too much.

After 11am I could sense the heat reaching an unsustainable level. Pushing on too much further would make recovery difficult the following day. An hour or so later, just after the Bungabinni native well turn-off, I conceded that we needed to stop. My work was done for the day – I had completed seven hours on the road by 1pm, and could afford to find a campsite and put my feet up under the filtered shade of a desert oak. Due to the hoards of marauding ants which, within an instant, would find their way into anything that could be eaten, feet had to be off the ground, as did all food supplies...that pet thorny devil would have come in very handy! Just as we started to settle down for lunch, parking on the track to take advantage of the shade, two vehicles arrived from the opposite

A thorny devil

direction. Helen and Frank Quicke and their friends had travelled the CSR many times and said that they never ceased to be captivated by the route. Helen, who was making a documentary film about the wildlife of the Canning, explained that, as it wound its way north-south across the latitudes of the four deserts, the track gave an unparalleled snapshot of the fauna and flora. We learned that it had been a particularly good season for the wildlife of the deserts. Food was bountiful, which explained the proliferation of ant-eating lizards in particular. They must have surely been in heaven.

The heat and the insects made the afternoon siesta uncomfortable. It was nice to know that I didn't have to push any further that day, but as the temperatures cooled in the mid-to-late afternoon, I started feeling guilty. My mind became restless, and I became a little tetchy at the thought that I could have made the most of the more manageable temperatures by moving on.

Day 18, Sunday 10 October
Bungabinni Native Well to Libral (Well 37) + 15 km
Distance – 48 km
Distance from Wiluna – 1079 km
Total distance – 13 113 km

Away at first light, I was immediately confronted with a conundrum of what I classified as low-to-medium height sand ridges. In the relative cool of the morning, I was able to cycle up the lower dunes, averaging a mesmerising speed of nearly 10 km per hour to Well 36, or Wanda. There I became frustrated and confused, disorientated by the maze of tracks which circled the previously flooded claypan. In the absence of sign-posts, I searched for any fresh vehicle tracks which I thought should signify the correct path out. I loathed wasting time and energy, particularly in the precious cool of the day.

I could have done with finding one of Snell's compasses, one of the many legendary bush skills he had developed from years of wanderings and learning from the Indigenous population. To make his compasses, which were engraved on hilltops between his pastoral leases and which must have saved several lives over the years, Snell would find a flat rock and on it mark the points of a compass. Between the north, south, east and west indicators he would scratch an arrow showing the direction travellers would find water and next to it a number giving the distance in miles to the source.

After a couple of circuits I finally navigated my way out. There was a choice of route: either directly north over the lesser used track past Mt Shoesmith or veering east, taking in a longer and more historic route via Wells 37 and 38. I chose the latter path, which had actually been created by Don about three seasons earlier. Small claypans along the original route were in flood, and to get through, he had led his group on a convoluted path along the crests of the sand ridges, away from the mud. With 4WDs in low ratio mode and tyre pressure low, drivers would comfortably pass over the track with an elevated view of the landscape.

For me, this was nightmare terrain. I attacked the challenge by switching into overdrive, like a boxer sending in volleys of frenzied punches as he senses a victory. Bludgeoning my way up the shorter slopes, with far less grace and balance than a boxer, I tried to maintain a rapid cadence by driving my legs extra hard to keep momentum. If I lost it, I would often have to drag the bike some distance to find somewhere firm enough to restart.

By 10am, I was satisfied with the morning gains, reaching a shady grove of desert oaks just short of Well 37. I may have done well but the extra energy requirements extracted a high price. I was shattered physically and overcome with a feeling of hopelessness: it had taken nearly five hours to do thirty-three kilometres – so much energy expended for such little distance. I was concerned that if I didn't keep moving, we would not make it to the next reliable water supply – Well 46 – in time, and if I took too long we would run out of food before Billiluna. According to Don, this was the last shade he could remember before Well 38. Discouraged that the previous day I had been frazzled after 11am, I could not push myself any further. My idea of doing all the work in the morning meant I would never reach my destination on time, so once more I had to re-think my daily routine.

I had plenty of time to consider this as I wandered around the nearby Well 37, also known as Libral. A gentle walk in the heat of the day was far more manageable than what I was usually doing at this time. Like the two previous wells, Well 37 had also been flooded, and we had to take care not to be enveloped by patches of deep mud disguised under the salty film. Investigating behind the tea-tree bushes, we found a depression which would once have been the native well. This was not a surprise as many wells, including Well 37, were located near native water holes; Canning used his local guides to lead his party to them. During the survey expedition, Canning and his second-in-charge, Trotman, recognised the value of the local Aboriginals; without the help of a succession of native guides, the team may well have perished. The guides were treated harshly, being chained up at night, and often during the day, to prevent them from escaping.

In the course of its work, the expedition crossed the boundaries of approximately eleven tribes. With each new territory, a new guide was enlisted. In general, the Aboriginals were reluctant to leave their land as they could be fatally punished by neighbouring tribesmen for trespassing. Small rewards were given as tokens of appreciation for their work, but overall Canning's team showed little respect for the local inhabitants. After the 1906-07 expedition the situation came to a head when Edward Blake, the expedition cook, accused Canning, Trotman and the team of cruelty to the Aboriginals in general, and of immorality towards the women. A Royal Commission was appointed and, after three weeks of emotional hearings, Canning and his men were cleared of any wrongdoing although the use of chains was condemned.

Libral is often referred to as the Haunted Well, a term most likely introduced in more recent times by travellers. The four graves nearby are testimony that early droving journeys were fraught with danger, as had been the explorations of the route in preceding years. In April 1911, the first drovers of the CSR, George Shoesmith and James Thomson, along with one of their Aboriginal stockmen named 'Chinaman', were fatally speared near Well 37. The Aboriginal drovers were highly regarded team members, in particular for their sense of direction and tracking skills, which were invaluable when shifting stock at night. 'Chinaman's' fate is proof that they also lived in fear of the 'bush blackfellows', who would equally regard them as invaders of their territory. The men's bodies were discovered on the next drive two months later by Tom Cole, who found the cattle wandering back up the route. The three graves are positioned on a sandy

The graves of drovers Shoesmith, Thompson and Aboriginal stockman, 'Chinaman', overlooking Libral, Well 37 – the Haunted Well.

rise overlooking the mud flat. To the north-west of the well is the lone grave and misspelt 'headstone' of John 'Jock' McLernon, an oil prospector who was speared in 1922.

Don and I returned to the shade of the desert oaks to get some rest. Although I couldn't get comfortable, I must have received some benefit from the semi-conscious daze I usually reserved for long flights between Europe and Australia. Faint puffs of breeze stirred movement overhead, branches creaking as they swayed. The moving air eddied among the fine, needle-shaped foliage, the resultant eerie, haunting sounds an appropriate ambience to our location.

The peace was interrupted by the noise of two vehicles labouring over the sand. After a short conversation with the occupants, we were invited to join Maureen and Charles, Maureen's son, Luke, and his friend, Greg, for lunch. Luke and Greg were spending a year working at the Balgo Community at the northern end of the Tanami Track. As a triathlete, Luke was particularly interested in how I was coping with the sand. He could relate to my efforts more than most, because he struggled to train in the sand around Balgo.

Hailing from Melbourne, Maureen and Charles were a long way from home but still made every effort to live well. There we were, in the middle of the Great Sandy Desert, in 43-degree temperatures, lunching in a civilised manner beside a clothed table! I refrained from any alcohol, but the roast beef sandwiches were far more gourmet fare than we were accustomed to. Having been out in the wilds for so long, table manners were a distant memory. I endeavoured not to make too much of a glutton of myself.

The good company and food boosted my morale, and my mind was stimulated beyond thinking how the hell I was going to get through the next stage. Summonsing the energy to have another go at the track, I set off after 3.15pm, the time when I had observed that the temperature started to drop. The region had been denuded by a wild fire fairly recently, exposing the bare, wind-swept dunes. I was now travelling perpendicular to the ridges, which seemed to be much higher and closer together than earlier. It had been a wise move not to try this section during the heat of the day – I would have expired.

We chose to camp that night on top of a sand ridge in order to make the most of any rare zephyrs of evening breeze.

Libral (Well 37) + 15 km to Murguga (Well 39)

Distance – 52 km

Distance from Wiluna – 1131 km

Total distance - 13 165 km

My refined daily plan, which I hoped would see me through to Halls Creek, now involved rising at 4am to cook breakfast and leave by 5.30am, cycling through to between 11am and noon, resting until 3.15pm, and then cycling through to dusk at about 5.45pm.

This day started with a 'surf' down a 12-metre wave of sand. From the frequency of the waves in this sea of sand – the dune crests were only about 250 metres apart – it seemed as if the land was engaged in a permanent storm. A welcome first destination for the morning was Wardabunni Rockhole, or Water 38, not only because it is in the middle of about five kilometres of stony ground but also because it is definitely worth a little investigation. I parked my bike near the old, rusty trough and wandered down the slope. A mob of galahs which had probably not sensed my quiet arrival suddenly launched themselves noisily into the air, the native sentinels warning other wildlife of my presence. A dingo kept an eye on proceedings from a safe distance. No doubt I had dashed any chance of it stalking unsuspecting prey for the time being.

Set back in a rocky fissure (Canning's number two, Hubert Trotman, had carved his initials there), the rockhole has an intermittent water supply. The stagnant pool contained enough water for Don to fill a 20-litre container when he came through later during the morning. We only used the water for washing and boiling, but it was enough to alleviate the pressure of reaching Well 46 in time.

Route between Well 37 and Water 38, Wardabunni Rockhole. The higher than usual frequency of sand dunes intensified the workload

Back on the track, which rejoined the old, now alternative route (heading straight back to Well 36), I was immediately faced with open, scorching plains of constantly corrugated soft stuff. This soon gave way to the soul-destroying sand ridges. It was dusk before I reached Well 39 on the edge of a samphire flat. Not so long ago, I would have been dissatisfied with achieving just fifty kilometres in a full day, my present attitude a reflection of the difficulty of the conditions and my debilitating fatigue. It was a war of attrition, the efforts of each day gradually grinding away at my physical and mental condition. I fell asleep sitting upright at the table, mid-sentence while writing my diary.

Day 20, Tuesday 12 October
Murguga (Well 39) to near Gunowarba Native Well turn-off
Distance – 53 km
Distance from Wiluna – 1184 km
Total distance – 13 218 km

For the last couple of days I had been longing to reach Tobin Lake just 4 km through the sand from Well 39. The promise of being able to skim at almost normal pace for about 16 km over the dry ephemeral lake bed buoyed my spirits. And in the main, the experience lived up to expectations although there was only 12 km of normal pace with a couple of sand islands to negotiate in the centre. Beside the island a herd of camels grazed among a range of giant termite mounds. The lake crossing was over all too soon as huge red dunes invaded, lapping over its shores.

The lake was named in honour of Michael Tobin, the well-boring specialist who was fatally speared by an Aboriginal during Canning's survey expedition. He was buried near Waddawalla, Well 40. During the return leg of the well-sinking expedition, Canning's party lugged a marble cross, traversing some of the highest sand dunes, for erection at Tobin's grave.

No respite from the extreme conditions

Conditions north of Waddawalla up to Well 42 degenerated into what I can safely say in retrospect were the worst on the stock route for a cyclist. My 'cross to bear' involved struggling over *the* tallest, most awkward dunes with long, convoluted ascents in *the* softest sand and in *the* hottest temperatures. I had reached a new echelon of tiredness, toiling in temperatures which were around 45°C in the shade. Shade, however, remained particularly elusive and goodness knows what the temperatures were radiating off the sand. The conditions put my emotions on a knife edge, and caused my perspiration to evaporate the moment the droplets hit the ground.

By 11am, I was pushing through triple-headed 'monster' dunes, desperately searching for shade for the long break. Adding to my frustration were two successive punctures which I repaired while partially entwined in a tea-tree bush to keep out of the direct sunlight. In the end, Don and I created our own shade by clearing away some of the spinifex from under a bush. After some food, Don dug himself a little 'nest' under his vehicle to have a kip, muttering repeatedly, 'Far too hot', 'This is far too difficult'. He too was really struggling.

Wrapping myself in my trusty piece of shadecloth, which now doubled as a fly net, I too tried to rest. I managed to relax and started to reason everything out once more in my mind. Many times during the morning and over the previous few days I had thought of throwing in the towel, totally fed up. Then I would remind myself of what I had so nearly achieved. I was at least three-quarters of the way there. Successful completion of the CSR was paramount to selling the whole expedition because it was the trump card; the one section which distinguished the GRACE Expedition from many other Australian cycle expeditions before it. Just five more days, if I continued at the current pace, to get through the worst of the sand – five days left (hopefully) and I would never have to deal with such conditions again.

In the afternoon back on the track, I fared a little better. A gentle breeze which prevailed in the late afternoon was the highlight.

Day 21, Wednesday 13 October
Near Gunowarba Native Well turn-off to Guli Water Tank (Well 42) + 14 km
Distance – 57 km
Distance from Wiluna – 1241 km
Total distance – 13 275 km

I needed to regroup after the ordeals of the previous day. I couldn't go on like that. I took extra time to check the bike over at first light. Even though I was wrecked at the end of each day, I was still brushing the chain and working parts and applying 'dry lube'. My bike was taking a terrible hammering and, although it was holding up remarkably well, I realised that I had to nurse it along to have the best chance of making it through. I noticed a problem with what I thought was the chain slipping, and deduced this was probably due to the constantly grinding sand. Unable to detect anything specifically wrong, I pushed off down the sand ridge.

Adopting a more positive mental approach, I broke the day into 5-km sections as my way of dealing with the continuous hard grind. By the time I reached the turn-off to the lonely Helena Spring, 89 km to the east, the ridges had become more uniform and distantly spaced. The track tended to cross each dune at a low point and then dog-leg to follow the line of the ridge before turning again to cross the 'valley'. The long, flat sections of track which ran parallel to the ridges were the most dreaded, as sand spilled down the slope filling the tyre tracks.

The mechanical problem on my bike worsened as I went. Baffled, I asked Don, an expert mechanic, to have a look. He identified it as the 'clutch', which in cycling terms means the enclosed free-wheel unit, the part which normally allows the bike to glide effortlessly when the rider is not pedalling. As it wore down, engaging the gears became increasingly difficult, especially when trying to put on the power. Starting off was particularly frustrating as I had to spin the pedals through a number of revolutions before I could get the drive train to catch. Moving forward was already a very stop-start affair and this problem really tested my patience. At times I wanted to pick my machine up and hurl it down the sand dune.

Guli Tank, Water 42, was yet another silted-up water point but it did signify the start of the dried-up Guli Lake bed. The ancient claypan was gradually succumbing to shifting desert sands – its surface was not as smooth as Tobin Lake. Ploughing my way through the sand patches, the free-wheel kept disengaging and I would have to pedal like mad, spinning fruitlessly until I could get the gear to catch again. This was worrying because I was still 600 km from Halls Creek and a long way from Broome, where I would be able to receive a new part. I hoped I would not be carrying my bike into Halls Creek.

By dusk I was pleased with myself for surpassing my minimum planned distance. Don seemed more tired and negative than usual. After erecting my tent, trying to be helpful, I offered to cook dinner.

There must have been a fire somewhere in the distance. The insects had been in a hyperactive, agitated state all day and the sun had graduated to a deep crimson before setting. The flies went to bed as the light faded, but this seemed to signify party time for the ants. Tiny black ants invaded my tent through a minute hole which I couldn't find. They continued to plague me through the night despite my desperate attempts to murder them in their hundreds.

The torment inflicted by these little buggers unfortunately comes with the territory. They are particularly hostile during the 'build up' to the Wet. Travelling at a similar time of year to ourselves, the first successful expedition to cross the Great Sandy Desert, led by Peter Egerton Warburton, suffered immense discomfort. In Egerton Warburton's 1875 book, *Journey Across the Western Interior of Australia*, Charles Eden, a pioneer and writer who contributed additional comments for Warburton, wrote a footnote about the ant situation the men endured:

> A small black ant seems to have been the avowed enemy of this expedition. The ground literally swarmed with them, and a stamp of the foot brought them up in thousands. When the wearied men threw themselves down under the shade of a bush, to snatch the half hour's slumber their exhausted frames required, the merciless little insects attacked them, and not only effectually routed their sleep, but even rendered a recumbent position impossible. The scanty clothing possessed by the travellers was no protection; so feeble a bulwark was speedily under-run by the enemy, and their successful invasion announced by sharp, painful nips from their mandibles. Often when the vertical sun poured down in full fierceness on their heads, and the poor shade afforded even by a bush would have been an inestimable blessing, the travellers were driven away from the shelter by their relentless persecutors, and in despair flung themselves down on the burning sand, where it was too hot for even an ant. By day or by night the little insects gave no respite.

By electing to miss the bypass to Wells 43 and 44, I had the privilege of cycling on the lesser used track. There was no sign-post; the turn-off was merely marked by an old tyre and a white-tipped post partially hidden behind some scrub. Unsure at first which way to go, I spent several minutes assessing the tyre tracks, and in the end, took the left-hand turn. After about three kilometres, it made an obvious turn to the north. Only then was I certain I had made the right choice.

It had been a while since a vehicle had driven up this section, churning up the thin crust which had formed after a sprinkle of rain. There were just as many corrugations and sand dunes as before but the fractionally more coherent surface made a significant difference: about two kilometres per hour faster on average. When the free-wheel behaved itself, I found I was able to get enough grip to cycle over some of the smaller dunes.

The absence of vehicles gave spiders the opportunity to construct their webs across the track, between the tea-trees. Rolling fast down the dunes, my bike accelerated to speeds to which I had become unaccustomed in the last three weeks. The undulations at the base of the dunes, caused by the excess power of ascending vehicles, resembled a BMX track and on occasions sent me airborne. After one such descent I came within centimetres of collecting a giant golden orb spider around my neck. I would certainly have provided the spider with far more than the meal it was used to snaring. Although not life-threatening, a nip from this palm-sized, master-weaving spider could have made circumstances very uncomfortable.

The web of a golden orb spider can be strong enough to trap small birds

I had done seven days straight since Well 33, and it seemed I existed under a constant veil of tiredness, which gnawed away at my wellbeing. I struggled to roll out of bed, trying to decide whether I was still dreaming or whether this was reality. As I shuffled around on the sand ridge preparing breakfast in the dark, the cool sand gradually filled my shoes, but I didn't care any more. Drawing energy from the first morning rays, flies revved up their activity and were at maximum annoyance levels by the time the kettle had boiled and the milky rice was cooked. Yes, I was still in the middle of the Great Sandy Desert.

The first hour to Gravity Lakes was a gruelling 9 km, after which conditions hardened slightly. There I rejoined the over-used track, pushed on a further 15 km to Well 45, and waited for Don. The plan was to separate there. Don was to head north to Well 46 to replenish the water supply as we were down to our last ten litres and I was to take the easterly route, which bypassed the other track when it flooded. Don would then to rejoin me by driving the connecting track between Well 46 and Crescent Ridge. My route past Mt Ford was 6 km shorter.

The dry and partly caved-in Well 45 is set among the most substantial stand of shady eucalypts I had seen for some days. A sign welcoming travellers to the Halls Creek Shire was faintly inspiring. I was definitely in the Kimberley region now. Getting there!

I loaded up with extra water and food to see me through the next four or five hours. Parting company from Don felt like I was heading for the dark side of the moon, especially as I would be out of radio contact until we re-united. There was uncertainty about the condition of both tracks. Don had never travelled on the connecting track and hoped it would be a viable option; not only that, the lake that often formed between Wells 45 and 46 could cause hazardous, boggy conditions for driving. I had to assume that my own rate of progress would remain constant. Any improvement would be a bonus.

In the absence of flood waters, travellers usually elected to drive past the wells. My own path, which followed parallel with the low sand ridges, was reasonable in parts, while other sections were covered with sand drifts. As usual, I was confined to the single tyre ruts, and changing across the central island was often hazardous. Branches had grown across my lane and I often had no choice but to crash through them – thankfully, the new growth was relatively elastic. When I occasionally misjudged the sturdiness of the natural barriers, I was flung off as if launched from a sling shot.

Approaching Mt Ford, an ancient tabletop mound, the vegetation, and with it the shade, petered out and I was forced to take a brief rest fully exposed to the late morning sun. Now that I was on the fringe of the South Esk Tablelands, the land became more gravelly. Dehydration was a greater concern – I had used three out of five water bottles to get to Mt Ford by 11am and was increasingly nervous about running short. Above the rocky outcrop majestic kites soared, scanning the land for lunch, small lizards most likely the preferred meal.

Lunch was very much on my mind too. I still had about twelve kilometres to reach the junction, but there was no telling when Don would arrive. Although I was still out of range, I tested my two-way at regular intervals just in case. I pondered whether I should stop and wait in order to conserve water, or keep going. If I stopped, conditions would be intensely uncomfortable as there was meagre protection from the elements and the marauding flies and ants would not let me rest. The ground was fairly soft, but certainly not deep sand. I decided to keep moving at an easier, steady pace, but I would closely monitor the water situation and stop when I was down to my final bottle. I was starting to worry that something may have happened to Don and kept trying the radio. Finally, just two kilometres from the junction, I made contact and, miraculously, we arrived there simultaneously just after midday. Covered in scratches and grazes, I took refuge in the vehicle, out of the furnace for a few minutes. Back on the bike after lunch, I didn't manage much more distance in the afternoon session. The topography reverted to uniform ridges, although they were definitely lower. Don reckoned that from this point on, the ridges would gradually diminish in height.

I was in a fragile state when I phoned Arnaud and my father that night for my weekly 'check in'. They had both been worried about me. Despite being relatively close to the finish, there still seemed an insurmountable task ahead. Doubts as to whether I would make it started to surface: it was difficult to see the 'wood for the trees', or in this case, the 'sand for the sand dunes'. My body was screaming out for a proper break, but there was nowhere to stop. The only thing to do was to push on.

Totting up the distance totals, I realised that during the course of the day I had surpassed the distance of the Trans-Siberian Cycle Expedition. I had pedalled further than from St Petersburg to Vladivostok in about the same time, but I was only just over halfway through.

Day 24, Saturday 16 October
Crescent Ridge + 11 km to Well 49
Distance – 72 km
Distance from Wiluna – 1 440 km
Total distance – 13 476 km

I set off knowing that the worst of the sand dunes were behind me. The stormy 'ocean' lay to the south and between that point and Billiluna it was to be the graduated 'ripples of a pond'. I rolled off down the sandy slope of our final sand ridge campsite fully expecting to make easier headway as I had been told that approaching the Breaden Hills there would be solid ground.

A vile wind from the north-west resisted every pedal revolution. Although the sand hurdles were certainly lower, until I was within a few kilometres of the stark hills, any rocky patches, often disguised under sand drifts, were sporadic. I seemed to be in a particularly negative mood, the worse-than-expected conditions eroding my patience. By about 10am, I could see the white LandCruiser behind me in the distance as it bobbed up on the crest of each ridge. Thinking Don would soon catch up to me, I polished off the last of the water. Strangely, he didn't seem to be getting any closer nor did he respond to the radio. I started to become annoyed – why was he following me? I was in no mood for cat and mouse games. By now I really needed the water and there wasn't an iota of shade.

A rare solid patch of track approaching the Breaden Hills

Breaden Hills

After about half an hour Don finally arrived and explained he was running out of fuel. He had been stopping to check the fuel tank and engine for leaks. As there were no mechanical problems, he deduced that he had miscalculated the amount of fuel required to reach Billiluna. He had used 40 litres more than usual, mostly due to spending too much time going slowly over the soft ground. From now on, he was in maximum fuel conservation mode – no crawling or idling, no air conditioning and no side-trips. He would travel at about 30 km an hour and then stop as required.

The region plays host to a confluence of routes of the earliest European explorers. Augustus Gregory reached as far west as the lake which bears his name (70 km to the east) and Warburton, Carnegie and Canning all left their marks over the following fifty years. I would really have liked to investigate the Breaden Hills, Breaden Valley and Breaden Pool and Godfrey Tank, all of which were named by David Carnegie. Godfrey Tank – a large natural rockhole above Breaden Valley – has the names and initials of many of the early explorers and drovers, such as Canning, Trotman and Ben Taylor, carved into its sandstone walls. But to see them would have involved an extra side-trip and there was nothing extra left in my tank either.

I had passed the route of Peter Egerton Warburton's expedition of the first crossing of the continent from the Northern Territory to Western Australia during the morning session. His journey was one of the toughest ever made by an Australian explorer. The party had to cope with demented Afghan camel-drivers, festering scorpion bites, marauding ants and, of course, flies. In desperation, at one point Egerton Warburton tried to improve the health of one of the sick, constipated camels by administering an enema from his double-barrel breech-loading shotgun. Given the rock-hard little pebbles usually expelled by camels, I can't imagine what constitutes a constipated camel!

Bad fly day

All along I had had my own battle with the flies. This day, however, will always be remembered as a 'bad fly day'. The worst fly day imaginable. They clung to every moist part of me, which in such hot conditions meant my body was coated from head to foot. They crawled under my sunglasses, in my ears, up my nose and I had to keep my mouth shut at all times. Insect repellent was ineffective. I pulled up my Buff, which usually sat around my neck, over my mouth and nose so I could breathe without inhaling the black nemeses. The sandy and rough track meant that I rarely had the opportunity to let go of the handlebars to shoo them away. I could only shake my head and contort my lips into weird and unattractive positions to puff jets of breath up my face to momentarily deter the persistent buggers. I guess that's how four-legged animals cope all the time.

The flies would not let us rest under the shade of the tarpaulin during the midday break. They clung to anything, nestling in single file up the guy ropes which held the square of canvas in position, clutching on to strands of spinifex grass as they wavered in the breeze, and crawling over our food and tired bodies. One slap of my leg would usually catch a number of the blighters, but most had the annoying knack of sensing danger and eluded my hand with only nanoseconds to spare. They found their way under the shadecloth which I had wrapped around my body like a giant fly net. Don gave up and went for a walk. Eventually I followed suit.

'Fire management' around the northern perimeter of the Breaden Hills on the way to Well 49

The local Aboriginals had been burning off around the hills. Soon after setting off again, I passed through the fire front which was allowed to run its course over the grass-covered plains and hills. The smoke was most probably the catalyst for the excessive fly activity. I made good time, pushing over some better ground, just making it to Well 49, renowned for its good water, in dimming light.

Day 25, Sunday 17 October
Well 49 to Lake Gregory Camp (Weriaddo + 18 km)
Distance – 70 km
Distance from Wiluna – 1510 km
Total distance – 13 544 km

I struggled to get away from Well 49 by 7am, heading due east between two parallel sand ridges. The track was constant soft corrugations (like between Wells 32 and 35) all the way past the burnt-out Well 50. Conditions were slightly better as I noted my average speed had rocketed to eleven kilometres an hour! From here, the ground became fractionally firmer but remained abominably rough.

Originally, Don had said that I could expect good ground all the way to Billiluna from before the Breaden Hills. During the course of the expedition, he had gained a greater appreciation of the surfaces on which I struggled but which he had barely noticed driving. In light of this, he had adjusted his prediction of track condition. This was just as well, because if he was wrong again I was ready to deal with him as I had dealt with the flies!

Just before reaching the final well, Weriaddo, I came to a lonely crossroad. The track off to the right skirted the southern end of Lake Gregory to the Mulan

Werriado, Well 51, the final well sunk by Canning before Lake Gregory, is now merely a depression beside an out-of-order windmill and dam belonging to Lake Gregory Station

Community and on to the larger Balgo Community. To the left, the track bypassed Well 51 when in flood. I continued straight over the intersection towards the well. Just before Weriaddo, the land changed abruptly and I was pedalling through low, grass-covered plains and white, gypsum-rich sand. The well itself was merely a depression. A large windmill and dam next to the depression were part of the Aboriginal-run Lake Gregory Station; they were not maintained.

Reaching the final well induced feelings of satisfaction, although mechanical concerns about both my bike and Don's vehicle were starting to dominate. Running out of fuel with just over 100 km to reach Billiluna would have been very frustrating. Food was also a concern – lunch at Weriaddo was down to sardines and dry damper. The fly situation was mildly better than the previous day.

There is always a sting in the tail. After lunch, sand dunes arose to crease the land around Lake Gregory, their defiant ridges ensuring I didn't get it too easy. It was strange seeing cows again after being so long away from pastoral land. I caught glimpses of the tranquil waters, well known for its abundant bird life. Hitting more red dunes in the afternoon was like a slap in the face – I thought I had left that behind. Overcome later by both an energy 'bonk' and by emotion, I had to stop and sit down. I was so near and yet I was still being punished. What had I done to deserve this? Back on the bike, I tried to fill my head with songs to pass the time. *Telegraph Road* lodged itself in my mind, and as I was longing to reach the superior surface of the Tanami Track, now just 100 kms away, my version turned into the *Tanami Road*. I managed to string out the 14-minute epic to last the rest of the afternoon. This lyrical bastardisation appealed to my warped sense of humour and brought a smile to my face every time I thought of it.

Day 26, Monday 18 October
Lake Gregory Camp to Stretch Lagoon
Distance – 66 km
Distance from Wiluna – 1576 km
Total distance – 13 610 km

In the knowledge that we would not be able to stay in the Billiluna Community, I planned an easier day. Assuming that the track really was going to improve, we would reach Stretch Lagoon, twenty kilometres short of the head of the CSR. Starting out, I couldn't be certain whether the car or I would run out of juice first so I took it steadily as if 'taxiing' down a runway. Fortunately, the station track had been graded and was in better condition. As during earlier times on the expedition, I was able to sneak down edges, skimming over the fine crust like an insect walking on water, treading carefully to avoid breaking the surface tension.

Much of the land had been recently burnt and many of the majestic desert oaks were singed; some were badly scorched, but hopefully not past the point of no return. The soil switched dramatically between red sand and rocky white limestone. Occasionally I would catch a glimpse of the lake and water birds such as brolgas and ibis. A slow puncture plagued my progress. I had to stop several

times to pump the tyres to see me through to Bloodwood Bore, our shady lunch stop. Both the cattle-yards and two large windmills with storage tanks were a wreck.

Stretch Lagoon, situated on Sturt Creek at the northern end of Lake Gregory, is a magical place to camp. Sturt Creek was named by Augustus Gregory in 1856 after fellow explorer, Charles Sturt (even though Sturt's explorations never ventured this far west). Drovers used the series of permanent waterholes between Halls Creek and the start of the stock route to water their animals. During the Wet, Sturt Creek discharges large volumes of water into Lake Gregory.

Arriving early for a change, I had plenty of time to relax and reflect on my last night on the Canning. I tried to ignore the rubbish synonymous with many permanent Indigenous communities, and enjoy the tranquillity. I pictured the lagoon bustling with thirsty cattle, oblivious of the arduous course over which they were about to be driven.

I thought about what I had done and was overcome with a mixture of pride and relief. My mind flashed back to the pivotal point on the journey on Day 10 when I had sat down in the sand, swamped with self-doubt about my ability to keep going, exhausted and emotionally drained from the dehydration saga. I realised it was all about how I perceived the desert and my existence in it. If I thought of the desert as a God-forsaken, fiery cauldron where life clings on grimly in the hot sand, I was never going to make it. If I concentrated on the same land as a place of beauty – the rich palate of colours, the delicate flowers and foliage, the untainted, clean landscape, the clarity of the light and the sharpness of the images – I became filled with a positive energy; inspired, clear, unpolluted like the desert. Although it was a constant battle out there, I learned that it was paramount to work with the conditions rather than fight against them. This was key to my mental survival.

In cycling the Canning Stock Route, I developed a rare bond with the desert. Having been so close to the harsh environment, it was easy to understand why the CSR was never used to the extent that the Kimberley pastoralists had predicted. The brutal conditions are the same today as they were a century or more ago, and those who do not respect the desert are just as likely to be

Reflecting on the journey, Stretch Lagoon on Sturt Creek

consumed by it. These days, easier access gives more people the opportunity to venture into the desert, but if something goes wrong, many travellers are ill-equipped and less versed in survival skills than earlier generations.

Cycling the CSR was a fine balancing act, like pedalling a tight-rope between Wiluna and the Billiluna. All sorts of forces prodded and tested my physical and mental resolve, threatening to unsettle me enough to 'fall off' my line, literally at times. I had experienced what it was like to teeter on the edge in the unforgiving, inhospitable lands. Fortunately, I was relatively unscathed and, apart from extreme exhaustion, basically in good health.

It was a comforting thought that even if the 4WD ran out of fuel over the final twenty kilometres, I would still make it. I could always phone for someone to bring a can of petrol to see Don through.

Day 27, Tuesday 19 October
Stretch Lagoon to Wolf Creek Meteorite Crater turn-off + 20 km
Distance – 84 km
Distance from Wiluna – 1660 km
Total distance – 13 694 km

To my surprise, Don was up before me. He was nervous about running out of fuel before Billiluna. Although I felt heavy with tiredness, to a degree the sense of occasion over-rode my condition.

The final leg of the CSR took only an hour. I passed the ruins of the old Billiluna homestead; its original lessee, Robert Falconer, was one of the prime movers in lobbying for the construction of the stock route. The track was the best I had encountered since the first 40 km out of Wiluna.

Don passed me and made it safely into the community store, where he waited. The locals were astonished when I arrived a little later. A group of Aboriginals whom Don had met while retrieving water from Well 46 had just arrived back from their excursion to visit sacred sites in the region around Well 46. Their families had vacated the land long ago, opting for community life in Fitzroy Crossing. It was they who were responsible for some of the fires we had seen over the previous few days.

Back on the road, the Tanami Track, which had seemed a struggle two months earlier, was a delight in comparison with what I had just endured. I danced along at a constant 20 km per hour with my revised version of *Telegraph/Tanami Road* revolving in my head. It was definitely something to sing about. Just 170 km to go to reach Halls Creek.

While in the region I could not go past the Wolfe Creek Meteorite Crater. Thought to be over one million years old, the world's second largest crater of its kind is 850 metres in diameter and 50 metres deep. The impact of the meteorite made a hole about 120 metres deep and must have had a catastrophic effect on the region.

We camped near a dry creek bed well away from the road. Thunderstorms lit the night sky and, combined with the steamy temperatures, they were a reminder that we were on the cusp of the Wet.

Wolf Creek Meteorite Crater

I was very excited about the prospect of finishing the stage and thus conquering the world's longest stock route. The road passed through the pastoral country of Ruby Plains, another station which had used the stock route. I welcomed the rocky undulating terrain and breezed over a small pass.

Suddenly, there was a lot more traffic on the road. Hitting the tarmac, the transition was all so sudden and complete. After encountering a grand total of eight cars on the Canning Stock Route, it was weird to be following the white lines of Highway No. 1, having to think about evading the road trains and passing traffic, which at least served to drown out the unhealthy groans from my worn-out bike.

At the town boundary, Don and I paused to record the moment of our arrival in front of the Halls Creek sign before rolling down the hill and into civilisation. I must have looked pretty grubby and unkempt when I walked into the shire offices. My brother-in-law had set up a meeting with Peter McConnell, the shire CEO, who had arranged for us to stay in the Kimberley Hotel. The hotel management, in turn, generously agreed to sponsor my stay and so I was able to relax in luxury for a couple of days and enjoy good food, a comfortable bed, swimming pool and air conditioning.

Don sorted out his vehicle and equipment, pleased to have made it through to Halls Creek with most things intact. He'd done well to support me and survive his own battle with his health and the heat. He'd endured the worst conditions he had ever experienced on the stock route. I assured him that the resultant scratches and minor dents on his 4WD only added to its character. One of the heavy-duty shock absorbers had broken a few hundred kilometres before the finish, but at least he would not need them on his journey of over 3000 km on the highway back to Perth.

Made it!

Kalumburu

Indian Ocean

Wyndham

Kununurra

The Kimberley

Ord River

Derby

Windjana Gorge

Purnululu N.P.

Fitzroy River

Fitzroy Crossing

Geikie Gorge

Halls Creek

Great Sandy Desert

Billiluna Settlement

WA | NT

Canning Stock Route

Tanami Road

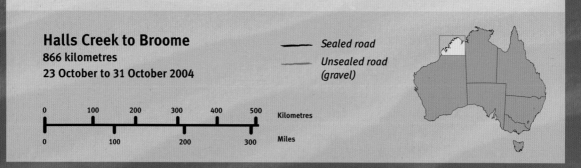

Halls Creek to Broome
866 kilometres
23 October to 31 October 2004

Sealed road
Unsealed road (gravel)

| 0 | 100 | 200 | 300 | 400 | 500 | Kilometres |

| 0 | | 100 | | 200 | | 300 | Miles |

12

Diamonds, pearls and a spirit of gold

(The Kimberley: Halls Creek to Broome)

The colours of Broome

Outside the Halls Creek shire offices is a sculpture of Russian Jack, believed in his time to be the strongest man in Australia. His heroic feats symbolised the qualities of mateship and endurance of the pioneers of the region, then lacking in all the amenities of civilisation. His legend is representative of the spirit and sense of community of the folks of the North West.

Aged twenty-two and hailing from Archangel beside the frozen White Sea in Arctic Russia, 'Jack' arrived in the searing deserts of the far reaches of Western Australia in 1886, looking for gold. To transport his worldly possessions during the search, he constructed an abnormally large wheelbarrow, with shafts over two metres long and a wooden wheel 12 cm thick. He used the barrow like a sled over the sand dune country, where he regularly commuted back and forth. As many of his feats are preserved only in oral history, some of the stories may be exaggerated, but Russian Jack was reputed to have possessed 'the strength of a lion and the tenderness of a woman'. He was, it seems, about seven feet tall, with 'forearms as thick as the thigh of an ordinary man'.

The unlikely 'Angel from Archangel' quickly developed a reputation for performing superhuman feats of strength and compassion, such as rescuing from Hell's furnace fellow prospectors stricken with illness in the middle of nowhere. Perhaps his most famous feat was saving a dying gold prospector suffering with typhoid fever. He simply loaded the ailing man on to his wheelbarrow and pushed him and their combined camping gear over 300 km to Halls Creek, where the man received treatment and lived to tell the tale.

Russian Jack would be a good candidate for a modern comic strip; everything about him was larger than life, including the amount he ate. His massive frame required massive feeding, and he loved eating – three pounds (1.5 kg) of steak, a dozen eggs, a loaf of bread and a pound of butter would disappear in no time, and he would still be hungry.

When I settled in for breakfast, delirious with tiredness and with an insatiable hunger to rival Russian Jack's, the management at Kimberley Hotel in Halls Creek must have been wondering what kind of monster they were supporting. They noted that at one sitting I consumed a bowl of fruit, a bowl of yoghurt, a bowl of muesli and a deluxe omelette with a couple of extra eggs thrown in followed by eight slices of toast, all washed down with plenty of juice and a couple of pots of tea! They were probably relieved when breakfast time was up and I could no longer be served, or I may have dented their daily profit margins severely.

It was already 30-odd degrees and uncomfortably humid at 6.30am when I pushed back up the hill and out of Halls Creek into a nagging headwind. It felt like I was starting over—just 11 000 km to go! But for the first time on the expedition I was completely alone. I needed the strength of Russian Jack to propel what seemed a ridiculously heavy load. When I was travelling with Greg, we had shared between us the items we only needed one of: stove and fuel, water filter, video recorder, tent, first aid kit, tools, spare parts, satellite phone and numerous smaller bits and pieces. Before Greg had left Wiluna, in preparation for this part of the trip, I had swapped my smaller front panniers for his larger rear bags. The over-sized 'buckets' now attached to the front wheel were so full that it required some forceful persuasion to close them.

Being alone meant I had no back up whatsoever. There was no one to remind me if I forgot something and no travelling water or food supply to draw on. There was no one to talk to and no one to help in times of difficulty. It was all up to me and I knew I really had to keep my wits together and remain alert to survive.

Safety is mostly about being self-aware – knowing one's capabilities. Expecting to travel daily distances in excess of 150 km in extreme heat meant I was pushing the boundaries of my personal sustainability. I had already learned how dehydration and hypoglycaemia could, as in guerrilla warfare, creep up out of nowhere and overpower me. Not thinking clearly, feeling weak, or even passing out on Highway No.1 could prove fatal. I didn't fancy being unconscious on the side of the road in the middle of nowhere or ending my days under the wheels of a road train. On the positive side, sticking to the main road meant that there was always a good chance of flagging down a passing vehicle in times of trouble.

As I glided over the bitumen, the white lines passed hypnotically beneath my wheels. Time went more slowly when I didn't have to concentrate on avoiding potholes and sand patches. The mental approaches I cultivated to cope with such long days on the road became something of an art form. I had to be careful to keep my mind occupied to avoid slipping into counting pedal revolutions and analysing the amount of energy required for each pedal stroke. At the same time, I had to remain alert enough not to miss a turn-off, a landmark or an opportunity to top up the water supply.

My original plan was to cycle from Halls Creek to Purnululu (Bungle Bungles) and up to Kununurra before taking the Gibb River Road west to Derby. After six months I was still on schedule, but as I had started the expedition late, I remained behind where I had planned to be at that point. As a result, I had been taking the full brunt of the 'build up' to the Wet for most of the way up the Canning Stock Route. The intensity of the heat and humidity was unlikely to let up until I left the Pilbara region and was out of the North West. I had been looking forward to my tour through the Kimberley region, but there was no way that I could have appreciated it in such oppressive conditions. Every afternoon, the storm clouds shed their load in the form of violent, isolated storms, which were spectacular as long as they didn't become too close – then it all became dangerous. The unsealed Gibb River Road, which bisects the Kimberley, an area the size of France, was likely to be cut off by flash flooding at any time. I had had grand ideas of venturing off the Gibb River Road as far north as I could go in Western Australia, to Kalumburu. My great-grandfather, George Waters Leeming (after whom the Perth suburb is named), surveyed the region around the Kalumburu Community. Named in his honour is Mt Leeming, by all reports a fairly innocuous mound just south of the Aboriginal community. On reflection, I decided there was too much at risk if I deviated to see it, and so I took a literal rain check on the northern Kimberley plans and altered my route.

In the North West, distances between any form of settlement are in a different league from other places. About 35 000 people live in the Kimberley, the bulk of the population concentrated in Broome, Derby, Kununurra, Wyndham, Fitzroy Crossing and Halls Creek. According to one local, even Queenslanders feel freaked by the isolation and that is just on the main road. I had arranged to stay that night at Larrawa Station, which divided the 300 km between Halls Creek and Fitzroy Crossing almost exactly in two. By the time I pushed up the long, dusty drive in the last light, I realised that once again I had exceeded my sustainable physical limit. A splitting dehydration headache prevented me from feeling totally numb, and my heart raced. I thought I had been drinking enough, but now that I was moving at a faster pace, perspiration evaporated effectively and I didn't notice just how much fluid I was losing.

Kevin and Wendy Brockhurst bought Larrawa Station about fifteen years ago and in that time developed the infrastructure and land from scratch. It is a 'small holding' for a Kimberley station – just half-a-million acres (200 000 hectares). Like Michelle and Garry Riggs at Mataranka, they are open to new and progressive pastoral developments and management techniques, and there never seems to be enough hours in the day to squeeze in all their projects.

Particularly heartening for me was the fact that Wendy, who was actively involved in the Isolated Children's Parents' Association, had heard about the

Collecting a bottle of iced water from the Christmas Creek Station mailbox. Travelling alone, I took the extra time to set up the tripod to take photos of myself

GRACE Project from Richard Huelin, the principal of the Cairns School of Distance Education, whom Greg and I had met almost four months before. Wendy promised to spread the word.

I was concerned about being able to carry enough water over this part of the trip. Every litre added a kilogram to my load and so carrying too much water, especially in the heat, was a waste of energy. Before I pushed off the next day, Wendy kindly phoned the family's neighbours at Christmas Creek Station, 70 km down the road, and arranged for them to drop some water in their mailbox for me.

With my spirits singed not only by the previous day but from the accumulated stress and stain of the past month, it was a mental tussle to set off. On the way into Fitzroy Crossing, the mercury reached its usual dizzying heights. At the entrance to Christmas Creek Station, I found a two-litre bottle of iced water – sheer luxury – in the letter-box as promised. I pressed the iced bottle to my forehead and then to the core of my body, savouring the cool. I never met my benefactors, who would have driven a round trip of approximately 40 kms for my benefit, and had to be content with leaving them a 'thank you' card. Tying the bottle to my load, I moved on. Within half an hour on being in the direct heat, the ice block had completely thawed so I persisted with fitting a damp sock over the drinking bottle, the only way I could keep fluids palatable. I could have fried eggs on the bitumen.

A little further along, where the karst (limestone) outcrops gave way to open plains, I bumped into Mark Sewell, administrator of the Mulan Aboriginal Community located beside Lake Gregory. Although we had never met before, he recognised me, having been made aware of my attempt on the Canning Stock Route before I left Wiluna. He had sent me an email warning that, given the conditions he knew I would face, he considered my proposed feat impossible. Fortunately, I did not receive the message until I arrived in Halls Creek. I replied to him from there, thanking him for his concern but saying that I had made it – just. Prior to taking up his post at Mulan, Mark had been a teacher at Wesley College, Melbourne. Seeking a new challenge, he was now on his way to Fitzroy Crossing to meet the management of his former school, who were endeavouring to create an educational exchange program for their students with the Fitzroy Crossing Indigenous communities. We all met up later in the town for a drink and supper.

Walking back later to my campsite, I started chatting to an Aboriginal woman who had just returned from a spiritual journey to Well 39 on the CSR. Her group had driven to their southern tribal boundary to meet up with a group from Port Hedland who had once inhabited the neighbouring tribal territory. They had noticed my tracks in the sand and a tribal elder had identified them as a woman's tracks. Knowing the land intimately, the woman I met was amazed at my feat. As Don's vehicle had wiped out many of my foot and tyre prints, she hadn't realised that I had managed to cycle the stock route in its entirety.

As the name suggests, Fitzroy Crossing sprang into existence as it was the only place for hundreds of kilometres where the immense Fitzroy River could be crossed. The township is now predominantly home to a number of Aboriginal communities, which are spread out more like a series of loosely connected settlements. It also provides services for the pastoral, mining and growing tourist industries.

Before European settlement, there were an estimated 600 Aboriginal languages spoken throughout Australia. As the majority of these were never recorded, most were lost after colonisation. Of the approximately 170 000 people of Aboriginal descent in Australia, 47 000 now have some knowledge of the remaining 263 different languages. Only a handful of these languages are spoken by more than 1000 people. The Kimberley region is one of the most diverse Indigenous regions in the country. The area around Fitzroy Crossing and north to Windjana Gorge and the Napier Range, where I was due to travel over the next three days, is home to the Bunuba people. Of the 600 Bunuba people there are only about 100 speakers of their language left, mostly the older generation living in Fitzroy Crossing. At least their language has been saved from extinction, as it has now been written down and registered in the UNESCO Endangered Languages Program.

◆　◆　◆

I had pushed myself to the limit from Halls Creek so I could spend more time focusing on the region. At Geikie Gorge, or Darngku, flood waters of the Fitzroy River have carved a chasm 30–50 metres deep through the limestone at the junction of the Oscar and Geikie ranges. These ranges are part of an ancient, 1000-km long, 20-km wide coral barrier reef which developed in the Devonian period, 350 million years ago. Johnson crocodiles, Leichhardt's sawfish and coach-whip stingrays, whose saltwater ancestors swam up the Fitzroy River millions of years ago, now reside in the freshwater pools. Cruising on an open barge toward the upper reaches of the tranquil waters, it was difficult to comprehend the astounding transformation the river undergoes every Wet season. The most incredible feature of the mighty Fitzroy River is that, when in flood during the Wet, it has the second highest flow rate of any river on the planet, surpassed only by the Amazon. Water flows at an estimated rate of 30 000 cubic metres (an Olympic-sized swimming pool) a second. The lower 16-metre-high, bleached-looking band on the gorge wall depicts the average annual flood level. Fitzroy Crossing itself can become a virtual island at this time; in the past, residents were cut off for months at a time. Until the main bridge was built in 1974, the only way people could cross the flooded river was by flying fox.

The high floodwaters of the Fitzroy River wash the limestone walls of Geike Gorge, an ancient Devonian reef

Pandanus at the waterline of Geikie Gorge

The average high water mark, Geikie Gorge – about 16 metres up

A boab tree sprouting new foliage signifying the start of the Wet season, Windjana Road

I had far less difficulty leaving town on the main highway and crossing the enormous, fertile floodplain. About two hours later, I turned north onto the gravel towards Windjana Gorge and the Gibb River Road. As always, turning onto rough road instantly transforms the ambience and character of a location. My sense of balance was immediately challenged as I hit heavy corrugations and unavoidable sand patches which subsided under the load. At that stage, including my own body weight, I was pushing around 120 kg. The path, characterised by many dips and twists, wound its way through the Oscar Ranges, offering an intimate relationship with the spectacular karst formations, which were decorated by enigmatic stands of boab trees. Eventually I climbed up on to the open downlands, and decided to stop in at Leopold Downs Station. The homestead was just a kilometre off the road and I needed to top-up water supplies.

Even before the manager, Ned McCord, answered the door, I could see this station was somewhat different from others that I had visited. Once I explained what I was doing and that I had just cycled the Canning Stock Route, any initial reservations I sensed he may have had about a strange woman on a bicycle vanished. He asked me in for tea and a chat, then lunch.

Leopold Downs was purchased on behalf of the Bunuba Aboriginal Corporation (BAC) by the Aboriginal and Torres Strait Islander Commission (ATSIC) in 1991 and neighbouring Fairfield Downs Station was acquired four years later. Since then it has been a long road for the two stations, which inherited a total of about 400 000 hectares of previously mismanaged land with little infrastructure. The properties are now managed by the Bunuba Cattle Company (BCC) and Ned has been employed as the business coordinator.

It is rare that the stakeholders of an Indigenous-owned station are from a single language group. The Bunuba people not only had a traditional association with the country of Leopold Downs (Yarranggi) and Fairfield Downs (Yuwa), but many also have an historical association. The majority of Bunuba people aged in their forties and fifties grew up on the stations, and recall these days fondly – there were still many old people, culture was strong and alcohol out of the picture. While station owners may not have paid their skilled Aboriginal stockmen well in terms of money, I learned that, in many cases, they did have an otherwise holistic approach. They supported the extended families, providing a place to live, education, health care and structure in the lives of maybe 100 locals at a time. By the early 1970s, the Cattle Station Industry Equal Pay case of 1966 was starting to have a major impact, and eventually saw hundreds of people moved off stations in the Kimberley (and the Northern Territory) and into communities such as in Fitzroy Crossing. Under the changes, station owners could no longer afford to support the communities on their land.

As the Bunuba people have no management experience, they recognised that they needed help to be set on the right path. Through strong leadership, they are now finding their way to a balance between the commercial aspects of managing cattle stations and the cultural side. Their homeland contains important cultural sites which they need to look after in their own 'proper way'. Making the venture commercially viable, however, means both cultures need to make concessions.

As we sat out the heat of the mid-afternoon chatting, Ned suggested that I stay for dinner and overnight in order to meet more of the station people. I had some time up my sleeve, as long as I did a big day from Windjana Gorge to Derby, so I accepted his offer. Around the table that evening gathered some of the station staff, two helicopter pilots who had arrived in preparation for cattle mustering the following day, and two Swedish 'gap year' students – a very long way from home. Conversation topics were diverse, and included the characters, joys and hazards involved in heli-mustering. Out on the veranda later, keeping an eye

Pete dropping in for a break from heli-mustering on Leopold Downs Station, Windjana Road

on the violent storms as they gradually closed in, I was thankful that I had a roof over my head. It would have been a very wet and lonely campsite had I had pushed on to Tunnel Creek.

The thunderstorm had flooded the track in places, so my route forward involved a few cross-country excursions. Tunnel Creek, a 750-metre tunnel through the Napier Range, was completely closed due to the high water level. I had definitely made the right decision not to attempt the Gibb River Road at this time of year.

Like Geikie Gorge, Windjana Gorge (Bandilngan) displayed a white water mark showing the average flood level. Being a lesser stream than the Fitzroy, the Lennard River barely flowed at all; it was really more a series of interconnected puddles. From the lush tropical path along the river bank, I counted fifteen fresh-water crocodiles, either sunning themselves on a sand bar or keeping cool in the water, only eyes and nostrils visible. In the late afternoon, fruit bats stirred noisily, waking from their slumber. I ducked and weaved my way through the vines and bushes, constantly surveying the gorge to catch a glimpse of its spectacular 100-metre wall from a different perspective.

The ride from Windjana into Derby was another epic – not that I shouldn't be used to it all by this stage – 42 degrees, 80 km of unsealed road out of 152 km. Most of the route was along the Gibb River Road. The gravel section was most like the Tanami Track for width, soft in places but not so appallingly corrugated overall. It was hard work, but not a patch on the Gunbarrel or the CSR.

I was definitely nearing civilisation. A Swiss couple whom I had met back at Windjana carried some extra water which made my day slightly easier. As I repaired a puncture under a precious piece of shade, a German couple stopped to check I was all right, then another motor cyclist and then more German tourists who'd already passed me on the way to Fitzroy Crossing. Not far from Windjana, I had passed the entrance to the Ellendale Diamond Mine which, according to one of the employees who generously donated fruit juice, was producing the world's purest gem-quality diamonds. The bitumen finally kicked in, and I pushed along the boab-lined road toward the setting sun and into a brisk westerly breeze.

◆　◆　◆

The Derby region was first explored by William Dampier in 1688, when his ship, under the command of Captain Read, sailed around the King Sound area for three months. On his return to England he published a book, *A New Voyage Around the World*, recording his observations about the Aboriginals and the poor quality of the Western Australian land. These observations unwittingly ensured that no one in Britain took any interest in Australia for the next century.

Dampier wrote, discouragingly:

> The inhabitants of the Country are the miserablest People in the world. The Hodmadods or Monomatapa, though a nasty people, yet for Wealth are Gentlemen to these; who have no Houses and skin Garments, Sheep, Poultry, and Fruits of the Earth, Ostrich Eggs &c. as the Hodmadods have: And setting aside their human shape, they differ but little from Brutes. They are tall, strait-bodied, and thin, with small long Limbs. They have great Heads, round Foreheads, and great Brows. Their Eye-lids are always half closed, to keep the Flies out of their eyes; they being so troublesome here, that no fanning will keep them from coming to ones Face; and without the assistance of both Hands to keep them off, they will creep into ones Nostrils; and Mouth too, if the Lips are not shut very close. So that from their infancy being thus annoyed with these Insects, they do never open their Eyes, as other People: And therefore they cannot see far; unless they hold up their Heads, as if they were looking at somewhat over them.

I could relate to his anguish about the flies.

It wasn't until 1879 that Alexander Forrest explored the area more thoroughly. He sent back glowing, exaggerated reports that the Derby region was 'well watered land suitable for pastoral purposes, besides a large area suitable for the cultivation of sugar, rice or coffee'. The descriptions, like sugar lumps to a brumby, soon attracted pastoralists to the region. They quickly found, however, that tropical diseases, unreliable seasons, horrendous transport problems and antagonistic local Aboriginals made life in the West Kimberley virtually unbearable. The site of Derby, on King Sound, was a poor choice for a port because steering ships through the narrow channels off the islands of the Buccaneer Archipelago required remarkable skill. In addition, the area is swept by vicious rips and whirlpools and there are tidal variations of up to 11.3 metres.

Derby's short but volatile history, which includes being bombed by the Japanese in 1942, may be what fortifies its renowned spirit and sense of community. I wasn't quite sure what to expect as I trundled wearily through a rather nondescript suburban sprawl. The Derby Highway tapered into Loch Street and finally into a causeway at the mudflat shoreline. After what I had travelled through, the town itself, with a population of about 5000, seemed like a grand metropolis.

I spent much of my rest day at the Kimberley School of the Air, getting to know the small and committed staff group and joining in on lessons. The educational lifeline transmits to its sixty-five students (approximately) over an area of 450 000 square kilometres – three times the size of the UK. School of the Air classes originated in the early 1960s when teachers tapped into the Royal Flying Doctor Service radio network in Meekatharra, Derby, Port Hedland, Kalgoorlie and Carnarvon. Before that, correspondence and boarding school were the only educational options for isolated primary-age students.

Teaching staff at the Kimberley School of the Air, Derby

The school had just upgraded from its ageing UHF radio to a satellite system. The UHF radio had a poor sound quality and, although teachers and students could speak without delay, it was often difficult to communicate, especially on a humid day. When I spoke into the microphone of the new satellite system, the sound travelled to Perth, then to a receiver in Sydney, was beamed up to the satellite, then back to Sydney, Perth and Derby and out to each station 'classroom'. Not surprisingly, there is a short delay between speaker and listener, but the sound quality is consistently clear. Other benefits of the upgrade include a range of effective teaching aids.

A typical line of questioning from the young, unseen audience went something as follows.

Q: What kind of dangerous animals did you see on the Canning Stock Route?

A: The most dangerous were the three King Brown snakes I saw in two days. They are one of the most poisonous snakes in the world.

Q: How long were they?

A: About five or six feet – at least 1.5 metres.

Q: Were you scared?

A: A little, but I stood there very quietly and waited for them to wriggle away.

Q: Did you try to kill any of them?

A: No, snakes are an important part of the environment just like all the other animals and plants.

Q: Did you carry a gun?

The questions kept coming until the lesson time was up.

A few kilometres south of Derby, I paid a visit to the 1000-year-old Prison Boab Tree. For thousands of years the Aboriginal people used boab trees for shelter, food and medicine, while the early police found another function – they used one of the oldest trees as a prison cell to lock up Aboriginal prisoners on their way to Derby for sentencing. During the turbulent history of early settlement of the region, young native men were routinely rounded up, usually put in chains and forced to march up to 48 km per day. The standard charge was stealing and killing cattle. A number of other Aboriginals were put to work as pearl divers – a particularly hazardous job. It was generally believed by the white population that fewer young Indigenous men in the area would mean less trouble.

The skeletal-looking deciduous tree that I saw has a hollow trunk over 14 metres in circumference, and a slit for a door one metre wide by two metres high. Now protected, it stands as a stark symbol of inhumanity – a result of two cultures not understanding each other.

From Derby, my direction had a very single-minded focus. Broome, just 220 km away, was firmly in my sights. My body was screaming out for a proper rest, my bike was in dire need of an overhaul and I couldn't wait to see Arnaud, who was flying up to spend a week with me. Apart from crossing the 30-km Fitzroy River floodplain at Willare Bridge and Yeeda Station (one of the first Kimberley stations), there was nothing to divert my focus. The highway was flanked by uniform and unremarkable bush and I tried not to let a defiant headwind get the better of me. I looked out for a suitable place to camp for my first night completely alone but there was nothing. My only option was to pull in at a travellers' rest stop, designed for long-distance drivers to have a powernap. I chose the most inconspicuous spot I could find, but didn't sleep easily knowing that anyone could drive in there off the highway at any time.

The next day, taking my final break before Broome at the Roebuck Plains Roadhouse at the junction of the Great Northern and Broome highways, I suddenly felt like just another tourist again. People weren't so friendly and personal. Tourists stared as if I was a real fruit cake. I must have looked pretty rough, but they had no idea.

On the way into Broome I passed the international airport and a smattering of new housing developments. A cricket match was in progress on a beautifully manicured green oval. The temperature had dipped to a pleasant 35 degrees, and the pure turquoise water lured me toward Moonlight Bay – this time it was not a mirage. I would have given anything for that sight a couple of weeks back. And now, for the first time since Canberra, I had a full week's rest off the bike. I could completely relax and spend time with Arnaud when he arrived the following day.

The settlement at Roebuck Bay had very humble beginnings. When the then governor of Western Australia, Sir Frederick Broome, learned that the new township was to be named in his honour, he initially refused to be associated with it, claiming it was nothing more than three graves and a few itinerants. In 1888, '…the only water was a native well, the mangrove swamps were full of mosquitoes, and high up on the sand hills a few struggling camps were pitched'. Two years later, due to volcanic activity in the Arafura Sea, the submarine telegraph cable, which was originally connected through Darwin, was rerouted through the new town of Broome.

The town grew rapidly, becoming very cosmopolitan as Malays, Chinese, Japanese, Filipinos and Europeans were drawn there in the search for pearls. The 'golden age' of pearling was the period before World War I when over 400 luggers operated out of Roebuck Bay, producing about 80 per cent of the world's mother-of-pearl. It was during this time that Broome gained a reputation aptly described by an old pearler when he wrote:

> Broome in its early days was probably the most unique town in Australia. It was an affluent, sinful and tolerant community, in which the Clergy's frequent references to Sodom and Gomorrah were regarded as appropriate tributes to civic progress, rather than warnings of future divine retribution.

In the lay-off season, there were over 3000 Asian divers in the town and Chinatown (the remnants of which are still preserved) was awash with gaming houses, pubs, eating places, and brothels. By World War II, there were more Japanese than Australians and when the coastline was threatened (and subsequently bombed), the entire Japanese population was interned.

Modern Broome may have lost some of its rough frontier charm, but as Arnaud and I walked the streets of the centre, a few relics of the bygone era, such as the corrugated iron buildings with shady verandas, could be spotted tucked in next to cafes, restaurants and modern amenities. The pearling industry is now centred on cultured pearls, and tourism is the region's oyster. Due to the foresight and entrepreneurship of Lord Alistair McAlpine, Broome has been reinvented as a resort town at the western terminus of the Savannah Way. Tourists flock to the warm weather, miles of broad white sand at Cable Beach and beyond, and the contrast of the azure water against the fiery red-orange pindan soils such as at Gantheaume Point. It is a tropical oasis now, with plenty of creature comforts. In 1986, the population of the Broome shire was approximately 6000. By the end of 2006, numbers had trebled to 18 000, with over a quarter of a million annual visitors.

All too soon my time in Broome with Arnaud was over and I had to say goodbye to my husband again. This time I took comfort in the fact that, although I still had 10 000 km ahead of me, I would be nearing the finish in just over three months. I was on the downhill run. I felt low as I retraced my route out of Broome to the junction with the Great Northern Highway. I was already missing Arnaud, but with my rested body and reconditioned bike, I was ready for the open road to Perth.

Pindan soils at
Gantheaume Point, Broome

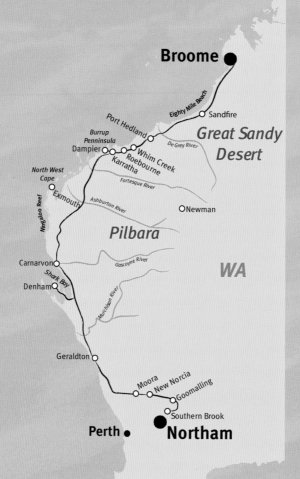

Broome

Eighty Mile Beach

Sandfire

Port Hedland

*Great Sandy
Desert*

*Burrup
Penninsula*

Dampier Whim Creek
Roebourne
Karratha

De Grey River

*North West
Cape*

Exmouth

Ningaloo Reef

Ashburton River

Fortesque River

Newman

Pilbara

Carnarvon

Shark Bay

Gascoyne River

WA

Denham

Murchison River

Geraldton

Moora New Norcia
Goomalling
Southern Brook

Perth

Northam

Broome to Northam
2638 kilometres
8 November to 3 December 2004

——— *Sealed road*

——— *Unsealed road
(gravel)*

| 0 | 100 | 200 | 300 | 400 | 500 | Kilometres |
| 0 | 100 | | 200 | | 300 | Miles |

13

The homeward run
(Broome to Northam)

Many cyclists who circumnavigate the Australian continent claim that the 570-km stretch of the Great Northern Highway between Broome and Port Hedland is the loneliest and most mentally arduous of their tour. It is certainly a flat and featureless landscape, almost devoid of shelter as the winds prevail from the north-west. What I remember about this section of the trip, however, was how friendly I found it. Despite the nondescript physical environment, I was well looked after on the four cattle stations I visited and met some great people. Western Australia is a huge state but a small world. At each station, I was able to find some sort of connection, often facilitated by having friends or relatives in common, as well as shared experiences such as boarding school or growing up in a pastoral environment.

My bike positively purred along the highway's recently upgraded tarmac strip, which melted into a mirage and then seemingly vanished into infinity. New, more efficient road tyres and working parts – bearings, drive train (gears, chain, derailleur) and a free-wheel mechanism – made the going more fluent. I played a game of 'chicken' with the 50-metre-long, three-carriage road trains by pulling out towards the centre of the lane when I heard them roaring up from behind. As the drivers spend countless hours on the road, mostly between Perth and the Kimberley, I wanted to alert them to my presence well in advance so he/she could steer an appropriate line for giving me enough breathing space. As they drew near I would swerve back to the hard shoulder. If one of these monsters has to make a sudden diversion, the third trailer can whip around and take out a cyclist without the driver knowing. Needless to say, timing is everything with this manoeuvre. I have lived to tell the tale.

I had received an invitation from Buss Morris to stay at Munro Springs Station when I had joined in on one of her daughter's lessons at the Kimberley School of the Air in Derby. The Morris family had just moved from Mia Mia Station near Carnarvon to the Kimberley station, keen to make use of its more abundant and reliable underground water supply. They have a lot of work ahead of them developing the 400 000 hectares (a million acres). I very much enjoyed their company and wished I could have stayed longer than overnight and had time to look around.

Day 2 out of Broome was an easy one – just 85 km to the Anna Plains turn-off, where I had arranged to be collected. Anna Plains, another 400 000-hectare property, is owned by John Stoate, the father of David who joined Greg and me cycling out of Sydney. Since then I had cycled a distance equivalent to almost halfway around the world in my quest to reach the diagonally opposite corner of my country. Even though John was away, I was still looked after like a long-lost friend and was able to learn a little about the station, the strip of land between the highway and the coastline being particularly good cattle country.

The third day was again only a simple 109-km ride to get to the Mandora Station turn-off. Mongrel headwinds made it less straightforward. As this coastline is regularly battered by cyclones and strong winds during the Wet, trees do not grow well and in some places not at all. I stopped at Sandfire Roadhouse, the sole services stop, 320 km from Broome, to give the people at Mandora an estimated time of arrival. On the frontier of the Great Sandy Desert, Sandfire received its name because the sand dunes were so hot it seemed as though they were on fire.

At smoko (afternoon tea) at Mandora it didn't take long to establish that the dePledge family are good friends of some cousins of mine, and we soon discovered we had a lot in common. After dinner, Polly Edmonds (née dePledge) pulled out some old photo albums, showing some of the good times she had at boarding school with my cousin back in the early 1980s. Most station kids receive their primary education from the regional distance education organisations, and are then sent away to boarding school (usually in Perth) for their secondary schooling. Although not so isolated, I too received my secondary education at a Perth boarding school.

I appreciated staying at the old Mandora homestead, whose stone buildings and design made perfect sense for the seasonal conditions. My quarters had an open veranda with beds lined up for musterers and workmen to sleep out,

Starting early from the front entrance of Anna Plains Station

Cob dePledge breaking in some stray horses, Mandora Station

Rounding up the pet lambs; they start young at Mandora

OUT THERE AND BACK

unprotected, in order to make the most of the cooling evening breeze. The window of my room was also completely open to the night, with a corrugated iron shutter which could be easily secured if battening down the hatches was called for. Attracted by my bedroom light, great fat green frogs had free rein, entering as they pleased through the window. Although they are completely harmless, I removed a few from my room before I settled down for the night. I had already learned earlier in the expedition that these frogs were an indication of a healthy environment and I took comfort in that. The dePledge family have adopted some important sustainable grazing practices such as cell grazing, in which livestock are put into smaller paddocks (about 800 hectares) and rotated regularly, ensuring even grazing patterns and preventing over-grazing.

◆　◆　◆

Happy frogs – indicators of a healthy environment

Back on the road, views may have been lacking but the scrubland was nonetheless alive, chirping with bird activity. Anna Plains and Mandora stations contain most of the Eighty Mile Beach coastline. Ecologically, this beach is a very important breeding ground for a number of species of birds. Eighty Mile Beach has been identified as an internationally significant wetland for migratory shore birds. Approximately half a million birds belonging to some twenty different species of waders arrive from their breeding grounds above the Arctic Circle, and spend the entire northern winter feeding and resting on the beach and the dunes at Eighty Mile Beach. The Bar-tailed Godwit, Red-necked Stint, Eastern Curlew, Great Knot, Greater Sand Plover and the Curlew Sandpiper are just a few of the shorebirds that migrate to this part of the world. The birds are said to fly at several thousand metres, and to average about 70 km an hour on their continuous 18-day flight via Japan and South-east Asia. That's a journey of between 10 000 and 15 000 kilometres! Even more remarkable is that some of these birds are only a few months old. Not surprisingly, the intrepid aviators are totally spent on arrival.

The prime reason for this extraordinary feat of endurance is to feed on the rich diversity of marine invertebrates found on Eighty Mile Beach, the birds building themselves up for the return flight to the Arctic to breed. Some researchers claim that the biodiversity of the coastline here may be the richest in the world. The freshwater lagoons behind the coastal dunes also provide a plentiful source of food for some of the species of migratory waders. The survival of these species depends entirely on their ability to successfully feed, rest and return to the Arctic to continue breeding. I shudder to think what devastation the bird flu could have on these populations if it got a hold.

Opposite Eighty Mile Beach is the turn-off to the Kidson/Wapet Track which leads directly across the Great Sandy Desert to the Canning Stock Route and the Kunawarritji Community at Gunowaggi, Well 33. The very thought of going back there on a bicycle made me feel very fragile in the pit of my stomach. I was happy to glide over the tarmac toward Pardoo Station, the next link in the chain.

My first memory of Port Hedland was a family trip when I was fourteen to visit my sister and her young family, who had lived there for several years. The road trip from our farm of almost 2000 km each way seemed to take forever for my younger brother and me, who found it difficult to sit still for such long periods. Worried that I was losing fitness before the athletics season, my parents let me run in front of the car first thing in the morning until the odometer clicked over five kilometres. This suitably sedated my energy levels and probably ensured peace for my parents for the rest of the day. Over twenty years on, I wondered how my memories would compare with my fresh perspective from a bicycle.

I was also looking forward to spending a day off and catching up with another old friend from the British hockey tour, Justin 'Kilts' McKirdy, whom I hadn't seen for years.

The town exists because of its natural harbour, set in among the mangrove coastline explored in 1863 by Captain Hedland. Early on, being a base for pearl luggers and crews, Port Hedland had a reputation as a wild frontier settlement. Given the lack of timber for building, the scarcity of drinkable water, and the fact there were no roads, few could have foreseen that the initial tiny settlement would grow into one of the largest and busiest mineral ports in the world. Up until the mid-1960s the port handled wool, livestock, gold and pearl shells. A few years previously, in the late 1950s, massive iron ore deposits had been discovered inland, including at Mt Whaleback in the Ophthalmia Range, the site of William Snell's first pastoral lease. Hedland was the chosen port facility for exporting this mineral wealth, and in 1965 the small town of some 1200 people was thrown into a frenzy of activity and expansion.

The first familiar landmark I recognised were stockpiles of salt, which protruded above the coastal flat like blinding white homing beacons in the shimmering heat haze of the mid-afternoon furnace. Hedland's second biggest industry, Dampier Salt, produces over three million tonnes of industrial salt annually for export from solar salt ponds. It seemed to take forever to skirt the evaporation ponds and the uninspiring marshlands, which isolate the townsite in times of flood. Navigating my way through a maze of streets and roundabouts, I finally arrived at Justin's place in the new suburb of Pretty Pool. It was great to be reunited with a familiar face and meet his family. The following day I was able to reacquaint myself with Hedland as we took a drive around town.

Much of Port Hedland, however, is not so pretty. It looks as though half of the 5.5-km by 1.5-km hole in the ground which is now Mt Whaleback has been dumped on the port, as everything is permanently coated with red dust. The scale of the operations from mines to port is difficult to comprehend. The ore trains normally contain up to 336 cars, but in 2001, BHP Billiton Iron Ore ran the world's longest and heaviest train on its privately owned railway. It stretched 7.4 km, had 682 ore cars, eight locomotives, and moved 82 262 tonnes of ore! At Hedland, the ore is stockpiled, crushed and loaded into about 500 container ships each year; these vessels are roughly a quarter of a kilometre long and carry a quarter of a million tonnes.

There isn't a great deal to entice travellers to the port town, apart perhaps from the fact that, along with Karratha just down the road (from an Australian perspective of distance) and Kalgoorlie, Port Hedland has the highest ratio of young single men in the country. Maybe they should advertise that to attract the girls.

The Pilbara region is called 'Bilybarra' by many different Indigenous groups and means 'dry country'. The actual word 'Pilbara' is an Aboriginal word meaning 'mullet'. It was first applied to Pilbara Creek because of the variety of fish found there. Nowadays it should refer to the popular 1980s hairstyle which is still far too prevalent in this rugged region. No wonder they are struggling to pull in the sheilas!

Perhaps I was feeling a bit soft from spending a day in air conditioning or maybe my will was gradually being wilted by the conditions, but I really did not want to venture on to Whim Creek. I felt all too conscious the body is made up of 90-odd per cent water, which in my case seemed to be leaking at an alarming and unsustainable rate. Was I going to evaporate or spontaneously combust?

Iron ore-rich, 'shiraz-coloured' Chichester Range, source of the Yule River

The only slit of shade I could find after 40 km was the thin shadow provided by the sign-post at the junction of the Great Northern Highway and the North West Coastal Highway, which I was following. I took a break to eat my umpteenth fruit cake for the journey, standing so at least my head was protected from the sun.

The mighty rivers of the Pilbara seem to have a character of their own. I paused on top of each bridge to appreciate the major oases. To the south, the iron ore-rich Chichester Range, the source of the Yule, Peewah, Sherlock, Harding and Maitland rivers, exuded a rich, velvety hue of shiraz. A glass of shiraz? That would be nice. It always helped to fantasise about favourite pleasures which I could look forward to enjoying when the expedition was over.

Conditions on the flat, barren landscape between the ranges and the coast were like being in a fan-forced oven. Panniers were loaded to the hilt with extra kilos of water, and demanded the sum of my God-given strength to propel all forwards. It was a pity my powers did not extend to turning some of the water into wine! The more water I carried, the more it became a compounding economy. Greater effort was required to push the weight and the larger surface area of the baggage meant more wind resistance. As my pace slowed, the time and effort required to turn the pedals increased. Consumption of food and water went up and I would have to carry more. All these thoughts eddied about in my already overheated brain. I put my head down and tried to think about something else.

At first sight of the lone Whim Creek Hotel, any refined thoughts about sipping a glass of shiraz rapidly degenerated into guzzling a middy or two of very cold lager. The back of my throat felt as parched as the Mungilli Claypan (Gunbarrel Highway). The mere anticipation of the moment when the icy beer would soothe the rawness was enough to temporarily erase the hardships of the day. I surged toward my destination with newfound energy.

My arrival at the bar was reminiscent of a classic scene from a spaghetti Western. Heads turned and conversations paused as I wheeled my over-laden machine on to the veranda, leant it against a post and hobbled into the bar with seized-up cycling legs and hard-soled cycling shoes. All I needed to do was swap my bike for a horse and cycling shoes for hob-nailed boots and I was there. A typical menagerie of jackeroos (cowboys), miners and travellers were propped up by the bar, by poker machines and by their pool cues.

'Jeez, mate, d'ya know its 43 degrees out there?'

'I thought it was bloody hot. My thermometer gave up the ghost ages ago.'

'Ya must be mad!'

A two-storey building prefabricated in England and transported by ship to the old port of Balla Balla nearby, the hotel had once been the social hub of a colourful community, whose population rose to four hundred after the discovery of copper in the 1870s. Its walls bore witness to the town's oscillating fortunes, and to its characters, as well as the hotel's destruction by several cyclones and idiosyncratic reconstructions. Whim Creek had now clearly turned another page as the pub and its hilly backdrop were a dusty hive of activity. A large Australian mining company was preparing a new infrastructure over the old copper mine workings which were soon to be reopened. The company had recently purchased the classic, heritage-listed pub and set up rows of temporary workers' huts behind. All visitor accommodation, including the campsite, had been closed, although I was kindly allowed to stay, quietly tucked away in the courtyard. I was also permitted to use the facilities and stock up on the calories at an 'on the house' smorgasbord staff breakfast.

During its heyday, when ore was exported from Balla Balla, sails were attached to the rail wagons to make the most of the constant trade winds. I too wished I could have hoisted a spinnaker to make the most of the morning session to Roebourne. I had noticed there was a general pattern to the wind conditions. In the early morning, warm, surging blasts of air tended to be more favourable coming off the land, but as the sun moved high in the sky, the wind revealed the full extent of its Jekyll and Hyde personality, switching to a nightmare headwind.

I didn't have high expectations of Roebourne, the oldest settlement between Geraldton and Darwin and the one isolated community on the whole vast and lonely Kimberley and Pilbara coastline. Its reputation as a rough town is exemplified by the historic stone buildings which are still fortified with iron bars across the windows and the barbed wire around the police station. Nevertheless, I was pleased to reach Roebourne if only for its shelter. For Peter Egerton Warburton and his party, who arrived in the town barely alive on Australia Day in 1874 after their epic first crossing of the Great Sandy Desert, the same stone buildings must have been their Arc de Triomphe. Of the expedition, Warburton later concluded: 'I may safely say no exploring party ever endured such protracted suffering as we have done, nor did anyone cross, with their lives, so vast an extent of continuous bad country'.

The first European settlers, John and Emma Withnell, had landed in Roebourne ten years earlier than Warburton accompanied by their two children, 1000 ewes, fifty rams, ten horses and ten head of cattle. They had travelled inland up the Harding River until they arrived at Eramuckadoo Pool, and camped at the base of a hill, which Emma named Mt Welcome. There they later built a one-room house made of mud and grass – the first building in Roebourne.

Concurrently with its pastoral history, Roebourne had been a trading centre for Indigenous slave labour. As the colonial government would not allow convicts to be shipped to the North to help in its development, Indigenous people of the region were subject to some of the worst treatment handed out anywhere. From the 1860s, 'blackbirders' rounded up Aboriginals and sold them as indentured labourers in the burgeoning pearling and pastoral industries. When smallpox and measles further decimated local communities in the 1860s, Emma Withnell, widely known as the 'Mother of the North-West', became involved with the victims, nursing them as best she could.

Roebourne has been plagued with a notorious reputation for strained relations between Indigenous and non-Indigenous communities for most of its existence, but according to the young manager of the Roebourne supermarket to whom I spoke, the town had recently cleaned up its act. He was upbeat about the revitalised spirit of Roebourne. The streets had been tidied, graffiti removed, alcohol distribution regulated and residents were endeavouring to improve the town's image. The local Yindjibarndi elders are leading a cultural revival, re-establishing traditional links with the land and re-connecting their grandchildren with their roots.

◆　◆　◆

Any brownie points that the wind had notched up in the first half of the morning were well and truly negated by the mid-afternoon session, and by the time I reached Karratha, I was owed some serious down-time. In the morning, I had sat high in the saddle, but heading towards Karratha I flattened my back and leaned so far forwards that I could have kissed the handlebars. I tilted into the cross-headwind to prevent the gusts sending me into the traffic. Passing motorists may have thought I was intoxicated as I could not hold a straight line.

Karratha is an Indigenous word meaning 'good country' but etched in my mind are the barren, windswept expanses I saw from over the handlebars. William Dampier was equally as scathing about this land as he was about the King Sound/Derby region and Europeans only ventured here after exaggerated reports designed to entice the most adventurous and hardy of settlers. Geologists and industrial developers of the late 1950s and '60s may have meant by 'good country' the iron ore rich Hamersley Ranges to the south, but a deep water port was needed to ship the ore to overseas furnaces and onto the global market. When I was born in the late 1960s, Karratha was still just a cattle station. Its meteoric rise as the Pilbara's most important services and administrative township, along with the port towns of Dampier and Wickham (near Point Samson), is synchronised with the iron ore boom. Hamersley Iron is to Karratha and Dampier as BHP Billiton is to Port Hedland. Ore is railed from Tom Price and Paraburdoo to Dampier. Wickham, the port for the third major iron ore company, Robe River Iron Associates, receives ore railed from Pannawonica.

The 'good country' – a conflict of interests. Flares burn 24/7 from the natural gas treatment plant with a backdrop of the barren rocks of the Burrup Peninsula

Karratha's second major growth spurt occurred when the Woodside Petroleum's North-West Shelf Natural Gas Project got underway in the early 1980s. The project collects gas from an offshore platform 135 km north-west of Dampier, from where it is piped 1500 km to Perth or liquefied for export to Japan. I was fortunate to be shown around the area by Jane Grieve, a fellow Perth College (younger) 'Old Girl' and ABC radio journalist. In the late afternoon we visited Dampier, passing kilometres of loaded wagons of ore and huge stock piles of salt produced by Dampier Salt, all waiting to be exported.

Just beyond Dampier, we reached the limit of our tour at the security gates of the natural gas

treatment plant nestled between the barren scree slopes and Mermaid Sound. The futuristic-looking domes, mazes of silvery pipes and continuously burning gas flares could not be a starker contrast to its ancient backdrop – the Burrup Peninsula. If the first Europeans had spent more time scratching the surface, they would have discovered why the Aboriginal people referred to this land as the 'good country'. They had been scratching surfaces there for at least 18 000 years. Until recent times, local groups visited this spiritual and religious 'Mecca' and carved between 500 000 and a million petroglyphs. Compared with the other main regions in Australia with high concentrations of Indigenous art, such as the Kimberley, Arnhem Land, Victoria River, Central Australia and Central Queensland, the Burrup Peninsula has the greatest density and diversity of subject and style. In fact, nowhere else in the world contains such an array and intensity of Indigenous art. The artists used the natural colours and features in the stone as part of their composition, for example, specks of quartzite were incorporated as stars in the sky. Alongside the petroglyphs, the rocky burrows also contain the world's largest concentration of standing stones, as well as shell middens, stone quarries, grinding stones, grinding patches and stone artefacts.

All this creative activity points to the fact that the Burrup religious sites are as important to groups of Aboriginal people as Delphi to the ancient Greeks, or the Vatican to Catholics. The region is yet to be fully documented and the clues to a complete history of events are yet to be unravelled. Burrup is the reason why Mary and Judith, whom Greg and I had met at the Docker River campsite back at the NT–WA border, had driven all the way from Sydney – to discover undocumented artwork and contribute pieces to the jigsaw puzzle. Despite the fact that the significance of the area is not yet fully understood, major industry was given the go-ahead in the 1980s to develop parts of the area. Proposals for further industries to be built here are in the pipeline (the world's largest ammonia/fertiliser plant of its kind opened in April 2006).

Although many of the original inhabitants of the area were totally wiped out due to a horrendous chain of events, mainly diseases and conflicts, three groups now have been granted Native Title: the Wong-goo-tt-oo, the Ngarluma Yindjibarndi and the Yaburara Mardudhunera. The signing of the Burrup and Maitland Industrial Estates Agreement in early 2003 and its joint management with CALM (Department of Conservation and Land Management) and the ABC (Approved Body Corporate) will restore to the Aboriginal people the ability to exercise their responsibilities for their country.

At the Burrup Peninsula Forum in April 2003, Wilfred Hicks, spokesperson for the Wong-goo-tt-oo Group, eloquently expressed the position of his people:

> ...Like you the Wong-goo-tt-oo people want to see development in the Pilbara. We believe that we are all Australians together and, like your families, so also do ours need jobs, education and the prospects for the future for our young people. In no sense are we against development.
>
> However, development has to be planned carefully and in such a way that it does not destroy our quality of life. We, the traditional owners of the lands between the George and Maitland rivers, have a special duty also for the country, as holders of the spiritual energies. On the Burrup that spiritual force is alive in the thousands of rock engravings that surround you here. They were placed here by our ancestors, and we receive from earlier generations the duty to protect them and must pass that on to our successors. The engravings are to us a spiritual source of energy – we can hear and see this energy when we are among them. It ties us to the land and the land to us.

The Traditional owners of country cannot sell it to third parties, such as the State Government, who intend to destroy it. The country is not ours to sell. As Traditional owners, the country owns us as much as we own its Traditional aspects. Nowadays we have an added duty to think of all you people who are permanent neighbours of ours. We reject the Land Council nonsense that only Aboriginal people are permanent here. We attend the celebrations and funerals of our white friends; your children marry into our families; our children marry into yours; your dead lie alongside our dead...we, the Wong-goo-tt-oo people accept you as our neighbours and welcome you to live in our Traditional lands.

But you must realise that we cannot allow the spiritual side of our lands to be destroyed by building factories that will hide forever some of our rock engravings and will pour acid rains on others, destroying them in less than a century. We cannot hand that disaster on to our descendants; if we do they will look back on us and despise us. To offer us money for that is to try to pay us to commit a crime. If the spiritual side of the land dies, then our spirits also will die and evil and death will come to your people as well as ours, especially those that break our ancient laws by dealing in a wrong way with our culture such as the Burrup Rock art...

The Wong-goo-tt-oo refused to sign an agreement to allow blanket industrial development on the Burrup that was being offered by the state. They would have been happier to leave the 88-km-square Burrup completely untouched. However, they saw the need to compromise so that they can have a voice in plans for the area, and remain in touch with their land. Their agreement allows heritage surveys to be carried out for five years of areas under consideration for development, and of areas being considered for World Heritage listing.

As I stepped outside the Karratha ABC building after a breakfast radio interview the next morning, it was as if someone had switched a giant hairdryer on to full blast. Back on the highway, the landscape seemed like an immense burnt ocean vaporising into the Big Sky. The hills were a combination of bare escarpments and scree slopes, which supported only tufty hummocks of spinifex, and the vast plains looked denuded and suspiciously overgrazed. The pure blue sky was broken only by wispy, high level cloud, indicating that the wind was not only at ground level. No matter how hard I pedalled, my efforts seemed futile – I was only inching forward as vehicles of all shapes and sizes thundered by at breakneck speeds. I felt overwhelmingly small and insignificant, like Gulliver arriving to the Land of Brobdingnag (the Giant People) after fleeing

Exposed plains appear over-grazed between the hills and the coast

the Lilliputians. This sensation magnified as I turned the corner towards the Fortescue River to take the full brunt of the persistent south-westerly.

The generosity of the locals inspired me and kept my spirits up. Five people stopped to offer water and soft drinks. Firstly, my friend from Port Hedland, Justin, had heard my radio interview and caught up with me near the Yan Yare River. As a Main Roads engineer, he is responsible for the road quality over a vast region. I can verify his claim that the road quality of the Pilbara is probably the best in the country, built to service the big dollars of the mining industries. Next, a truckie travelling in the opposite direction pulled over. I felt honoured. This was a particularly unusual thing to happen because of the effort it takes to stop and park a huge road train. The driver pulled a cold Coke out of his icebox and passed it down to me. Normally I didn't drink carbonated or highly sugared drinks on the road because they occasionally had an adverse effect, making me feel weak, even hypoglycaemic. But I couldn't refuse his kind gesture and decided under these circumstances to accept anything wet.

I was just finding a good rhythm again when a tourist van pulled over. It was a Danish guy who hailed from Greenland. Being more used to −40 degrees rather than the 40+ degree temperatures we were experiencing, he was really feeling the conditions. He had planned to cycle around Australia but after a couple of weeks of pedalling up the east coast he had given it away as being too difficult. Next to stop were some Karratha residents heading off for a few days fishing – the coastline is renowned for its great angling opportunities. Finally, the proprietor of the Fortescue Roadhouse donated another Coke and a Gatorade.

Feeling a little wobbly, I was running only on goodwill as I arrived at my destination. The mighty Fortescue was in a sedate mood in the late afternoon. The only disturbances ruffling the calm, ink-blue stream were superficial ripples from the persistent breeze. I paused in the middle of the massive bridge, itself engineered to withstand all but an atomic bomb. Any localised thunderstorms upstream could transform the ripples into turbulent waves spilling over the banks, the immense power flattening everything in its path. Flotsam and jetsam on the broad floodplain included clusters of uprooted mature trees.

◆　◆　◆

The mighty Fortescue in a sedate mood

The five principal rivers which segment the North West corner – the De Grey, Fortescue, Ashburton, Gascoyne and Murchison – all originate in the uplands which form the frontier to the Great Sandy and Little Sandy deserts. Crossing each river was an important landmark as I headed south, now desperate to escape the North West to beat the heat. I planned to cycle from the Fortescue to the Ashburton in a long day. There are absolutely no services or stations beside the road and the 165 km, even into an average headwind, would have been tough but achieveable, had I stuck at it.

I awoke at the Fortescue Roadhouse campground to the first squawks of the sulphur-crested cockatoos and with the idea of clocking up some good distance before the wind strengthened. Even before I unzipped the tent, I could hear the gale blowing. The circular Hills clothes hoist squeaked as it spun as furiously as a fairground ride, the walls of my tent bowed, doors slammed and an empty can rattled as it was blown across the campground. I prayed that the wind be a northerly but, as I ventured out, my worst fears were realised.

Setting off uphill, I rode into the gale with a full load of water. The six hours until lunch I spent hunched over the handlebars averaging 15 km an hour. It was soon evident I was not going to make Nanuturra Roadhouse on the Ashburton in a day. The afternoon south-westerly strengthened further, I became fatigued and as the sun disappeared, scoured the roadside for a sheltered spot to camp. Eventually I found a patch of old road which had been left to return to nature, barely out of sight of the highway. The gravel made a perfect place to pitch the tent and was protected enough to fire up my stove. It had taken me ten hours to pedal 131 km. At 35 km short of my destination I felt completely stuffed, but at the same time strangely elated. The adrenaline produced by the extended exercise period put me on a natural high. In the past, being totally alone in the middle of nowhere, with no one knowing where I was hiding out, would have frightened me, but at this point I really didn't care. The Parry Range to the east glowed spectacularly, reflecting the last of the sun's warm glow.

The generosity of those with whom I shared the road continued all the way down the coast in the same vein as the day out of Karratha. After asking around at Nanuturra and making a few phone calls, I arranged to stay the following night with one of the more interesting families I encountered on the expedition. The Tate family home encompassed the converted buildings of the old Barradale service station on the Yannarie River. Bruce Tate is the resident regional professional kangaroo shooter. At first, he seemed defensive and reluctant to discuss details of his job, probably assuming that I wouldn't understand his side of the emotive issue. Once I started to talk about the purpose of the expedition, Bruce opened up, explaining that his profession is very important in maintaining a sustainable kangaroo population. For every one kangaroo that was alive when

A night's work for Bruce, a professional kangaroo shooter. The kangaroos are culled to maintain a sustainable balance

Europeans first arrived in Australia, there are at least fifty now. In the past, the kangaroo population has been controlled by the climate; many thousands always perished during drought and bushfires. Reliable water and food supplies have meant that numbers have increased to unsustainable levels. Bruce helps maintain the balance and his work, along with kangaroo population levels, is monitored by CALM. Nothing is wasted as each carcass is prepared and loaded before he can continue. The meat is refrigerated and transported by truck to Geraldton; it is sold mostly as pet meat.

Sand dune country north of Mia Mia Station

Of immediate concern to me was that I was ravenously hungry, thanks to my struggle with the weather conditions. Bruce and his wife, Gian, made feel very welcome, but as they were both so thin I was concerned as to whether there would be enough food. As it turned out, there was barely enough to touch the sides, but fortunately for me, Bruce was so keyed up before work he was not hungry, so I polished off his meal as well. I spent the evening with Gian and their youngest daughter, Lissie, who was enrolled at the Carnarvon School of the Air.

It was a great comfort knowing that I had just 100 km to do before my next station visit and new friends, Kirsty and John Forsyth at Mia Mia. The desolate sand ridge country before neighbouring Winning Station did not seem so imposing from the bitumen strip. I had plenty of opportunity to lift my head and appreciate the harsh yet fragile landscape, although it felt like I was cheating. The ease of my path made me feel slightly removed from the land in comparison with the rough desert tracks I had traversed over the past months. Dragon and tartar lizards darted out ahead playing 'chicken' with my front wheel. They were far more daring than my efforts with the road trains – it was as if they had a death wish. Even though I was moving at a reasonable speed, the little creatures still managed to out-pace me for a short distance and then would stop and wave furiously as if I was competing in the Tour de France. I blasted my way through to the Mia Mia front entrance, stopping only once. The natural elements may have been against me, but somehow I was completely in my own element. I felt totally secure in this country.

A quick call on the satellite phone at the station entrance and Kirsty drove down to meet me. By the time we reached the homestead, we had established some of the people we knew in common. John's family also own the Three Rivers Station in the upper Gascoyne region and are successfully producing and marketing their organic beef. They had recently bought Mia Mia from Todd and Buss Morris (Munro Springs) and seemed excited by the challenge ahead, developing their cattle breeding program on the 200 000 hectares (half a million acres). With a young family (new arrival Hamish was just seven weeks old when I visited) and being at the end of mustering, they had plenty on their plate. After a couple of beers, I thankfully had plenty on my plate too.

Waiting to be collected at the entrance of Mia Mia Station

By the time I reached Minilya Roadhouse the next day, after crossing the Tropic of Capricorn for the fourth time on the journey, Kirsty had left a message to confirm that it would be fine for me to stay at Boologooro Station, 80 km north of Carnarvon. When I explained to one of the Minilya managers about the expedition and its purpose, I obviously struck a raw nerve. Being a pastoralist and dealing with the tourist trade he could really identify with the topic. One of his greatest concerns was controlling the development of tourism on the 280-km Ningaloo Reef, the world's longest western fringing reef. Bordering the nearby North West Cape, it is one of the last healthy major coral reef systems in the world. In near pristine condition, Ningaloo supports a staggering abundance species of fish, corals and many other marine invertebrates.

The roadhouse, strategically located near the junction with the main access road to the reef, has certainly benefitted from the recent explosion in tourism as the beauty and endemic qualities of the region are promoted. 'Beautiful one day, perfect the next' the advertising slogan boasts. Every year increasing numbers of people come to swim with the whale sharks (the world's largest fish), giant manta rays (which span about three metres), dugongs and various species of whales as well as to witness the rare coral-spawning phenomena. Even though his business benefits from increasing numbers of passing trade, the manager is very much into sustainable development of the natural treasure. He wants his children to be able to grow up appreciating the unique environment, as he has.

It being late in the renowned wildflower season, I was surprised at the colourful sprays of delicate wildflowers which decorated the scrubland, gradually upgrading in intensity as I pushed south of the sand ridge country and into the Gascoyne region. Yellow, purple and white everlastings carpeted the red earth, and mulla mulla, wattles, grevillea, eucalypts and various acacias started to appear among the gnarled mulga scrub: it had obviously been a good season. Just before Boologooro I spotted a few emus, mobs of feral goats and a large feral tabby cat, no doubt growing fat on a constant supply of tartar lizards and other small native animals.

On arrival I had already figured out my connection with the next link in the chain at Boologooro. The station is owned by Jo and Bob Symonds. I knew Jo was a Maslen and that the Maslen family are friends of my uncle. I was quick to insert this fact into the conversation when I finally managed to catch Jo and her daughter, Billie, as they hared back and forth between paddocks and sheep-yards. There was a mob of at least 12 000 sheep sitting in the yards. Many station owners have converted to cattle, due to a greater demand and easier care, and Boologooro is one of the few remaining sheep stations, traditional to the region. Mustering, shearing and overall care of sheep requires more effort than cattle, and handling of greater numbers of animals to get the returns.

I kicked back as invited, dangled my aching feet in the swimming pool, and used the water to mend a punctured tube. At dusk, the old, rustic homestead came to life: vehicles returned and people and dogs piled out. Even though they were flat out, Jo, Bob and their daughters, Brock and Billie, welcomed me. In no time, everyone was cleaned up, the girls had prepared a roast and fourteen of us sat on the veranda around the dinner table, no drama.

When I awoke at 5.30am, everyone was up and off. I could hear vehicles buzzing around like angry mosquitoes, dogs barking as they worked the sheep and people shouting, cursing at the dogs and stock alike. I felt as though I was the lazy one. There was no need to rush as I only had a half-day ride to reach Carnarvon, my focal point since Port Hedland, and then a full day off the bike.

◆ ◆ ◆

Carnarvon may have initially grown in prosperity off the sheep's back, but in the late 1920s it was realised that a combination of its hot, dry climate and the waters of the Gascoyne also made it ideal for growing tropical fruit. Bananas thrived initially but more recently market gardens have diversified, growing avocadoes, coconuts, dates, jojoba, macadamia nuts, mangoes, pawpaws, pecans, tomatoes, pineapples, melons and various varieties of beans. I had fully expected to be able to stock up on some of the succulent fresh produce when I reached the packing sheds on the banks of the dry Gascoyne River. But there was nothing for sale – all local produce is bought by the southern market and freighted straight down to Perth. Most fruit available in the Carnarvon supermarkets has done a 2000-km road trip to Perth and back, an expensive and ridiculous waste of fuel and labour.

From the main bridge a few kilometres before town, it was difficult to imagine how the dry river of sand can supply enough water to irrigate the plantations and market gardens. On average, water flows for about 120 days of the year. For the rest of the time, the river literally flows upside down. The mouth of the Gascoyne River is a 300-km tongue of sand which acts as a huge water storage system. The aquifers lie below the sands and local growers tap into it to pump out their water quotas.

Caitlin and Adam, friends of my brother and sister-in-law, made me feel at home in Carnarvon and showed me the main sights. Perhaps the biggest event in recent Carnarvon history was the establishment of the NASA tracking station in 1964. From the Carnarvon base command was given for the Trans Lunar Insertion (TLI), which sent the Apollo missions in to land on the moon. Its greatest moment came on 20 July 1969 when astronaut Neil Armstrong stepped out of Apollo ll. His famous words, 'One small step for a man, one giant leap for mankind' were relayed to the world via the tracking station at Carnarvon. It was finally closed down in 1974 because it became outmoded.

Wind power at Wooramel Station

Before setting off from Carnarvon, I arranged a visit at the School of the Air where I sat in on a class. The Year 6 students, including Lissie Tate, were well primed as the principal and I had sent out a fax the day before. The class began with the school song, recorded by one of the teachers with his acoustic guitar to the tune of Boney M's *By the Rivers of Babylon*, which had been changed to *By the River of the Gascoyne*. By the time the teacher had played the full version in my honour, which involved a verse for all seven classes, my mind had been tainted with the chorus, which proceeded to haunt me as I continued my journey, all the way to Wooramel Station.

Fortunately, the hours for torment were reduced as, for the first time in quite a while, the wind was now in my favour and the temperature had dropped off. I sat as high as possible to make the most of the north-westerly and arrived at the front gate of Wooramel Station just five hours and 125 km after leaving the School of the Air. Kirsty Forsyth back at Mia Mia Station had organised for me to stay with her and John's friends, Rachel and Justin Steadman, at their 200 000 hectare property. Halfway up the front drive I could hear their wind turbine whirring like a giant Aboriginal bull roarer. It was spinning so frantically in the gale it sounded as though it might take off. The Steadmans have opted for a wind turbine in conjunction with solar panels to produce most of their energy needs at the homestead. Given the amount of sun and wind in the region, it is an astute long-term investment. The diesel generator is only fired up when the renewable energy sources do not provide sufficient power.

Like Kirsty and John and others I met on the trip, Rachel and Justin are part of the new generation of station managers; well educated, energetic, full of innovative ideas, the concept of sustainability an integral feature of their practices. Having taken over the reins from Justin's father in the last year, the couple have numerous projects on the go – cattle, sheep, trapping wild goats, table grapes and now a citrus orchard.

Before I left Wooramel, Rachel arranged my next stop, at Hamelin Station. With the wind at my back, it was a straightforward day's ride to Hamelin Pool, although a snapped spoke ensured I didn't get things all my way. Mary and Brian Wake, owners of this historic property for twenty-five years, welcomed me warmly. The homestead itself is built of solid blocks of coquina shells carved from a quarry on the nearby beach. When I arrived, Brian was preparing for shearing and loading vermin goats which they had trapped. At $46 each, the goats were worth more than sheep and the land was far better off without them.

These owners also had many projects on the go. Mary showed me their hydro-electric generator which produces all their power needs. Basically, they use 10 per cent of the potential flow of their bore to drive a turbine and produce electricity. In more recent times, all free-flowing bores in the region had to be capped by law to protect the artesian supply. The water is channelled down to an artificial lake which has been there since 1915. Hamelin Station has been granted a special licence to allow the restricted flow to maintain the lake because it has become an important habitat for local birdlife.

Hydro-electric power scheme at Hamelin Station

Visiting Hamelin Station aside, the two main reasons for the long diversion off the North West Coastal Highway were to learn more about the Shark Bay World Heritage site, inscribed in 1991, and to reach the most westerly point of mainland Australia. After the station, my first port of call was a visit to the stromatolites near the Old Hamelin Pool Telegraph Station.

Stromatolites represent the oldest form of life on earth, dating back some 3500 million years. Hamelin Pool contains the most diverse and abundant examples of stromatolite forms in the world. Formed by single-celled organisms, stromatolites are often referred to as 'breathing rocks'. They were essential for releasing oxygen into the atmosphere, gradually building the levels up to 20 per cent, the necessary level for air-breathing life. The tide was in when I arrived and as I studied the submerged life-forms from the purpose-built walkway, I could see trails of oxygen bubbles rising to the surface. Conditions here are well suited to harbouring the stromatolites, the hyper-saline qualities of the water of the shallow, semi-enclosed Hamelin Pool supporting an abundance of rare and endemic species. The 4000-km-square Wooramel Seagrass Bank, the largest seagrass meadows of its kind in the world, forms an extensive ecosystem attracting 12 per cent of the world's dugong population as well as dolphins, sharks, rays, turtles and an abundant and diverse population of fish.

I had been timing my journey very precisely since Broome, as I needed to give dates of my arrival in Perth to Alcoa so that the company could organise school visits and various other community engagements. With such a strict schedule, I had only limited time to try to reach Steep Point, the most westerly point of Australia. To save two days and back-tracking an extra 150 km over some isolated and sandy tracks, I decided to pedal up the main road through the Peron Peninsula to Denham. I had a contact I could to stay with there, and from Denham I could arrange to catch a boat across to Useless Loop on the most westerly peninsula.

Unfortunately, the winds that had blown me all the way from Carnarvon continued from the north-west with great force, turning what would have been a moderate day into a war of attrition over the exposed, bone-dry peninsula. The colour of the sea which contrasted against the flame-orange sands graduated through every hue of the blue-green spectrum during the course of the day; pale turquoise blue at the shallow shoreline of Hamelin Pool, deep green in the middle of the day looking out over the hyper-saline l'Haridon Bight, and ranging from bottle green to violet blue looking west over the deeper Denham Sound in the mid-afternoon. The beauty of this ever-changing kaleidoscope helped ease the severity of the long grind.

As I crossed a standard-looking cattle grid, just before another of Shark Bay's treasures, Shell Beach, a deep-throated growling bark made me nearly jump out of my skin. My heart skipped a beat as I looked around, fully expecting to find a rabid, drooling rottweiler sizing up my ankles. Fortunately, there was no dog in sight. Then, as a car crossed the barrier, I realised it was a recording. The grid and audio deterrent form part of a 3.4-km barrier fence separating the Peron Peninsula at the narrowest point, creating an ecological island for Project Eden.

In 1990, CALM purchased the 1000-km square Peron pastoral station with the intention of not only slowing but actually turning the tide of extinction and ecological destruction on a small slice of mainland Australia. Project Eden is an ongoing attempt to reconstruct and rejuvenate an entire, ailing ecosystem on the Peron Peninsula. When Project Eden began in 1995, the ecosystem was vastly different from that observed and recorded by the brilliant French naturalist, François Péron, and his colleagues on Nicholas Baudin's exploration voyage, which visited the shores of Shark Bay in 1801–3. Within two hundred years, less than a third of the species Péron recorded could still be found inhabiting the landscape. Habitat loss and degradation due to grazing pressures and land clearing, the competition for food and habitat from introduced herbivores like sheep, goats and rabbits, and the predation by introduced predators such as cats and foxes, have all contributed to the crisis. A program of eradication of the feral herbivores and predators was the first step to rejuvenating the peninsula, allowing the slow recovery of indigenous species. Marginalised and endangered species such as mallee fowl, the woylie and the greater bilby were then re-introduced back to their old stomping ground. The red-tailed phascogale, rufous hare-wallaby, banded hare-wallaby, western barred bandicoot and chuditch are next on the list. Obviously, the process of creating a future ark for native wildlife is a long-term project.

Coquina shells in their billions at Shell Beach

Shell Beach – the vermin-proof fence in the distance extends into the shallows, sectioning off the Peron Peninsula for Project Eden

Shell Beach is a 10-metre-thick layer made up of billions of tiny coquina bivalve shells. This broad, snow-white expanse extends for about 110 km around l'Haridon Bight. The barrier fence I encountered protrudes right across Shell Beach and out to sea to ensure animals cannot swim around it.

I spent a day in Denham, kindly looked after by Tim, the principal of the Denham Primary School, and a complete stranger except he was a friend of a friend. He took me on a quick tour of the area and I spent the rest of my time trying to organise my route to Useless Loop – a township owned by Shark Bay Salts. I needed to apply for permission to land at the company's port and to cycle across its property – the shortest route to Steep Point. I would have been able to get across by boat, but even after explaining the purpose and achievements of my expedition, and emailing off a UNESCO letter, Shark Bay Salts would not allow me to do so on two wheels. I was disappointed at this refusal which I understood was because of the risk that an accident may have occurred on their small pocket of land. Useless Loop lived up to its uninviting name. Time lost while trying to organise my way to Steep Point meant I was unable to visit Monkey Mia on the east side of the peninsula, one of only two places in the world where wild bottle-nosed dolphins regularly choose to interact with humans. I decided that, as I could not afford to add another three days to the schedule, I would have to be content with reaching the most westerly town in the country, and returned to the main highway.

◆ ◆ ◆

The south-west corner of Western Australia, from Shark Bay to Esperance, has been identified as one of the world's thirty-four 'Biodiversity Hotspots', the only part of Australia to be so recognised. These hotspots are defined as the most biologically rich and most threatened terrestrial regions on earth. To qualify, a region must have at least 1500 endemic species of vascular plants and have lost at least 70 per cent of its original habitat. Collectively, the Hotspots of the world contain half the planet's species of endemic plants in 16 per cent of the land area, while almost 80 per cent of the terrestrial species live in a remaining habitat covering 2.3 per cent of the land surface. Identifying these regions allows resources to be targeted where they are most urgently needed. Unless we succeed in conserving this small fraction of the planet's land area, we will lose more than half of our natural heritage.

Mallee flower

Australia's south-west corner has nearly 6000 species of endemic plants and large numbers of unique vertebrates. This is attributed to millions of years of isolation from the rest of the country due to the vast central deserts, which I now know all about. Extreme climate shifts and poor soils have also promoted specialisation of the region's flora. Only 30 per cent of the original vegetation remains in more or less pristine condition. These principal vegetation types – eucalyptus woodlands, mallee scrublands and Kwongan heath formations (an indigenous word referring to the open, scrubby vegetation on sandy soil) – have been cleared mostly for agriculture.

During the course of a very long 'into the wind day' between the Overlander Roadhouse and the Murchison River, the land I rode through, and its associated use, changed notably. The first third of my day was more of the same: a deadpan straight road across stunted mulga scrub and red earth. Then, as I approached Nerren Nerren Station, I entered a more prosperous-looking woodland. Majestic eucalypts towered over the roadside, providing welcome patches of dappled shade over my path. About thirty kilometres before the Murchison, the soil colour of the now gently rolling hills changed to lighter grey, and through the broad roadside nature reserve strip I could see open, cleared paddocks of recently harvested wheat crops. I had arrived at the far northern reaches of the Wheatbelt. Each paddock (about 100-200 hectares) had been almost totally cleared for broad-acre cereal farming, except for the bands of natural vegetation, often about 20 metres wide, which had been left as a border. The nature strips are important to reduce wind erosion, provide shade for stock and a haven to protect wildlife. With the scent of recently harvested wheat and the open paddocks, I was suddenly back in familiar territory – just four more riding days and I would be home!

I arrived at the Galena Bridge on the Murchison in the dullest of light to find Jean, whom I had initially met ten days before at the Fortescue, parked up in her converted minibus for the night. Since then, we had been travelling down the west coast at roughly the same speed. Living frugally off her age pension, she travelled with her little dog in a vehicle which was as rickety as her elderly legs. I felt far more secure camping in an exposed picnic stop in the company of Jean and her little 'guard dog' than I did on my own.

South of the Murchison, the land took on even more of a familiar flavour for me: long rolling hills, large grain bulk-handling receival points at Binnu and Northampton, and vivid yellow Christmas trees flowering in the paddocks. But the wind was soul destroying. I had to struggle just as hard to pedal down the hills as up. The same persistent trade winds, the 'Roaring Forties', have made the adjacent coastline perilous to ships since European discovery, which is why it received its touristy name, 'the Batavia Coast'. When François Pelsaert's ship, the *Batavia*, was wrecked on the reefs of the Houtman Abrolhos Islands in 1629, some two hundred years before the founding of the Swan River Settlement (Perth), the mutiny, rape and murders which followed were a most grisly chapter of early Australian history. Two of the mutineers were punished by being marooned on the mainland coast. They are believed to be the first European 'settlers' in Australia. Many decades later, there were reports of early explorers sighting blue-eyed Aboriginals, suggesting that at least one of the mutineers survived for a time.

There must be something rebellious in the winds. About fifty kilometres south of Binnu, I passed an unremarkable-looking road-sign pointing to the Hutt River Province. A more recent chapter of eccentric defiance, tenacity and guile in Australia's history is the story of the formation and continued existence of the Hutt River Province. In 1969, Leonard Casley, owner of a large wheat farm, was dictated absurd quotas for wheat production by the Australian Wheat Board. Having tried, in vain, to convince the administration to go back on its decision, one which could only lead his family and staff to ruin, the 'bush lawyer' proposed the dispute be settled by arbitrage, and then that the estimated losses be made the object of a financial compensation. None of these proposals elicited a satisfactory answer. The government administration even threatened to seize a part of his land. Casley and his associates resorted to a purported provision in British common law which they felt allowed them to secede and declare their independence from the Commonwealth of Australia. Leonard Casley was elected administrator of the new 'sovereign state' by his family and later styled himself His Royal Highness Prince Leonard I of Hutt. His wife became HRH Princess Shirley and their seven children received their own titles: Prince Ian, successor to the throne, Duchess Kay, Prince Wayne, Duchess Diane, Prince Richard, Prince Graeme and Duchess Sherryl.

Although the major port of Geraldton markets itself as the Sun City, it has become a modern epicentre for chasers of wind. Windsurfers and lovers of some

Trees near Greenough sculpted by the persistently strong 'Roaring Forties' which prevail from the south-west

of the world's finest rock lobsters are drawn to Geraldton and its surrounds, centre of the Mid-West and the largest town since I left Darwin. Friends of my mother, retired pastoralists Wanda and Roderick O'Connor, looked after me here as one of their own and helped me make use of the administrative centre for publicity – regional radio and local newspapers.

The Brand Highway was a brand-new beast. The main drag between Geraldton and Perth is a notorious accident hotspot, its weight of over-sized traffic far too heavy to be constricted into two narrow lanes. I often felt intimidated, squeezed out by the large semi-trailers carrying mineral sands between the Eneabba mine sites and port.

It was frustratingly appropriate that I was made to struggle into appalling head winds out of Geraldton. Any exposed trees near Greenough, just south of the Sun City, have been famously sculpted by nature so that they are completely doubled over, contorted as if in pain. I mirrored the form of the tree trunks as I pushed head first into the south-westerly in an effort to streamline my shape. To passers-by it must have looked as though I was blending, perhaps unharmoniously, with the landscape. I was back down to fifteen kilometres per hour. Double gees – spiky burrs, also known as 'three-cornered jacks', 'devil's eggs' or 'centurions' depending on which state you are in – which had blown off the hay pastures or off the back of stock trucks, lay camouflaged on the bitumen like mini-land mines. In conspiracy with the wind, this was like nature's version of guerrilla warfare. I blew three tubes during the course of the morning. The high quality road tyres which I had been using had meant that prior to this point I had only collected one puncture on the tarmac since Canberra; after Dongara, my tyres remained puncture-free for the remainder of the expedition.

By day's end it was apparent that I was going to fall short of Eneabba. I had hoped to find an accessible farmhouse, but the roadside was flanked with wildflower nature reserves for as far as I could see. Eventually I chose a firebreak track and followed it out of sight of the highway. Enthusiasts flock from as far away as Japan to this region during spring. Any other time of the year, the low scrub, or Kwongan heath, which grows in poor, gutless, white sandy ground, would not attract a second look. I had noticed a few specks of colour from the road, but being 1 December, I didn't expect to see anything much. The dense, head-high scrub provided a sheltered micro-environment, which I soon discovered had protected the last of the seasonal blooms. The heavy morning dew which condensed on my tent flysheet must also serve to prolong the flowering season. I have never seen such a variation of delicate flora. Surrounding my camp were various species of banksias, orchids and leschenaultia alongside the papery everlastings, waxy acacias, grevilleas and eucalypts I had also seen in the deserts and the North West. There are estimated to be about 2000 species of flowering plants in the immediate region around Eneabba.

For the next 100 km, all the way to Badgingarra, the road was lined with nature strips and reserves, giving the impression that someone had planted a continuous garden. At my slow pace, I had more time to notice what was there. At Badgingarra, I turned away from the coast off the Brand Highway and through some prosperous-looking farmland towards Moora. Finally there was some respite from the wind.

One of the main reasons for choosing this particular route home was so that I could include New Norcia, Australia's only monastic town, in the journey. Founded in 1846 by Dom Rosendo Salvado, the mission was originally created to convert the Indigenous population to Catholicism. The Benedictine monks built the Spanish mission with their bare hands. The only aspect the region has in common with Spain is the Mediterranean climate, and the traditional architecture, more usual in Spanish-colonial Central and South America, is an odd sight among the dry grasslands and gum trees. Life was unbelievably tough in the beginning for the monks, and the Aboriginals did not easily convert to their religion. Then this self-contained outpost of the Mediterranean slowly began to prosper, developing its own micro-economy by producing silk and the usual agricultural fare. Nowadays, the community has diversified into tourism, olive oil and wine and runs a renowned bakery.

I was particularly interested in finding out more about the Spanish handball game the monks played with their bare hands – their own *pelota*. This is a general name for a variety of court sports played with a ball using either the hand, a bat, a racquet or a basket 'propulsor'. *Pelota* is played against a wall, or more traditionally, two teams compete face to face, separated by a line or a net. My *pelota*, real tennis, is still known as *jeu de paume* in France because it evolved on the streets of France and central Europe using the hand, long before a racquet was developed. There are many 'cousins' of the game still played,

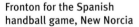
Fronton for the Spanish handball game, New Norcia

Almost home. The road between Calingiri and Goomalling

particularly in Spain and France, and also in rural pockets of Belgium, Holland, Ireland, Northern Italy, Mexico, Argentina and the USA. In my quest, I was directed behind the monastery, where I found an outdoor court in need of some restoration. The free-standing, double-sided fronton (wall) looked a little like the front wall of a squash court but more than double the size. The monks used this open style of court for their game, whereas at St Ildephonsus College nearby the boys played on smaller courts with high side-walls. The open version requires greater skill to control the hard ball. From what I could understand, the game most resembles the modern game of Valencian Pelota, where the ball is played with the bare hand and only minimal protection is used.

With the wind at my back, I sailed towards home along the quieter roads. The harvest was in full swing and my main concern was to keep clear of unsuspecting wheat trucks on the narrow back roads. Finally, just before Goomalling, I could put the map away: I knew the roads like the back of my hand. I turned off along the Goomalling–Meckering Road and on a high point, just before the turn-off to my brother's farm, I could see on the horizon the bush paddock which was my home farm, about twenty kilometres away as the crow flies. I stopped to take it all in and video the moment. It was a strange feeling to have pedalled over 17 500 km through some of the most inhospitable parts of the country and to connect it with familiar territory – my childhood home. I had managed to catch up a day by pushing extra hard from Geraldton, and so was able to spend more time at my brother's farm, twenty-five kilometres from Ullaring Rock, my parents' farm, and where I grew up.

The following day, I accompanied my brother, Rick, for a few rounds of a paddock in the harvester. My fifteen-year-old nephew, James, decided he would like to cycle with me across to Ullaring Rock. Having never pedalled any sort of distance before, James did very well, especially pushing up some of the sharp little hills, which he attacked with gusto, steaming ahead of me as he got a run-up.

Amazingly, between Halls Creek and home, a distance of 3 500 km, I had only had to camp 'wild' four times and had used two commercial campsites. The rest of the time I had stayed on stations and farms and with various contacts.

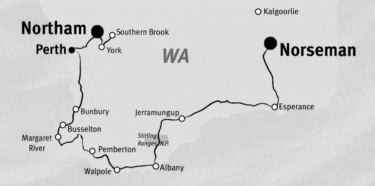

Kalgoorlie

Northam ○ Southern Brook

Perth York

WA

Norseman

Bunbury Jerramungup Esperance

Busselton

Margaret
River

Stirling
Ranges N.P.

Pemberton

Walpole Albany

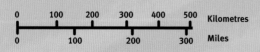

Northam to Norseman
1649 kilometres
6 December to 29 December 2004

Sealed road

Unsealed road
(gravel)

| 0 | 100 | 200 | 300 | 400 | 500 | Kilometres |

| 0 | 100 | 200 | 300 | Miles |

14

The great South West:
a hot spot
(Northam to Norseman)

Natural patterns in the
granite of Ullaring Rock
show prehistoric lava flows

As James and I entered the bush paddock through the back gate to the home farm, we passed the 'Old Camp', now virtually indistinguishable among the wild oats and York gums. Almost a century ago, my grandfather set up the remote outpost – a stable and a shed. There he lived for twelve years, clearing and developing the scrubland with a disc plough pulled by a team of horses. In common with all the pioneers of the region, his existence was harsh and extremely isolated. Our farm was, and still is, at the end of a line. The nearest neighbours are about five kilometres away and the nearest main town, Northam, is thirty-two kilometres distant. The front half of the farm lies in the Northam Shire, the back half in the Cunderdin-Meckering-Tammin Shire and the boundary is shared with the Goomalling Shire.

Nowadays, town is only a 25-minute drive away, but when my father was growing up it was a very different story. A journey into Northam may have been undertaken about once a month. The family travelled to the big smoke – Perth – once a year, if they were lucky. As a result of this isolation, local communities such as Southern Brook, Grass Valley or Jennapullen were the social hub, and one-teacher, one-room schools, such as Southern Brook State School, provided a primary education for the sparse rural population. It is difficult to comprehend that, only a generation back, my father and his older brother had to ride a horse to school, ten kilometres each way, opening and closing seven 'cocky' (wire) gates across our neighbour's property as they went. At lunch-time, the boys had to feed their horses before they were allowed to eat their own meals. Times were so tough during the years of the Great Depression that Dad had to ride a blind horse to school. That can't have earned him much kudos among his peers.

Primary school for the five children in my generation of the family involved an hour-long bus trip each way, give or take depending on how many families needed to be collected on the bus run. As our sandy front drive is about four kilometres long, we would usually be driven to and from the front gate until we were old enough and responsible enough to drive ourselves – at about ten years of age, or when we could reach the foot controls and see over the dashboard at the same time. One of my early memories is of my first day at school as a five-year-old and my grandfather forgetting to pick me up from the gate. There was no shelter and it was a searing-hot February day. After waiting what seemed an eternity, I started to walk home. I knew how to get water from the sheep troughs by sliding off the cement lid and pushing the float down to turn on the tap so I filled my lunch box, being careful not to disturb the redback spiders. Within a couple of hundred metres of home, I heard a car reverse out of the garage and roar off towards me as Papa planted his foot. I wasn't too concerned about being forgotten. My sisters and brothers all experienced the same situation a few times.

The two things I always try to make time for when I am home are a run down the front drive to the mail-box and back and a walk on The Rock directly behind our house. Both actions evoke a spiritual sense of place in my heart. The Rock, 'Ullaring Rock', is like our family's Uluru. ('Ullaring' is one of the many Indigenous terms meaning 'a place of water'). The granite outcrop covers a total of about five hectares in three major lumps. It is exactly 1000 feet (330 metres) above sea level and is used as an easily identifiable trig point for aircraft.

The Rock saved our house from a bushfire in the 1960s, and we like to think it helped protect the bricks and mortar during the 1968 Meckering earthquake, the fault line of which is only about 15 km away as the crow flies. My father engineered a water channel to catch the run-off which supplies us with drinking water, and we have collected the flat stones, which are gradually exfoliating away from the weathering surface, to use as paving stones in the garden. As kids we spent endless hours there, usually barefoot, catching tadpoles and building dams in the pools (in winter), making cubby houses or race tracks for the push-carts we constructed.

'Kitchen window' view of the front paddocks of my home farm

OUT THERE AND BACK

Above all, I value The Rock for its peace and solitude. It is a place to think and a source of energy. Things become clear and simple from there. Time permitting, I would wander up on The Rock if I was stressed, upset, in trouble, if I needed to psych myself up for a big event such as an athletics carnival or a squash match, before exams or if I just needed to make plans. Sometimes I would lie down on The Rock like a lizard, absorbing warmth, and close my eyes. Granite can be surprisingly comfortable. No vehicles can be heard at all and there is no one, apart from family, for miles. The silence is deafening, which usually freaks out friends visiting from the city or overseas. When we take them out to watch the sunset or look at the night sky, they are overwhelmed with the space and peace. Without light pollution from any urban glow, the usually clear night sky is so bursting with stars it feels heavy.

Strangely enough, this time I didn't feel the usual burning desire to go for a run down to the front gate. It had been a long stint since Broome. I had never pedalled down the front track before but cycling creates a similar relationship with the land as being on foot, and I was sure this would be sufficiently satisfying for my soul. Loaded as usual and with only my thin road tyres, I really struggled to negotiate the sand patches and corrugations. I snaked all over the track, slipping from one soft patch to another. It was impossible to tell when the surface was going to subside. At one point, I came flying off and landed very heavily. It should have been embarrassing but, of course, there was no one in sight. Even the nearest mob of sheep had bolted at first sight of me bouncing along the track.

Cycling the farm track with a load twenty years earlier, however, would have been completely impossible – more like the Canning Stock Route. The land is naturally sandplain country and, by the end of summer, the poorer patches more closely resembled Cottesloe Beach (or any of the Perth beaches for that matter). Over about twenty-five years, our family has planted pockets and rows of trees in selected areas, and these have gradually helped stabilise the land and protect the topsoil from being blown away. Summer holidays were spent carting full water tanks, and lugging buckets of water to keep the trees alive. There also used to be a wetland at the lowest point on the farm, which could not support a crop or produce good pasture and, if left unchecked, would have turned salty. A long-term tree-planting program by us and our neighbours has resolved the problem, lowering the water-table so the land can now be used. With better land management practices, technology and a greater understanding of the threshold of the local conditions, my father and now my brother, Rick, have the land in good heart. Today it produces 50 per cent more wheat on average than twenty years ago.

Rising levels of salinity in surface and groundwater are among the greatest environmental challenges facing Western Australia. In the south-west of the state, 18 million hectares of the 25 million originally covered by native vegetation have been cleared. About 1.8 million hectares (10 per cent) are now salt-affected. The clearing of native vegetation and planting of shallow-rooted crops can cause groundwater to rise and pass through the soil carrying with it dissolved naturally occurring salts. This highly saline water can eventually appear on or near the ground surface, causing 'dryland salinity', damaging soil structure and natural plants, and becoming unsuitable for drinking or irrigation. The water may also find its way directly to rivers and streams, where it severely damages plant and animal life.

A few undulating kilometres from the front gate, I crossed the dry Southern Brook. The ephemeral waterway is flanked, in part, by salt-affected land

Dryland salinity, the cancer of the Wheatbelt. Salt-affected flats at Meckering with the wheat bin in the distance. The water-pipe connects a main reservoir in the Darling Range (at Mundaring) to Kalgoorlie, supplying water to the arid goldfields over 500 km away

characterised by bulrushes, saltbush and dead tree trunks. Patches of bare ground are topped with stark white salt crystals like icing on the cake of long-term misguided land use. Salty run-off is drained from the land via the Brook into the Mortlock River, which in turn flows into the Avon River, which continues a convoluted path to become the Swan River and finally meander out across the Perth coastal plain before entering the sea at Fremantle Harbour. Clearly, whatever happens upstream may have an effect hundreds of kilometres downstream.

The salinity problem is not new: it has taken the best part of a century to reach its current scale. All farmers 'worth their salt' are active in their attempts to manage the problem before they lose their land altogether. I could see plenty of promising efforts to stem the cancer of the Wheatbelt. Planting salt-resistant vegetation, fencing off areas in need of rehabilitation from stock and controlling run-off with contour drainage banks all help send dryland salinity into remission. It requires a prolonged cooperative effort and investment from all in the region to kick the epidemic. I am not qualified to judge whether enough is being done, but most are certainly on the right track.

◆   ◆   ◆

The path I had chosen between home and Perth, like most of my expedition, was not direct. Instead of heading straight for the city, which would have been an average day's ride, I wanted to make a feature of the Avon Valley region, site of the first inland settlements from the Swan River Colony. I continued by following my old school bus run as far as Grass Valley, and then cut through to York. Although the first inland town is a 65-km cycle to the south-west from my home, Mt Bakewell, which stands 457 metres above the farmland, is clearly visible when standing on top of The Rock. On my way into York, the dark green mound – an important remnant bushland – remained in my sights like a guiding beacon.

The Aboriginal people of the region, the Nyoongars, were no less impressed than were the later explorers with Mt Bakewell's bold topographical presence, giving it and neighbouring Mt Brown their own Dreaming legend. The legend tells us that the taller mountain, Mt Bakewell, was called Walwalling, or 'place of weeping', and the lower hill, Mt Brown, was called Wongborel, or 'the sleeping woman'. Long ago in the Dreaming, the Hill People used to meet the Valley People at the foot of Walwalling for sports and games. Wundig, a handsome young warrior from the Hill People, who excelled at games and spear throwing, fell in love with Wilura, a beautiful young girl from the Valley People. This relationship between their family groupings was forbidden, so they eloped. When the Valley People discovered that the girl was missing, they demanded her return, but the Hill People did not know where the couple had gone. A great battle ensued between the two groups. The Valley People, who were outnumbered, called on their wise man for help. He used his magic powers to change the Hill warriors into grasstrees as they surged down the slopes of Walwalling. The wide band of grasstrees can be seen to this day on Mt Bakewell, where the warriors were magically changed. The wise man then put a curse upon the two young people who had caused so much bloodshed. Their dead bodies were found later, and the curse sent the spirit of Wundig to stay on Walwalling, and the spirit of Wilura to Wongborel, so that their spirits would not meet again until the mountains crumbled together.

I hugged the curves of the Avon River as it slipped between the two hills and into town, and was just in time to talk to children at the York Primary School. Years 4 and 7 gave me their full attention and were bursting with questions. My parents were following me for the day in their car, so it was fitting that they could spend some time with me here to get a feel for what it was all about.

Before pushing off to Perth the next day, I also visited my old primary school in Northam where once again the students were captivated, and brimming with questions at the end. Just as I was finishing, Andrew Campion, who had accompanied Greg and me out of Sydney, arrived as promised, to cycle with me on the 100-km leg to Perth. He even had the same bike, albeit a competition model.

While York now thrives as a tourist township with well-preserved historical buildings and a growing number of boutique cafes and restaurants, Northam is a much larger commercial centre. Officially a year younger than York, Northam's development surged ahead when the Trans-Australian Railway was pushed through. The town also became a base for fossickers and miners before they headed to the goldfields about 500 km to the east.

Although I have driven the Great Eastern Highway many times over the years at 110 km per hour, I noticed so much more detail from the bicycle saddle at 22 km per hour. We paused for a breather at the top of the Darling Scarp and marvelled at the vast expanse of the shining young city below.

Ready to cycle to Perth with Andrew Campion after talking to the students at my old primary school

In 1962, a lone astronaut orbiting the earth sighted a small cluster of lights on the dark silhouette of Australia's western coastline – the people of Perth had switched on all their lights as a token of friendship, the gesture prompting inter-national media to dub the world's most isolated city the 'City of Light'. Since then, due largely to a mineral boom in Western Australia, Perth's urban sprawl has more than doubled, insatiably devouring the country-side. The Mandurah region, just to the south of Perth, now surpasses the Gold Coast as the fastest growing region in the country. The Perth metropolitan area is much larger than London's, with about one-sixth of the population. It has the lowest population density of the main Australian cities at 164 people per square kilometre. Sydney has 690 people per

Question time at Subiaco
Primary School

square kilometre, London averages 4700 and New York 9700 people per square kilometre.

The 5-km descent down Greenmount was far less intimidating than the route down the road's eastern terminus, the Great Western Highway into Sydney. At 60 km per hour it was my turn to fly past the huge trucks which are forced to crawl down the slope in low gear. With so much momentum, I even freewheeled faster than Andrew towards the bottom of the hill. That all changed on the flat. As we were both wearing the same sponsor's tee-shirts we were obviously a team, which led to Andrew receiving some strange looks as he surged ahead effortlessly at the traffic lights on his unladen wheels. He copped a few derogatory comments implying that he was a 'slacker' in allowing me carry all the weight. Of course, I genuinely appreciated Andrew's support. He had got off his butt and pushed himself to join me for the day.

We made our way along the Swan River foreshore, through the CBD and into Kings Park via Fraser Avenue, which is lined with gum trees, each one dedicated to a soldier killed in World War II. Overlooking the ever-changing skyline, the memorial to the Bali victims seemed an appropriate meeting place. Here we were greeted by close friends, family and press. Even though I have not lived in Perth for fourteen years, I still feel such a close bond with my 'home city' and particularly with my ever-reliable long-time friends. My only disappointment was that Arnaud couldn't make it. He had planned to fly over for the occasion but couldn't afford the time away from studies and work. A week was spent giving presentations to schools and community, before pushing off south and more engagements at North Dandalup, the Alcoa bauxite mine and alumina refinery, and at Yarloop.

The small North Dandalup Primary School is a special environment school. After giving a talk to all the students and staff, I was shown some of their projects. Environmental education is an important part of the curriculum here, like mathematics or English. Students learn to separate their rubbish into various bins for recycling; the organic matter is processed as compost which

Students at North Dandalup Primary School

Planting shrubs at Yarloop Primary School

feeds the worm farm. The worm castings are used to fertilise the vegetable garden and nursery plants, which the children maintain in the greenhouse, and the produce is sold to make money to plough back into the projects. Chickens and a frog pond are also kept. The small school's latest project, the development of an educational nature trail through surrounding bushland – the 'Pathway to Nature'– was recognised by the United Nations Association of Australia on World Environment Day with a Special Commendation Award.

As the students take responsibility and work together to reap the rewards, they get to see the results of their pro-active involvement, and the whole education process becomes intrinsically motivational. By taking their sustainable habits home, they help to educate their parents, or at least gnaw away at their environmental conscience. The community in turn becomes involved in supporting the school projects. It's all about sowing seeds for the future. The sustainable habits being embedded into the children's psyche embrace the important concept that their actions should be a normal way of life, not a chore. We shared a giant cake to commemorate the expedition, but I was celebrating their achievements, confident that my words were not falling on deaf ears.

After participating in an organised tour of Alcoa's alumina refinery and bauxite mining operations near Pinjarra, where I learnt of the company's pioneering, internationally recognised efforts to rehabilitate the jarrah forest, I continued south through Pinjarra, Waroona and Harvey towards Bunbury. The mature trees and richly fertilised pastures of the Swan Coastal Plain benefit from a higher rainfall and run-off from the Darling Escarpment, and as I pedalled, paddocks became smaller and farming practices more intensive. I hadn't seen any green pastures for a long time. The gently undulating farmland, often bordered by irrigation channels and electric fences, supports herds of lot-fed beef and dairy cattle, fat lambs, olive groves, grapes, citrus and apple orchards.

Just near Bunbury, the largest town in WA outside the Perth metropolitan area, my cousin, Greg, met me with his two sons on their bicycles and escorted me the last kilometre or so to their new home. Then aged five and two respectively, Nick and Adam qualify as the youngest participants of the GRACE Expedition.

◆　◆　◆

The Gillett's olive plantation, North Dandalup. There is more intensive land use in WA's South West

Kangaroo paws among the dense undergrowth in a tuart forest

Kangaroo paws, the state flower emblem of Western Australia

I left for Busselton via the Bunbury television studios where I taped an item about the expedition for the state news. Between Capel and Busselton lies the Tuart Forest National Park, the largest remaining area of pure tuart trees left in the world. Tuart Forest is one of the rarest ecosystems left on earth, endemic to the limestone soil of the Swan Coastal Plain. The rough-barked trees can live up to 500 years, grow up to 33 metres tall and, prior to protection, were prized for the quality of their dense, fine-grained hardwood.

Named after the first settlers of the region, the Bussell family (more relatives), Busselton had changed beyond recognition from when we used to spend summer holidays there. Busselton was where I saw the movie *Jaws* as a seven-year old. It utterly terrified me. I could not dip my toes into the eerily tranquil waters of Geographe Bay without the dreaded music fuelling my imagination and complete paranoia. When I did pluck up the courage to get wet, the only bites I received were from the swarms of stingers which washed in with the tides, infesting the shallows. Nine days after I left Busselton, the devastating Indian Ocean tsunami struck, and the usually calm waters of Geographe Bay experienced tidal surges which swept three people into the bay.

Far more famous for its waves, my destination for the day, Yallingup, on the unprotected western coastline, is one of the world's premier surf spots. The prime real estate of the township are the houses and weekend getaways nestled in the steep hillside, forming a residential amphitheatre which drops away dramatically to the rocky headland, sandy beaches and pounding surf. I was fortunate to be staying that night in a friend of a friend's holiday home.

At 5.30am the following morning I awoke suddenly, feeling very ill. My whole alimentary tract was fizzing and foaming as violently as the boiling Yallingup surf. Completely alone in the house, I divided the morning between bathroom and bedroom. As I lay on the bed, I felt as washed up as an empty shell on the beach.

Waves crashing into the rocky headland at Yallingup

What to do? I had a strict schedule to maintain if I was to reach Esperance – where I planned to meet friends – for Christmas in a week's time. Every day had been carefully calculated for my tour of the south-west. By midday I was able to keep a banana down and decided that I would try to cycle back up the steep hill to the general store and see how I felt. My body was quivering, oscillating between hot and cold, and I was incredibly weak but persevered to the top. I decided that if I could get to Margaret River, just 45 km away, I would be able to adjust my route, cutting off the diversion to Cape Leeuwin, the country's most south-westerly tip, and not lose a day – providing I was well enough to cycle the next day. I hadn't planned to stay at Margaret River, but had a telephone number of the parents of someone I barely knew from Northam. I didn't like to impose myself on them, but this was an emergency. Fortunately, Shirley and Keith said it would be fine for me to stay in their caravan so I continued with Plan B and set off down Caves Road for Margaret River armed with a bunch of bananas.

The hills are probably not as severe as they seemed to me at the time, but I had nothing in the tank and my ribs were burning. I did my best to conserve energy, but I was definitely teetering on the boundaries of my personal sustainability. The ride itself was beautiful, passing some of the most famous wineries in the state: Amberley, Evans and Tate, Vasse Felix and Mad Fish. At that point, I think I was probably a mad fish out of water. Three bananas and three hours later, the ordeal was over although that night I still could not keep any food down. I defiantly dressed for action the following day, but after being unable to manage breakfast, I had to concede that I was going to lose a day and therefore would not reach my friends in time for Christmas.

The next morning I managed to retain some food and felt stronger, but was still washed out. I had to go. It was all or nothing to cover the 145 km to Pemberton. The only settlement en route was Karridale, 33 km from Margaret River. I took it easy to Karridale where I could still not face any food, loading up on Gatorade and fruit juice. I also bought some fuel for my stove in case I really bombed out and needed to camp in the bush. The crosswind as I travelled east along the Brockman Highway and over the Blackwood River pushed me around like a school bully. Somehow I survived the day on fruit, electrolytes and plenty of short breaks. Every time I restarted, I felt feverish, and had to cycle through a cold sweat.

The karri forest near the Gloucester Tree, Pemberton, would have once been logged

Nearing Pemberton, the geography of the Vasse Highway showed little understanding of my condition, metamorphosing into what seemed a monster – a defiant rollercoaster. Dwarfed by dense karri forest, I could have been back to the Land of Brobdingnag, developing a crick in my neck as I ogled at the majestic giants of Karri Valley. Just before the logging town of Pemberton, I passed through tracts of forest which had been clear-felled 75 years ago. There were no massive trees as the world's third tallest hardwood species can take a century to grow up to 90 metres tall, but the forest appeared and sounded vibrant – stately straight white trunks contrasting against the lush green understorey.

I couldn't leave Pemberton without revisiting the Gloucester Tree – the famous climbing tree which towered above the timber town and which was used as a fire lookout. As a kid I remember ascending the 61 metres into the canopy as a white-knuckle experience. Those who can cope with heights ascend to the platform shelter via 300 metal pegs which have been hammered into the trunk. The only protection climbers have to break their fall if they faint or succumb to vertigo is a flimsy wire cage, whose precious few strands of wire do little to instil confidence. I guess fear is what the management relies upon to weed out those who are unsuitable from attempting the climb – they simply freeze with sheer terror. As I ascended now, I was careful to focus directly on each peg as I grasped it, rung by rung. Looking up was fine but looking down was to be avoided at all costs. The tree swayed in the breeze, and gazing out over the sea of green from the platform I felt a little sea-sick. The queasiness was due in part to my location, partly to my state of health and partly because I knew I had a long, hilly day ahead if I was to reach Walpole.

The idea of cutting kilometres off my route was extremely attractive at this point and when a ranger described a short-cut from the Gloucester Tree through to the South West Highway by following forestry tracks, I was all ears. He assured me there were no serious hills on the Barma Road, and as we were standing on a high point in the landscape when he spoke, it was all too easy to get ahead of myself and assume it must be mostly downhill to the coast from there.

OUT THERE AND BACK

Wrong. The ranger either was not a cyclist, or had some sort of sadistic streak. After a short distance, the 'no caravans' and 'steep descent' signs were a dead give-away. Then the ridge dropped straight down to a creek and then straight back up and into the gravel. The pattern repeated for most of the twenty kilometres. Some of the climbs were so steep I had to zigzag back and forth across the loose gravel in my granny gears, the rear wheel spinning out as I fought to keep traction. There were no signs and the mud map I had been drawn was hopelessly inaccurate. It would have been easy to lose my bearings as the karri, marri and jarrah trees towered above and the intense midday sun beat down on my back. Doubts crept into my head as I crossed a succession of nameless intersections, keeping an eye out for unsuspecting logging trucks. This situation could have turned ugly. I navigated by watching the sun, reasoning out that if I continued to head east, I would hit the main road eventually. I did not crave the extra adventure at this point, but it was a case of 'Where's the cheese?'. Finally, I could hear vehicles and found my way out of the maze. Only 100 km to cover to reach the next town! I had lost a fair amount of time and only just made it to Walpole, running out of light and strength simultaneously.

◆   ◆   ◆

The Walpole and Nornalup inlets are where the karri forests meet the sea. My connection in Walpole was Gary Muir, a friend and former work colleague of my cousin Greg from Bunbury. With his parents he runs the multi-award winning WOW (Wild on Walpole) Wilderness cruises and safaris. Gary's innovative and educational boat tours aim to generate understanding, appreciation and stewardship of the natural and cultural environment. The crux of his ethos is that everything is connected: 'It's all about connections'. The interactive cruises he runs promote a perception of the Walpole environment as 'the centre of the earth', as a way to respect and comprehend issues on a continuum all the way up from the local to the global scale. A quote from Kemal Ataturk on Gary's website encapsulates the responsibility we all need to have for each other, and for our physical and cultural environment.

> Mankind is a single body and each nation is a part of that body. We must never say 'What does it matter to me if some part of the world is ailing?' If there is such an illness, we must concern ourselves with it as though we were having that illness.

Gary Muir with Lukas (visiting from Austria), propping up my bike

By the time I hit the road again the next morning, feeling only slightly stronger, Gary had done his daily 15-km cross-country run and was ready for work – another educational performance. The route to Albany via Denmark was what I called a 'video camera' day – when I wished I could roll up the whole experience of the day and store it with me forever. I pulled out my camera and had a go. I had to be careful not to get too carried away, as I was simultaneously struggling to hold a straight line, pedal, steer and operate the camera. The region I filmed receives the highest rainfall in the state and can therefore support the largest trees. The Walpole-Nornalup National Park is the only place

A window on to the Nornalup Inlet near Walpole

where the red tingle tree is found. The largest-based of all the eucalypts, with a girth of up to 26 metres, the buttressed, rough-barked red tingle can grow up to 75 metres tall and can live to over 400 years old. The coastal road wove a path through these giants, plus karris, marris and jarrah, and climbed up and over some sharp undulations. Occasionally, vistas of the Nornalup Inlet and then, as I approached the town of Denmark, the Wilson Inlet would be revealed – cameo appearances between gaps in the trunks and dense understorey.

After leaving Denmark's tidy streets, the country opened out into heathland and farmland exposing me to the full force of the southerly. Just as I arrived in the outer suburbs of Albany, Western Australia's oldest settlement, a storm had whipped up from the Southern Ocean and I took refuge in a bus shelter.

Although we had never met prior to the expedition, the story of how I came to stay with the Grieve family in Albany involved a complex state-wide web of connections. Separate strands included my brother-in-law, my old school, and Sue and Peter Gillett, with whom I stayed with in North Dandalup. Jane Grieve, whom I had stayed with in Karratha, had just flown down to spend Christmas with her parents, Jenny and Owen. She said it felt like she had cheated by flying as it had taken me about a month to cycle from Karratha to Albany. Before setting off from Albany, Owen arranged the next link in the chain, staying with the Sounness family near Borden, just over the Stirling Range.

I left town after another ABC breakfast radio interview. At the King River Roadhouse, where I turned off the South Coast Highway for Borden, someone recognised me from the television news – the story shot in Bunbury had just been aired – and then another customer said that she had just heard me on the radio. I headed towards the 'Alps of the South West' satisfied that things were working.

Tree plantations, mostly blue gums, dominated the scene between the coast and the Porongurups. These sterile-looking monocultures have an important role to play in taking the pressure off the native timbers, particularly in old

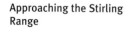

Approaching the Stirling Range

growth forests. As the tree-farming industry continues to grow, there should be no need to use the precious, diverse, old growth forests for wood chipping. Most of the species planted thrive on poor sandy soil, so farmers who put part of their land under trees can benefit from land which produces little otherwise. Deep-rooted trees also serve to lower the water table and therefore ease problems with salinity. Wind erosion is significantly reduced as well.

On the rare occasion that snow falls in Western Australia, it usually lands on the Porongurups and the higher Stirling Ranges to the north. The 1100 million-year-old granite domes of the Porongurups, which rise 670 metres above the coastal plain, are thought to be the oldest hills in the world. I barely noticed any incline as I skirted the base. Between the Porongurups and the Stirling Ranges, the land opened up and I was suddenly back into wheat country. The Stirling Ranges provided a spectacular landscape but in the valleys lay tell-tale evidence of salinity and soil erosion problems.

Although only 40 km away from the Porongurup hills, the much larger Stirling Range is a completely different beast. The sedimentary layers were exposed over millions of years and gradually sculpted into the jagged peaks which remain. As far as diversity is concerned, the ranges are a hotspot within the hotspot. More floral species occur in the Stirling Range than in the entire British Isles, and eighty-seven of those occur nowhere else on earth. Given the size of the mountain barrier, I was fully expecting a steep climb over the Chester Pass. The road, however, slips between the two major massifs and I was only confronted with civilised gradients. Just over the pass, I turned away from Bluff Knoll (the highest peak) and towards Mount Trio. Initially I missed the turn-off to the Sounness family farm, where I was to stay, but to my surprise met Richard Sounness cycling up the hill towards me with two friends on their regular run. He

Natural bushland in the Stirling Range National Park. Bluff Knoll (1065 metres) is the highest peak in the South West directed me down a sandy track through the edge of the National Park, the back entrance to their 2500-hectare (6000 acre) farm.

At the base of the Stirling Range National Park, Nanette and Richard's farm certainly has a spectacular setting. We were definitely on the same wavelength as we shared a love of cycle touring and travelling. Nan also set me up with a place to stay the following night, Christmas Eve – with her friends, Di and Geoff Bee, in Jerramungup.

I called in at the Borden Co-operative Store, the first stop on the way to Jerramungup, to bolster my biscuit supply. Just as I was about to leave, a couple of French cyclists arrived from the opposite direction. Rémy and Valérie had started in Perth, with the aim of crossing the Nullarbor to Adelaide. Having battled into persistent ferocious headwinds all the way to Esperance, they had decided to turn around and cycle back through the South West instead. Pushing into such terrible wind was not a holiday, they said. I agreed, but I was not on holiday.

After Borden, I turned due east and was confronted with the same oppressive head winds which had repelled Rémy and Valérie, prolonging what would have been a simple day. Occasionally, I would glance over my shoulder back to the mighty Stirling Ranges, which gradually diminished beyond a horizon of golden cereal crops. Harvest in the Great Southern district is later than 'up north'.

The change of scenery as I approached Ongerup was also dramatic. The ranges form a rain shadow initially, but then I was back into mallee scrubland, which continued until I reached the coastal heathland again near Esperance. The area only receives an annual rainfall of 400 mm compared to Albany's almost 1000 mm. The sparse towns in the area may only be small, but they are all extremely well kept and can boast an impressive range of sporting facilities: football/cricket ovals, hockey pitches, tennis courts, basketball and netball courts, and swimming pools. Sport is a very important component of the social structure of these farming communities.

By the time I reached 'Jerry', Di was waiting to escort me into town just in time to catch the Co-op before it closed. I would not be able to buy anything the next day, Christmas Day. The Sounness and the Bee families have become friends, as they share a common interest in growing lucerne as a sustainable farming practice. After dinner, Geoff took the time to explain the basis of his pioneering land management systems. He had recently won the Australian Landcare Primary Producer Award for developing his projects to combat soil erosion and salinity. Over many years of trials and personal investment, he has pioneered the use of lucerne to lower the water table, reduce salinity, and prevent soil erosion. The deep-rooted perennial originated in the ancient Mediterranean region and so it makes sense that it can thrive in a similar climate and soil conditions on the other side of the world. Lucerne also makes great summer feed and fixes nitrogen into the soil, improving fertility. In addition, it provides a carpet of shelter to stop topsoil blowing away and with careful stock rotation can be used to prevent over-grazing which makes land susceptible to wind erosion. Many farmers in the Great Southern region grow lucerne for the purposes mentioned, but as a life-long commitment to improving Landcare systems, this modest farmer has developed groundbreaking methods of maximising its virtues. The Bees have succeeded in lowering the water table by four metres and reversed the environmental problems which have threatened their land since it was cleared in the 1960s.

◆　◆　◆

I felt strange cycling out of town on Christmas Day, and sad to be on my own. If all had gone to plan, I would have been in Esperance with my friends. As it was, I made my phone calls to Arnaud and family, and then left the tinselled houses of Jerramungup behind. The white 'frosting' which is traditionally sprayed on windows to convey the notion of a Northern Hemisphere 'white Christmas', along with silhouette cut-outs of reindeers and Santa Claus, seemed surreal in relation to the battle ahead. The day promised to be another scorcher and the wind showed no Yuletide spirit. The road was eerily deserted, like the uneasy calm before an air raid. I tried to erase from my mind the idea that it was Christmas, but the Band Aid song, *Do They Know It's Christmas?* circulated as restlessly inside my head as the swirling gusts outside. I reminded myself that in creating and performing the GRACE Expedition, I was luckier than most in this world, and got on with it.

One of the most famous Western Australian bands, The Triffids, wrote one of their best-known songs, *Wide Open Road*, about this stretch of road. I can fully appreciate what they were on about. The scenery was certainly vast, but not particularly eye-catching. Broad-acre wheat and sheep farms intermingled like an archipelago in a sea of mallee scrub. Early explorers concluded that the region was 'worthless'. Considered a marginal area, places like Jerramungup were eventually opened up as 'soldier settlement' farms providing returned servicemen with a fresh start after World War II.

Nowadays, this region is internationally recognised as being ecologically priceless. The smoky-green, gently rolling topography and gutless-looking sandy soil totally belies its importance. Between Jerramungup and Ravensthorpe I travelled through the heart of the Fitzgerald River National Park and Biosphere Reserve. A Biosphere Reserve is a region where economic activity and conservation coexist in an area recognised for its diverse environment. Biosphere Reserves are the keystone of UNESCO's Man and the Biosphere Program which was created to catalyse a greater support for sustainable relationships between people and their environment. The Fitzgerald Biosphere consists of an undisturbed core, which is enclosed by the majority of the Fitzgerald River National Park. Surrounding the core area is a 'buffer zone' of uncleared bush, which I spent most of the day travelling through. Beyond this are the areas used for day-to-day human activities called the 'zone of cooperation'.

Geoff and Diane's farm lies within the cooperation zone, making their sustainable farm practices even more significant. Reversing the salinity levels, reducing and even phasing out the need for chemicals for weed control and fertilisers, which would normally wash down the waterways flowing through the national park, helps preserve its ecological health. More than 1800 beautiful and bizarre species of flowering plants, as well as a myriad of lichens, mosses and fungi, have been recorded in the Fitzgerald River National Park; this is nearly 20 per cent of the total number of plant species in Western Australia in an area that covers only a tiny fraction of the state. Included are sixty-two endemic species and a further forty-eight species which are virtually confined to the park. Threatened animal species such as the dibbler, woylie, tammar wallaby and ground parrot are also protected in the park.

In normal circumstances, I would have considered the 120 km to the mining town of Ravensthorpe into a stiff headwind as being a respectable day's work. To have any chance of reaching Esperance the following day, though, assuming the wind direction and intensity were the same, I needed to knock off a few more kilometres.

Ravensthorpe sprang into existence after gold was discovered in the surrounding large rolling hills, its population topping out at about 3000 before World War I. The same hills, which have been depleted of their mineral riches over the last century, in turn extracted all the energy from my tired legs as I traversed them. Christmas night was spent camping wild among rare, secluded shelter beside the Jerdacuttup River. I felt very alone dining on another bland pasta meal.

Knowing Boxing Day was going to be huge, I set off early, hoping to sneak in a couple of hours before the wind woke up. No such luck. Pedalling downhill was almost as punishing as the long uphills. Despite keeping the lowest, most aerodynamic position possible, it took one-and-a-half hours to cover the 24 km to the Rabbit-Proof Fence and by the time I made Munglinup, four-and-a-half hours and 64 km later, I was suffering from backache.

Rabbits were introduced into Victoria in 1859 for hunting purposes, but by 1894 they were crossing the Nullarbor Plain and posing a threat to Western Australia. The WA government set up a Royal Commission in 1901 to defeat the menace, and the result was that Alfred Canning, accompanied by Hubert Trotman and an Afghan cameleer, set out on an expedition to survey a line from Starvation Boat Harbour, just to the south, to Wallal on the Pilbara coast (near Pardoo Station). Canning and Trotman's next major assignment was the survey of the Canning Stock Route. Over 400 men were employed in labour gangs, and they completed the 3256-km Rabbit-Proof Fence in 1907. One fence proved inadequate and two more fences were built to protect the south-west agricultural region. The fences, 1219 mm-high (4ft), were built of three plain and one barbed wires and wire netting. The bottom section of the netting was dipped in coal tar to prevent it from rusting and buried 15 cm underground. The longest continuous fence in the world at the time was manned by twenty-five boundary riders who patrolled 240-km stretches using camels, horses and carts or bicycles. There were ingenious water catchments and huts every 32 km, and every eight kilometres trap-yards were placed to catch foxes and dingoes as well as rabbits.

With the decline of the rabbit population during the 1950s due to the impact of poisoning and myxomatosis, the fence has been modified and realigned to protect the south-west agricultural area from emu infestations. Now renamed the State Barrier or Vermin Fence, it provides a poison-baiting trail for wild dogs and feral cats and prevents the entry of feral goats. The fence that for a century has protected the agricultural and native environment alike is tucked away in the mallee scrub, so blending in with the extensive farming landscape that most people would barely notice its existence.

When I walked into the Munglinup Roadhouse, the manager deduced that I must be in good shape. Most cyclists coming from the Ravensthorpe direction arrive totally spent. He described how he sometimes walked outside to find Japanese cyclists collapsed on the grass and had to bring them water. Such visitors have no conception of the distances involved, and no one is prepared for the wind which prevails all year round. I headed out into the blustery conditions at noon with 107 km to do in eight hours. Normally this would be easy, but the wind strengthened and my average speed dropped to 12 km per hour. The side-headwind forced me into the gravel a couple of times. Keeping on the road required full concentration and a vice-like grip. By the end of the day, I was struggling to manage 10 km per hour, my fingers were no longer functioning and my right hand was totally numb. After 12 hours of pedalling, I had managed 155 km at just under 13 km per hour, my longest day on the bike ever.

◆　◆　◆

The rusting Rabbit-Proof Fence near Jerdacuttup

Although the Dutch were the first Europeans to discover the Esperance region in 1627, it was the French who named many of the coastal features when they explored the region about 160 years later. Captain Bruni d'Entrecasteaux commanding *Le Recherche* and Captain Huon de Kermandec of *L'Esperance* landed at Esperance Bay, seeking shelter from a storm. They were searching the southern waters for a missing explorer, and at the same time charting and exploring the coastline of the 'new' continent. D'Entrecasteaux named the harbour after the first frigate to enter it. A loose translation of the French word *espérance* means 'hope, with confidence and faith in the future'.

A great-great-grandfather of mine, Charles Edward Dempster, along with his brothers Andrew and William, showed plenty of optimism and faith in the future when they explored the area looking for pastoral land in the 1860s. Andrew and William became the first settlers at Esperance, droving sheep, cattle and horses there from Northam in 1863, and taking up a grazing lease of 126 000 hectares (304 000 acres).

Needing to find a place to stay the second night in Esperance and exhausted from the efforts and illness of the last week, I sat in a cafe like a zombie, trying to decide what to do. A couple of leads I had followed up didn't pull through. Then a brainwave – I remembered my mother mentioning that we had a distant relative in Esperance, Alan Leeming. We had never met because he was connected to the Victorian side of the family. Leeming being an uncommon name, I simply looked up his number in the phone book, called and introduced myself. 'Blood is thicker than water,' he said, and soon I was heading for Wireless Hill, a suburb of Esperance overlooking the stunning coastline.

Because of its isolation, Esperance does not draw the hoards of interstate and international tourists one might expect to some of the best beaches in the country. Instead, the port town of about 14 000 depends mainly on holiday makers from the western goldfields, which stretch due north from Norseman (200 km) to Wiluna (1000 km).

Alan took me for a drive around the not-to-be-missed Great Ocean Drive, a 40-km loop west of town. The impossibly white sands, the gently rounded granite cliffs, and the ocean changing from aquamarine near the shore to a deep

One of the 'pearls' of the Great Ocean Drive, Esperance

Pink Lake on the inland part of the Great Ocean Drive circuit receives its colour from high concentrations of the salt-tolerant algae, *dunalella salina*

blue out near the islands of the Archipelago of the Recherche are as good as it gets. Like a string of pearls, every successive beach has its own special appeal: West Beach, Second Beach, Blue Haven Beach, Salmon Beach, Fourth Beach, Twilight Beach, Nine Mile Beach and Eleven Mile Beach.

On the bald coastal heath-covered hills behind Salmon Beach stand the turbines of Australia's first wind farm. Judging by my experience of cycling to Esperance and the constant white caps speckling the ocean blue, the turbines are set in a prime location. Esperance's isolation also means that it is not connected to the state power grid and so power produced by the wind turbines significantly subsidises the diesel-powered generators, and at a lower cost of production.

Assuming that the 'Esperance Doctor' would continue with the same force as it had for the last few days, I was looking forward to being blown all the way to Norseman. As I gazed out at the tireless view from the Leeming's balcony, I noticed the white caps had gone and the sea looked calm. In a dismaying development, the wind had done a full 180-degree turn and hot air was blowing straight off the desert from the north-east. As I set off, I wondered what I had done to deserve such a farewell.

Despondently pushing away from the coast towards Norseman, I entered the eastern limits of the wheat and sheep-producing country. The land there is naturally higher in salt which blows in from the ocean, and combined with extensive farming practices, the cleared areas are more susceptible to salinity problems. I passed almost continuous patches of salt-damaged land between Gibson and Grass Patch.

The motto of the Grass Patch Primary School is 'Undaunted' – not exactly how I felt that night trying to knock my tent pegs into compacted gravel in the municipal park, which doubles as a camping-ground. There was no grass in Grass Patch! I found out from one of the few residents of the hamlet, Rozz, that the water supply was insufficient for the community needs and any greenery had to be let go.

OUT THERE AND BACK

Not long after Salmon Gums the next day, the vast paddocks of wheat gave way to mallee scrub and salty claypans. The surging north-easterly blasted hot dry air directly at me, and the daily temperature topped out at 40°C. About 50 km out from Norseman, I stopped for lunch in a shady parking bay. I was a little dehydrated and probably guzzled too much water down too quickly before eating. I will never know whether it was this action, the conditions, or the fact that I had not fully recovered from my illness, but I lost the lot.

Just as I was being ill, a retired English couple pulled up in the bay to retrieve another bottle of champagne out of their caravan. Seeing that I was in trouble, they generously donated a couple of bottles of water and waited to see that I was okay. As they drove off sipping their champagne, the man tossed an empty plastic bottle into the bush just in front of me. I couldn't believe it. There was even a brightly painted yellow rubbish bin 20 metres ahead of them. I said nothing, although I am sure my incriminating gaze aptly expressed my sentiments. Picking up the bottle and placing it into the bin, making sure they saw me do it, I felt disappointed. What hope have we got if 'educated' people cannot be bothered looking after the environment they were supposed to be appreciating? The wondrous biological diversity of the South West 'hotspot' does not include plastic bottles.

The incident served to stir up some passion and I channelled my anger into energy for pushing forward. Powered as well by fruit, water and glucose tablets, I made for Norseman at a steady pace. I wasn't sure the past few days had been the best preparation for tackling the Nullarbor Plain.

WA   SA
Nullabor Plain

○ Leonora

○ Menzies   Nullabor
                                             Roadhouse
○○ Kalgoorlie   Eucla ○━━━━━○   ○ Yalata
Coolgardie   Cocklebiddy ○   Penong ○
                               ○ Madura   ● **Ceduna**
Norseman ●━━━○━━━━○
         Balladonia Caiguna

                              Great Australian Bight

○Esperance

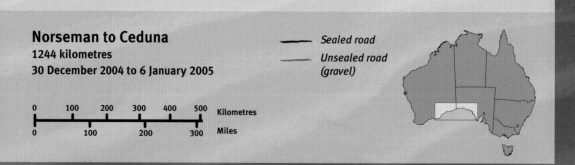

Norseman to Ceduna
1244 kilometres
30 December 2004 to 6 January 2005

━━━━━ *Sealed road*
━━━━━ *Unsealed road*
      (gravel)

0   100   200   300   400   500   Kilometres
0   100   200   300   Miles

15

In the tyre tracks of William Snell

(The Nullarbor: Norseman to Ceduna)

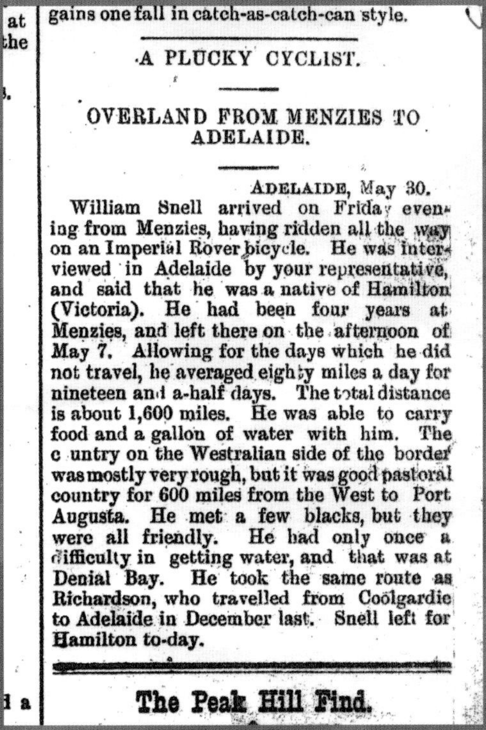

'A Plucky Cyclist',
Coolgardie Miner, 31 May
1897

> gains one fall in catch-as-catch-can style.
>
> ·A PLUCKY CYCLIST.
>
> OVERLAND FROM MENZIES TO ADELAIDE.
>
> ADELAIDE, May 30.
>
> William Snell arrived on Friday evening from Menzies, having ridden all the way on an Imperial Rover bicycle. He was interviewed in Adelaide by your representative, and said that he was a native of Hamilton (Victoria). He had been four years at Menzies, and left there on the afternoon of May 7. Allowing for the days which he did not travel, he averaged eighty miles a day for nineteen and a-half days. The total distance is about 1,600 miles. He was able to carry food and a gallon of water with him. The country on the Westralian side of the border was mostly very rough, but it was good pastoral country for 600 miles from the West to Port Augusta. He met a few blacks, but they were all friendly. He had only once a difficulty in getting water, and that was at Denial Bay. He took the same route as Richardson, who travelled from Coolgardie to Adelaide in December last. Snell left for Hamilton to-day.
>
> The Peak Hill Find.

On 24 November 1896, Arthur Richardson, son of a Kalgoorlie doctor, left Coolgardie for Adelaide. He arrived there thirty-one days later, claiming the status of being the first person to pedal across the Nullarbor Plain. Richardson, an unassuming, highly independent and determined character, went on to become the first man to cycle around the Australian continent in 1899-1900 – an astonishing achievement given that his journey would have mostly been on isolated tracks of poor quality, without any kind of services.

Five months after Richardson left Coolgardie, William Snell set out from Menzies, almost 300 km to the north of Coolgardie, on what was to be the second successful bicycle crossing of the Nullarbor. He stopped off in Adelaide and Hamilton before arriving in Melbourne twenty-eight days later. Over the next ten years, about two dozen men undertook a series of widely publicised overland rides, most of them commencing from the western goldfields.

During the century which has passed since these cyclists first trail-blazed from west to east, the challenge of pedalling across the Nullarbor Plain has remained an iconic symbol of achievement. Cycling across this arid expanse conjures up simplistic yet romantic images of the humble leg-powered machine versus endless, flat, empty plains; of dead-straight roads stretching beyond the horizon. Endurance cyclists and budding endurance cyclists are attracted from all over the world, fascinated by the notion of riding for days across 'nothing'. For some, the thought of such isolation is so overwhelming that the arrow-straight road remains a pipe-dream. For others, the crossing of the flat limestone block – the world's largest – becomes their Everest. Some are motivated by the personal journey; others raise money for charity or awareness for a cause. All types of bicycles are used for the crossing, from high-tech racing machines accompanied by a support vehicle, touring bikes and mountain bikes down to 'happy shoppers'. Some riders are endeavouring to sheer seconds off the various category records while others just do it because they can. At any one time it would be unusual for there not to be at least one cyclist braving the tyranny of distance somewhere on the 1240-km stretch between Norseman and Ceduna.

I was looking forward to sinking my teeth into this part of the expedition, attracted by the notion of the pure cycling, and excited by the idea that I would be retracing the tyre tracks of my great-great-uncle. Compared with some of the 19 000 km I had covered since Canberra, I believed the route of Highway No.1 across the Nullarbor would be literally and figuratively a straightforward affair. At the same time, I was mindful that I was still crossing a desert, where there would be up to 200 km between service points, and that I needed to remain highly respectful of the task ahead. My passage would be easier than Snell's as I had a smooth tarmac road and service stops, but I would be presented with different types of dangers. An American cyclist had been sucked under a road train and killed three weeks before, a warning of how alert I had to be.

The wind largely dictates the fortunes of the cross-continental cyclist. High and low pressure systems which move north from the Southern Ocean over the Bight jostle with the continental systems at the coastal zone – at about the line of the road. Apart from the obvious motivation of cycling east to get married, Snell's fast pace was probably attributable to the prevailing westerly winds predominant in May. Richardson was likely to have been retarded by the easterlies which dominate over the summer period. At Norseman, I crossed paths with a British cyclist who had just made an express-paced journey from Ceduna in five-and-a-half days, fanned by gale-force easterly winds. This alarming piece of information verified what I had already suspected.

Stocking up: the extra food carried in my panniers from Norseman

Still feeling washed out from my illness, I had decided to have a rest day at Norseman but when I ventured outside the wind had swung around to the south-west, bringing cool, overcast conditions. I felt obliged to take advantage of this and forego the projected break. Administration work done and loaded up, I set off, passing a road sign showing numbers which looked more like dates in history than distances which should be cycled. My panniers bulged at the seams with food for the next week;

any items which did not fit were strapped on with elastic bungies. Just as I set off for a half-day to Fraser Range Station, the wind, which had coerced me into the saddle like the Pied Piper, swung to the south, negating any benefit it had promised. The southerly stirred up some wild weather which seemed to be straight from Antarctica, and for the last hour before the Fraser Range turn-off I was chased by a thunderstorm. Like a celestial stock-whip, lightning cracked on the ground all around me and the heavens opened. In a mad dash to reach shelter I squinted to see my way on the dirt road through the driving rain.

Fraser Range Station was initially developed by the Dempster brothers, Andrew and William, to whom Esperance owes its existence. The pastoral land around Esperance turned out to be deficient in certain trace minerals important for grazing sheep, so they explored further afield and found what they needed at Fraser Range. The new proprietors now provide tourist accommodation, but once I established in conversation my connection with the property's history, they donated a room for the night.

I could not have foreseen being so cold cycling across the arid plains on New Year's Eve, the height of summer. Balladonia was a slow morning's grind away into the chilly south easterly, the long, gradual hills of Fraser Range the only notable variations in terrain for the 92 km. The Balladonia Roadhouse does a roaring trade, as travellers flow through, making either their first or last break on their monotonous journey. I received some bemused looks as I parked my bike against the wall, swinging the awkward load around on my hip as I did so. I took a few minutes to check out the little museum. The display includes a number of remnants from Skylab, the satellite that crashed to earth scattering parts over the region in 1979. Amusingly at the time, the local Dundas Shire Council presented NASA with a littering fine, and President Jimmy Carter even rang the roadhouse to make his apologies. The whole issue was something of a good-natured diplomatic event, with the US ambassador visiting the region from Canberra to inspect any damage that may have been done. I made polite conversation with a well-presented woman customer while checking out the range of tacky souvenirs. Just as I was filling my last water-bottle before pushing on, her husband slipped me a $100 note, encouraging me to keep up the good work, before the couple sped off in their Porsche.

The weather closed in again by the time I reached the Old Balladonia Telegraph Station, 28 km further along the Eyre Highway. The crumbling limestone building was closed to the public but, knowing a little of the importance of the place, I climbed through the barbed wire fence for a closer look. Judging by the vandalism, I was not the first to do this – although I remained far more respectful. Windows were smashed and sheets of corrugated iron were strewn on the ground. Loosely translated, the Indigenous term 'Balladonia' means 'big red rock', referring to the lichen-covered granite outcrops behind the telegraph station. Rocks were used to produce the impressive dry stone walls, which will no doubt be standing long after the building has returned to nature.

The Balladonia Telegraph Station was an integral part of a network of telegraph stations that operated between 1877 and 1927, linking Western Australia with the eastern states and overseas through Adelaide. The original link was connected by a dusty track which provided a route for Richardson and Snell. The modern Eyre Highway was only first pushed through in 1941, and remained a rough track until it was finally completely sealed in 1976, a graphic indication of just how isolated the south-west corner is from the rest of the country.

Sun setting on 2004.
Campsite in the gnarled
scrub alongside the 90
Mile Straight

I was glad to be back out on the highway, as the intermittent showers and
south easterly sapped body heat from my core. The 90 Mile Straight (146.6 km),
the longest straight stretch of road in the country and one of the longest in the
world, loomed out of the gloom. For the next two hours, until I decided to stop
for the night, kangaroos ventured cautiously to the roadside to drink from the
puddles. At the first sound of an approaching vehicle, they would bound off into
the scrub. I could sometimes creep up within 20 metres before their twitching
radar ears would detect my presence, masked also by the headwind, and they
would hurriedly disappear into the safety of the bush. It is natural phenomena
like these which people travelling in the cocoon of a vehicle miss out on. I found
a secluded campsite out of view of the highway in time to watch the sun set on
2004 in spectacular pink and mauve technicolour.

The Decade of Education for Sustainable Development began just as
peacefully in the tranquil bush morning. As I worked my way through some
lumpy semolina, I contemplated what the New Year might bring. Back out on the
highway the answer was...nothing different. The road did not bend and the
scenery did not change for another 100 km. For much of the first five hours, I
kept my mind busy trying to calculate just how much paint it would take to paint
the white lines marking the road. I had to consider the width of a single straight
line, double lines, broken lines and a combination of one single and one broken
line. I have Andrew Campion to thank for introducing me to that idea.

Just before Caiguna the scrub petered out. Little grows at all on the bare karst
landscape, and I was left exposed to the opposing elements. Below the surface
is a labyrinth of caves which give the limestone block the texture of Swiss
cheese – on a scale about five times the area of Switzerland itself. The Caiguna
Blowhole, five kilometres west of the roadhouse, acts as a pressure release vent
for the cave system below. Air flow has been measured at 72 km per hour as it
escapes into the atmosphere. Since the Nullarbor Plain receives less than
250 mm of rain annually, the landscape has little erosion. In a wetter climate,
water erosion would have sculptured gorges and a more rugged landscape.

There was little to divert my mind as I tussled with the phantom enemy
between Caiguna and Cocklebiddy. No living kangaroos made themselves
visible, but I noticed an unusually high frequency of dead roos and I entertained
myself by counting the carcasses which lined the built-up verges like fallen
soldiers. Pedalling out in the open over this section of road required the breath

control of an opera singer, because for the first 35 km east of Caiguna, I counted 301 dead kangaroos. It was often difficult to distinguish which configurations of scattered bones constituted a whole animal, so I made the rule that they had to have at least some fur. A single paw didn't count either. As the twilight encroached, I found myself chasing my shadow which gradually elongated before fusing with the early evening. The beautiful glow of dusk brought out uncountable numbers of live kangaroos for their night shift. I wondered how many more would end up splattered across the roo-bars (bull-bars) of road trains before the night was over.

By the time I finally reached Cocklebiddy, site of another of the original telegraph stations, my legs were numb and turned the pedals on autopilot, as if they were detached from the rest of my body. Having just taken ten hours and twenty-two minutes to cover 182 km into persistent winds, I'd had enough of being exposed to the elements and decided to give myself a New Year treat by taking a room in the motel. Understanding that the owners have a business to run and that they are regularly approached by people crossing the Nullarbor for all sorts of worthy causes, I fully expected to pay. But when I explained the purpose of the expedition and what I had achieved so far, I was given a free room. Even the chef got carried away, piling my plate with more than I could eat, which meant an awful lot. It was ridiculous: after three days on the Nullarbor, I had made a profit! Even more ridiculous was that the truckie I met over dinner happened to be Eddie Riggs, uncle of Garry from Mataranka and brother of Muriel, whom Greg and I had met at Burke and Wills Camp 119.

◆ ◆ ◆

Exhausted from the previous couple of excessive days which collectively involved pedalling for nearly twenty hours, I delayed my departure from Cocklebiddy in order to watch the start of the test match. Over the next few days I was eager to reach each roadhouse, not only as a refuge from the conditions but also to find out the cricket score. Madura, the next opportunity to watch the cricket, seemed to take an eternity – it was 10 km further than my map suggested, adding a cruel twist to the morning. Drivers would not notice the gentle gradients all the way to Madura Pass which subtly added to my workload. Fortunately the scrub, although sparse, reappeared, acting as a partial wind break; it also allowed the full force of the sun's rays to concentrate on and radiate off the bitumen. At 35 degrees, it was back to proper summer conditions.

Roe Plains from Madura Pass

At 150 km per day, sunburn cream was not the only type of cream I needed to apply on my body!

Madura Pass was perhaps marginally more exciting than Bang Bang Jump-Up. As on the Burke Development Road, my expectations had been building for days. The escarpment, which drops away steeply from the Hampton Tablelands, would once have marked the shoreline and the meagrely vegetated Roe Plains, which stretched out of sight to the coast, would once have been part of the sea-bed. Nestling in a little oasis set attractively against the hilly backdrop, Madura was originally settled in 1876 as a place to breed horses for the Indian Army; they were shipped to their destination from the nearby coast.

I could feel my body was precariously balanced at its sustainable threshold and if I pushed over the limit, it would take days rather than hours to recover. I dawdled along the plain at a reduced intensity, the wind not helping as it was funnelled along the Hampton escarpment. By sunset I reached my 130 km 'minimum distance' and started to search for a bush campsite.

The spot I finally settled on was not well protected nor particularly comfortable. I awoke annoyingly early, and lay in my sleeping bag frustrated that I hadn't had the proper rest my body was screaming out for. The wind boasted about its strength like a spoilt child and the bushes which had provided precious protection through the night pushed against the flimsy walls of the tent. My heart sank and I put off facing the day for as long as possible. Finally, I sucked my index finger and unzipped the tent flysheet enough to poke it outside to determine wind direction, as if I was holding up a white surrender flag to the weather. To my delight I realised the blustery conditions came from the south-west – finally, a tailwind.

My original plan was to reach Eucla at the border of Western Australia and South Australia, which would have been a long 150-km grind had I been presented with the conditions of the previous few days. As I flew along the tarmac in an excitingly high gear, I ignored the fact that my legs were severely drained and started to think instead about heading into a new state. Three hours and 80 km later, I arrived at Mundrabilla, site of the first pastoral station on the Nullarbor, in time to catch the start of the day's play.

OUT THERE AND BACK

The monotony of my path between the escarpment and the Roe Plains was broken just before Eucla. Gradually becoming more prominent in my field of view were the famous white coastal sand dunes. The Eucla dunes proved to be a mid-expedition salvation for John Eyre's first crossing of the Nullarbor in 1840-41. Heading west, the party had struggled for about 200 km over the waterless plains above the Bunda Cliffs. The men adopted many Indigenous techniques to keep themselves alive during the journey, including finding water by excavating into sand dunes. Upon turning into the sand hills, Eyre was fortunate to strike the very place where Aboriginals had dug little wells. Here the men camped for a week, recuperating and building strength to continue their brave struggle. Four months later, Eyre and his faithful Aboriginal companion, Wylie, arrived at King George Sound (Albany) minus his second-in-command, John Baxter, who had been murdered by the other two Aboriginals in the party under the most desperate of circumstances.

Today, the sand dunes have virtually consumed the original manual repeater station for the Overland Telegraph, established in 1877. Originally, Eucla's Delisser Sandhills were considerably smaller. The dunes were denuded when the great rabbit plague of the 1890s passed through, causing the large sand drifts which now repeatedly cover and uncover the telegraph station. To rid the land of rabbits, some bright spark decided to introduce cats, so the area was in due course over run with an infestation of feral cats – a devastating outcome for native wildlife.

At the time both the South and Western Australian colonial administrations operated out of Eucla's telegraph station. Before the invention of Morse Code, South Australian staff employed what was known as the 'Victorian Alphabet', and Western Australian telegraphers used what was known as the 'Universal Code'. This disparity illustrates how each of the country's colonies developed as independent entities prior to federation in 1901, fuelling the interstate rivalry that still endures, although thankfully mostly on the sporting arena.

My rhythm was only broken when I hit the Eucla Pass rising above the Roe Plains and rode into the largest settlement on the Nullarbor. I made the 68 km without even a breather, covering 150 km by lunch. Because of the sand dunes, the town, population fifty, is set five kilometres from its original coastal site. Eucla police officers have a special role because of its location as a frontier town which has become a bottleneck for fugitives.

Although I was very tired, it would have been a sacrilege to waste the wind so I considered pushing on. Between the Border Village, 12 km further along, and the next services stop at the Nullarbor Roadhouse lay 190 km of exposed plains, and if the wind switched back to its usual prevailing direction, then this may have been more than I could do in a day. After three hours of hesitation, I decided to load up with enough water for camping that night and for all of the next day, and headed off into South Australia. Even with the long break, this was an opportunity to surpass my all-time cycle touring distance record. Back in 1991, I managed 227 km in one day in Austria, riding out of Vienna, along the Danube River and then into the rolling hills towards Salzburg. The memory of such varied and inspiring scenery and the challenge of beating my record tipped the scales from staying in the comfort of Eucla in favour of moving off into the wilds with all the uncertainties of not knowing where I would end up.

I willed my leaden legs on and was still going as the moon started to illuminate the white lines, which lured me east into infinity. My body was wishing my mind was not so competitive. I was competing against myself in the middle of nowhere. I won in the end, hitting my target after nine hours of

A distinct lack of shelter. Cooking breakfast the morning after my 228-km ride the previous day

pedalling. Just to be certain, I rolled on for another kilometre into unchartered territory before calling it a night. With the scrub only reaching about four or five feet high, it was difficult to find cover out of sight of the road. As I sat huddled below the scrub line, cooking another uninspiring family pack of pasta, I could hear the waves of the Southern Ocean crashing into the Bunda limestone cliffs about 90 metres below. The endorphins still running riot through my veins, I buzzed with satisfaction. I couldn't buy this moment – but I felt it was totally earned. One part of me couldn't help wondering, however, that if I had ridden a day as long as the horror 12-hour stretch into Esperance, would I have topped the 300-km mark? Dangerous thoughts.

◆   ◆   ◆

A new day and, finally, a new state. I had covered my home state comprehensively since first entering from the Docker River Road on 8 September. The wind had turned again, but at least the pressure to reach the Nullarbor Roadhouse had eased. I could afford to take my time to explore the Bunda cliffs from several vantage points just off the road. The world's longest continuous limestone wall, once part of the sea bed, stretches from Eucla to the Head of the Great Australian Bight. The vegetation gradually petered out until I reached the true Nullarbor Plain just before the roadhouse.

The local Aboriginals, the Mirning people, referred to the Nullarbor area as 'Oondiri' which is said to mean 'the waterless' – as Eyre had discovered. When Alfred Delisser surveyed the Nullarbor Plain in 1866, he derived the term from the Latin 'nulla' for no, and 'arbor' for tree, hence the term Nullarbor, meaning 'no trees'. Although people usually refer to the road crossing of the Nullarbor as being the stretch between Norseman and Ceduna, this route only touches the region completely void of trees for about 20 km on either side of the Nullarbor Roadhouse. The true Nullarbor Plain lies to the north of the road and is bisected by the Trans-Australian Railway Line, which runs parallel 100 km or so inland. As I paused to take in my surroundings, a rare black dingo pup, which had been sniffing around probably hunting lizards, was momentarily startled by my

presence and then darted away into the naked plain – there was no cover so its defence was to put distance between us.

In keeping with the generous attitude I had experienced all the way across what truckies call affectionately 'the paddock', the chef at the Nullarbor Roadhouse loaded me up with a breakfast fit for three. As I cleaned the plate the smile disappeared from his face. He had lost a $5 side bet with one of his staff that I wouldn't finish it all.

Cycling on the eastern fringe of the plain, I noticed a figure moving toward me and on my side of the road, head bobbing up and down. Jasper Olsen, a Danish ultra-marathon runner, was midway

Bunda Cliffs – where the Nullarbor limestone block meets the Southern Ocean

through the Australian leg of his run around the world. To qualify for *The Guinness Book of Records*, he had to cross four continents. He had chosen Europe, Asia, Australia and North America. We stopped to chat and he told me that when he finished he would have run 25 000 km – the same distance as I would cover on my expedition – running about 50 km a day. After a quick stretch, he trotted off into the treeless plain and I headed into the bush which abruptly re-appeared. Even more of a shock was the sudden emergence of rolling hills – I thought the Nullarbor was meant to be flat!

With Jasper Olsen on his run around the world

Just after the Aboriginal community of Yalata, my odometer clicked over the 20 000-km mark – a particularly gratifying moment. There was obviously no one to share this with, but it was very satisfying for my soul. A little before Nundroo the bush gave way to extensive cereal cropping – a bit like the northern Wheatbelt in WA. Fowlers Bay on the coast south of Nundroo was the starting point for Eyre's epic journey. Just one more day and I would reach the end of the Nullarbor stage at Ceduna.

Between Nundroo and Penong, I noticed what I thought was a cyclist in the distance. As I gradually closed the gap, I realised it was actually a tandem and thought it strange that I should be travelling faster. With two people driving the chain, tandems normally are much quicker than single cyclists. When I finally caught up with the riders and found out more, I realised that Ross and Ann Pearson are an amazing couple. Ross had a life-threatening brain haemorrhage in 2001, and unable to walk, talk or read as a result, spent two years in a wheelchair. He and Ann's Able2Ride journey was an 18 000-km, twelve-and-a-half month odyssey around Australia, during which they visited local hospitals and community groups to raise awareness about strokes. Their journey to me was an uplifting celebration of life as they followed their dream.

We pulled over for what Ann called a much-needed 'bum break'. When they had first left Sydney, she had had to do most of the work, but gradually over the course of the trip Ross had developed more strength and had rehabilitated considerably. His right side still had very limited function and so their journey posed a different set of challenges to mine – mounting and dismounting the tandem, for example, involved a complex, well-coordinated sequence of manoeuvres. I pushed on, leaving the pair to pedal at their own speed. They planned to stop in Penong whereas I still had a further 75 km to reach Ceduna that day.

At Penong, I phoned my relations to give an estimated time of arrival at Ceduna. There always seems to be a sting in the tail. Headwinds strengthened and I had nothing left. By the time I reached the quarantine station, fully prepared to relinquish my one remaining tomato into the fruit fly bin, the officer waved me through saying that my uncle was very worried about me. I was just an hour late. It had been a long stint since Esperance – 1500 km in ten days, mostly into a raging headwind. Ceduna is a corruption of the local Aboriginal word 'Chedoona' and is said to mean 'a place to sit down and rest'. I fully intended to follow this advice, and was very fortunate to spend time with the Hughes families – Ben and Brenda, Tim and Joy (Ben and Tim are brothers) – relations with whom my family had always kept in contact but whom I had never met. Ben and Tim both farm in very marginal country north-east of Ceduna. A boundary of Ben's farm is the dog fence which is Australia's longest continuous fence. Over 5000 km long, it runs from the coast near Ceduna right through to Roma in Queensland. Built to keep the wild dingoes out of pastoral lands and away from livestock, it is more sophisticated than the Rabbit-Proof Fence. The two-metre high electrified barrier is charged by solar panels every twenty kilometres.

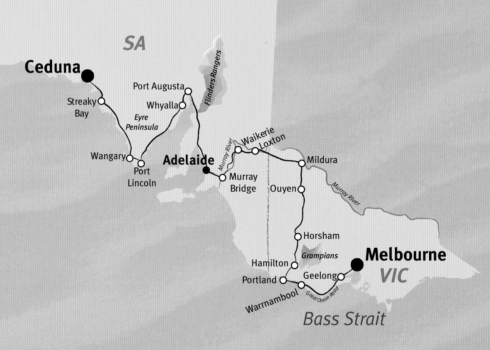

SA

Ceduna

Streaky
Bay

Port Augusta

Whyalla

Eyre
Peninsula

Wangary

Port
Lincoln

Adelaide

Murray
Bridge

Flinders Rangers

Murray River

Waikerie
Loxton

Mildura

Ouyen

Murray River

Horsham

Grampians

Hamilton

Melbourne
VIC

Portland

Geelong

Warrnambool

Great Ocean Road

Bass Strait

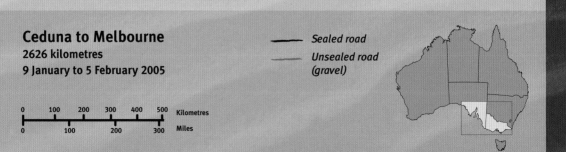

Ceduna to Melbourne
2626 kilometres
9 January to 5 February 2005

—————— Sealed road

—————— Unsealed road
(gravel)

| 0 | 100 | 200 | 300 | 400 | 500 | Kilometres |

| 0 | | 100 | | 200 | | 300 | Miles |

16

The fifth element
(The south-east corner:
Ceduna to Melbourne)

My load was not getting any smaller as I neared Adelaide

By the time William Snell reached the eastern frontier of agricultural land, he must have been excited. He was supposed to be 'leisurely looking for pastoral land', but he also had his childhood sweetheart, Mary Jane Duncan, from Cavendish (near Hamilton), in his sights. I imagine he may have upped his already impressive pace as he neared his destination. On arriving in Ceduna, I too felt like I was coming home with a wet sail. I had just under 5000 km to go through what I called 'civilisation', by which I mean the most populous south-east corner of the country. For the remainder of the journey I was almost continuously in mobile phone range, a modern indicator of 'civilisation'. Like Uncle Willy, I had romantic notions of returning to Melbourne in three weeks to be with my husband whom I had been missing terribly throughout the expedition. I would then have to leave again for a two-week circuit of Tasmania, and then back to Melbourne before the final week back to Canberra to complete the expedition.

Unfortunately, there was to be no personal fairytale ending for me. When I called home from my uncle's place in Ceduna, my high spirits were catapulted to the opposite extreme, as if they were flung over the Bunda Cliffs into the icy swells of the Southern Ocean.

Arnaud announced that he had decided to leave me.

I was in complete shock, totally caught without warning. The news made no sense: only two days earlier Arnaud and I had been discussing how we were going to spend the next New Year's Eve together. If fact, since Broome, where we had had shared a special time two months previously, we had been constantly

295

talking, making plans for the next chapter in our lives as a couple. The reasons Arnaud gave for his change of heart all seemed very fixable to me. I couldn't understand why he wouldn't wait for me to come home and at least try to work things out together. He cut me off in mid-air.

My impulsive response to my changed situation was to stop in my tracks and to fly straight to Melbourne. The expedition could be put on hold for a short time. But Arnaud insisted that there was no point in doing so – and that I had to finish the last few weeks off.

I felt completely drained and numb. The GRACE Project had drawn so much energy out of me, its organisation and its execution. I was finally starting to relax, feeling that its and my purposes were being realised and that the whole thing was a complete success. Such was my level of fitness I felt almost indestructible...and then, smack. I lay awake for most of the night – it would have been the whole night if I hadn't been so physically exhausted.

As would remain the pattern over the coming weeks, I awoke with my heart racing, thinking this could not really be happening and that it was just a nightmare. Unfortunately, reality hit shortly after – it was actually happening. I chose not to tell anyone, at least until after I reached Melbourne and Arnaud and I could talk face to face. My first reaction was to protect any chance our relationship might have; if I started telling my family and closest friends I knew they would be very upset with Arnaud. If I told people I met along the way to Melbourne – people whom I didn't know well – I knew I would break down and I did not wish to dump my problems on anyone, not even my Ceduna relations. In going on, I made the best choice for the expedition; honouring sponsors and supporters and doing justice to the project as a whole. But the situation festered, eating away inside while I was 'keeping up appearances'. In retrospect, this was not a very good way to deal with the situation.

All of a sudden, the path which before Ceduna had started to seem a little easier and under control became worse than the deepest sand of the Canning Stock Route. As I waved goodbye to the Hughes families and their friends, it seemed I was heading into the unknown – a void, even though I was back in 'civilisation'. It felt as though Arnaud had let all the air out of my tyres and I would have to finish the final 5000 km pushing along the road with just the bare metal rims grating on the bitumen. It was difficult to steer a rudderless ship.

Fortunately the wind, although a hot one, whipped in from the north off the desert and blew me and my oversized spinnaker-like panniers in the right direction as I turned off the main highway down the west coast of the Eyre Peninsula. It was tempting under the circumstances to divert straight to Melbourne, but I decided to at least stick to the basic plan.

This route may have looked as though I was all at sea with my direction. I planned to go around the periphery of the Eyre Peninsula, through the southern end of the Flinders Ranges to Adelaide, along the course of the Murray River through the Riverina region of South Australia to Mildura in the north-east corner of Victoria, down through the Mallee region, pass west of the Grampians to Hamilton, then on to Portland, the Great Ocean Road, Geelong and Melbourne. But there was method in my madness.

Being the middle of summer, I thought it sensible to hug the South Australian coastline where the sea breezes keep average temperatures down. Doing so would add an extra 300 km to my journey, but the route promised much variation and I had friends of friends to stay with at Streaky Bay and Port Lincoln. Heading down the Flinders Highway, I felt I had made the right decision as I was treated to wonderful snippets of coastal scenery – rugged headlands battered by the full force of the Southern Ocean, white sand dunes and protected bays striated by thick, dark tracts of seaweed. The ocean here contains a smorgasbord of 'fruits of the sea': oysters, crustaceans and all sorts of fish. It seems that everyone who resides on the peninsula is an expert in fishing; with my hosts in Streaky Bay, Jenny, Anthony and friends, I enjoyed a decent feed of freshly caught trevally and whiting. As I headed for Port Lincoln, the agricultural land which dominated the east side of the road appeared to become increasingly more productive.

Out of Elliston, a raging vortex of wind whisked me along. My plan, to reach Port Lincoln (about 170 km away) by day's end, was looking highly possible as I was propelled along at 30 km per hour, even if the ferocious 44°C temperatures upped the 'fan-forced oven' effect to 'high'. The oppressive conditions were extracting every available molecule of moisture from my body. Fluid leaked as readily as I drank in a never-ending cycle to maintain equilibrium.

Then, as I skirted a chain of salt lakes near the Cummins Lookout, the wind direction abruptly switched to a westerly. The cooler sea breeze brought instant temperature relief, but it soon swung around to the south and strengthened. I spent the remainder of the day tucked over the handlebars, as the Medusa wind gusted unpredictably, swirling and changing directions. Debilitated by my emotional state, I would have preferred the hot tailwind to the cooler headwinds. At this point I noticed the bellowing white smoke of a crop stubble fire to the south and thought that in these conditions any fire would be difficult to contain.

As I neared Wangary, two drivers stopped in turn to warn me that the road to Port Lincoln was closed. The smoke which now figured prominently in my field of view was from a massive bushfire raging out of control. I decided to push on from Coulta through a stunning green valley – mountains on either side of the road – to the small hamlet of Wangary where I could find out the latest information.

On my arrival at the village store, the news was grim; five deaths so far (the number was to rise to nine) as the fire surged west across the tip of the peninsula. I checked in at the community hall where the emergency services had set up base. The policeman in charge warned it was too risky to cycle on – the road had re-opened but conditions were volatile. As I would never have been able to outrun the flames if the wind changed, to push on would have been totally irresponsible. I called my contacts in Port Lincoln who were expecting me that evening and they offered to collect me.

In the meantime I observed the activity in the makeshift control centre. The State Emergency Services were calm and efficient in the time of crisis, conducting an orchestra of ambulance staff and community volunteers as if it were a sombre musical score. Everyone knew everyone and so it was likely that the victims could be friends, relatives or locals. Some volunteers, just returned from the fire front, sat around quietly with blackened faces, bloodshot eyes and smoked clothing, stunned and exhausted. Others waited anxiously for their call-up. The local women had set up a sandwich production line and the local priest hovered, ready to comfort anyone in need. I tried to stay out of the way. By the time Greg collected me, I had developed a healthy respect for and confidence in the way a small Australian community can respond to a disaster.

Port Lincoln, reminiscent of Esperance in terms of size, spectacular coastal location and prosperity, had to be vigorously defended from the fire. Flames came within a few kilometres of the town, which only narrowly escaped the 'Black Tuesday' inferno due to a timely change of wind direction. Built on one of the world's finest natural harbours (more than three times the size of Sydney Harbour), Port Lincoln nearly became the capital of South Australia. But its relative isolation on the tip of the Eyre Peninsula and a shortage of potable water meant that Adelaide became the preferred site for development. Today, Port Lincoln's economy is based on huge grain-handling facilities, canning and fish processing works, and the farming of fat lambs, wool, beef and tuna. The Mediterranean climate is matched by the large number of extravagant Mediterranean-style homes located in prime positions along the waterfront. Italian fishermen have cornered the lucrative Japanese market for sashimi-quality blue fin tuna and, as a result, have become Port Lincoln's *nouveau riche*.

I spent an extra day there with Penel and Greg Jones, looking around and allowing time for the fires to be brought under control. Back on track, my ride out of town was spectacular as the Lincoln Highway hugged the curves of Boston Bay. About eight kilometres north of the Port Lincoln boundary, I entered the area of devastation. As is so often the case, the fire had been totally selective: some houses were completely razed while the neighbours were miraculously spared. The town of North Shields and the North Shields Caravan Park are graphic examples of this. I stopped to have a look at the caravan park where three fatalities had occurred. The southern end of the park was totally destroyed as huge fireballs vaporised everything in their path. Flames from the worst-rated fires in Australian history raged over the hills from the west at up to 80 km an hour and out over Boston Bay, boiling its surface water before fizzling out. Some residents had managed to cheat death by diving into the sea. Others didn't even make it out of their vans. The heat of the inferno was so great it melted the steel joins on the water pipes. Incredibly, the northern section of the caravan park remained untouched.

A little further on I stopped to photograph the scenes and talk to some of those milling around. As I was about to move on, Brian, who owned a small farm across the road, wandered over, clearly in shock. He and his elderly mother had narrowly escaped with their lives. He told me that in fleeing from the fire, he had driven through a 10-metre wall of flames which liquefied his tyres. The dense

Devastation at the North Shields Caravan Park – where the fire melted the steel joins of the mains water-pipes

This could have been my bike – North Shields

smoke caused him to crash and the pair had spent the night recovering in hospital from smoke inhalation. 'I thought I had nerves of steel,' Brian said, his face creasing and tears welling in his eyes. I suddenly found myself consoling a complete stranger. As we talked, he realised that although he thought he had lost everything he had worked for, it was, in fact, all replaceable. Starting again was an opportunity to build things better than before.

I could see 'lucky' surviving sheep huddled together for support, traumatised, in a paddock which had been burnt to a cinder – blackened and totally denuded like a desert wilderness. The fire had devastated 80 000 hectares and about 50 000 sheep were lost. Work was going on throughout the area to repair badly affected water pipes and power lines.

Fire is selective – some homes and stock were spared, others razed. The 'lucky' sheep have nothing to eat

Back on the road, these scenes played havoc with my own vulnerable mental state. I couldn't accept or understand my husband's decision. If my feelings and emotions could be compared with such a horrendous bushfire, then I was still back at Wangary where the bush had been ignited by a welding spark. I hoped to put out the flames before they were fanned out of control and certainly wasn't seeing 'the fire' as an opportunity to start anew – to build something better. I wasn't able to heed the very advice I gave to the distraught farmer. I pedalled through paddock after paddock of charred farmland as if I was in my own 'Black Hole', drawn along numbly by the anti-matter. There was no 'anti' in me, though. I was not angry, but became increasingly fragile and upset as Arnaud and I traded text messages.

The hot breeze continued to swirl from all directions, stirring the ash and soot 'matter' into the air. By the time I reached Tumby Bay, the northern limit of the devastation, the fine particles, which sent my throat raw and combined with my perspiration to form a dirty black paste on my skin, were a reality check. Beneath the grief at Arno Bay, where I stayed that night, was a mild level of satisfaction. There may have still been about 4000 km to go but, despite the situation, I had managed a good day's work and was a step closer to fulfilling the expedition goals. It was something concrete to cling to.

Just after Cowell, the coastline veered away from the straight(ish) road and I re-entered pastoral station country. Open paddocks of gently rolling wheat crops and pastures gave way to mid-level scrub. To the west, the purple iron ore-rich Middleback Range presented some variation on the horizon. The highway appropriately followed parallel with the hills all the way to the steel town of Whyalla, South Australia's largest provincial city (population, 22 000). It could have been a function of my psychological condition, or the fact that it started to drizzle as I arrived, but I perceived Whyalla to be a large, sad sort of place, reddened like a bruised eye by the powdery iron ore which is blown over the city from the steelworks. I didn't feel the industrial iron ore town had the same type of energy as Port Hedland or Karratha in the Pilbara.

Whyalla markets itself as the place 'where the desert meets the sea'. Leaving my campsite beside the bay, I headed for the sparse, gnarly scrubland in increasingly heavy rain. The desert absorbed the moisture, perhaps appreciating a good drink far more than I welcomed the soaking tepid dollops.

I left for Port Augusta in a 'molten steel' state, rejoining the Eyre Highway, whose endless stream of oversized traffic was intimidating. There was often no hard shoulder to provide sanctuary. I was constantly squeezed off the crumbling edges by disrespectful drivers whom I feared may be relying too much on No-Doze (tablets) for the last few kilometres of their trans-Nullarbor trek.

Port Augusta is often referred to as the 'Crossroads of Australia', its strategic location the major reason for the town's development. Just before crossing the head of Spencer Gulf, I passed the main east-west, north-south junction, where the Eyre Highway meets the Stuart Highway to become the Princes Highway. I had cycled in and out of Darwin at the Stuart Highway's northern terminus, rejoined it for a short section out of Alice Springs and now I had met its southern limit. For me, reaching Port Augusta signified the end of the sweeping desert plains where cycling was uncomplicated and the openness evoked such a sense of freedom.

Approaching Horrocks Pass

The wind, which had been my friend all morning to Port Augusta, strengthened as I rounded the Gulf. Channelled along the base of the southern Flinders Ranges, the south-westerly whipped unimpeded over the coastal plain. I was flung around like a rag doll as heavy industrial traffic thundered by, sending destabilising eddies of air my way. Fortunately, I did not have to stay on the coastal highway for very long. Twenty-two kilometres on from Port Augusta I turned east into the Flinders Ranges for Wilmington. It had been a grey, overcast day but as I headed for the Horrocks Pass, the late afternoon sun peeped through, illuminating patches of the mountain barrier. Against a moody leaden backdrop, I was treated to a velvet curtain of spectacular hues: golden sage, and dark green and purple where the hills were bare.

I paused to polish off the last of the morale-boosting treats I had bought at a Port Augusta bakery, hoping they would see me through to the day's end. A rocket-booster, however, would have been more appropriate to send me up the Horrocks Pass. I hadn't pedalled over anything much bigger than a termite mound for many weeks, and had encountered nothing like the four-kilometre climb since I was last crossing the Great Dividing Range. The path wriggled past iconic stands of eucalypts which gave the upper reaches of the valley a character very different from anything I had seen up the east coast. Steep-sided bald hills with well-worn sheep and cattle trails furrowed into the thick grassy carpet of pasture are a result of about 150 years of grazing. Alarming signs of gully erosion are an indication that more of the vegetation needs to be replaced.

The first European settlers had been so impressed with the richness of the region, the small town of Wilmington had started life known as Beautiful Valley. The broad main street has no footpath, just a buffer zone of shady trees between the road and the buildings. Cold and soaked to the core, I was searching for shelter rather than shade. I managed to catch the owner of the general store as he was closing to ask about my accommodation options. Without hesitation, John offered the back-room of the store for sleeping and a shower at his home. Perfect.

The next morning, I chose an inland route away from the busiest highway through the heart of the southern Flinders Ranges, hoping this would better protect me from the prevailing headwinds. Maybe it was slightly better, but I struggled to average 15 km an hour, a slow, painstaking grind. Fortunately, a string of charming old rural towns divided the day into manageable portions: Melrose, Murray Town, Wirrabara (best bakery in Australia), Stone Hut, Laura, Gladstone, Georgetown, Gulnare and Yacka all have proud local histories and characters of their own.

Near Melrose I noted a small sign beside the road denoting that I was crossing Goyder's Line. Most people would have not blinked an eyelid and continued past the shady clump of gum trees, but I had heard of the line and stopped to investigate. In the 1860s, when pastoralists were struggling with severe drought, the surveyor-general of South Australia responded by evaluating the lands they had settled. His line of travel, which amounted to nearly 5000 km on horseback, marked off the limit of drought and became known as Goyder's Line of Rainfall. The line coincided with the southern boundary of saltbush country.

This Australian version of the African Sahel (southern transition zone between the Sahara Desert and the tropical savannahs) separates lands suitable for agriculture from those fit for pastoral use only. It also marks areas of reliable and unreliable annual rainfall. The line extends across the south-east corner of South Australia, the driest state in the country, from the Victorian border to Ceduna. It divides the Eyre Peninsula from near Cowell Bay, where I had noted an obvious change, north-west to Ceduna. My cousins there live just to the north of the line and so have to rely on modern extensive farming techniques to make a living. They would not survive if they budgeted for a profitable crop every year. I wondered how global warming and increased climate variability will affect Goyder's Line.

I was well short of my planned destination for the day but by the time I reached Yacka (an appropriate name considering the difficult conditions), I was within range of Adelaide, and decided I'd had enough. Nestled in the shallow valley of the Broughton River, this tidy little town (population 90, according to the sign) didn't take long to cycle through. There were no shops, no pubs and no people around. On my second run through I saw signs of movement and knocked on the door of the second last house to ask where I could stay. Jim

Jim and his scarecrow, Yacka

opened the door, and invited me in for a cup of tea and a shower. He was a keen cyclist and later showed me his high-tech racing bike. He used to cycle competitively and I suspected he was pretty good even though he kept his achievements to himself. In the end, he offered the spare bed, which certainly beat another cold night alone in the tent.

Reaching Adelaide from Yacka involved another gruelling ten hours of pedalling. I trusted Jim's recommendation of the flatter, quieter road through Balaklava because he was a fellow cyclist and knew the roads like the back of his hand. For most of the way, I travelled between two parallel ridges of hills through vast wheat-producing country. The fertile plain of red-chocolate soil supported other, more intensive forms of land use as I headed south, culminating in market gardens on the Adelaide periphery. I was definitely south of the Goyder Line.

◆　◆　◆

Like Perth, Adelaide has also been called the 'City of Light', but for a very different reason. In 1836, Colonel William Light planned the city on a grid pattern, interspersed with squares and surrounded by a garland of parklands. I navigated through the broad, leafy streets of the centre to finally arrive in the inner suburb of Kensington in the dark. Cath, the daughter of Penel and Greg from Port Lincoln, had kindly agreed for me to stay.

In addition to my usual admin work, in Adelaide I started making plans for the finish. Exact dates for my arrival in Canberra were required so we could coordinate publicity and people arriving at Parliament House. In these days of increased security, I needed permission to have a public gathering there. Prior to that, the dates of my arrival in Portland, Anglesea and Geelong in Victoria had to be confirmed so that Alcoa could set up various school and community visits.

Also like Perth, Adelaide is strung out along a coastal plain with hills rising sharply to the east. Leaving the city, I ascended to the point known as 'Eagle on the Hill', and quickly discovered that the Mount Lofty Ranges are on a slightly grander scale to the Darling Range and are more generously sprinkled with pockets of development; touristy towns full of boutique shops and cafes, geared for day trippers from the city.

Paddle-wheel of the *Murray Princess*, Murray River, Mannum

At Murray Bridge, I left the Old Princes Highway, the original route of Highway No.1 which circumnavigates the continent, to follow the course of Australia's greatest river from near its mouth, through the Riverina region and into the extreme north-west of Victoria. The Murray-Darling River system is almost exactly the length of the Mississippi River in the United States and, although it transports only a fraction of the Mississippi water flow, it has a parallel importance in cultural heritage before and after European settlement. In fact, all the rivers in Australia combined (in the Dry season) would not fill the Mississippi.

The Murray-Darling Basin area, shaped like a shallow saucer (500 km across and about 600 metres deep in the centre), covers about 14 per cent of the continent's surface area. Deposits of sand and fine clay over the last 65 million years have made the Murray Basin relatively flat – only 200 metres above sea level. For at least 40 000 years, the Aboriginal people have been relying on the permanent water supply and its abundance of food, ceremonial centres and raw materials for shelter, clothing, tools, weapons and transport.

The development of a European way of life resulted in unintentional degradation of many of the river's natural resources. This lack of knowledge about soil, climate and geology of the Murray Basin has led to serious environmental problems through salinity, rising water-tables and vegetation clearances. Two million people now live and work in the region; one million more rely on its water. I was interested to examine the Murray, its floodplains and hinterland to put the river and at least some of its conflicts into perspective.

In 1824, Hamilton Hume and William Hovell were the first Europeans to discover the Murray River. Five years later, Charles Sturt, assigned to solve the great mystery of why so many rivers flowed westward from the Great Dividing Range (many thought the Murray may have led to an inland sea) rowed a whale-boat down the Murrumbidgee River (from near Canberra). He reached the junction with the Murray River in January 1830, and continued down the 'Big River' to arrive a month later at Lake Alexandrina, and then the mouth of the river. Over the next twenty years, squatters settled on the river frontage and sheep and cattle were introduced to the Murray Valley. During the 1840s all land along the Murray had been taken over for grazing.

My first port of call upstream from Murray Bridge was Mannum, 'Birthplace of the Murray River Paddle Steamer'. The construction of steamers opened up large areas in New South Wales, Victoria and South Australia, providing many settlers with a source of supply and contact with the outside world. They plied the Murray's full length, carrying wool, wheat and goods. Gradually, the more efficient railway took away the business and the river has never made it back as a highway of trade.

Near the river banks, everything appeared green and prosperous, from the manicured lawns of the well-kept historic town to out along the narrow floodplain sandwiched between ancient limestone cliffs. The water's edge was fringed with reeds so thick it was at times difficult to see across the great river expanse. That all changed as I climbed out of the valley and followed the snaking curves – according to the Dreaming legend, this was the work of Ponde, the Giant Murray River Cod, which widened the river with sweeps of its tail. In the context of the wider horizons, the river was just a narrow green artery providing life to the arid brown lands. From Walker's Flat, I followed a plateau as flat as a billiard table; being summer and in the midst of a drought, the treeless paddocks of the South Australian Mallee region looked desperately barren. There were few sheep – I imagine many would have been sold off to cope with the drought. Near the main towns, such as Swan Reach and Blanchetown, pockets of irrigated orchards contrasted with the parched landscape. Here I was well outside of Goyder's Line.

I had organised to stay at Waikerie with Denise and Bill Walding whom I had met on the Gunbarrel Highway. About 10 km out, the mallee scrub was replaced by irrigated orchards and market gardens of grapes, citrus, olives, stone fruit and a range of vegetables. Bill collected me in town; we crossed the river by barge and drove out to their property at Taylorville as the sun, like an enormous blood orange, bled into a western horizon of unbroken orchards and vines. We talked about our Gunbarrel experiences, what had happened since then and about life beside the Murray River. Like all the towns of the Riverina region, South Australia's orchard, Waikerie depends on the Murray's year-round water supply for all its water needs, including irrigation.

Trays of apricots ready for drying

In its natural state, the Murray River was an unreliable supplier of water and during droughts it could be reduced to a chain of saline ponds. In order to provide a reliable source of water, in the 1920s the river was regulated by a series of locks and weirs, including one at Waikerie. Their construction enabled year-round navigation for commercial cargo and passenger paddle steamers. Each weir raises the level of water behind it by an average of three metres, to create a continuous series of stepped pools between Blanchetown and Mildura. River flows are now regulated and so there is no seasonal flow, with the result that summer flows are higher and winter flows are reduced, and the incidence of flood lessened. The manipulation of the river's natural state and the management of the water and land use have contributed towards some of the Murray's major environmental problems.

Denise Walding and friends – preparing apricots from their orchards for drying, Riverina region, SA

Irrigation in the Basin accounts for more than half of all water used in Australia. Bill believes that there needs to be more stringent controls on water quotas, especially with the doling out of water licences to broad-scale cotton, rice, sugar cane and fruit farming corporations. In his view, the Riverina region, being downstream of these large businesses, suffers from the consequences of over-generous water allowances. About 90 per cent of South Australia depends on drinking water piped from the Murray, including Whyalla and Woomera in the central desert region.

The introduction of alien fauna and flora, such as carp and willow trees, has threatened the existence of native species as well as challenged water quality. Originally from central Asia, carp, also known for good reason as 'rabbits of the Murray', were introduced to Australia in the 1850s as a food to help settlers struggling with the 'harsh' environment. During the 1960s, carp which had been illegally imported from Germany escaped in the Murray River during a flood. They are now the most common fish found in the Murray-Darling Basin, able to thrive in water of poor quality, and highly prolific.

Introduced willow trees are another major player threatening local diversity and water flow. The trees are abundant because they can reproduce asexually, meaning they don't need a female and male plant in order to reproduce. Broken-off branches and twigs take root and soon a whole new plant establishes itself. Since they take root so easily, willows quickly colonise and spread, providing unhealthy competition for the natural environment, and choking the river banks.

Before I left Waikerie, Bill loaded me up with freshly picked peaches, nectarines, apricots and oranges from their orchards. Fuelled on the juiciest fruits of the Murray, I followed one of the river's most pronounced meanders to Loxton, the major town at the base of the Riverina cradle. With an easy half-day planned to reach the next link in the chain, I could afford to take my time.

◆ ◆ ◆

A river in distress – the Murray and its floodplain between Loxton and Berri

Loxton, a much larger centre than Waikerie, owes much of its development to an influx of soldier settlements after World War II. The Murray waters offered veterans a fresh start after the horrors of war. My hosts, Ken and Rosalie, friends of my cousins in Ceduna, proudly showed me around the exemplary streets and down to the river banks where majestic river red gums provided almost unbroken shade.

Away from Loxton, towards Berri, the river and its vast floodplain did not appear in good heart. Few of the red gums survived their artificially regulated environment, their austere skeletons protruding from the landscape as if they were crying for help. Dead and dying trees along the river may be a result of changed water regimes and increased salinity levels within the river. While River Red Gums are able to withstand some flooding of their roots, they also need periods where their roots are free from flooding, a cycle altered by river regulation.

OUT THERE AND BACK

Sprinklers operating in the heat of a summer's day on the edge of the Riverina region – an avoidable misuse of the Murray's water

The Murray River is particularly susceptible to salt problems because it flows through a highly saline groundwater environment. Most of the salt comes from deposits that were laid down when the land was under the sea. As with the Western Australian Wheatbelt, prolonged misguided land use has been the root cause of the Murray-Darling dryland salinity problems. The Murray region suffers the additional consequences associated with the high level of demand for its water.

Despite all these major issues, the future of Australia's greatest river basin is not all gloom and doom. South Australia is investigating alternatives to reduce its reliance on the river for drinking water. Steps are being taken to control carp and other vermin species, and to reintroduce deep-rooted vegetation. Irrigation techniques are gradually being made more efficient by improving watering regimes, lining (and hopefully soon enclosing) water channels, and using trickle systems and micro-sprinklers rather than wasteful overhead sprinkler systems.

Rejoining the Sturt Highway east of Renmark, I left the irrigated farmland behind for the time being and entered a new state. Most people think of Victoria as the state with the most prosperous farmland; 'Australia Felix', or 'the lucky country' as it was described by explorer Major Mitchell. The north-west corner is the exception as Victoria has its own 'wide brown land'. In 1991, the Murray-Sunset National Park was reclaimed from pastoral country in an effort to return the land and preserve its natural wilderness state. I fleetingly brushed the tip of the park before the rather monochromatic-looking mallee scrub gave way to desolate grazing land – more of a 'wide red land'. The drought had a stranglehold as sand drifts collected at the fence lines. Willy-willies accelerated the destructive processes as they twisted chaotically over the ground, funnelling red dust into the atmosphere. The pasture and topsoil had mostly been lost, and there was limited vegetation to shelter the ground, only sparse crop stubble in some paddocks. The Big River meandered 10-20 km to the north, and yet at Lake Cullulleraine, a remnant of the ancient floodplain, drinking water was in such short supply that I had to buy bottled water to see me through to Mildura.

Although on a grander scale, the Sunraysia district is to Victoria as the Riverina is to South Australia. The irrigation sprinklers were on full throttle when I arrived in the Murray hinterland in the late afternoon, the cooler mist-filled atmosphere a soothing relief to my parched throat. I was dog tired by the time I made it into the provincial city of Mildura after another day of almost ten hours of pedalling into a headwind in 40°C temperatures. All the cheap accommodation was booked out due to the seasonal influx of fruit pickers, so unable to treat myself, I resorted to a campsite on the edge of town.

With names like Orange, Lemon, Lime, Valencia, Avocado, Cherry, Muscat, Vineyard, Olive and Walnut, the streets of Mildura provide a clue as to the economic basis of the area. The district supplies 80 per cent of Australia's dried fruit, 15 per cent of its citrus fruit, and 85 per cent of the Victoria's winemaking grapes. The name Mildura was derived from a local Indigenous term for 'red earth'. After Red Cliffs, about 20 km south of Mildura, the vines and orchards ended abruptly and the productive 'red earth' was reduced once more to fly-away red sand. The pattern of thirsty broad-acre paddocks interspersed with patches of mallee scrub continued through to Ouyen, then south along the Sunraysia Highway before gently graduating to more fertile country along the Henty Highway to Warracknabeal.

Feeling somewhat heat stressed in the early afternoon of my fourth 40°C plus scorcher in a row, I took refuge by dropping in at Beulah Primary School. It was just at the end of the school summer holidays and the teachers were preparing for the start of the new school year. Marg, the principal, explained that Beulah Primary was in the process of becoming an 'environment school'. The staff were developing a number of initiatives as part of the children's education, similar to the program at the North Dandalup Primary, south of Perth. One of the teachers, Maureen, invited me to stay that night at her home in Warracknabeal, my 'minimum distance' for the day. Feeling physically and emotionally fragile, I was in dire need of some spoiling: a proper bed, good food, good company. I didn't hesitate to accept.

Soon after leaving Warracknabeal, the jagged rock formations of the Grampians (Gariwerd) appeared to the south-east. As I drew nearer to Horsham, the town at their western gateway, the imposing sandstone mounds, the westernmost extension of the Great Dividing Range, increasingly dominated my field of view. There weren't too many other distractions in the landscape.

When American author Mark Twain visited Horsham in 1895 he described it as 'a country town, peaceful, reposeful, inviting, full of snug homes, with garden plots, and plenty of shrubbery and flowers'. The plains of the Wimmera region he described 'as level as a floor…grey, bare, sombre, melancholy, baked, cracked, in the tedious long droughts, but a horizonless ocean of vivid green grass the day after a rain'. Compared with where I had just been, even in the summer drought this land looked like a 'Garden of Eden'. It was this region – the Grampian Ranges and the south-western districts of Victoria – that Major Mitchell had referred to as 'Australia Felix' when he discovered and mapped it in 1836.

As I left the streets of Horsham behind, and the last of the satellite hobby farms phased out, a farmer stopped to warn me that there would be no facilities whatsoever until I reached Cavendish, 105 km away. I assured him that it was all in hand. There was little traffic to disturb what would be one of my Top 10 favourite rides for the whole expedition. The scenery was totally inspiring as the road took a course roughly parallel with the waves of sharp-peaked cuestas which rise dramatically to about 1000 metres. The alluvial flood plain supported the thick-trunked eucalypts which towered overhead. I was excited at the prospect of arriving in what was William Snell's old stomping ground before he left for the West in 1892. Snell had worked as an engineering contractor building mostly bridges and roads in the area. I paused for a break beside a beautiful waterhole on the Glenelg River near Woohlpooer, where in 1890 he had built the Woohlpooer Bridge.

Grapes growing under plastic sheeting to minimise water loss

OUT THERE AND BACK

The humid atmosphere, which had been draining for most of the day, bubbled up into a grumpy-looking sky. With about 30 km to go, I could see the heavy grey clouds to the south had erupted into a full-blown thunderstorm. Lightning strikes ignited a number of spot fires – I counted six trails of smoke but could not tell how far they were away. Farm utes equipped with fire-fighting gear raced to attend the outbreaks and I was asked to stop and await further instruction. Once the roadside flames were controlled I was waved through, with no option but to head into the teeth of the storm. The heavens opened and water fell in sheets, making it difficult to discern where I was going. Torrents gushed down the road and lakes formed over the flat paddocks but I didn't bother with my rain jacket as the temperature was warm. Within a few kilometres of Cavendish, the rain ended as if someone turned off a tap. Another farmer checked to see that I was all right and suggested that I camp out at the sports club in the town. I sheltered under the football grandstand and showered in the unlocked umpires' room.

Camping under the grandstand of the Cavendish Country Football Ground after the storm

Hamilton, the agricultural hub of the region, prides itself on being the 'Wool Capital of the World'. The district is considered to have the densest population of broad-acre sheep farming per hectare on earth, allowing a diverse range of quality wool, from over twenty different breeds, to be grown. Reaching the giant wool bale monuments (built to commemorate the region's wool-producing heritage) completed a major personal chapter for the expedition for me – although Uncle Willy must have been far more excited to reach Hamilton than I was. Another box ticked.

Heading down to Portland concluded my cross-section trip of western Victoria. Suddenly I was in a coastal climate mild enough to support lush summer pasture for sheep and dairy cattle. Within two days, I had gone from red dust and intense dry heat to temperate coastal summer breezes, the smell of fresh cut hay and green meadows. Arriving in Portland, Victoria's oldest permanent settlement, I was on schedule for the community appointments Alcoa had arranged. There I upheld my end of the bargain which included three school visits and some publicity. It was another hectic day off the bike, but at least I was well looked after. En route to Melbourne I also had engagements to keep in Anglesea, on the Great Ocean Road, where the company has a power station, and at its Victorian headquarters and smelter at Point Henry near Geelong,

It was probably best that my mind was kept busy so as to give me little time to dwell on what lay ahead when I returned to Melbourne in four days. I had been going hard since Adelaide and needed the physical rest, but a day off the bike was another tortuous day of waiting. I really needed to get there to confront the situation. It seemed that the closer I came to Melbourne, the more the pressure compounded within.

The path along Highway No.1 to Warrnambool, passing the Codrington Wind Farm and Port Fairy, looked quite un-Australian. Had Greg been cycling with me, I am sure he would have claimed that the open, rolling green hills, the small paddocks of freshly mown grass and the whitewashed houses reminded him of

Ireland. He would not have been the first to make this claim. The fishing town of Port Fairy, set on a bay which once provided a sheltered base for sealing and whaling boats, was at one stage called Belfast. About half-way from there to Warrnambool lies a sleepy hamlet called Killarney – an antipodean's recognition of the original Killarney I visited on my first bumbling attempt at cycle touring in south-west Ireland. If I totalled the distances I have covered on my major bicycle adventures since then, I would have ridden from Killarney to Killarney and back, then back again.

Nearby, I stopped to admire Tower Hill and its crater lake. Compared with the Tweed and Focal shield volcanoes on the NSW-Queensland borders and most of the volcanic chain which stretches down the backbone of the Great Dividing Range, Tower Hill is a comparatively young volcano. Although now extinct, the crater formed only 7500 years ago. The volcanic earth has formed the base for the fertility of the soil for 'Australia Felix'.

Bay of Islands near Peterborough, Great Ocean Road

I passed light industry, large warehouses and heavy traffic on the way in and out of Warrnambool, the largest port in Western Victoria. After a short warm-up ride out of town, I turned off the Princes Highway and on to the Great Ocean Road. It was a picture-book summer's day and I lapped up the opportunity to see perhaps Australia's most well-trodden tourist route in the best of light. I could smell the salt of the sea well before the road joined the coastline at the Bay of Islands a few kilometres from Peterborough. Bass Strait was in one of its more tranquil moods. The scene was simply light blue on dark blue – Cambridge versus Oxford as the clear sky met the ocean. The limestone cliffs and stacks, however, bear the scars of the most notorious weather conditions, when Bass Strait throws a tantrum. The same gales and massive waves which have eaten out the Great Australian Bight also constantly sculpt the spectacular debris of the sea which studs the Great Ocean Road, from the Bay of Islands to their more famous cousins, the Twelve Apostles.

A tumultuous history lies beneath the surface as the stretch of water between Port Fairy and Cape Otway is known as the Shipwreck Coast. The sea floor is littered with the wrecks of hundreds of ships – victims of wild weather, human error and a rugged coastline. I took time to appreciate the beautiful afternoon light, watching the waves gnaw away at stacks of the Twelve Apostles – too much time, in fact. I still had 50 km to go to reach Lavers Hill. I laboured hard across the undulating heathland before the road turned away from the coast at Princetown and deep into the Otway Range. Having only driven this stretch of road before, I had little appreciation of just how long and arduous the section through Lavers Hill to Apollo Bay was. I tried to concentrate on the beauty and

Twelve Apostles – or what is left of them – in the late afternoon, Great Ocean Road

finer details of the verdant rainforest, which I could well appreciate at my snail's pace, rather than how I was really feeling inside – washed up like another casualty of the Shipwreck Coast.

East of Cape Otway, the coastline changed character. The eroding limestone cliffs and rolling heathlands were behind me and ahead the Otway Range dropped vertically to the shore, thick forest clinging to the slopes protected from the ocean front. The scene was like a dinky version of the Amalfi Coast (south of Naples, Italy), except the beach sand was pearly white rather than fine volcanic charcoal. The road, an incredible feat of engineering, is engraved into the cliff faces, often in

The beach at Apollo Bay

a tangle of switchbacks dropping down to sea level at creek intersections and then back up to crow's-nest vantage points. On the narrowest passages of road, converging tourist buses skilfully danced the closest of tangos to pass by each other. I proceeded with caution, relying mostly on sound to negotiate the blind corners. The severe climbs around Lavers Hill had injected my legs with a top-up of steel and I pedalled strongly over the inspiring section to Lorne and on to Anglesea.

The hoards of travellers around would have not noticed the echidna which I stopped to rescue as it threatened to cross the busy road. There weren't too many ants beside the road for it to eat and there was nowhere for it to go, just cliff, gutter, road, cliff, ocean. I hoped it might work its way along the gutter until it found a way back into the bush, but as I had seen plenty of squashed wildlife, feared the shy creature would be another casualty.

Vulnerable roadside wildlife – drivers would miss such details as an echidna beside the busy Great Ocean Road

My final day into Melbourne was a long one, starting with a school visit in Anglesea. The traffic steadily built up as I pushed on to the industrial city of Geelong for a sponsor's lunch. It was tough keeping up appearances and posing for the press with such a big knot inside. I thanked the Alcoa representatives and pushed off down the Princes Freeway beside Port Phillip Bay towards Melbourne. Even my backside felt numb as I was sucked along with the flow the traffic. At least the raging tailwind was on my side although I noticed it was dragging some heavy rain clouds. It was a relief to finally hit the busy Melbourne streets. The wait was over.

From Ceduna to Melbourne, a stretch of over 2600 km, I had explored and been presented with the extremes of all four elements: I had witnessed the horrific Eyre Peninsula fires and their effects and persisted through the hottest of temperatures fanned by desert winds. I had followed some of the country's most spectacular coastline and explored a good chunk of Australia's mightiest river. I had travelled through barren and drought-affected country to the most fertile of farmland, but by the time I reached Melbourne, perhaps fittingly in a torrential downpour, it was the fifth element that seemed insurmountable.

Bass
Strait

Wynyard Burnie **Devonport**

Tamar River

Launceston

Perth Fingal

Cradle Mtn.
-Lake St Clair
Nat.Pk. **TAS**

Zeehan Avoca Bicheno

Queenstown Tarraleah Swansea

Franklin-Gordon
Wild Rivers
Nat. Pk. Hamilton Freycinet
Peninsula *Tasman
Sea*

Derwent River

Hobart

Southwest
Nat. Pk. Dover

Cockle Creek

South East Cape

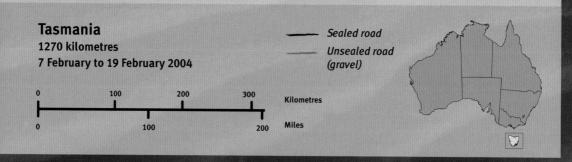

Tasmania
1270 kilometres
7 February to 19 February 2004

| | Sealed road |
| | Unsealed road (gravel) |

| 0 | 100 | 200 | 300 | Kilometres |
| 0 | 100 | | 200 | Miles |

17

Heart to heartland
Tasmanian loop: Devonport to Devonport

Cockle Creek, at the terminus of Australia's most southerly road, is closer to Antarctica than Cairns

The island state has been known by several different names throughout its history, including, in order: Trowunner (Indigenous), Van Diemen's Land, Tasmania and such touristy terms as 'The Apple Isle'. If, as in the introductory chapter, Australia is equated as representing a human body, its roads and tracks its blood vessel network and the act of bicycle travel as the flow of life-giving blood all the way to its extremities, then cycling a lap of the 'heart-shaped island' would be like pumping life via the coronary arteries to the cardiac muscle. All I had to do was control some haemorrhaging. A brochure that I flicked through to pass the time on the *Spirit of Tasmania* across Bass Strait described Tasmania as an 'Island of Rejuvenation'. I hoped so.

Given my personal situation, it was tempting to skip Tasmania and continue the line directly back to Canberra. What lured me on was the spirit of the expedition and the will to complete what I had promised to do. An email from Robert Swan encouraging me to keep going and to take extra care all the way through to the end of the journey was welcome and helpful. When I had rolled onto the *Spirit of Tasmania* at the Melbourne docks for the 240-km overnight crossing I felt like a convict condemned to the once-notorious Van Diemen's Land penal colony, wrongly sentenced without a fair trial. Back in Melbourne, I had hoped Arnaud would at least keep an open mind about our relationship, but he had shut up shop and was not prepared to even try to work things out.

I had chosen to take the ship to Devonport on the north coast rather than a short flight to Hobart in the far south as I felt there was more of a connection with the mainland this way. It was as recently as the last Ice Age (12 000-15 000 years ago) that Tasmania was physically separated from Victoria, leaving about three hundred or so islands as debris in its wake. In keeping with European comparisons, 'Tassie' is almost exactly the size in area of Ireland and about the same size as Holland and Belgium combined. The first known European to discover the state later named in his honour was the Dutch explorer Abel Tasman, who mapped its south-west tip in 1642, before crossing what we now know as the Tasman Sea to discover New Zealand and on to Fiji. Tasman had been sent into unchartered waters by Anthoony van Diemen, the then governor-general of the Dutch East Indies (Indonesia), to piece together the isolated discoveries of earlier Dutch explorers and, of course, to search for anything of economic importance. The intrepid sailor recorded that at a latitude of 42 degrees he had sighted a mountainous island and that, on landing, his men found tall trees with notches cut at five-foot (1.5 metre) intervals. In this strange place, which Tasman subsequently named Van Diemen's Land, his men had heard the sounds of trumpets and small gongs and found the paw-prints of an animal like a tiger.

I had allowed thirteen days to ride the 1300 km around the island. Normally this wouldn't have been a big deal, but on leaving the Devonport streets, I soon discovered that the physical conditions, combined with my stressed state, amounted to a serious challenge. The island may be small in area, but for a heavily laden cyclist, it sure packs a few decent punches. For a start, there are twenty-eight peaks over 1250 metres high – twenty-seven more than in the whole of Western Australia. If the terrain was ironed out, the state would cover a much larger area! In the height of summer, the cool temperate maritime climate has a less-than-cool temperament. I hadn't expected to be suffering from the effects of wind chill in early February in Australia. Blood drained from my fingers and toes regularly over the two weeks' ride even though my heart was doing a job beyond its usual call of duty.

From Devonport I took the quieter and more steeply graded forestry road rather than the highway to Exeter in the Tamar River Valley. The chocolate earth was carved into small paddocks producing a variety of crops not seen, or at least not in such abundance, on the mainland: various types of berries and fruit, vegetables, irrigated pastures and – opium poppies. In 1961, the United Nations decided to allow the production of opium in Tasmania, which now produces 40 per cent of the world's legal crop. Morphine and thebaine which are obtained from the poppy sap are essential in the production of pain-relieving medicine. Morphine, a depressant, is the precursor to codeine and heroin. With its relatively sparse population and good security, Tasmania's northern coastal region provides the right growing conditions for the plants. To decrease opportunities for illegal harvesting, indistinguishable mutant poppies, such as 'Norman' (no morphine), are grown along side the real thing.

As the road wound a convoluted path up and over a series of taxing hills, through forestry plantations, I had to remain particularly alert to the high numbers of logging trucks, especially on the steep descents. Even the empty semi-trailers, with their trays folded up like oversized Meccano sets, I found intimidating as they rattled along at breakneck speeds through the forest. At Exeter I entered the Tamar Valley, where grape-vines dominated the land use, and followed the busier West Tamar Highway beside the estuary into Launceston. Tasmania's northern capital was founded at the confluence of the North and South Esk Rivers (which then become the Tamar) early on in Australia's European development. The region became the site of the third

Opium poppies

European settlement – after Sydney and Hobart – when the British colonials feared that the French had their eyes on the region. Georgetown, 50 km to the north at the mouth of the Tamar, was settled in 1804, Launceston the year after that. I whisked by Australia's greatest concentration of nineteenth century buildings and out of town along the Midland or 'Heritage' Highway as I had organised to stay on a farm south of Perth (the first 'Perth' in Australia) on the South Esk River.

The connection to meeting and staying with Gwendolyn Adams and her husband Viv on their farm, Leighlands, was Geoff Bee (Jerramungup) and Landcare. Both parties had represented their states at the 2002 national Landcare awards of which Geoff was the overall winner. Gwendolyn's set-up and achievements on her 330-hectare (800 acre) property are very different from Geoff's approach for managing his 4200 hectares (10 000 acres) in Western Australia. She took over the running of the family property in 1969, a highly unusual move at the time as farm management was not then considered an appropriate vocation for women. With the assistance of Viv, Gwendolyn has successfully built the business while also becoming a strong advocate of environmental management.

On a late afternoon tour, I was privileged to be shown the main projects. A major effort has been to clear the banks of the South Esk River, which flows through part of the property. As with the Murray River, introduced plants such as willow, gorse and other weeds had choked the flow. All have been removed thanks to a cooperative program with the neighbours, the waterway protected by fences and native plants reintroduced. Soil structure has been improved and the threat of dry land salinity minimised. I learned that Gwendolyn's work extends far beyond the boundary fences. She is a leader in the larger community and contributes to the environmental curriculum of the local primary school and to the education of disadvantaged children.

When I was staying at Leighlands I stumbled across an important historical association between Tasmania and Victoria. The farm and its original cottage, which still stands near the sheep-yards, were once owned by John Wedge, a surveyor and colleague of John Batman, accredited as the founder of Melbourne. From their respective Van Diemen's Land properties, Batman and Wedge planned an expedition across Bass Strait to look for suitable land for a settlement. When Batman returned in June 1835 from his first visit to the Port Phillip District (as the area around the future Melbourne was known), Wedge resigned from the Survey Department and crossed to Port Phillip where he explored along the Barwon River and surveyed the land 'acquired' for settlement from the Aboriginals by Batman's Port Phillip Association. It was he who gave the Yarra River its name after he misheard local Aboriginals using the words 'Yarrow yarrow' to refer to how the water flowed over the rapids.

The 'treaty' that Batman's Port Phillip Association and eight tribal leaders had signed involved the exchange of approximately 250 000 hectares of land for a barrow-load of trinkets: 'blankets, knives, looking-glasses, tomahawks, beads, scissors, flour and other basic items' and in addition the newcomers agreed to pay a yearly rent of quantities of similar items. The local Aboriginals were as unable to comprehend the idea of selling their land as Batman was of appreciating the value it held for them. The exchange that took place, and the 'treaty' that marked it, were at best the result of a cultural misunderstanding by both sides.

◆ ◆ ◆

Kelvedon River looking across towards the Freycinet Peninsula

My own misunderstanding, marital in nature, continued to plague my thoughts. It was essential that I kept my mind as busy as possible. Waking at Leighlands after limited sleep, and with a tension headache and suppressed appetite, was far from optimum conditions for facing another 160-km day, mostly uphill.

Setting off, I basically followed the course of the South Esk River along the main Launceston–Hobart artery, turning east at the Esk Highway. The road climbed steadily up the beautiful grassy valley of open farmland through Avoca to Fingal, where the main stream veered north toward Ben Lomond, whose craggy peaks looked a bit sinister partially hidden by swirling grey clouds. I continued to ascend, following a tributary and the old railway track to St Mary's. The finale to the day's climbing was Mount Elephant, so-named because of its shape. To a cyclist, that translates to being very steep, but fortunately it was not such a long pass. I was coaxed to the summit, 450 metres above the Tasman Sea, by signs advertising the Mt Elephant Pancake Restaurant and promptly rewarded myself by indulging in the most exquisite pancakes. The snack injected just enough energy and raising of spirits to see me down the hairpins to Chain of Lagoons and along the stunning coastline to Bicheno.

The safe, tranquil beaches and modern resort charm belie the settlement's rugged beginnings. Sealers and whalers were the first Europeans to set up outposts such as Waub's Boat Harbour (Bicheno's original name) along the north and east coasts of Van Diemen's Land. Pre-dating the first official settlement of the island, they lived a primitive and dangerous life and were known to be particularly cruel to the local Aboriginals, whom they enslaved and prostituted.

Tasmania's isolation has resulted in the island being home to a high degree of endemism at many levels – its Indigenous people, plants and animals. Many were and are highly susceptible to alien influences. As tragically occurred here

Dry-stone work, the Spiky Bridge

On the convict-built Spiky Bridge

as in other parts of the 'new world', when the Europeans arrived, they brought diseases for which the Indigenous people had no immunity. The Tasmanian Aboriginals were especially vulnerable to respiratory diseases, influenza and pneumonia. The Bass Strait sealers first introduced these illnesses to Trowunner in 1798, the year Flinders and Bass circumnavigated Van Diemen's Land, proving it was an island, and before colonial settlement in 1803. From that point, the fate of the full-blood Tasmanian Aboriginals was sealed: by 1876 they had become extinct with the death of Truganini, a 'princess' from the Bruny Island tribe, the last of her people. Tasmanian Aboriginals of today are all of mixed decent.

For about 36 000 years the land had sustained a population of between 5000 and 10 000 Aboriginals; all were wiped out in less than eighty years of European colonisation. While there was no agenda of genocide by the new settlers, a combination of circumstance, susceptibility, appalling maltreatment and violent conflict stemming from the unfortunate official attitudes of the era, loss of fertility from venereal disease, reduction in the population of women and social deprivation combined to bring about a most a shameful chapter in Australia's early history.

Some of the more famous landmarks and attractions between Bicheno and Hobart, and, in fact, in the whole of Tasmania, I decided to reserve for when I had more time and conditions were more conducive for appreciating them. The Freycinet Peninsula, Maria Island and Port Arthur were all put on hold. There were still tantalising snippets of the history, ecology and beauty to be experienced without diverting too far: pristine, white beaches bisected by creeks and rivulets originating in the hills to the west; convict-built architecture such as the 'Spiky Bridge', just south of Swansea.

Heading inland from Orford the climbs were particularly rude and after Buckland I was introduced to another form of local endemism – the Tasmanian sense of humour. The three successive passes were signposted; 'Break-Me-Neck', 'Bust-Me-Gall' and 'Black Charlie's Opening'. Fittingly, as I descended Break-Me-Neck Hill, I noticed two squashed Tasmanian devils beside a sharp bend. They had most likely been feasting on other forms of road kill; carrion being a preferred meal of the world's largest surviving carnivorous marsupial.

Break-Me-Neck Hill

Apple orchards near
Geeveston

Huon River

The devils, like their larger extinct cousins, the Tasmanian tiger or thylacine, once inhabited the whole of the continent. (I mentioned evidence of the thylacine's existence on the mainland by citing the petroglyph in the Calvert Range off the Canning Stock Route.) The introduction of dingoes by the Aboriginals caused the extinction of both creatures from the mainland. But the rising of the ocean at the end of the last Ice Age proved to be their saviour – until the Europeans arrived. The more versatile and populous devils barely survived the bounty hunters, the thylacine did not. The whole of Tasmania could only support a population of about 4000 tigers and once they were blamed for attacking livestock, they were doomed. The last shy creature died in the Hobart Zoo about seventy years ago. Some believe the thylacine still exists and unsubstantiated sightings are regularly reported.

Thankfully, after Black Charlie's Opening, it was mostly downhill to Sorell and then busy traffic all the way over the River Derwent and into Hobart. I followed the main road into the city centre, connecting with well-trodden territory at the Hobart Real Tennis Club on Davey Street where I have played in a couple of Australian Opens. I was pleased to link up with some familiar faces and spend a recovery day out of the saddle, staying with a real tennis friend in Sandy Bay.

From Hobart, I headed for Cockle Creek, as far south as the road would take me. The South East Cape, about four hours return walk from Cockle Creek, is Australia's most southerly point. (I would have to sail to Heard Island or the Australian Antarctic Territory to reach the most southern Australian outposts.) Grinding through my lowest gears to climb out of Hobart, I was glad of my decision to take an extra day off. Over the first 40 km to Huonville, there were three massive climbs, all into a biting Antarctic south-westerly, and as I skirted the foothills of Mount Wellington I started to doubt whether I would reach Cockle Creek by day's end.

A Huonville bakery provided welcome refuge from an icy downpour and allowed blood to reintegrate with my extremities. This cool, wet climate may have made conditions difficult for me but it has proved to be optimum for the 'Apple Capital' of the Apple Isle. As I followed the river downstream towards the

At the Lune River train
station – the end of the line

D'Entrecasteaux Channel, most of the level ground was taken up with orchards
of ripening fruits: apples, apricots, berries, plums and pears. The river had been
a busy artery for timber-laden ships removing the region's most prized natural
resource, the Huon pine, which once graced the banks in dense, towering
stands.

Huon pine, a relic of Gondwana, is one of the slowest-growing and longest
living plants in the world. Advancing upwards at an average rate of one
millimetre a year, they can attain heights greater than 40 metres, and live for
3000 years or more. This means that some of the trees alive today could be older
than Christianity and Islam and almost as old as Judaism.

The softwood, highly prized by artists, fine furniture makers and boat
builders, is endemic to the west and south-west of Tasmania. During 'recent'
times of human intervention, stocks have been diminished by Indigenous fire
regimes, logging, mining, inundation and drought (Huons need a cool, wet
climate to survive.) Today, most of the remaining stands are protected within
reserves and with closely monitored harvest quotas. The majority exist within
the World Heritage Area which covers almost a third of the island; their future is
assured unless the effects of climate change take hold.

With the landscape's sharp, frequent peaks and troughs, an altitude profile
graph of the route from leaving the Huon Valley through to Dover, Southport,
Lune River and Recherche Bay would have mirrored a cardiograph, had I bothered
to connect up to my heart rate monitor. Even with the longer summer days of the
southern latitudes, the sun was low by the time I reached the old Lune River
Railway Station and the end of the tarmac. Fortunately the final 20 km of gravel
was respectably surfaced – up and over logged forests, at various stages of
harvesting, and finally back to sea level at Recherche Bay. I continued to the
'End of the Road' and looked back.

In every direction I was surrounded by vistas of mountains, forests and
ocean. The whole of Australia was above me – in fact, I was closer to Antarctica
than Cairns. Reaching the fourth major geographical landmark of the expedition
was immensely satisfying, even with all the other difficulties. I was nearly there,
even if it was 'uphill' all the way back to Hobart the next day and on to Canberra
two weeks after that.

At the end of Australia's
most southerly road

◆   ◆   ◆

As with Launceston and Albany, on the southern coast of WA, the initial *raison d'être* for the establishment of Hobart was to keep the French out of Australia at a time when the countries were at war. A little over a century ago, on the same journey which included the afore-mentioned visit to Horsham, Mark Twain also ventured down to Hobart Town, by then an important port. His description eulogised its charms:

> How beautiful is the whole region, for form, and grouping, and opulence, and freshness of foliage, and variety of colour, and grace and shapeliness of the hills, the capes, the promontories; and then, the splendour of the sunlight, the dim, rich distances, the charm of the water-glimpses! And it was in this paradise that the yellow-liveried convicts were landed, and the Corps-bandits quartered, and the wanton slaughter of the kangaroo-chasing black innocents consummated on that autumn day in May, in the brutish old time. It was all out of keeping with the place, a sort of bringing of heaven and hell together.

Many of the buildings Twain would have admired, around the docks of historic Sullivans Cove, the harbour of the Derwent River and Battery Point, still stand and are today much valued. The 200 000 residents of Hobart are fortunate – waterside views so sought-after in other cities are the norm for them as the urban area is strung out along the Derwent. From my friend's place in Sandy Bay, it took about an hour to escape the city traffic which filtered out gradually through the industrial fringe. At Bridgewater, the Midland Highway branched north toward Launceston and I continued west along the Lyell Highway.

The main road follows the Derwent River from its mouth to its source, then over the central highlands plateau to the west coast. Loosely translated, this promised two huge days of ups and downs; virtually all ups on the first day to Tarraleah and then a mixed bag to Queenstown. Although there were plenty of undulations as the road roughly aligned with the valley, I had only ascended about 50 metres by the historic village of Hamilton. The open grassy plains served as no protection as I battled into polar squalls of wind and horizontal rain. The summer must bring some hospitable weather soon, or so I thought. The serious climbing started after Ouse, through the forest into the Central Highlands. It was virtually dark as I crossed a large aqueduct and followed a network of canals and water pipes into the hydro-town of Tarraleah, 600 metres above Hamilton. In a day I had cycled almost the length of the Derwent.

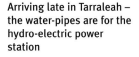
Arriving late in Tarraleah – the water-pipes are for the hydro-electric power station

The river's catchment is not only the source of Tassie's longest river, but also the source of almost a third of the state's power. Tasmanians originally found their way around at night by the light of candles and oil lamps – one of the reasons for the importance of whaling in the early days of European settlement. Whale oil was superseded briefly by coal and gas, but more than a century ago hydroelectric power began production. Now, except for a small thermal power station on the north coast, used only in times of severe and prolonged drought, Tasmania's electricity comes entirely from hydro-power.

The Tarraleah camping-ground was as sodden and spongy as the button grass meadows on the central highland plains. Rather than have everything become soaked through, I cooked and slept on the laundry floor – not a particularly idyllic location, but at least I would face the next day dry. Barely escaping the clutches of rigor mortis after another frustratingly insufficient sleep on cold concrete, I set off knowing there could be no half measures on the task ahead. Fingers and toes refused to follow instructions as I left the streets of pre-fab houses and immediately dropped away through the hairpins to the power station at the bottom of the Nive River valley. The water which powers the Tarraleah turbines is diverted 25 km overland from Butlers Gorge, just below the source of the Derwent River at Lake St Clair, tumbles 300 metres down the penstocks at Tarraleah to the Nive River and finally flows back into the Derwent. After Derwent Bridge, 50 km from Tarraleah, I entered the Franklin-Gordon Wild Rivers World Heritage Area, where camping was not permitted until Queenstown 90 km further on.

The King William Range at the eastern edge of the World Heritage Area forms a geographical frontier between the island's east and west. A little further on I paused for a breather at the Franklin River Bridge. Appearing enigmatically out of the misty rain, the fast-flowing river, as black as coal, reflected a leaden, gloomy sky while angry-looking white caps perhaps symbolised its more turbulent recent history. On the back of the inundation of Lake Pedder (first

Mt King William I – the division between eastern and western Tasmania

discovered by John Wedge) in 1973 for hydro-power, the proposal for damming the Franklin stirred environmental passions to a level unseen just about anywhere in the world. On the positive side, a hydroelectric power plant uses a renewable source of energy that does not pollute the environment. However, the construction of dams to enable hydroelectric generation would cause significant environmental damage. A carefully orchestrated political campaign gradually gained momentum from local to national and international levels, from mass on-site resistance to the law courts and finally to Canberra. The issue ultimately had a significant bearing the 1983 federal election and after a change of power the project was abandoned. Saving the Franklin provided proof that if enough people really care about an issue they can make a difference.

I continued over the Victoria Pass and out of the World Heritage Park as the highway rounded Lake Burbury, another hydro lake. The downpours gradually eased off and the low-level clouds dissipated, opening a window of clear views in the deepening twilight. I could have been in the Twilight Zone as the road slipped through the West Coast Range between Mt Lyell and Mt Owen. The pristine wilderness landscape abruptly changed to more of a moonscape. I had not witnessed such total devastation since cycling through the copper mining town of Karabash in the Ural Mountains. Tickling the granny gears once more as I ventured by Gormanston and up another steep slalom course, I experienced at close quarters a profound reminder of humanity's capacity to destroy and pollute. I could smell the sulphurous bare earth as I gulped in the cool, moist evening air.

The largest settlement on the west coast, Queenstown started with the discovery of gold, but turned to the exploitation of its copper reserves once the gold ran out. It is the copper smelters which have wreaked havoc on the

Girl playing in the wastelands of the Karabash Copper Mine, Siberian side of the Ural Mountains, Russia. This toxic island, surrounded by lush forest, is a similar blot on the landscape to that at Queenstown.

surrounding landscape ever since. Not only did the sulphur fumes kill off plants in the area but the eleven furnaces required vast quantities of timber and the mining company simply cut down the forests to fuel the fires. At Queenstown's peak, the furnaces were consuming 2040 tonnes of wood each week. The combination of timber felling, the sulphur fumes and the heavy rainfall in the area (which washed away the top soil) ensured that since 1900 the whole valley has looked like a desert. I saw some evidence of a regeneration program but the denuded hills of coloured earth have become an attraction in themselves, and a stark reminder of complete environmental abuse.

The promise of further appalling weather conditions, and physical and emotional exhaustion, caused me to trim planned diversions to the west coast from my schedule and head straight for the north coast via the Murchison Highway. To my lactic acid-filled legs, which by now felt as useful as two hindquarters of roast beef, even the main road was unforgiving. Physically and metaphorically I was cycling along the edge of the wilderness. A string of mountains, including mounts Tyndall, Read, Murchison and Black, form the virtually impenetrable western boundary of the Cradle Mountain–Lake St Clair National Park. Historically, this area of Tasmania was inaccessible and therefore resisted early European exploration. The forests were dense, the cold winds – as I well knew – blew rain clouds straight off the Southern Ocean, and the undergrowth with its leeches and dense scrub made travelling through the area difficult and unpleasant. As with Queenstown, the discovery of gold followed by that of other minerals – tin, copper and zinc – was the economic bait which led to the establishment of settlements such as Zeehan, Renison Bell, Rosebery and Tully.

About 40 km from the north coast, the high button grass plains gave way to agricultural land and thousands of hectares of tree plantations. Thanks to some persuasion from my friend in Hobart, a photographer from *The Hobart Mercury*, Tasmania's biggest newspaper, met me on the road. By the time I had wandered – finally in rejuvenating sunshine – back along the coast from Wynyard to Devonport for the return trip to the mainland, the pending publication of the article meant there was some recognition in the wings of the effort I had made to include a 'quick lap of Tassie' in the expedition.

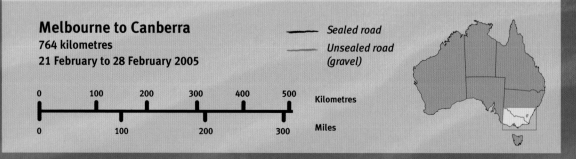

Sydney

NSW

Canberra

ACT

Murray River

VIC

Cooma

Jindabyne

Mount Kosciuszko

Snowy Mountains

Snowy River

Melbourne

Bairnsdale

Drouin

Melbourne to Canberra
764 kilometres
21 February to 28 February 2005

———— *Sealed road*

———— *Unsealed road (gravel)*

| 0 | 100 | 200 | 300 | 400 | 500 | Kilometres |

| 0 | | 100 | | 200 | | 300 | Miles |

18

And back

The Finish: Melbourne to Canberra

Pink bark shedding from a young snowgum on the Monaro Plain

When I first pushed out on my own – to confront the Canning Stock Route with a support vehicle, and then completely alone out of Halls Creek – I enjoyed the freedom of doing exactly as I pleased. I cycled at my own pace and didn't have to make any concessions for anyone. No one had to make concessions for me. Now the reverse was in order. I was looking forward to some company, someone to share the last few days.

When I returned to Melbourne after cycling around Tasmania, Greg was waiting to rejoin me for the final week to Canberra. He had returned to support the expedition and give closure to the project he had committed so much to. It had been five months since I had last seen him in Wiluna and a great deal had passed beneath my tyres in that time. In the interim, Greg had returned to England and settled back into normality – well, almost. He had even found a new 'proper' job as he'd had to resign from his last one in order to take part in the expedition.

On meeting up again, Greg discovered that the support I needed extended beyond the usual cycle touring partnership. Each time I had seen Arnaud, it opened the wounds a little further, and so pushing off for the final week was even more heart-wrenching than in earlier, happier times. I had invested complete trust in our personal relationship, and the GRACE Project had only come into being through mutual consensus. We had always shared everything, so to suddenly see Arnaud with someone else, taking my place in his life, was too much to bear. He didn't hate me, in fact, he said he still loved me – as a friend. I had done nothing wrong, it seemed – he was the one who had changed with his new life and new opportunities in his newly adopted country.

Now I had to somehow dig even deeper than before to find the strength to complete the last week of the expedition. Although I had managed to follow my planned route and was scheduled to finish on time after nine-and-a-half months, I certainly hadn't bargained for the personal journey I was faced with. It was the 'spinifex scenario' in a different guise; the barbed spines were embedded under the skin and the scars destined to remain long after the wounds appeared to have healed.

In the early stages of the Russian expedition, when we were exhausted after a 200-km day from Moscow to Vladimir, a hotel took over two hours to accept us in, charging us triple because we were non-Russian, and then the restaurant refused to serve us any food so that we were forced to cook pasta-reinforced soup on our camp stove in the room. George, one of our accompanying Russian cyclists, dealt with our exasperation by proclaiming, 'Problems will make us strong!' I reminded myself of this as Greg and I worked our way through the far eastern reaches of Melbourne's sprawl and around the base of the Dandenong Ranges. I was looking forward to finishing, not because of the traumas but because I would be completing what had I set out to do. I could have chosen a simpler path for the final run, but I was still fired by some adventurous sparks, and I needed to keep things interesting. The plan was to wend our way through the rich dairy pastures of Gippsland, then into the Snowy Mountains, pick up the Barry Way, a classic course beside the iconic Snowy River to Jindabyne, then across the Monaro Plains and into Canberra.

We finally escaped the urban peninsula which stretches along the Princes Highway. Just after Pakenham we opted for the original road beside the railway line. Apart from this being more relaxing than the highway, I was intrigued to find out what a village with a name such as Nar Nar Goon had to offer. It sounded as though the founders of this settlement had pre-empted a line out of a Spike Milligan sketch by about a century. The general store, where we both sought morale-boosting treats, advertised copies of *Goon News*. As it turns out, Nar Nar Goon is a local Indigenous term for 'koala'; like the names of the towns we sailed through that afternoon, this reflects the region's pre-European history. Our line was along the undulating transition between the ranges and marshlands – the Koo-Wee-Rup ('plenty of blackfish') Swamp. We passed Tynong ('many fish') and Bunyip ('mythical swamp creature') before arriving at Drouin ('where north winds blow'). We were specifically aiming for Drouin so we could look up Viv and Ron whom we had met at Hell's Gate along the Gulf Track. Ron was away and, at short notice, Viv collected us and took us back to their farm for the night. Another strand woven into the web of connections.

Greg is a strong cyclist and by the start of the second day he had obviously become re-acquainted with his cycling legs. True to the Indigenous name of the town, a north-easterly persisted as we left Drouin's hilly avenues lined with colourful displays of flowering gum trees: red, salmon pink and orange. We were funnelled back on to Highway No. 1 until Moe where we again opted for the quieter alternative. We picked a route along the Latrobe River Valley, then out into the foothills of the Great Dividing Range. There we could be much more in touch with the land rather than being concerned with avoiding juggernauts. The road, which stepped like a staircase through the back blocks, was more like a 'D' (*départementale*) road in France, quiet but still relatively direct, with gently rolling countryside to perhaps match parts of Normandy or the Loire region.

The minor roads brought us more in touch with the locals too. Deciding we'd had enough for the day, we pulled into a pub in the small village of Tinamba and in no time were offered a place to stay a few kilometres down the road. Greg may have felt at home as we passed through Stratford on the Avon River, the scenery not totally unlike the original. At Bairnsdale, we again diverted off the highway, this time along a cycle path created from an old light tramway track, travelling for 30 km over increasingly larger hills inland to Bruthen. Whichever road we took, we were resigned to the fact that it was going to be all uphill from there.

◆   ◆   ◆

During the expedition I had covered most of the icons the country is famous for: white sandy beaches from Broome to Cottesloe, Port Douglas to Bondi, Uluru and the Red Centre, Kakadu and the Great Barrier Reef. I had just one more famous region to complete the set – the Snowy River, a nationally and internationally recognised symbol of a wild and free river. Flowing from the high country down to the coast, it is part of Australia's folklore heritage. The Snowy Mountains and the Snowy River are the locale of Australia's legendary man of the mountains.

The Man from Snowy River is one of Australia's most famous poems written by one of Australia's most famous poets. It tells the story tells of a valuable horse which escapes to the bush. When its owners offer a princely sum for its safe return, the 'best' riders in the area gather to pursue the wild bush horses and separate the valuable horse from the mob. But the rough countryside defeats them all – except for The Man from Snowy River. His personal courage and skill has turned The Man into a legend.

An ominous sign – turning towards Buchan and the Snowy Mountains

Our route was to take us deep into the Australian high country, through the Alpine and Kosciuszko national parks, along the banks of the Snowy River and then up and out, rejoining the river once more at Jindabyne. The journey into the highland wilderness on a dirt track was the final adventurous clause. I was determined that this last high hurdle was not going to defeat us either.

The somewhat inauspicious start involved an easy, steady ascent through bushland and small holdings before dropping down to Buchan, one of Victoria's oldest towns, set beside a river of the same name. The degree of difficulty wound up a few notches out of the Buchan valley, then down again to Murrindal Creek before ascending all the way up on to Butcher's Ridge.

Now only four days from the finish, I had to coordinate our arrival at Parliament House with various arrangements for greeting us. As we ascended and descended in and out of mobile phone range, I kept tabs on the situation, often compelled to stop to answer a call just as I was busting myself near the summit of a long climb. Usually out of breath, I conversed, to name a few, with the head of security at Parliament House, with the secretary of Senator Bob McMullan, the politician who was going to greet us, with a representative from the Australian Association for Environmental Education, who was helping to arrange for a group of school children to meet us, and with my PR person. It was all becoming quite complex, and I needed to get it right.

My office was different with every stop. I could only get a reception on the high ground and as I spoke I looked out on spectacular vistas across the valleys. It was always difficult to restart and find a rhythm again. The road dropped down, down, and further down from Butcher's Ridge to Butcher's Creek and then Gelantipy Creek. As usual, there is always a sting in the tail and the final climb for the day to Karoonda Park at Gelantipy was as steep as a scorpion's tail in defence mode.

Just before the Snowy River Road turn-off we reached the recently defunct Wulgulmerang service station, now marked by a heap of scrap metal and junk – rusting petrol bowsers, a boat, some old caravans and, more worryingly, a cluster of wrecked bicycles. The bitumen gradually phased out over the next few kilometres, and it was gravel all the way after the Benambra turn-off. The open farmland also petered out as we ascended once more and at Hamilton Gap the scenery changed dramatically. The devastating fires, fuelled by eucalyptus vapours, which swept through the region in 2003 had temporarily tamed the wild mountains. Tipped with the delicate new foliage, the bush was slowly restoring itself to its former glory.

We had to take care descending to Suggan Buggan, the most isolated hamlet on the Victorian frontier. The narrow track dropped away steeply and missing a turn could have spelt the end for one of us over the cliff face. We listened carefully for any oncoming vehicles and then realised there was no need to do so as the roar of an engine labouring up the pass would echo, ping-pong fashion, between the mountains. As on the Bloomfield Track up in the Daintree, the path away from the old school house beside the idyllic Buggan River was so steep in places that it had to be tarmacked to prevent it from washing away. At the most vertical stage I almost lifted my laden front wheel off the ground as I applied power.

Once over the Monaro Gap, we were able for the first time to view the broad Snowy River valley in all its glory. But the amount of heavy braking to control our 'mechanical horses' down the slopes of the past couple of days had taken its toll: both of us were aware of an alarming depreciation in brake function. Halfway down to the valley floor, I realised that Greg, who had been following behind, was nowhere to be seen. I waited for many worrying minutes before he re-appeared at a snail's pace from around a curve. In the antithesis of the spirit of the Snowy River horsemen, both feet dragged along the ground to prevent him careering over the edge. Inserting a new single brake pad did the trick. My brakes were only marginally better but I decided not to waste the daylight hours, to continue conservatively, and to fix the problem at the end of the afternoon. We dropped a long way down to the valley through a proliferation of Cypress Pine trees on the lower slopes and to the Snowy River at Gattamurg Ford. After all that effort, we had descended to just 205 metres above sea level.

Someone at Gelantipy mentioned that once we reached Willis at the state border, we could expect to enjoy a flat run beside the symbolic river. They were partially right. The scene was awe-inspiring and because the track was a slow, difficult road, we enjoyed it all to ourselves. Our informant, however, failed to mention that the track was spiked with continuous energy-sapping sorties up into the hillsides.

In light of only my front brake working, I was travelling with the utmost of care. All the same, just after the New South Wales border, I came unstuck – without warning, my wheels disappeared from under me as the steep hairpin dropped away. I had no chance to react before I pitched onto the road, where sharp grit skinned my elbow, wrist, shoulder and hip. In shock, I lay motionless, head first down the slope. Taking, stock of my situation, I assessed that all bones seemed to be intact and that my head and feet still pointed in the same direction. I was lucky: it could have been much worse. My bike was fine too. Greg raced back to see what had happened. Over the last ten years spent working as a mountain bike tour guide, he had become pretty good at patching up grazed bodies. The elbow wounds were deep and I preferred to look the other way as he scrubbed hard to dig out the stones before dousing the affected parts with antiseptic. I was fortunate to have such a friend to help share the load, in all respects, during the last few days.

The crash had dashed my confidence. For the rest of the afternoon I tensed with fear, moving like a novice with wobbly trainer wheels. I rounded each bend with the turning circle of a 50-metre road train rather than a Snowy Mountains thoroughbred. What did Robert say about taking extra care towards the end of the expedition? The incident had caused us to lose a fair bit of time and as we paused at Jack's Lookout we could see menacing-looking grey clouds gathering down the valley. The river valley at that point was so enormous that its trickle of water appeared almost insignificant in comparison. The Man from Snowy River may have tamed the hillsides, but it was the Snowy Mountains Hydro-Electric Scheme which tamed the waters. By the time the 25-year project was complete in 1974, the mighty river had been dammed, some say damned, so that only one per cent of its original flow escaped below the final barrier at Jindabyne. With its flow and ecology so severely altered, the river no longer represents the symbol of a wild and free waterway. Many claim its folklore heritage and its ideology of courage, skill and spirit barely survive with the miserly trickle of today.

After the crash

The Snowy River from Jack's Lookout – a shadow of its former glory

The Snowy Mountains Hydro-Electric Scheme is by far the largest engineering project ever undertaken in Australia. It is also one of the biggest and most complex hydro-electric schemes in the world. Its sixteen dams, seven power stations, a pumping station and 225 km of tunnels, aqueducts and pipelines cover an area of over 5000 square kilometres. The system's construction is seen by many as a defining point in Australia's history, an iconic symbol of a different kind, signifying Australia's identity as an independent, multicultural and resourceful country. When Europe was reeling from the effects of World War II, the scheme provided opportunities for more than 100 000 people from over thirty countries who came to the mountains to work on the project. The purpose of the scheme is to collect water from melting snow and rain in the Snowy Mountains. Where once most of this water used to flow into the Snowy River, it is now diverted through tunnels in the mountains and stored in dams. The water is also used for irrigation that makes drought-prone regions in the western rain-shadow of the Great Dividing Range productive. The bulk of the water eventually flows into the Murray and Murrumbidgee rivers.

In relation to the economic and political components of the sustainability issue(s), the Snowy Mountains Hydro-Electric Scheme is very much a success. The environmental and social viewpoints are more divided. The non-polluting, renewable hydro-energy produces enough power to displace more than 5 million tonnes of greenhouse gases that contribute to global warming every year. The irrigation sustains dozens of communities, some new in the region. Inundation of the land upstream from Jindabyne caused a major loss of heritage for Indigenous Australians and existing towns and farms. Below the dams, the ecology of the river has been collapsing ever since and those who once relied on its flow for their water supply have been seriously disadvantaged. From our vantage point, the river flow certainly looked low, a shadow of its former glory, even though the McLaughlin, Jacobs, Pinch and Quidong rivers feed into it upstream of that point.

In 1998, the New South Wales and Victorian governments set up the Snowy Water Inquiry to find a solution that balanced these environmental, economic and social factors. The governments agreed to restore 21 per cent of the original flow to the Snowy River by the year 2010. Much of the increase could be returned by improving the efficiency of the scheme's water use, adjustments similar to those I witnessed being made on the Murray River. Eventually, the river flows will be restored to 28 per cent, the minimum amount that scientists say the river needs to return it to good health.

◆ ◆ ◆

We made it to Jacob's River with little light left and pitched the tent for the last time. A family of eastern grey kangaroos, obviously accustomed to campers, blended in with the bush as they grazed nearby, rather less nervously than most wild kangaroos. Greg hit the sack straight after (thankfully) our final 'Pasta Mediterranean', and was soon snoring away as usual. Restless, as had been my usual state over the past few weeks, I sat out in the moonlight, observing the possums scavenge the campsite for morsels. They were far bolder than the roos. After a refreshing dip in the chilly river, I listened to the water as it babbled away toward the Snowy. My fresh war wounds throbbed a bit but my mind now occupied itself by running through landmark events and places I had visited during the last nine-and-a-half months.

It was an inspiring train of thought. I started by singling out specific places of beauty, but then realised (and came to appreciate to an even greater degree

Delicate alpine flowers

later) that what I most enjoy is the memory of the actual journey to reach them. The expedition had linked all these wonderful highlights together. My satisfaction comes from making a line on a map come to life, seeing an idea through to its fruition. Cycling through my own country connects the best and the worst times, joins the deserts to the great forests, mountains to the sea, history to the present, Dreamtime to folklore, environmental blunders to foresight and positive innovations, farms to the cities and the extremes of weather conditions. The Blue Mountains, Kata Tjuta, the Twelve Apostles, Cable Beach, Sydney Harbour or the Ubirr Rock paintings in Kakadu are no longer separate picture postcards; rather they are pieces of a wider picture. The photographs I took of the people I met are not just faces – they are real Australians, whose

Greg recording the scene from Wallace Craigie Lookout

interactions, typically of kindness and generosity, helped form a multi-dimensional, constantly evolving portrait of the whole country.

Perhaps in light of these thoughts, the following morning I approached Jacob's Ladder, the first obstacle on the penultimate full day of cycling, with a little more vigour than the previous day. We climbed through the cloud line and out of the Snowy River Valley to the Wallace Craigie Lookout, almost 900 metres up. The track continued to ascend for five or six kilometres before levelling out somewhat, then broke into a testing roller-coaster course to completely finish my legs off. Ingebyra signified the end of the wild country with the reappearance of small properties. We celebrated the start of the tarmac by polishing off the last of the ginger nuts. (I wouldn't be eating ginger nuts for quite some time post-expedition – or sachets of 'Tuna Tempters' or family packs of pasta.) Making good time to Jindabyne and 'civilisation', we quickly sought the comfort of the cafes in the centre of the relatively up-market ski village for some classier treats – well-deserved cake and a latte. The original town was lost with the inundation of Lake Jindabyne. Its remains, submerged beneath the lake, can

Lake Jindabyne

occasionally be glimpsed when water levels are low. We crossed the main barrage wall, rounded the southern shores of the lake and rode out of town on the Kosciuszko Road, destination Berridale – apparently the 'Crossroads of the Snowy Mountains'.

The Monaro region embraces roughly from where we crossed into New South Wales on the Barry Highway virtually up to Canberra, a long strip between the Snowy Mountains, which form its western border, and the coastal Kybean Range. 'Monaro', an Indigenous word meaning 'treeless plains', specifically describes the dominant natural temperate grasslands which carpet the high country, rising and falling between 800 and 1400 metres above sea level. On our final full day, it seemed fitting that we crossed the Great Divide for the last time, going over the Monaro Range on the way to Cooma, the principal town in the region. Trees struggled to push up through the subterranean layer of volcanic rock as the shallow crust of fertile soil mainly supports the grassland. Vast, open paddocks were studded with outcrops of granite boulders and graced with the odd snowgum. The most ancient snowgums stood tortured and gnarled, sculpted by the weight of snow, the ferocity of the wind, the severity of the Cooma winter frosts and the heat of summer. They had been clinging precariously to life for a century or more. Others had lost the fight altogether but remained as glorious memorials even in death. In contrast, the younger, healthier trees stood tall and proud. They were in the midst of shedding their sun-damaged pink-orange bark, gradually giving birth to a fresh 'winter coat' in preparation for repelling the cold.

My emotions undulated with the lie of the land. From Berridale and sporadically throughout the day, my thoughts resembled the contorted old snowgums, struggling to survive. This unsettled mental state really affected my strength and stamina: my legs felt like planks of dead wood and I spent most of the day in a lather of perspiration. This was not how it was meant to be. I tried to gather up all those debilitating thoughts and shove them in the 'too hard basket', to be dealt with after the expedition. This was a time when I should have been soaking up the final few hours in the saddle, taking it all in. The landscape should have been passing by in slow motion and I should have been flooded with feelings of elation and pride. Those feelings were certainly in there, I just had to search a little harder to locate and release them.

Certainly the weather and the scenery helped. We had a warm tailwind encouraging us along and the landscape was inspiring as we followed the tree-lined valley of the Murrumbidgee River. I occupied my mind compiling lists of things I would and wouldn't miss when the expedition was over – in less than twenty-four hours. In no particular order, I certainly wouldn't miss: the flies, a constantly sore backside, headwinds, the rigmarole of packing and unpacking – squeezing everything into those four small panniers – wearing the same worn-out, smelly clothes every day, the almost constant veil of tiredness, camping food, and people claiming that I was mad without at least trying to understand what I was doing. I would miss the things which make all those annoyances worth bearing: the adventure, the space and time, the simplicity, the clarity of the desert, the characters I met along the journey, the supreme, 'indestructible' feeling of fitness, the satisfaction and the natural high at the end of every day's effort. This last-mentioned was to the fore by the time we reached Greg's friend's place in Queanbeyan. My thoughts at that point more resembled the younger, healthy snowgum, shedding its old weathered shell to reveal a fresh, more resilient coat. I had pruned the dead wood and was excited, ready for the finale.

◆　◆　◆

The Big Day was finally here. All we had to do was to cycle about twenty kilometres from Queanbeyan into the capital city, make an appearance on the ABC's Breakfast radio program and then complete the final run up Parliament Hill to meet a welcoming party in the forecourt of Parliament House. The plan was straightforward, the theory simple.

We set off in plenty of time and carved our way through the traffic, handling our loads a little more adeptly than when we had made our way to Parliament House for the start of the journey. Some parts of both bikes and bodies were beautifully worn in, others were plain worn out. Body and bike had virtually become one. Judging by the state of both, no one would have needed to call on forensics to determine the authenticity of my journey. Scratched and dented, the bike no longer gleamed as it did on the frosty autumn morning last May. Grazed and bruised, my bronzed skin held together a body that had changed composition somewhat. I didn't look haggard or gaunt as many expected; in fact, I was more of a strong, well-oiled fighting machine – with a little extra oil required for my right knee. The great wads of dressings which covered my battle scars were the only physical clue to my vulnerability. Perhaps these would serve to attract more of a sympathy vote when I reached Parliament House.

My mind was so busy it almost short circuited. One part had to concentrate on the task at hand: staying alive and keeping the morning schedule on track. Another part 'looked over my shoulder', randomly flashing back to experiences and events of the journey, rewinding and fast forwarding. A *mélange* of emotions unravelled like a trail of DNA, an individual genetic fingerprint. Yet another part 'looked far ahead'. For me, it wasn't a question of what I would do when I finished, but what I should do first. I had all those valuable 'raw materials' to make sense of and then communicate. At the same time there were more ideas and new plans evolving. In choosing to undertake the GRACE Expedition, I had to leave behind my comfort zone. During its nine-and-a-half months' length, the expedition had become my way of life and I had slotted into a different comfort zone. Now I was going to have to break out of that to re-establish 'normality' – whatever that was. Going home wasn't going to be as I had expected but I needed to face that too.

The trouble with looking behind for too long, or looking too far ahead, is that you either fall off or lose your way. I had already done the falling off trick but in trying to find the ABC radio station, we lost our way and took the wrong bridge over the lake. The circular street plan of Canberra was just as confusing as the thoughts and feelings which revolved in my head. Eventually establishing our location, we realised we had a further seven kilometres to go to reach the studio. It was a mad dash and we took the law unto ourselves to make the interview on time, wheeling our bikes straight in to the studio, only slightly late. I started by claiming that I had found my way cycling 25 000 km around the country to be there, through remote desert tracks in the outback, over the mountains, through cities and even through bushfires, only to be defeated by the Canberra road system.

In the meantime, my sister had phoned to say that her flight had been delayed. Mum and Jane were flying in from Perth and it was going to be touch and go as to whether they would arrive in time for the official finish. Greg and I found a cafe within easy range of Parliament House and tried to chill out while we waited. We couldn't delay our arrival because there were others with busy schedules waiting for us. There were definitely going to be some press there this time. As before the official start of the journey, I tried to rehearse some of the answers to the likely questions: Why have you just you just pedalled 25 000 km?

What is sustainability? Why is it important? What was the highlight of the expedition? What was the worst experience? Did you ever want to give up? These were all simple-seeming questions, but the project was so big and my mind so clouded with emotion that it was often difficult to summarise in a few sentences what I wanted to say.

The plane arrived, a hire car collected and my sister also probably took liberties with the traffic laws as she practised her rally-driving skills through unfamiliar streets and into town, my mother navigating. They were going to make it in the nick of time – or that is what we hoped as we set off back over the lake, passing the Old Parliament House and up the hill.

Like a Pro Hart composition, at the last minute all the parts of the reception party seemed to fall into place to produce a memorable scene. Children from the Campbell Primary School formed a guard of honour and politicians Bob McMullen and Mick Gentleman waited at its head to greet us. The end of the expedition was celebrated with a fitting representative collection of people. The children, future voters, are the ones most affected by how we approach issues of sustainability. Education from a young age forms habits for life and if the GRACE Project has contributed towards inspiring at least some to be proactive, then the effort has been worthwhile. Meeting the politicians was a publicity stunt aimed at getting the message across to the people who make the decisions. There were members of supporting groups such as the Australian Association for Environmental Education and representatives from television stations and newspapers.

My mother and sister made it – just. They were all smiles and waited patiently, proudly holding my bike until I had met everyone else and we could share some quality time. I am fortunate to have such unconditional love and support. Greg was the most important other member of the team. There were many who contributed but Greg was also prepared to leave his comfort zone, be away from his partner for four months and resign from his job because he believed in the cause (and has a healthy sense of adventure).

The success of the project is difficult to quantify. The concept worked. I had to fight hard to maintain that cycling unsupported is a model for sustainability. Various extremes in conditions made it a fine balancing act at times. I couldn't have done it on my own, without a network of team members, supporters, sponsors and the many wonderful Australians who put me up, fed and watered me, and generally took care of me. There is a high level of mutual respect out there.

An essential part of making decisions on sustainability issues is realising that everything is connected. In the same way, the environmental, economic, social and political components of each issue are linked, although it is often a real struggle to strike the optimum balance, more like dragging the bike over the fiery desert sands rather than cruising down smooth tarmac with a tailwind. The project has certainly made a contribution toward motivating people to be more proactive: I've tried to spread the message during the school visits, via radio, television and newspaper appearances at local, state and national levels, and through the website. Determining the level of that effect is a bit like asking how long is a piece of string. My answer would be: take a piece of string – a good arm span's length – yank it a few times to test its tensile strength. Then take a map of Australia and arrange the string so that it represents the route of the Great Australian Cycle Expedition, and so that the ends meet in Canberra. The few strands which frayed when the cord was tugged represent the hiccups – not everything ran perfectly smoothly. By and large, the string retains its strength so that when the ends are tied, the energy can continue to flow around the loop. I hope, as with this analogy, the energy I have invested in this project has a long-lasting effect.

The word GRACE has many meanings. In the case of this project, GRACE not only serves as an acronym for the Great Australian Cycle Expedition, grace is also a mantra which can help make our world a better place. When dehydrated and exhausted on the Canning Stock Route, when shaken to bits and short of water on the Gunbarrel Highway, when enduring all the ten-hour, into-the-wind days, when at the base of a long, steep climb, when personally distraught as I was for the last 5000 km, it was the ability to find the beauty and the positive side of each challenging situation which carried me through. With grace we can find beauty in everything, at every level. That is what GRACE is about.

The small group posed together for photographs standing on the mosaic in front of the entrance of Parliament House – an Indigenous representation of 'Kamberry'; a meeting place and where the ends of the expedition came together – *out there and back*.

All that was left to do now was to roll back down the hill to the same cafe so that we could crack open a bottle of champagne.

At the finish with Senator Bob McMullen (left), Mick Gentleman, MLA, my mother and sister, standing on the Indigenous mosaic depicting Canberra as a meeting place

Epilogue

While this book provides a snapshot of many of the issues concerning sustainable development which I encountered on my journey, Australia is, of course, just one 'state' of the global community. In February 2007, Koichiro Matsuura, the Director-General of UNESCO, outlined the world-wide situation during an important speech entitled, 'Let us make peace with the Earth'. Here is an edited version of what he said.

We know now that our civilisation, our species, and even our planet may not be immortal. This is not the first ecological crisis that humanity has lived through, to be sure; but there can be no doubt it is the first that is so wide – indeed, world-wide – in scope.

What are we doing to safeguard the future of the Earth and its biosphere? What are the challenges to be met? What solutions can we offer?

First and foremost, climate change and global warming: by the end of the century this planet could be hotter by an amount between 1.5°C and 5.8°C. Such a warming of the climate threatens many parts of the world, and is liable to provoke further disasters from the proliferation of tropical storms to the drowning of whole island states or coastal regions.

Next comes desertification, already affecting a third of the world's land. At the end of the 20th century almost one billion people in 110 countries were threatened by encroaching deserts: the figure might well double by 2050, when two billion could be affected.

Deforestation is continuing, too, though primary and tropical forests are home to the greater part of the world's biodiversity, and we know they help to combat climate change as well as slowing soil erosion.

The whole biosphere is threatened by pollution: pollution of air and water, oceans and soils, chemical pollution and invisible pollution. In Asia alone, the World Bank estimates the cost in human life of atmospheric pollution at 1.56 million deaths a year.

There is a world water crisis that cannot be ignored. Two billion people will face water shortages in 2025 – three billion, in all likelihood, by 2050. Lastly, biodiversity is endangered: species are becoming extinct a hundred times faster than the mean natural rate, and 50 per cent of all species could be gone by 2100. Yet biodiversity is essential to the cycle of life, to human health and to the security of our food supply.

This situation brings a serious risk of war and other conflicts, and demands a global response. Sustainable development concerns us all: it is a necessary condition for any effective fight against poverty, not least because it is the poorest who will suffer the worst of the droughts and other natural disasters to come.

Today, though, we understand that our war on nature is a world war. That is the meaning of the Stern Report on the economic consequences of climate change. If we do not take immediate action to combat global warming, we can expect to forgo between five and twenty per cent of world GDP. Who says sustainable development costs too much? 'Business as usual' is what threatens to ruin us! Javier Perez de Cuellar began our 21st Century Dialogues with a clear warning: 'How can we know, yet be unable – or unwilling – to act?'.

It can no longer be argued that 'sustainability' and 'development' are conflicting goals, nor that tackling poverty is incompatible with conserving ecosystems. We are going to have to fight on every front at once.

We shall also have to invent new and far more wisely restrained modes of growth and consumption. The idea is not, of course, to stop growth entirely, to bring about the quickest possible shift in its nature towards less material forms of wealth, reducing our consumption of raw materials in every area of production. There must also be far greater awareness of the devastating potential of global warming; and that awareness must result in compliance with the measures laid down in the Kyoto protocol.

It would also be useful to promote a right to clean drinking water, laying a proper foundation for the ethical governance of water so that it becomes possible both to control demand and to manage it better, as well as improving water quality through careful use, proper treatment and recycling.

UNESCO is actively engaged on many fronts in promoting sustainable water policies, fostering education in this area and encouraging the global protection of biodiversity not least through its world-wide network of 'biosphere reserves'. They have truly become experimental laboratories for ecosystem conservation and the rational use of natural resources at local level.

I have also in mind UNESCO's many operations in the South (developing countries) to help with the training of experts and managers; for there is a cruel lack of trained professionals and educated policy makers properly aware of the links between water, poverty, health, culture and development. Cultural aspects and education are often neglected in environmental thinking and policy: yet education and culture are two essential factors in any sustainable development.

The call for us, today, to put an end to the War on Nature is a call for an unprecedented solidarity with future generations. Perhaps, in order to achieve this, humanity needs to make a new pact, a 'Natural Contract' of co-development with the planet, and an armistice with nature?

We need the wisdom to champion an ethic of the future, for such an ethic must prevail if we are to make peace with the Earth. This planet is our mirror image: if it is wounded, then we are wounded; if it is mutilated, human kind is mutilated as well. To change direction, we have to create knowledge societies that can combine tackling poverty with investing in education, research and innovation; in doing so, we lay the foundations of a true ethic of responsibility.

Appendix

GRACE Expedition distances

Date	From	To	km (tarmac)	km (gravel)	Total km
May-10	Canberra	Goulburn	99		99
11	Goulburn	Abercrombie River	70	10	80
12	Abercrombie River	Hampton	91	15	106
13	Hampton	Sydney	163		163
14-15	Sydney				0
16	Sydney	Wollombi	132		132
17	Wollombi	Hawks Nest	138		138
18	Hawks Nest	Gloucester	70	38	108
19	Gloucester	Nowendoc	80		80
20	Nowendoc	Armidale	141		141
21	Armidale	Yaraandoo Env. Centre	77		77
22	Yaraandoo	Coutt's Crossing (Grafton)	121		121
23	Coutt's Crossing	Woodburn	119		119
24	Woodburn	Byron Bay	82		82
25	Byron Bay	Wiangaree	108		108
26	Wiangaree	Brisbane	124		124
27-28	Brisbane				0
29	Brisbane	Ravensbourne	103		103
30	Ravensbourne	Dalby	122		122
31	Dalby	Miles	131		131
		May totals	1971	63	2034
		GRACE totals	1971	63	2034
Jun-01	Miles	Roma	145		145
2	Roma	Ridgelands (Injune + 25 km)	117		117
3	Ridgelands	Carnarvon Gorge	113	18	131
4	Carnarvon Gorge				0
5	Carnarvon Gorge	Rollerston + 30 km	103		103
6	Rolleston + 30 km	Anakie	151		151
7	Anakie	Alpha	132		132
8	Alpha	Barcaldine	145		145
9	Barcaldine	Longreach	113		113
10	Longreach	Winton	185		185
11	Winton				0
12	Winton	Kynuna	168		168
13	Kynuna	McKinley + 45 km	125		125
14	McKinley + 45 km	Cloncurry	66		66
15	Cloncurry	Quamby	50		50

Maximum daily temperatures (°C)

	40+		35-39		30-34		25-29		20-24		Below 20

Date	From	To	km (tarmac)	km (gravel)	Total km
16	Quamby	Burke and Wills R/house	141		141
17	Burke and Wills R/house	Flinders River	141		141
18	Flinders River	Leichhardt's Lagoon	90		90
19	Leichhardt's Lagoon	Croydon	135		135
20	Croydon	Georgetown	152		152
21	Georgetown	Mt Surprise	96		96
22	Mt Surprise	Mt Garnet	126		126
23	Mt Garnet	Malanda	84	11	95
24	Malanda	Cairns	82		82
25	Cairns				0
26	Cairns	Port Douglas	74		74
27	Port Douglas	Woobadda River (Daintree)	70	39	109
28	Woobadda River	Cooktown	46	41	87
29	Cooktown	Old Laura	16	95	111
30	Old Laura	Hann River R/house		104	104
		June totals	2884	290	3174
		GRACE totals	4855	353	5208
Jul-01	Hann River R/house	New Bamboo Station		81	81
2	New Bamboo Station	Coen		93	93
3	Coen	Archer River + 40 km	25	84	109
4	Archer River + 40 km	Bramwell R/house		124	124
5	Bramwell R/house	Eliot Falls		87	87
6	Eliot Falls	Bamaga	5	94	99
7	Bamaga	The Tip		44	44
8-14	Thursday Is/Horn Is	Cairns/Perth/Cairns/Karumba	7	2	9
15	Karumba	Burke + Wills camp 119	77	38	115
16	Burke + Wills camp 119	Leichhardt Falls		120	120
17	Leichhardt Falls	Tirranna R/house	40	68	108
18	Tirranna R/house	Hell's Gate R/house		148	148
19	Hell's Gate	Calvert Road junction		117	117
20	Calvert Road junction	Snake Lagoon		135	135
21	Snake Lagoon	Borroloola		80	80
22	Borroloola	Batten Creek		85	85
23	Batten Creek	Butterfly Spring		97	97
24	Butterfly Spring	Lomarieum Lagoon		129	129
25	Lomarieum Lagoon	Roper Bar + 40 km		115	115
26	Roper Bar + 40 km	Mataranka Station	157		157
27	Mataranka Station				0
28	Mataranka Station	Katherine	94		94
29	Katherine	Nitmiluk (and return)	61		61
30	Katherine	Mary River R/house	151		151
31	Mary River R/house	Maguk (Barramundi Gorge)	54	12	66
		July totals	671	1753	2424
		GRACE totals	5526	2106	7632
Aug-01	Maguk	Jabiru	98	13	111
2	Jabiru	East Alligator River (return)	92		92
3	Jabiru	Bark Hut Inn	138		138
4	Bark Hut Inn	Darwin	117		117
5-7	Darwin				0
8	Darwin	Wangi Falls (Litchfield NP)	97	44	141

Date	From	To	km (tarmac)	km (gravel)	Total km
9	Wangi Falls	Adelaide River	118		118
10	Adelaide River	Pine Creek	130		130
11	Pine Creek	Katherine	91		91
12	Katherine	Willeroo Station	125		125
13	Willeroo Station	Buchanan Highway camp	140	4	144
14	Buchanan Highway camp	Victoria River Downs Station		109	109
15	Victoria River Downs				0
16	Victoria River Downs	Pigeon Hole Station		73	73
17	Pigeon Hole Station	Lajamanu turn-off + 5 km	40	71	111
18	Lajamanu turn-off + 5 km	Lajamanu		101	101
19	Lajamanu	Suplejack Road camp		74	74
20	Suplejack Road camp	Suplejack Downs Station		79	79
21	Suplejack Downs Station	Tanami Mine		92	92
22	Tanami Mine	The Granites (via Rabbit Flat)		102	102
23	The Granites Mine				0
24	The Granites Mine	Renahan's Bore + 23 km		125	125
25	Renahan's Bore + 23 km	Yuendumu		135	135
26	Yuendumu	Tilmouth R/house		107	107
27	Tilmouth R/house	Hamilton Downs turn-off camp	100	39	139
28	Hamilton Downs camp	Alice Springs	54		54
29-31	Alice Springs				0
		August totals	1340	1168	2508
		GRACE totals	6866	3274	10 140
Sep-01	Alice Springs	Finke River camp	124		124
2	Finke River camp	Mt Ebenezer	133		133
3	Mt Ebenezer	Curtin Springs	105		105
4	Curtin Springs	Yulara	88		88
5	Yulara	Uluru/Kata Tjuta/Docker River Rd	90	6	96
6	Docker River Road camp	Little Puta Puta Road camp		98	98
7	Little Puta Puta Rd camp	Docker River camp		88	88
8	Docker River camp	Warakurna		99	99
9	Warakurna	nr Jamieson Rd turn-off camp		110	110
10	nr Jamieson Rd turn-off camp	Warburton		122	122
11	Warburton				0
12	Warburton	Heather Highway camp		104	104
13	Heather Highway camp	28 km before Camp Beadell		61	61
14	28 km before Camp Beadell	nr Mt Everard		76	76
15	nr Mt Everard	Geraldton Bore + 21 km		66	66
16	Geraldton Bore + 21 km	88 km before Carnegie		97	97
17	88 km before Carnegie	Carnegie Station		88	88
18	Carnegie Station	Wongawol Station		129	129
19	Wongawol Station	Leaman's Bore		102	102
20	Leaman's Bore	Wiluna		113	113
21-22	Wiluna				0
23	Wiluna	The Granites, Tank 2A		82	82
24	The Granites, Tank 2A	Well 4A		100	100
25	Well 4A	Well 8		92	92
26	Well 8	Lake Aerodrome		85	85

Maximum daily temperatures (°C)

40+	35-39	30-34	25-29	20-24	Below 20

Date	From	To	km (tarmac)	km (gravel)	Total km
27	Lake Aerodrome	5.7 km before Well 15		72	72
28	5.7 km before Well 15	Calvert Range turn-off		51	51
29	Calvert Range turn-off	Durba Spring		30	30
30	Durba Spring				0
		September totals	540	1871	2411
		GRACE totals	7406	5145	12 551
Oct-01	Durba Spring	Well 19 + 3 km		63	63
2	Well 19 + 3 km	Well 21 turn-off		59	59
3	Well 21 turn-off	Well 24 (Curara Soaks)		82	82
4	Well 24 (Curara Soaks)	Canning camp 1907		58	58
5	Canning camp 1907	Well 28 + 17 km		66	66
6	Well 28 + 17 km	Nurgurga Soak		70	70
7	Nurgurga Soak	Well 33 (Gunowaggi)		61	61
8	Well 33 (Gunowaggi)				0
9	Well 33 (Gunowaggi)	nr Bungabinni native well		60	60
10	nr Bungabinni native well	Well 37 (Libral) + 15 km		48	48
11	Well 37 (Libral) + 15 km	Well 39		52	52
12	Well 39	nr Gunowarba native well turn-off		53	53
13	nr Gunowarba turn-off	Well 42 (Guli Tank) + 14 km		57	57
14	Well 42 (Guli Tank) + 14 km	FT 65 (survey marker)		61	61
15	FT 65 (survey marker)	Crescent Ridge + 11 km		66	66
16	Crescent Ridge + 11 km	Well 49		72	72
17	Well 49	Well 51 (Weriaddo) + 18 km		70	70
18	Well 51 (Weriaddo) + 18 km	Stretch Lagoon		66	66
19	Stretch Lagoon	Wolfe Creek Crater turn-off + 20 km		84	84
20	Wolfe Creek Crater turn-off + 20 km	Halls Creek	16	95	111
21-22	Halls Creek				0
23	Halls Creek	Larrawa Station	152	5	157
24	Larrawa Station	Fitzroy Crossing	143	5	148
25	Fitzroy Crossing	Geikie Gorge	24		24
26	Fitzroy Crossing	Leopold Downs Station	40	46	86
27	Leopold Downs Station	Windjana Gorge		70	70
28	Windjana Gorge	Derby	67	85	152
29	Derby				0
30	Derby	Nillibubbica roadside stop	120		120
31	Nillibubbica roadside stop	Broome	109		109
		October totals	671	1454	2125
		GRACE totals	8077	6599	14 676
1-7 Nov	Broome				0
8	Broome	Munro Springs Station	153	5	158
9	Munro Springs Station	Anna Plains Station	85		85
10	Anna Plains Station	Mandora Station	109		109
11	Mandora Station	Pardoo Station	152		152
12	Pardoo Station	Port Hedland	120		120
13	Port Hedland				0
14	Port Hedland	Whim Creek	119		119
15	Whim Creek	Karratha	126		126
16	Karratha	Fortescue River R/house	116		116
17	Fortescue River R/house	nr Parry Range camp	131		131
18	nr Parry Range camp	Barradale/Yannarie River	109		109

Date	From	To	km (tarmac)	km (gravel)	Total km
19	Barradale/Yannarie River	Mia Mia Station	96		96
20	Mia Mia Station	Boologooro Station	127		127
21	Boologooro Station	Carnarvon	80		80
22	Carnarvon				0
23	Carnarvon	Wooramel Station	125		125
24	Wooramel Station	Hamelin Station	112		112
25	Hamelin Station	Denham	119		119
26	Denham				0
27	Denham/Overlander Roadhouse	Galena Bridge (Murchison River)	169		169
28	Galena Bridge	Geraldton	117		117
29	Geraldton				0
30	Geraldton	Dongara + 55 km	124		124
		November totals	2289	5	2294
		GRACE totals	10 366	6604	16 970
Dec-01	Dongara + 55 km	Moora	164		164
2	Moora	Goomalling/Condering Farm	143	10	153
3	Goomalling/Condering Farm	Ullaring Rock	20	5	25
4-5	Ullaring Rock				0
6	Ullaring Rock	York/Northam	99	7	106
7	Northam	Perth	103		103
8-13	Perth				0
14	Perth	North Dandalup	77	2	79
15	North Dandalup				0
16	North Dandalup	Eaton/Bunbury	111		111
17	Bunbury	Yallingup	108		108
18	Yallingup	Margaret River	45		45
19	Margaret River	(ill)			0
20	Margaret River	Pemberton	146		146
21	Pemberton	Walpole	99	20	119
22	Walpole	Albany	122		122
23	Albany	Stirling Ranges	87	6	93
24	Stirling Ranges	Jerramungup	98		98
25	Jerramungup	Jerdacuttup River camp	136		136
26	Jerdacuttup River camp	Esperance	155		155
27	Esperance				0
28	Esperance	Grass Patch	99		99
29	Grass Patch	Norseman	129		129
30	Norseman	Fraser Range Station	106	2	108
31	Fraser Range Station	Balladonia + 70 km	163	2	165
		December totals	2210	54	2264
		GRACE totals	12 576	6658	19 234
1-Jan-05	Balladonia + 70 km camp	Cocklebiddy	182		182
2	Cocklebiddy	Madura + 40 km camp	134		134
3	Madura + 40 km camp	Border Village + 68 km camp	228		228
4	Border Village + 68 km	Nullarbor Roadhouse	125		125
5	Nullarbor R/house	Nundroo	148		148
6	Nundroo	Ceduna	155		155
7-8	Ceduna				0

Maximum daily temperatures (°C)

	40+		35-39		30-34		25-29		20-24		Below 20

Date	From	To	km (tarmac)	km (gravel)	Total km
9	Ceduna	Streaky Bay	119		119
10	Streaky Bay	Elliston	128		128
11	Elliston	Wangary/Port Lincoln	129		129
12	Port Lincoln				0
13	Port Lincoln	Arno Bay	125		125
14	Arno Bay	Whyalla	161		161
15	Whyalla	Wilmington	125		125
16	Wilmington	Yacka	115		115
17	Yacka	Adelaide	175		175
18-19	Adelaide				0
20	Adelaide	Murray Bridge	84		84
21	Murray Bridge	Waikerie	165		165
22	Waikerie	Loxton	79		79
23	Loxton	Mildura	176		176
24	Mildura	Tempy	137		137
25	Tempy	Warracknabeal	125		125
26	Warracknabeal	Cavendish	168		168
27	Cavendish	Portland	120		120
28	Portland				0
29	Portland	Warrnambool	110		110
30	Warrnambool	Lavers Hill	125		125
31	Lavers Hill	Anglesea	128		128
		January totals	3466	0	3466
		GRACE totals	16 042	6658	22 700
Feb-01	Anglesea	Melbourne	133		133
2-6	Melbourne				0
7	Melbourne/Devonport	Perth/Leighlands	129		129
8	Leighlands	Bicheno	156		156
9	Bicheno	Orford	105		105
10	Orford	Hobart	80		80
11	Hobart				0
12	Hobart	Cockle Creek	107	20	127
13	Cockle Creek	Hobart	107	22	129
14	Hobart				0
15	Hobart	Tarraleah	137		137
16	Tarraleah	Queenstown	142		142
17	Queenstown	Rosebery	57		57
18	Rosebery	Wynyard	126		126
19	Wynyard	Devonport	84		84
20	Devonport/Melbourne				0
21	Melbourne	Drouin	97		97
22	Drouin	Maffra	128		128
23	Maffra	Bruthen	76	25	101
24	Bruthen	Gelantipy	91		91
25	Gelantipy	Jacob's River camp	28	54	82
26	Jacob's Creek camp	Berridale	55	28	83
27	Berridale	Queanbeyan	148		148
28	Queanbeyan	Canberra	34		34
		February totals	2020	149	2169
		GRACE totals	18 062	6807	24 869

Index

Photographs indicated in italics